T0231912

Introduction to Privacy-Preserving Data Publishing

Concepts and Techniques

Chapman & Hall/CRC
Data Mining and Knowledge Discovery Series

SERIES EDITOR
Vipin Kumar
University of Minnesota
Department of Computer Science and Engineering
Minneapolis, Minnesota, U.S.A

AIMS AND SCOPE

This series aims to capture new developments and applications in data mining and knowledge discovery, while summarizing the computational tools and techniques useful in data analysis. This series encourages the integration of mathematical, statistical, and computational methods and techniques through the publication of a broad range of textbooks, reference works, and handbooks. The inclusion of concrete examples and applications is highly encouraged. The scope of the series includes, but is not limited to, titles in the areas of data mining and knowledge discovery methods and applications, modeling, algorithms, theory and foundations, data and knowledge visualization, data mining systems and tools, and privacy and security issues.

PUBLISHED TITLES

UNDERSTANDING COMPLEX DATASETS:
DATA MINING WITH MATRIX DECOMPOSITIONS
David Skillicorn

COMPUTATIONAL METHODS OF FEATURE
SELECTION
Huan Liu and Hiroshi Motoda

CONSTRAINED CLUSTERING: ADVANCES IN
ALGORITHMS, THEORY, AND APPLICATIONS
Sugato Basu, Ian Davidson, and Kiri L. Wagstaff

KNOWLEDGE DISCOVERY FOR
COUNTERTERRORISM AND LAW ENFORCEMENT
David Skillicorn

MULTIMEDIA DATA MINING: A SYSTEMATIC
INTRODUCTION TO CONCEPTS AND THEORY
Zhongfei Zhang and Ruofei Zhang

NEXT GENERATION OF DATA MINING
**Hillol Kargupta, Jiawei Han, Philip S. Yu,
Rajeev Motwani, and Vipin Kumar**

DATA MINING FOR DESIGN AND MARKETING
Yukio Ohsawa and Katsutoshi Yada

THE TOP TEN ALGORITHMS IN DATA MINING
Xindong Wu and Vipin Kumar

GEOGRAPHIC DATA MINING AND
KNOWLEDGE DISCOVERY, SECOND EDITION
Harvey J. Miller and Jiawei Han

TEXT MINING: CLASSIFICATION, CLUSTERING,
AND APPLICATIONS
Ashok N. Srivastava and Mehran Sahami

BIOLOGICAL DATA MINING
Jake Y. Chen and Stefano Lonardi

INFORMATION DISCOVERY ON ELECTRONIC
HEALTH RECORDS
Vagelis Hristidis

TEMPORAL DATA MINING
Theophano Mitsa

RELATIONAL DATA CLUSTERING: MODELS,
ALGORITHMS, AND APPLICATIONS
Bo Long, Zhongfei Zhang, and Philip S. Yu

KNOWLEDGE DISCOVERY FROM DATA STREAMS
João Gama

STATISTICAL DATA MINING USING SAS
APPLICATIONS, SECOND EDITION
George Fernandez

INTRODUCTION TO PRIVACY-PRESERVING DATA
PUBLISHING: CONCEPTS AND TECHNIQUES
**Benjamin C. M. Fung, Ke Wang, Ada Wai-Chee Fu,
and Philip S. Yu**

Chapman & Hall/CRC
Data Mining and Knowledge Discovery Series

Introduction to Privacy-Preserving Data Publishing

Concepts and Techniques

Benjamin C. M. Fung, Ke Wang,
Ada Wai-Chee Fu, and Philip S. Yu

CRC Press
Taylor & Francis Group
Boca Raton London New York

CRC Press is an imprint of the
Taylor & Francis Group, an **informa** business

A CHAPMAN & HALL BOOK

First published 2011 by CRC Press

Published 2019 by CRC Press
Taylor & Francis Group
6000 Broken Sound Parkway NW, Suite 300
Boca Raton, FL 33487-2742

© 2011 by Taylor and Francis Group, LLC
CRC Press is an imprint of the Taylor & Francis Group, an informa business

No claim to original U.S. Government works

ISBN-13: 978-1-4200-9148-9 (hbk)

Library of Congress Cataloging-in-Publication Data

Introduction to privacy-preserving data publishing : concepts and techniques / Benjamin C.M. Fung ... [et al.].
    p. cm. -- (Data mining and knowledge discovery series)
    Includes bibliographical references and index.
    ISBN 978-1-4200-9148-9 (hardcover : alk. paper)
    1. Database security. 2. Confidential communications. I. Fung, Benjamin C. M. II. Title. III. Series.

QA76.9.D314I58 2010
005.8--dc22
                                            2010023845

Visit the Taylor & Francis Web site at
http://www.taylorandfrancis.com

and the CRC Press Web site at
http://www.crcpress.com

To Akina, Cyrus, Daphne, and my parents
- B.F.

To Lucy, Catherine, Caroline, and Simon
- K.W.

To my family
- A.F.

To my family
- P.Y.

Contents

III   Extended Data Publishing Scenarios   129

List of Figures

List of Tables

List of Algorithms

Preface

Organization of the Book

The book has four parts. Part I discusses the fundamentals of privacy-preserving data publishing. Part II presents anonymization methods for preserving information utility for some specific data mining tasks. The data publishing scenarios discussed in Part I and Part II assume publishing a single data release from one data holder. In real-life data publishing, the scenario is more complicated. For example, the same data may be published several times. Each time, the data is anonymized differently for different purposes, or the data is published incrementally as new data are collected. Part III discusses the privacy issues, privacy models, and anonymization methods for these more realistic, yet more challenging, data publishing scenarios. All works discussed in the first three parts focus on anonymizing relational data. What about other types of data? Recent studies have shown that publishing transaction data, trajectory data, social networks data, and textual data may also result in privacy threats and sensitive information leakages. Part IV studies the privacy threats, privacy models, and anonymization methods for these complex data.

Part I: The Fundamentals

Chapter 1 provides an introduction to privacy-preserving data publishing. Motivated by the advancement of data collection and information sharing technologies, there is a clear demand for information sharing and data publication without compromising the individual privacy in the published data. This leads to the development of the research topic, *privacy-preserving data publishing*, discussed in this book. We define some desirable requirements and properties of privacy-preserving data publishing, followed by a general discussion on other closely related research topics.

Chapter 2 explains various types of attacks that can be performed on the published data, and the corresponding *privacy models* proposed for preventing such attacks. The privacy models are systematically grouped by their attack models. Industrial practitioners can use the privacy models discussed in the chapter to estimate the degree of privacy risks on their shared data. Researchers in the field of privacy protection may find this chapter as a handy reference.

Chapter 3 discusses the *anonymization operations* employed to achieve the privacy models discussed in Chapter 2. The chapter compares the pros and cons of different anonymization operations.

Chapter 4 studies various types of *information metrics* that capture different information needs for different data analysis and data mining tasks. Data can be anonymized in different ways to serve different information needs. These "needs" are captured by an information metric that aims at maximizing the preservation of certain type of information in the anonymization process.

Chapter 5 studies some representative *anonymization algorithms* for achieving the privacy models presented in Chapter 2 and systematically classifies them by their addressed privacy attacks without considering any specific data mining tasks. In contrast, the anonymization algorithms discussed in Part II are designed for preserving some specific types of data mining information in the anonymous data.

Part II: Anonymization for Data Mining

Chapter 6 uses the Red Cross Blood Transfusion Service as a real-life case study to illustrate the requirements and challenges of the *anonymization problem for classification analysis*. We present a privacy model to overcome the challenges of anonymizing high-dimensional relational data without significantly compromising the data quality, followed by an efficient anonymization algorithm for achieving the privacy model with two different information needs. The first information need maximizes the information preserved for classification analysis; the second information need minimizes the distortion on the anonymous data for general data analysis. The chapter also studies other anonymization algorithms that address the anonymization problem for classification analysis, and presents a methodology to evaluate the data quality of the anonymized data with respect to the information needs. Researchers and industrial practitioners may adopt the methodology to evaluate their anonymized data.

Chapter 7 studies the *anonymization problem for cluster analysis* and presents a framework to tackle the problem. The framework transforms the anonymization problem for cluster analysis to the anonymization problem for classification analysis discussed in Chapter 6. The framework includes an evaluation phase that allows the data holder to evaluate the quality of their anonymized data with respect to the information need on cluster analysis.

Part III: Extended Data Publishing Scenarios

Chapter 8 studies the scenario of *multiple views publishing* in which each data release is a view of an underlying data table serving different information needs. Even if each release is individually anonymized, an adversary may be able to crack the anonymity by comparing different anonymized views. Often, additional statistics are published together with the anonymized data. This chapter also studies the privacy threats caused by the published data together with the additional statistical information.

Chapter 9 studies the scenario of *sequential data publishing* in which each data release is a vertical partition of the underlying raw data table and may contain some new attributes. Since the releases could be overlapping, an adversary may be able to crack the anonymity by comparing multiple releases. This chapter provides a detailed analysis on the privacy threats in this scenario and presents an anonymization method to thwart the potential privacy threats.

Chapter 10 studies two scenarios of incremental data publishing. The first scenario is called *continuous data publishing* in which each data release includes new data records together with all previously published data records. In other words, each data release is a history of all previously occurred events. We illustrate the potential privacy threats in this data publishing model, succinctly model the privacy attacks, and present an anonymization algorithm to thwart them. The second scenario is called *dynamic data republishing* in which each data release is a snapshot of the current database. The privacy model for dynamic data republishing takes both record insertions and deletions into the consideration of potential privacy threats.

Chapter 11 studies the scenario of collaborative data publishing in which multiple data holders want to integrate their data together and publish their integrated data to each other or to a third party without disclosing specific details of their data to each other. We study the problem of *collaborative anonymization for vertically partitioned data* in the context of data mashup application, and present a web service architecture together with a secure protocol to achieve the privacy and information utility requirements agreed by all participating data holders.

Chapter 12 studies a similar scenario of collaborative data publishing but in the problem of *collaborative anonymization for horizontally partitioned data*. Each data holder owns different sets of data records on the same data schema, and would like to integrate their data together to achieve some common data mining task.

Part IV: Anonymizing Complex Data

Chapter 13 defines the *anonymization problem for transaction data*, discusses the challenges, and presents various anonymization methods for addressing the challenges. Transaction data can be found in many daily applications. Examples of transaction data include supermarket data, credit card data, and medical history, etc. The major challenge of transaction data anonymization is to overcome the problem of high dimensionality. The high dimensionality of transaction data comes from the fact that most transaction databases, for example a supermarket database, contain many distinct items. Every distinct item constitutes a dimension in the transaction data.

Chapter 14 defines the *anonymization problem for trajectory data*, and presents various privacy models and anonymization methods to address the problem. In addition to the challenge of high dimensionality discussed above, anonymizing trajectory is even more complicated due to the presence of sequences. The chapter also discusses how to preserve and evaluate the information utility in the anonymized trajectory data.

Chapter 15 discusses different data models and attack models on *social networks data*. Social network application is one the fastest growing web applications. In social network applications, e.g., Facebook and LinkedIn, participants share their personal information, preferences, and opinion with their friends and in their participated social groups. This valuable information precisely captures the lifestyle of individuals as well as the trends in some particular social groups. This chapter concerns the privacy threats and information utility if such data are shared with a third party for data mining.

Chapter 16 studies some sanitization methods on *textual data*. Textual data can be found everywhere, from text documents on the Web to patients' medical history written by doctors. Sanitization on textual data refers to the procedure of removing personal identifiable and/or sensitive information from the text. Unlike the structural relational data and transaction data discussed earlier, textual data is unstructural, making the anonymization problem much more complicated because the anonymization method has to first determine the identifiable and/or sensitive information from the textual data and then apply the anonymization. This research topic is still in its infancy stage. This chapter discusses two recently proposed methods.

Chapter 17 briefly discusses other privacy-preserving techniques that are orthogonal to privacy-preserving data publishing, and concludes the book with future trends in privacy-preserving data publishing.

To the Instructor

This book is designed to provide a detailed overview of the field of privacy-preserving data publishing. The materials presented are suitable for an advanced undergraduate course or a graduate course. Alternatively, privacy-preserving data publishing can be one of the topics in a database security or a data mining course. This book can serve as a textbook or a supplementary reference for these types of courses.

If you intend to use this book to teach an introductory course in privacy-preserving data publishing, you should start from Part I, which contains the essential information of privacy-preserving data publishing. Students with some data mining knowledge will probably find Part II interesting because the anonymization problems are motivated by a real-life case study, and the chapter presents both data mining and privacy requirements in the context of the case study.

Part III covers more advanced topics in privacy-preserving data publishing. For an undergraduate course, you may want to skip this part. For a graduate course, you may consider covering some of the selected chapters in this part. For this part, the students are expected to have some basic knowledge of database operations, such as selection, projection, and join. Chapters in this part are standalone, so you may selectively skip some chapters and sections, or change the order.

Part IV covers some recent works on addressing the anonymization problem for different types of data. The data models and challenges are explained in detail. The materials are suitable for a graduate course.

To the Student

This book is a good entry point to the research field of privacy-preserving data publishing. If you have some basic knowledge in computer science and information technology, then you should have no problem understanding the materials in Part I, which contains the essential information of the research topic. It will be beneficial if you already have some basic knowledge of data mining, such as classification analysis, cluster analysis, and association rules mining, before proceeding to Part II and Part IV. Han and Kamber [109] have written an excellent textbook on data mining. Alternatively, you can easily find lots of introductory information on these general data mining topics on the Web. In order to understand the materials in Part III, you should have some basic knowledge of database operations.

To the Researcher

If you are a beginner in the field of privacy-preserving data publishing, then this book will provide you a broad yet detailed overview of the research topic. If you are already a researcher in the field, then you may find Part I a good reference, and proceed directly to the more advanced topics in subsequent parts. Despite a lot of effort by the research community spent on this topic, there are many challenging problems remaining to be solved. We hope this book will spark some new research problems and ideas for the field.

To the Industrial Practitioner

Information sharing has become the daily operation of many businesses in today's information age. This book is suitable for industrial IT practitioners, such as database administrators, database architects, information engineers, and chief information officers, who manage a large volume of person-specific sensitive data and are looking for methods to share the data with business partners or to the public without compromising the privacy of their clients. Some chapters present the privacy-preserving data publishing problems in the context of the industrial collaborative projects and reflect the authors' experience in these projects.

You are recommended to start from Part I to gain some basic knowledge of privacy-preserving data publishing. If you intend to publish the data for some specific data mining tasks, you may find Part II useful. Chapter 6 describes a data publishing scenario in the healthcare sector. Though the data mining task and the sector may not directly be relevant to yours, the materials are easy to generalize to be adopted for other data mining tasks in other sectors. If you intend to make multiple releases of your continuously evolving data, then some of the data publishing scenarios described in Part III may match yours. Part IV describes the privacy models and anonymization algorithms for different types of data. Due to the complexity of real-life data, you may need to employ different anonymization methods depending on the types of data you have at hand.

The book not only discusses the privacy and information utility issues, but also the efficiency and scalability issues in privacy-preserving data publishing. In many chapters, we highlight the efficient and scalable methods and provide an analytical discussion to compare the strengths and weaknesses of different solutions. We would be glad to listen to your stories if you have applied privacy-preserving data publishing methods in real-life projects. Our e-mail address is bfung@ieee.org.

Acknowledgments

This work is supported in part by the Natural Sciences and Engineering Research Council of Canada (NSERC) Discovery Grant 356065-2008, RGC Research Grant Direct Allocation 2050421 of the Chinese University of Hong Kong, and NSF Grant IIS-0914934.

We would like to express our sincere thanks to our current and past research collaborators in the fields of privacy-preserving data publishing, privacy-preserving data mining, statistical disclosure control, and secure multiparty computation. These include Ming Cao, Rui Chen, Mourad Debbabi, Rachida Dssouli, Bipin C. Desai, Guozhu Dong, Amin Hammad, Patrick C. K. Hung, Cheuk-kwong Lee, Noman Mohammed, Lalita Narupiyakul, Jian Pei, Harpreet Sandhu, Qing Shi, Jarmanjit Singh, Thomas Trojer, Lingyu Wang, Wendy Hui Wang, Yiming Wang, Raymond Chi-Wing Wong, Li Xiong, Heng Xu, and Yabo Xu. We also specially thank the graduate students, Khalil Al-Hussaeni, Rui Chen, Noman Mohammed, and Minu Venkat, in the Concordia Institute for Information Systems Engineering (CIISE) at Concordia University for their contributions to this book.

We would also like to thank Randi Cohen, our editor at CRC Press/Taylor and Francis Group for her patience and support during the writing of this book. Finally, we thank our families for their continuous support throughout this project.

About the Authors

Benjamin C. M. Fung received a Ph.D. degree in computing science from Simon Fraser University, Canada, in 2007. He is currently an assistant professor in the Concordia Institute for Information Systems Engineering (CIISE) at Concordia University, Montreal, Quebec, Canada, and a research scientist and the treasurer of the National Cyber-Forensics and Training Alliance Canada (NCFTA Canada). His current research interests include data mining, databases, privacy preservation, information security, and digital forensics, as well as their interdisciplinary applications on current and emerging technologies. His publications span across the research forums of data mining, privacy protection, cyber forensics, and communications, including ACM SIGKDD, ACM Computing Surveys, ACM TKDD, ACM CIKM, IEEE TKDE, IEEE ICDE, IEEE ICDM, EDBT, SDM, IEEE RFID, and Digital Investigation. He also consistently serves as program committee member and reviewer for these prestigious forums. His research has been supported in part by the Natural Sciences and Engineering Research Council of Canada (NSERC), Le Fonds québécois de la recherche sur la nature et les technologies (FQRNT), the NCFTA Canada, and Concordia University.

Before pursuing his academic career, Dr. Fung worked at SAP Business Objects and designed reporting systems for various Enterprise Resource Planning (ERP) and Customer Relationship Management (CRM) systems. He is a licensed professional engineer in software engineering, and is currently affiliated with the Computer Security Lab in CIISE.

Ke Wang received a Ph.D. degree from the Georgia Institute of Technology. He is currently a professor at the School of Computing Science, Simon Fraser University, Burnaby, British Columbia, Canada. He has taught in the areas of database and data mining. His research interests include database technology, data mining and knowledge discovery, machine learning, and emerging applications, with recent interests focusing on the end use of data mining. This includes explicitly modeling the business goal and exploiting user prior knowledge (such as extracting unexpected patterns and actionable knowledge). He is interested in combining the strengths of various fields such as database, statistics, machine learning, and optimization to provide actionable solutions to real-life problems. He has published in database, information retrieval, and data mining conferences, including ACM SIGMOD, ACM SIGKDD, ACM SIGIR, ACM PODS, VLDB, IEEE ICDE, IEEE ICDM, EDBT, and SDM. He was an associate editor of the IEEE Transactions on Knowledge and Data Engineering, and an editorial board member for the Journal of Data Mining and Knowledge Discovery.

Ada Wai-Chee Fu received her B.Sc degree in computer science from the Chinese University of Hong Kong in 1983, and both M.Sc and Ph.D degrees in computer science from Simon Fraser University of Canada in 1986, 1990, respectively. She worked at Bell Northern Research in Ottawa, Canada from 1989 to 1993 on a wide-area distributed database project and joined the Chinese University of Hong Kong in 1993. Her research interests include topics in data mining, privacy-preserving data publishing, and database management systems. Her work has been published in journals and conference proceedings in both the data mining and database areas.

Philip S. Yu received Ph.D. and M.S. degrees in electrical engineering from Stanford University, the M.B.A. degree from New York University, and the B.S. Degree in Electrical Engineering from National Taiwan University. His main research interests include data mining, privacy-preserving publishing and mining, data streams, database systems, Internet applications and technologies, multimedia systems, parallel and distributed processing, and performance modeling. He is a Professor in the Department of Computer Science at the University of Illinois at Chicago and also holds the Wexler Chair in Information and Technology. He was a manager of the Software Tools and Techniques group at the IBM Thomas J. Watson Research Center. Dr. Yu has published more than 560 papers in refereed journals and conferences. He holds or has applied for more than 300 US patents.

Dr. Yu is a Fellow of the ACM and of the IEEE. He is associate editor of ACM Transactions on the Internet Technology and ACM Transactions on Knowledge Discovery from Data. He is on the steering committee of IEEE Conference on Data Mining and was a member of the IEEE Data Engineering steering committee. He was the Editor-in-Chief of IEEE Transactions on Knowledge and Data Engineering (2001-2004), an editor, advisory board member, and also a guest co-editor of the special issue on mining of databases. He had also served as an associate editor of Knowledge and Information Systems. He has received several IBM honors including 2 IBM Outstanding Innovation Awards, an Outstanding Technical Achievement Award, 2 Research Division Awards, and the 93rd plateau of Invention Achievement Awards. He was an IBM Master Inventor. Dr. Yu received a Research Contributions Award from the IEEE International Conference on Data Mining in 2003 and also an IEEE Region 1 Award for "promoting and perpetuating numerous new electrical engineering concepts" in 1999.

Part I

The Fundamentals

Chapter 1

Introduction

Data mining is the process of extracting useful, interesting, and previously unknown information from large data sets. The success of data mining relies on the availability of high quality data and effective information sharing. The collection of digital information by governments, corporations, and individuals has created an environment that facilitates large-scale data mining and data analysis. Moreover, driven by mutual benefits, or by regulations that require certain data to be published, there is a demand for sharing data among various parties. For example, licensed hospitals in California are required to submit specific demographic data on every patient discharged from their facility [43]. In June 2004, the Information Technology Advisory Committee released a report entitled *Revolutionizing Health Care Through Information Technology* [190]. One key point was to establish a nationwide system of electronic medical records that encourages sharing of medical knowledge through computer-assisted clinical decision support. Data publishing is equally ubiquitous in other domains. For example, Netflix, a popular online movie rental service, recently published a data set containing movie ratings of 500,000 subscribers, in a drive to improve the accuracy of movie recommendations based on personal preferences (New York Times, Oct. 2, 2006); AOL published a release of query logs but quickly removed it due to the re-identification of a searcher [27].

Information sharing has a long history in information technology. Traditional information sharing refers to exchanges of data between a data holder and a data recipient. For example, the Electronic Data Interchange (EDI) is a successful implementation of electronic data transmission between organizations with the emphasis on the commercial sector. The development of EDI began in the late 1970s and remains in use today. Nowadays, the terms "information sharing" and "data publishing" not only refer to the traditional one-to-one model, but also the more general models with multiple data holders and data recipients. Recent standardization of information sharing protocols, such as eXtensible Markup Language (XML), Simple Object Access Protocol (SOAP), and Web Services Description Language (WSDL) are catalysts for the recent development of information sharing technology.

The standardization enables different electronic devices to communicate with each other, sometimes even without interference of the device owner. For example, the so-called intelligent fridge is capable to detect the RFID-tagged food items inside, display the ingredients and nutritional data, suggest recipes, retrieve the latest information of the product from the producers, and allow users to browse the web for further information. The advancement of information technology has improved our standard of living. Though not everyone agrees that an intelligent fridge is useful, having such a fridge will at least make the kitchen more fun. Yet, detailed data in its original form often contain sensitive information about individuals, and sharing such data could potentially violate individual privacy. For example, one may not want to share her web browsing history and the information of items in her intelligent fridge to a third party. The data recipient having access to such information could potentially infer the fridge owner's current health status and predict her future status. The general public expresses serious concerns on their privacy and the consequences of sharing their person-specific information.

The current privacy protection practice primarily relies on policies and guidelines to restrict the types of publishable data, and agreements on the use and storage of sensitive data. The limitation of this approach is that it either distorts data excessively or requires a trust level that is impractically high in many data-sharing scenarios. Also, policies and guidelines cannot prevent adversaries who do not follow rules in the first place. Contracts and agreements cannot guarantee that sensitive data will not be carelessly misplaced and end up in the wrong hands. For example, in 2007, two computer disks containing names, addresses, birth dates, and national insurance numbers for 25 million people went missing while being sent from one British government department to another.

A task of the utmost importance is to develop methods and tools for publishing data in a hostile environment so that the published data remain practically useful while individual privacy is preserved. This undertaking is called *privacy-preserving data publishing (PPDP)*, which can be viewed as a technical response to complement the privacy policies. In the past few years, research communities have responded to this challenge and proposed many approaches. While the research field is still rapidly developing, it is a good time to discuss the assumptions and desirable properties for PPDP, clarify the differences and requirements that distinguish PPDP from other related problems, and systematically summarize and evaluate different approaches to PPDP. This book aims to achieve these goals.

1.1   Data Collection and Data Publishing

A typical scenario of data collection and publishing is described in Figure 1.1. In the *data collection* phase, the *data holder* collects data from *record owners* (e.g., Alice and Bob). In the *data publishing* phase, the data holder releases the collected data to a data miner or the public, called the *data recip-*

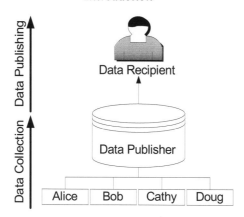

FIGURE 1.1: Data collection and data publishing ([92])

ient, who will then conduct data mining on the published data. In this book, data mining has a broad sense, not necessarily restricted to pattern mining or model building. For example, a hospital collects data from patients and publishes the patient records to an external medical center. In this example, the hospital is the data holder, patients are record owners, and the medical center is the data recipient. The data mining conducted at the medical center could be any analysis task from a simple count of the number of men with diabetes to a sophisticated cluster analysis.

There are two models of data holders [99]. In the *untrusted* model, the data holder is not trusted and may attempt to identify sensitive information from record owners. Various cryptographic solutions [258], anonymous communications [45, 126], and statistical methods [242] were proposed to collect records anonymously from their owners without revealing the owners' identity. In the *trusted* model, the data holder is trustworthy and record owners are willing to provide their personal information to the data holder; however, the trust is not transitive to the data recipient. In this book, we assume the trusted model of data holders and consider privacy issues in the data publishing phase. Every data publishing scenario in practice has its own assumptions and requirements on the data holder, the data recipients, and the data publishing purpose. The following are different assumptions and properties that may be adopted in practical data publishing depending on the application:

The non-expert data holder. The data holder is not required to have the knowledge to perform data mining on behalf of the data recipient. Any data mining activities have to be performed by the data recipient after receiving the data from the data holder. Sometimes, the data holder does not even know who the recipients are at the time of publication, or has no interest in data mining. For example, the hospitals in California publish patient records on the web [43]. The hospitals do not know who the recipients are and how the recipients will use the data. The hospital publishes patient records because it is required by regulations [43], or because it supports general medical research, not because the hospital needs the result of data mining. Therefore, it is not reasonable to expect the data holder to do more than anonymizing the data for publication in such a scenario.

In other scenarios, the data holder is interested in the data mining result, but lacks the in-house expertise to conduct the analysis and, therefore, outsources the data mining activities to some external data miners. In this case, the data mining task performed by the recipient is known in advance. In the effort to improve the quality of the data mining result, the data holder could release a customized data set that preserves specific types of patterns for such a data mining task. Still, the actual data mining activities are performed by the data recipient, not by the data holder.

The data recipient could be an adversary. In PPDP, one assumption is that the data recipient could also be an adversary. For example, the data recipient, say a drug research company, is a trustworthy entity; however, it is difficult to guarantee every staff in the company to be trustworthy as well. This assumption makes the PPDP problems and solutions to be very different from the encryption and cryptographic approaches, in which only authorized and trustworthy recipients are given the private key for accessing the cleartext. A major challenge in PPDP is to simultaneously preserve both the privacy and information utility in the anonymous data.

Publish data, not data mining results. PPDP emphasizes publishing data records about individuals (i.e., micro data). This requirement is more stringent than publishing data mining results, such as classifiers, association rules, or statistics about groups of individuals. For example, in the case of the Netflix data release, useful information may be some type of associations of movie ratings. Netflix decided to publish data records instead of publishing such associations because the participants, with data records, have greater flexibility to perform required analysis and data exploration, such as mining patterns in one partition but not in other partitions, visualizing the transactions containing a specific pattern, trying different modeling methods and parameters, and so forth. The assumption of publishing data, not data mining results, is also closely related to the assumption of a non-expert data holder.

Truthfulness at the record level. In some data publishing scenarios, it is important that each published record corresponds to an existing individual in real life. Consider the example of patient records. The pharmaceutical researcher (the data recipient) may need to examine the actual patient records to discover some previously unknown side effects of the tested drug [79]. If a published record does not correspond to an existing patient in real life, it is difficult to deploy data mining results in the real world. Randomized and synthetic data do not meet this requirement. Also, randomized and synthetic data become meaningless to data recipients who may want to manually interpret individual data records.

Encryption is another commonly employed technique for privacy protection. Although an encrypted record corresponds to a real life patient, the encryption hides the semantics required for acting on the represented patient. Encryption aims to prevent an unauthorized party from accessing the data, but enable an authorized party to have full access to the data. In PPDP, it is the authorized party who may also play the role of the adversary with the goal of inferring sensitive information from the data received. Thus, encryption may not be directly applicable to some PPDP problems.

1.2   What Is Privacy-Preserving Data Publishing?

In the most basic form of privacy-preserving data publishing (PPDP), the data holder has a table of the form

$$D(\text{Explicit\_Identifier, Quasi\_Identifier, Sensitive\_Attributes,}$$
$$\text{Non-Sensitive\_Attributes}),$$

where Explicit_Identifier is a set of attributes, such as name and social security number (SSN), containing information that explicitly identifies record owners; Quasi_Identifier is a set of attributes that could potentially identify record owners; Sensitive_Attributes consist of sensitive person-specific information such as disease, salary, and disability status; and Non-Sensitive_Attributes contains all attributes that do not fall into the previous three categories [40]. Most works assume that the four sets of attributes are disjoint. Most works assume that each record in the table represents a distinct record owner.

Anonymization [52, 56] refers to the PPDP approach that seeks to hide the identity and/or the sensitive data of record owners, assuming that sensitive data must be retained for data analysis. Clearly, explicit identifiers of record owners must be removed. Even with all explicit identifiers removed, Sweeney [216] shows a real-life privacy threat on William Weld, former governor of the state of Massachusetts. In Sweeney's example, an individual's name in a public voter list was linked with his record in a published medical database through the combination of zip code, date of birth, and sex, as shown in Figure 1.2. Each of these attributes does not uniquely identify a record owner, but their combination, called the *quasi-identifier* [56], often singles out a unique or a small number of record owners. Research showed

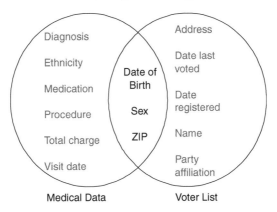

FIGURE 1.2: Linking to re-identify record owner ([217] ©2002 World Scientific Publishing)

that 87% of the U.S. population had reported characteristics that made them unique based on only such quasi-identifiers [216].

In the above example, the owner of a record is re-identified by linking his quasi-identifier. To perform such *linking attacks*, the adversary needs two pieces of prior knowledge: the victim's record in the released data and the quasi-identifier of the victim. Such knowledge can be obtained by observations. For example, the adversary noticed that his boss was hospitalized, therefore, knew that his boss's medical record would appear in the released patient database. Also, it is not difficult for an adversary to obtain his boss's zip code, date of birth, and sex, which could serve as the quasi-identifier in linking attacks.

To prevent linking attacks, the data holder publishes an anonymous table

$$T(QID', \text{Sensitive\_Attributes}, \text{Non-Sensitive\_Attributes}),$$

QID' is an *anonymous* version of the original QID obtained by applying *anonymization operations* to the attributes in QID in the original table D. Anonymization operations hide some detailed information so that mulitple records become indistinguishable with respect to QID'. Consequently, if a person is linked to a record through QID', the person is also linked to all other records that have the same value for QID', making the linking ambiguous. Alternatively, anonymization operations could generate a synthetic data table T based on the statistical properties of the original table D, or add noise to the original table D. The *anonymization problem* is to produce an anonymous T that satisfies a given privacy requirement determined by the chosen privacy model and to retain as much data utility as possible. An *information metric* is used to measure the utility of an anonymous table. Note, the Non-Sensitive_Attributes are published if they are important to the data mining task.

1.3 Related Research Areas

Several polls [41, 144] show that the public has an increased sense of privacy loss. Since data mining is often a key component of information systems, homeland security systems [208], and monitoring and surveillance systems [88], it gives a *wrong* impression that data mining is a technique for privacy intrusion. This lack of trust has become an obstacle to the benefit of the technology. For example, the potentially beneficial data mining research project, Terrorism Information Awareness (TIA), was terminated by the U.S. Congress due to its controversial procedures of collecting, sharing, and analyzing the trails left by individuals [208].

Motivated by the privacy concerns on data mining tools, a research area called *privacy-preserving data mining* (*PPDM*) emerged in 2000 [19, 50]. The initial idea of PPDM *was* to extend traditional data mining techniques to work with the data modified to mask sensitive information. The key issues were how to modify the data and how to recover the data mining result from the modified data. The solutions were often tightly coupled with the data mining algorithms under consideration. In contrast, privacy-preserving data publishing (PPDP) may not necessarily tie to a specific data mining task, and the data mining task is sometimes unknown at the time of data publishing. Furthermore, some PPDP solutions emphasize preserving the data truthfulness at the record level as discussed earlier, but PPDM solutions often do not preserve such property.

PPDP differs from PPDM in several major ways.

1. PPDP focuses on techniques for publishing data, not techniques for data mining. In fact, it is expected that standard data mining techniques are applied on the published data. In contrast, the data holder in PPDM needs to randomize the data in such a way that data mining results can be recovered from the randomized data. To do so, the data holder must understand the data mining tasks and algorithms involved. This level of involvement is not expected of the data holder in PPDP who usually is not an expert in data mining.

2. Both randomization and encryption do not preserve the truthfulness of values at the record level; therefore, the released data are basically meaningless to the recipients. In such a case, the data holder in PPDM may consider releasing the data mining results rather than the scrambled data.

3. PPDP primarily "anonymizes" the data by hiding the identity of record owners, whereas PPDM seeks to directly hide the sensitive data. Excellent surveys and books in randomization [3, 19, 21, 81, 158, 212, 232] and cryptographic techniques [50, 187, 230] for PPDM can be found in the existing literature. In this book, we focus on techniques for PPDP.

A family of research work [69, 71, 89, 133, 134, 228, 229, 259] called *privacy-preserving distributed data mining* (*PPDDM*) [50] aims at performing some data mining task on a set of private databases owned by different parties. It follows the principle of *Secure Multiparty Computation* (*SMC*) [260, 261], and prohibits any data sharing other than the final data mining result. Clifton et al. [50] present a suite of SMC operations, like secure sum, secure set union, secure size of set intersection, and scalar product, that are useful for many data mining tasks. In contrast, PPDP does not perform the actual data mining task, but concerns with how to publish the data so that the anonymous data are useful for data mining. We can say that PPDP protects privacy at the data level while PPDDM protects privacy at the process level. They address different privacy models and data mining scenarios. PPDDM is briefly discussed in Chapter 17.3. Refer to [50, 187, 232] for more discussions on PPDDM.

In the field of *statistical disclosure control* (*SDC*) [3, 36], the research works focus on privacy-preserving publishing methods for statistical tables. SDC focuses on three types of disclosures, namely identity disclosure, attribute disclosure, and inferential disclosure [51]. *Identity disclosure* occurs if an adversary can identify a respondent from the published data. Revealing that an individual is a respondent of a data collection may or may not violate confidentiality requirements. *Attribute disclosure* occurs when confidential information about a respondent is revealed and can be attributed to the respondent. Attribute disclosure is the primary concern of most statistical agencies in deciding whether to publish tabular data [51]. *Inferential disclosure* occurs when individual information can be inferred with high confidence from statistical information of the published data.

Some other works of SDC focus on the study of the *non-interactive* query model, in which the data recipients can submit one query to the system. This type of non-interactive query model may not fully address the information needs of data recipients because, in some cases, it is very difficult for a data recipient to accurately construct a query for a data mining task in one shot. Consequently, there are a series of studies on the *interactive* query model [32, 62, 76], in which the data recipients, including adversaries, can submit a sequence of queries based on previously received query results. The database server is responsible to keep track of all queries of each user and determine whether or not the currently received query has violated the privacy requirement with respect to all previous queries.

One limitation of any interactive privacy-preserving query system is that it can only answer a sublinear number of queries in total; otherwise, an adversary (or a group of corrupted data recipients) will be able to reconstruct all but $1 - o(1)$ fraction of the original data [33], which is a very strong violation of privacy. When the maximum number of queries is reached, the query service must be closed to avoid privacy leak. In the case of the non-interactive query model, the adversary can issue only one query and, therefore, the non-interactive query model cannot achieve the same degree of privacy defined by the interactive model. One may consider that privacy-preserving data publishing is a special case of the non-interactive query model. The interactive query model will be briefly discussed in Chapter 17.1.

In this book, we review recent works on privacy-preserving data publishing (PPDP) and provide our insights into this topic. There are several fundamental differences between the recent works on PPDP and the previous works proposed by the statistics community. Recent works on PPDP consider background attacks, inference of sensitive attributes, generalization, and various notions of information metrics, but the works in statistics community do not. The term "privacy-preserving data publishing" has been widely adopted by the computer science community to refer to the recent works discussed in this book. SDC is an important topic for releasing statistics on person-specific sensitive information. In this book, we do not intend to provide a detailed coverage on the statistics methods because there are already many decent surveys [3, 63, 173, 267] on that topic.

Chapter 2

Attack Models and Privacy Models

What is privacy preservation? In 1977, Dalenius [55] provided a very stringent definition:

> *access to the published data should not enable the adversary to learn anything extra about any target victim compared to no access to the database, even with the presence of any adversary's background knowledge obtained from other sources.*

In real-life application, such absolute privacy protection is impossible due to the presence of the adversary's background knowledge [74]. Suppose the age of an individual is sensitive information. Assume an adversary knows that Alice's age is 5 years younger than the average age of American women, but does not know the average age of American women. If the adversary has access to a statistical database that discloses the average age of American women, then Alice's privacy is considered to be compromised according to Dalenius' definition, regardless of the presence of Alice's record in the database. Most literature on privacy-preserving data publishing considers a more relaxed, more practical notion of privacy protection by assuming the adversary has limited background knowledge. Below, the term "victim" refers to the record owner targeted by the adversary. We can broadly classify privacy models to two categories based on their attack principles.

The first category considers that a privacy threat occurs when an adversary is able to link a record owner to a record in a published data table, to a sensitive attribute in a published data table, or to the published data table itself. We call these *record linkage*, *attribute linkage*, and *table linkage*, respectively. In all three types of linkages, we assume that the adversary knows the QID of the victim. In record and attribute linkages, we further assume that the adversary knows the victim's record is in the released table, and seeks to identify the victim's record and/or sensitive information from the table. In table linkage, the attack seeks to determine the presence or absence of the victim's record in the released table. A data table is considered to be privacy-preserving if it can effectively prevent the adversary from successfully performing these linkages. Chapters 2.1-2.3 study this category of privacy models.

The second category aims at achieving the *uninformative principle* [160]: The published table should provide the adversary with little additional information beyond the background knowledge. If the adversary has a large

Table 2.1:   Privacy models

Privacy Model	Attack Model			
	Record linkage	Attribute linkage	Table linkage	Probabilistic attack
k-Anonymity [201, 217]	✓			
MultiR k-Anonymity [178]	✓			
ℓ-Diversity [162]	✓	✓		
Confidence Bounding [237]		✓		
(α, k)-Anonymity [246]	✓	✓		
(X, Y)-Privacy [236]	✓	✓		
(k, e)-Anonymity [269]		✓		
(ϵ, m)-Anonymity [152]		✓		
Personalized Privacy [250]		✓		
t-Closeness [153]		✓		✓
δ-Presence [176]			✓	
(c, t)-Isolation [46]	✓			✓
ϵ-Differential Privacy [74]			✓	✓
(d, γ)-Privacy [193]			✓	✓
Distributional Privacy [33]			✓	✓

variation between the prior and posterior beliefs, we call it the *probabilistic attack*. Many privacy models in this family do not explicitly classify attributes in a data table into QID and Sensitive_Attributes, but some of them could also thwart the sensitive linkages in the first category, so the two categories overlap. Chapter 2.4 studies this family of privacy models. Table 2.1 summarizes the attack models addressed by the privacy models.

2.1   Record Linkage Model

In the attack of *record linkage*, some value qid on QID identifies a small number of records in the released table T, called a *group*. If the victim's QID matches the value qid, the victim is vulnerable to being linked to the small number of records in the group. In this case, the adversary faces only a small number of possibilities for the victim's record, and with the help of additional knowledge, there is a chance that the adversary could uniquely identify the victim's record from the group.

Example 2.1
Suppose that a hospital wants to publish patients' records in Table 2.2 to a research center. Suppose that the research center has access to the external table Table 2.3 and knows that every person with a record in Table 2.3 has a

Table 2.2: Original patient data

Job	Sex	Age	Disease
Engineer	Male	35	Hepatitis
Engineer	Male	38	Hepatitis
Lawyer	Male	38	HIV
Writer	Female	30	Flu
Writer	Female	30	HIV
Dancer	Female	30	HIV
Dancer	Female	30	HIV

Table 2.3: External data

Name	Job	Sex	Age
Alice	Writer	Female	30
Bob	Engineer	Male	35
Cathy	Writer	Female	30
Doug	Lawyer	Male	38
Emily	Dancer	Female	30
Fred	Engineer	Male	38
Gladys	Dancer	Female	30
Henry	Lawyer	Male	39
Irene	Dancer	Female	32

record in Table 2.2. Joining the two tables on the common attributes *Job*, *Sex*, and *Age* may link the identity of a person to his/her *Disease*. For example, *Doug*, a male lawyer at 38 years old, is identified as an *HIV* patient by $qid = \langle Lawyer, Male, 38 \rangle$ after the join. □

2.1.1 k-Anonymity

To prevent record linkage through QID, Samarati and Sweeney [201, 202, 203, 217] propose the notion of *k-anonymity*: If one record in the table has some value qid, at least $k - 1$ other records also have the value qid. In other words, the minimum equivalence group size on QID is at least k. A table satisfying this requirement is called *k-anonymous*. In a k-anonymous table, each record is indistinguishable from at least $k - 1$ other records with respect to QID. Consequently, the probability of linking a victim to a specific record through QID is at most $1/k$.

k-anonymity cannot be replaced by the privacy models in attribute linkage discussed in Chapter 2.2. Consider a table T that contains no sensitive attributes (such as the voter list in Figure 1.2). An adversary could possibly use the QID in T to link to the sensitive information in an external source. A k-anonymous T can still effectively prevent this type of record linkage without considering the sensitive information. In contrast, the privacy models in attribute linkage assume the existence of sensitive attributes in T.

Table 2.4:   3-anonymous patient data

Job	Sex	Age	Disease
Professional	Male	[35-40)	Hepatitis
Professional	Male	[35-40)	Hepatitis
Professional	Male	[35-40)	HIV
Artist	Female	[30-35)	Flu
Artist	Female	[30-35)	HIV
Artist	Female	[30-35)	HIV
Artist	Female	[30-35)	HIV

Table 2.5:   4-anonymous external data

Name	Job	Sex	Age
Alice	Artist	Female	[30-35)
Bob	Professional	Male	[35-40)
Cathy	Artist	Female	[30-35)
Doug	Professional	Male	[35-40)
Emily	Artist	Female	[30-35)
Fred	Professional	Male	[35-40)
Gladys	Artist	Female	[30-35)
Henry	Professional	Male	[35-40)
Irene	Artist	Female	[30-35)

Example 2.2

Table 2.4 shows a 3-anonymous table by generalizing $QID = \{Job, Sex, Age\}$ from Table 2.2 using the taxonomy trees in Figure 2.1. It has two distinct groups on QID, namely $\langle Professional, Male, [35\text{-}40) \rangle$ and $\langle Artist, Female, [30\text{-}35) \rangle$. Since each group contains at least 3 records, the table is 3-anonymous. If we link the records in Table 2.3 to the records in Table 2.4 through QID, each record is linked to either no record or at least 3 records in Table 2.4. $\square$

The k-anonymity model assumes that QID is known to the data holder. Most works consider a single QID containing all attributes that can be potentially used in the quasi-identifier. The more attributes included in QID, the more protection k-anonymity would provide. On the other hand, this also implies more distortion is needed to achieve k-anonymity because the records in a group have to agree on more attributes. To address this issue, Fung et al. [95, 96] allow the specification of multiple QIDs, assuming that the data holder knows the potential QIDs for record linkage. The following example illustrates the use of this specification.

Example 2.3

The data holder wants to publish a table $T(A, B, C, D, S)$, where S is the sensitive attribute, and knows that the data recipient has access to previously

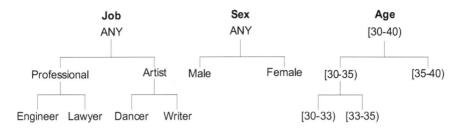

FIGURE 2.1: Taxonomy trees for *Job, Sex, Age*

published tables $T1(A, B, X)$ and $T2(C, D, Y)$, where X and Y are attributes not in T. To prevent linking the records in T to the information on X or Y, the data holder can specify k-anonymity on $QID_1 = \{A, B\}$ and $QID_2 = \{C, D\}$ for T. This means that each record in T is indistinguishable from a group of at least k records with respect to QID_1 and is indistinguishable from a group of at least k records with respect to QID_2. The two groups are not necessarily the same. Clearly, this requirement is implied by k-anonymity on $QID = \{A, B, C, D\}$, but having k-anonymity on both QID_1 and QID_2 does not imply k-anonymity on QID.

The second scenario is that there are two adversaries, one has access to $T1$ and one has access to $T2$. Since none of them has access of all of A, B, C, and D in a table, considering a single $QID = \{A, B, C, D\}$ would result in over-protection and, therefore, over data distortion.   □

Specifying multiple $QIDs$ is practical only if the data holder knows how the adversary might perform the linking. Nevertheless, the data holder often does not have such information. A wrong decision may cause higher privacy risks or higher information loss. Later, we discuss the dilemma and implications of choosing attributes in QID. In the presence of multiple $QIDs$, some $QIDs$ may be redundant and can be removed by the following subset property:

Observation 2.1.1 (Subset property) Let $QID' \subseteq QID$. If a table T is k-anonymous on QID, then T is also k-anonymous on QID'. In other words, QID' is *covered by* QID, so QID' can be removed from the privacy requirement [95, 96, 148]. ∎

The k-anonymity model assumes that each record represents a distinct individual. If several records in a table represent the same record owner, a group of k records may represent fewer than k record owners, and the record owner may be underprotected. The following example illustrates this point.

Example 2.4

A record in the table *Inpatient*(*Pid, Job, Sex, Age, Disease*) represents that a patient identified by *Pid* has *Job, Sex, Age,* and *Disease*. A patient may have several records, one for each disease. In this case, $QID = \{Job, Sex, Age\}$ is not a key and k-anonymity on QID fails to ensure that each group on QID contains at least k (*distinct*) patients. For example, if each patient has at least 3 diseases, a group of k records will involve no more than $k/3$ patients.   □

2.1.2 (X, Y)-**Anonymity**

To address the shortcoming of k-anonymity discussed in Example 2.4, Wang and Fung [236] propose the notion of (X, Y)-anonymity, where X and Y are disjoint sets of attributes. For a table T, $\Pi(T)$ and $\sigma(T)$ denote the projection and selection over T, $att(T)$ denotes the set of attributes in T, and $|T|$ denotes the number of distinct records in T.

DEFINITION 2.1 (X, Y)-**anonymity**   *[236]* Let x be a value on X. The *anonymity* of x with respect to Y, denoted by $a_Y(x)$, is the number of distinct values on Y that co-occur with x, i.e., $|\Pi_Y \sigma_x(T)|$. If Y is a key in T, $a_Y(x)$, also written as $a(x)$, is equal to the number of records containing x. Let $A_Y(X) = min\{a_Y(x) \mid x \in X\}$. A table T *satisfies* the (X, Y)-anonymity for some specified integer k if $A_Y(X) \geq k$. ∎

(X, Y)-anonymity specifies that each value on X is linked to at least k *distinct* values on Y. The k-anonymity is the special case where X is the QID and Y is a key in T that uniquely identifies record owners. (X, Y)-anonymity provides a uniform and flexible way to specify different types of privacy requirements. If each value on X describes a group of record owners (e.g., $X = \{Job, Sex, Age\}$) and Y represents the sensitive attribute (e.g., $Y = \{Disease\}$), this means that each group is associated with a diverse set of sensitive values, making it difficult to infer a specific sensitive value. The next example shows the usefulness of (X, Y)-anonymity for modeling k-anonymity in the case that several records may represent the same record owner.

Example 2.5
Continue from Example 2.4. With (X, Y)-anonymity, we specify k-anonymity with respect to *patients* by letting $X = \{Job, Sex, Age\}$ and $Y = \{Pid\}$. That is, each X group is linked to at least k distinct patient IDs, therefore, k distinct patients.   □

2.1.3 Dilemma on Choosing QID

One challenge faced by a data holder is how to classify the attributes in a data table into three disjoint sets: QID, Sensitive_Attributes, and Non-Sensitive_Attributes. QID in principle should contain an attribute A if the adversary could potentially obtain A from other external sources. After the QID is determined, remaining attributes are grouped into Sensitive_Attributes and Non-Sensitive_Attributes based on their sensitivity. There is no definite answer for the question of how a data holder can determine whether or not an adversary can obtain an attribute A from some external sources, but it is important to understand the implications of a misclassification: misclassifying an attribute A into Sensitive_Attributes or Non-Sensitive_Attributes may compromise another sensitive attribute S because an adversary may obtain A from other sources and then use A to perform record linkage or attribute linkage on S. On the other hand, misclassifying a sensitive attribute S into QID may directly compromise sensitive attribute S of some target victim because an adversary may use attributes in $QID-S$ to perform attribute linkage on S. Furthermore, incorrectly including S in QID causes unnecessary information loss due to the curse of dimensionality [6].

Motwani and Xu [174] present a method to determine the minimal set of quasi-identifiers for a data table T. The intuition is to identify a minimal set of attributes from T that has the ability to (almost) distinctly identify a record and the ability to separate two data records. Nonetheless, the minimal set of QID does not imply the most appropriate privacy protection setting because the method does not consider what attributes the adversary could potentially have. If the adversary can obtain a bit more information about the target victim beyond the minimal set, then he may be able to conduct a successful linking attack. The choice of QID remains an open issue.

k-anonymity and (X, Y)-anonymity prevent record linkage by hiding the record of a victim in a large group of records with the same QID. However, if most records in a group have similar values on a sensitive attribute, the adversary can still associate the victim to her sensitive value without having to identify her record. This situation is illustrated in Table 2.4, which is 3-anonymous. For a victim matching $qid = \langle Artist, Female, [30\text{-}35] \rangle$, the confidence of inferring that the victim has HIV is 75% because 3 out of the 4 records in the group have HIV. Though (X, Y)-anonymity requires that each X group is linked to at least k distinct Y values, if some Y values occur more frequently than others, there is a higher confidence of inferring the more frequent values. This leads us to the next family of privacy models for preventing this type of attribute linkage.

2.2 Attribute Linkage Model

In the attack of *attribute linkage*, the adversary may not precisely identify the record of the target victim, but could infer his/her sensitive values from the published data T, based on the set of sensitive values associated to the group that the victim belongs to. In case some sensitive values predominate in a group, a successful inference becomes relatively easy even if k-anonymity is satisfied.

Example 2.6

Consider the 3-anonymous data in Table 2.4. Suppose the adversary knows that the target victim *Emily* is a female dancer at age 30 and owns a record in the table. The adversary may infer that *Emily* has *HIV* with 75% confidence because 3 out of the 4 female artists with age *[30-35)* have *HIV*. Regardless of the correctness of the inference, *Emily*'s privacy has been compromised.□

Clifton [49] suggests eliminating attribute linkages by limiting the released data size. Limiting data size may not be desirable if data records, such as *HIV* patients' data, are valuable data and are difficult to obtain. Below we discuss several other approaches proposed to address this type of threat. The general idea is to diminish the correlation between QID attributes and sensitive attributes.

2.2.1 ℓ-Diversity

Machanavajjhala et al. [160, 162] propose the diversity principle, called *ℓ-diversity*, to prevent attribute linkage. The ℓ-diversity requires every *qid* group to contain at least ℓ "well-represented" sensitive values. A similar idea was previously discussed in [181]. There are several instantiations of this principle, which differ in what it means by being well-represented. The simplest understanding of "well-represented" is to ensure that there are at least ℓ distinct values for the sensitive attribute in each *qid* group, where *qid* group is the set of records having the value *qid* on QID. This *distinct ℓ-diversity* privacy model (also known as p-sensitive k-anonymity [226]) automatically satisfies k-anonymity, where $k = \ell$, because each *qid* group contains at least ℓ records. Distinct ℓ-diversity cannot prevent probabilistic inference attacks because some sensitive values are naturally more frequent than others in a group, enabling an adversary to conclude that a record in the group is very likely to have those values. For example, *Flu* is more common than *HIV*. This motivates the following two stronger notions of ℓ-diversity.

A table is *entropy ℓ-diverse* if for every *qid* group

$$-\sum_{s \in S} P(qid, s) log(P(qid, s)) \geq log(\ell) \qquad (2.1)$$

where S is a sensitive attribute, $P(qid, s)$ is the fraction of records in a *qid* group having the sensitive value s. The left-hand side, called the entropy of the sensitive attribute, has the property that more evenly distributed sensitive values in a *qid* group produce a larger value. Therefore, a large threshold value

ℓ implies less certainty of inferring a particular sensitive value in a group. Note that the inequality does not depend on the choice of the log base.

Example 2.7

Consider Table 2.4. For the first group $\langle Professional, Male, [35\text{-}40]\rangle$,

$$-\tfrac{2}{3}log\tfrac{2}{3} - \tfrac{1}{3}log\tfrac{1}{3} = log(1.9),$$

and for the second group $\langle Artist, Female, [30\text{-}35]\rangle$,

$$-\tfrac{3}{4}log\tfrac{3}{4} - \tfrac{1}{4}log\tfrac{1}{4} = log(1.8).$$

So the table satisfies entropy ℓ-diversity where $\ell \leq 1.8$. $\qquad\square$

To achieve entropy ℓ-diversity, the table as a whole must be at least $log(l)$ since the entropy of a qid group is always greater than or equal to the minimum entropy of its subgroups $\{qid_1, \ldots, qid_n\}$ where $qid = qid_1 \cup \cdots \cup qid_n$, that is,

$$entropy(qid) \geq min(entropy(qid_1), \ldots, entropy(qid_n)).$$

This requirement is hard to achieve, especially if some sensitive value frequently occurs in S.

One limitation of entropy ℓ-diversity is that it does not provide a probability-based risk measure, which tends to be more intuitive to the human data holder. For example in Table 2.4, being entropy 1.8-diverse in Example 2.7 does not convey the risk level that the adversary has 75% probability of success to infer HIV where 3 out of the 4 record owners in the qid group have HIV. Also, it is difficult to specify different protection levels based on varied sensitivity and frequency of sensitive values.

It is interesting to note that entropy was also used to measure the anonymity of senders in an anonymous communication system [61, 209] where an adversary employs techniques such as traffic analysis to identify the potential sender (or receiver) of a message. The goal of anonymous communication is to hide the identity of senders during data transfer by using techniques such as *mix network* [45] and *crowds* [197]. The general idea is to blend the senders into a large and characteristically diverse crowd of senders; the crowd collectively sends messages on behalf of its members. Diaz et al. [61], and Serjantov and Danezis [209] employ entropy to measure the diversity of a crowd.

DEFINITION 2.2 recursive (c, ℓ)-diverse *[162]* Let $c > 0$ be a constant. Let S be a sensitive attribute. Let $s_1, \ldots, s_m$ be the values of S that appear in the qid group. Let $f_1, \ldots, f_m$ be their corresponding frequency counts in qid. Let $f_{(1)}, \ldots, f_{(m)}$ be those counts sorted in non-increasing order. A table is *recursive (c, ℓ)-diverse* if every qid group satisfies $f_{(1)} \leq c \sum_{i=\ell}^{m} f_{(i)}$ for some constant c. $\blacksquare$

The recursive (c, ℓ)-diversity makes sure that the most frequent value does not appear too frequently, and the less frequent values do not appear too rarely. A *qid* group is recursive (c, ℓ)-*diverse* if the frequency of the most frequent sensitive value is less than the sum of the frequencies of the $m - \ell + 1$ least frequent sensitive values multiplying by some publisher-specified constant c, i.e., $f_{(1)} < c \sum_{i=\ell}^{m} f_{(i)}$. The intuition is that even if the adversary excludes some possible sensitive values of a victim by applying background knowledge, the inequality remains to hold for the remaining values; therefore, the remaining ones remain hard to infer. A table is considered to have recursive (c, ℓ)-diversity if all of its groups have recursive (c, ℓ)-diversity.

This instantiation is less restrictive than the entropy ℓ-diversity because a larger c, which is a parameter independent of the frequencies of sensitive values, can relax the restrictiveness. However, if a sensitive value occurs very frequently in S, this requirement is still hard to satisfy. For example, if $p\%$ of the records in the table contains the most frequent sensitive value s, then at least one *qid* group will have $|qid \wedge s|/|qid| \geq p\%$ where $|qid|$ denotes the number of records containing the *qid* value, and $|qid \wedge s|$ denotes the number of records containing both the *qid* and s values. This *qid* group could easily violate the recursive (c, ℓ)-diversity if c is small.

Machanavajjhala et al. [160, 162] also present two other instantiations, called *positive disclosure-recursive* (c, ℓ)-*diversity* and *negative/positive disclosure-recursive* (c, ℓ)-*diversity* to capture the adversary's background knowledge. Suppose a victim is in a *qid* group that contains three different sensitive values $\{Flu, Cancer, HIV\}$, and suppose the adversary knows that the victim has no symptom of having a flu. Given this piece of background knowledge, the adversary can eliminate Flu from the set of candidate sensitive values of the victim. Martin et al. [165] propose a language to capture this type of background knowledge and to represent the knowledge as k units of information. Furthermore, the language could capture the type of implication knowledge. For example, given that Alice, Bob, and Cathy have flu, the adversary infers that Doug is very likely to have flu, too, because all four of them live together. This implication is considered to be one unit of information. Given an anonymous table T and k units of background knowledge, Martin et al. [165] estimate the maximum disclosure risk of T, which is the probability of the most likely predicted sensitive value assignment of any record owner in T.

ℓ-diversity has the limitation of implicitly assuming that each sensitive attribute takes values uniformly over its domain. In case the frequencies of sensitive values are not similar, achieving ℓ-diversity may cause a large data utility loss. Consider a data table containing data of 1000 patients on some QID attributes and a single sensitive attribute *Disease* with two possible values, HIV or Flu. Assume that there are only 5 patients with HIV in the table. To achieve 2-diversity, at least one patient with HIV is needed in each *qid* group; therefore, at most 5 groups can be formed [66], resulting in high information loss in this case.

A common view in the literature is that ℓ-diversity should replace k-anonymity. In fact, it depends on the data publishing scenario. Usually linking attack involves data from two sources, one table T_1 containing names and identity of individuals (e.g., voter list), and one table T_2 containing sensitive attributes (e.g., medical data), and both containing QID attribute. k-anonymity is suitable for anonymizing T_1 and ℓ-diversity is suitable for anonymizing T_2. In this sense, these two privacy notions are not competitors, but rather are different tools to be used under different scenarios.

2.2.2 Confidence Bounding

Wang et al. [237] consider bounding the confidence of inferring a sensitive value from a *qid* group by specifying one or more *privacy templates* of the form, $\langle QID \rightarrow s, h \rangle$. s is a sensitive value, QID is a quasi-identifier, and h is a threshold. Let $Conf(QID \rightarrow s)$ be $max\{conf(qid \rightarrow s)\}$ over all *qid* groups on QID, where $conf(qid \rightarrow s)$ denotes the percentage of records containing s in the *qid* group. A table satisfies $\langle QID \rightarrow s, h \rangle$ if $Conf(QID \rightarrow s) \leq h$. In other words, $\langle QID \rightarrow s, h \rangle$ bounds the adversary's confidence of inferring the sensitive value s in any group on QID to the maximum h. Note, confidence bounding is also known as ℓ^+-diversity in [157].

For example, with $QID = \{Job, Sex, Age\}$, $\langle QID \rightarrow HIV, 10\% \rangle$ states that the confidence of inferring HIV from any group on QID is no more than 10%. For the data in Table 2.4, this privacy template is violated because the confidence of inferring HIV is 75% in the group $\{Artist, Female, [30-35)\}$.

The confidence measure has two advantages over recursive (c, ℓ)-diversity and entropy ℓ-diversity. First, the confidence measure is more intuitive because the risk is measured by the probability of inferring a sensitive value. The data holder relies on this intuition to specify the acceptable maximum confidence threshold. Second, it allows the flexibility for the data holder to specify a different threshold h for each combination of QID and s according to the perceived sensitivity of inferring s from a group on QID. The recursive (c, ℓ)-diversity cannot be used to bound the frequency of sensitive values that are not the most frequent. For example, if Flu has frequency of 90% and HIV has 5%, and others have 3% and 2%, it is difficult to satisfy (c, l)-diversity. Even if it is satisfied, it does not protect the less frequent HIV which needs a much stronger (c, l)-diversity than Flu. Confidence bounding provides greater flexibility than ℓ-diversity in this aspect. However, recursive (c, ℓ)-diversity can still prevent attribute linkages even in the presence of background knowledge as discussed earlier. Confidence bounding does not share the same merit.

2.2.3 (X, Y)-Linkability

(X, Y)-anonymity in Chapter 2.1.2 states that each group on X has at least k distinct values on Y (e.g., diseases). However, being linked to k persons does not imply that the probability of being linked to any of them is $1/k$. If some Y values occur more frequently than others, the probability of inferring a particular Y value can be higher than $1/k$. The (X, Y)-*linkability* below addresses this issue.

DEFINITION 2.3 (X, Y)-*linkability*   *[236]* Let x be a value on X and y be a value on Y. The *linkability* of x to y, denoted by $l_y(x)$, is the percentage of the records that contain both x and y among those that contain x, i.e., $a(y, x)/a(x)$, where $a(x)$ denotes the number of records containing x and $a(y, x)$ is number of records containing both y and x. Let $L_y(X) = max\{l_y(x) \mid x \in X\}$ and $L_Y(X) = max\{L_y(X) \mid y \in Y\}$. We say that T *satisfies* the (X, Y)-linkability for some specified real $0 < k \leq 1$ if $L_Y(X) \leq h$. ∎

In words, (X, Y)-linkability limits the confidence of inferring a value on Y from a value on X. With X and Y describing individuals and sensitive properties, any such inference with a high confidence is a privacy breach. Often, not all but some values y on Y are sensitive, in which case Y can be replaced with a subset of y_i values on Y, written $Y = \{y_1, \ldots, y_p\}$, and a different threshold h can be specified for each y_i. More generally, we can allow multiple Y_i, each representing a subset of values on a different set of attributes, with Y being the union of all Y_i. For example, $Y_1 = \{HIV\}$ on *Test* and $Y_2 = \{Banker\}$ on *Job*. Such a "value-level" specification provides a great flexibility essential for minimizing the data distortion.

2.2.4 (X, Y)-**Privacy**

Wang and Fung [236] propose a general privacy model, called (X, Y)-*privacy*, which combines both (X, Y)-anonymity and (X, Y)-linkability. The general idea is to require each group x on X to contain at least k records and the confidence of inferring any $y \in Y$ from any $x \in X$ is limited to a maximum confidence threshold h. Note, the notion of (X, Y)-privacy is not only applicable to a single table, but is also applicable to the scenario of multiple releases. Chapter 9 discusses (X, Y)-privacy in the context of sequential anonymization in details.

2.2.5 (α, k)-**Anonymity**

Wong et al. [246] propose a similar integrated privacy model called (α, k)-*anonymity*, requiring every *qid* in a Table T to be shared by at least k records and $conf(qid \rightarrow s) \leq \alpha$ for any sensitive value s, where k and α are data holder-specified thresholds. Nonetheless, both (X, Y)-Privacy and (α, k)-anonymity may result in high distortion if the sensitive values are skewed.

2.2.6 *LKC*-Privacy

In most previously studied record and attribute linkage model, the usual approach is to generalize the records into equivalence groups so that each group contains at least k records with respect to some QID attributes, and the sensitive values in each qid group are diversified enough to disorient confident inferences. However, Aggarwal [6] has shown that when the number of QID attributes is large, that is, when the dimensionality of data is high, most of the data have to be suppressed in order to achieve k-anonymity. Applying k-anonymity on the high-dimensional patient data would significantly degrade the data quality. This problem is known as *the curse of high-dimensionality on k-anonymity* [6].

To overcome this problem, Mohammed et al. [171] exploit the limited prior knowledge of adversary: in real-life privacy attacks, it is very difficult for an adversary to acquire *all* the information in QID of a target victim because it requires non-trivial effort to gather each piece of prior knowledge from so many possible values. Thus, it is reasonable to assume that the adversary's prior knowledge is bounded by at most L values of the QID attributes of the target victim. Based on this assumption, Mohammed et al. [171] propose a privacy model called *LKC-privacy*, which will be further discussed in a real-life application in Chapter 6, for anonymizing high-dimensional data. The assumption of limited adversary's knowledge has also been previously applied for anonymizing high-dimensional transaction data [255, 256], which will be discussed in Chapter 13.

The general intuition of *LKC*-privacy is to ensure that every combination of values in $QID_j \subseteq QID$ with maximum length L in the data table T is shared by at least K records, and the confidence of inferring any sensitive values in S is not greater than C, where L, K, C are thresholds and S is a set of sensitive values specified by the data holder (the hospital). *LKC*-privacy bounds the probability of a successful record linkage to be $\leq 1/K$ and the probability of a successful attribute linkage to be $\leq C$, provided that the adversary's prior knowledge does not exceed L values.

DEFINITION 2.4 *LKC*-privacy   Let L be the maximum number of values of the prior knowledge. Let S be a set of sensitive values. A data table T satisfies *LKC-privacy* if and only if for any qid with $|qid| \leq L$,

1. $|T[qid]| \geq K$, where $K > 0$ is an integer anonymity threshold, where $T[qid]$ denotes the set of records containing qid in T, and

2. $conf(qid \rightarrow s) \leq C$ for any $s \in S$, where $0 < C \leq 1$ is a real number confidence threshold. ∎

The data holder specifies the thresholds L, K, and C. The maximum length L reflects the assumption of the adversary's power. *LKC*-privacy guarantees the probability of a successful record linkage to be $\leq 1/K$ and the probability of a successful attribute linkage to be $\leq C$. LKC-privacy has several nice properties that make it suitable for anonymizing high-dimensional data.

- LKC-privacy requires only a subset of QID attributes to be shared by at least K records. This is a major relaxation from traditional k-anonymity, based on a very reasonable assumption that the adversary has limited power.

- LKC-privacy generalizes several traditional privacy models. k-anonymity is a special case of LKC-privacy with $L = |QID|$, $K = k$, and $C = 100\%$, where $|QID|$ is the number of QID attributes in the data table. Confidence bounding is also a special case of LKC-privacy with $L = |QID|$ and $K = 1$. (α, k)-anonymity is also a special case of LKC-privacy with $L = |QID|$, $K = k$, and $C = \alpha$. ℓ-diversity is also a special case of LKC-privacy with $L = |QID|$, $K = 1$, and $C = 1/\ell$. Thus, the hospital can still achieve the traditional models if needed.

- LKC-privacy is flexible to adjust the trade-off between data privacy and data utility. Increasing L and K, or decreasing C would improve the privacy in the expense of data utility loss.

- LKC-privacy is a general privacy model that thwarts both record linkage and attribute linkage, i.e., the privacy model is applicable to anonymize data with or without sensitive attributes.

2.2.7 (k, e)-Anonymity

Most works on k-anonymity and its extensions assume categorical sensitive attributes. Zhang et al. [269] propose the notion of (k, e)-anonymity to address numerical sensitive attributes such as salary. The general idea is to partition the records into groups so that each group contains at least k different sensitive values with a range of at least e. However, (k, e)-anonymity ignores the distribution of sensitive values within the range λ. If some sensitive values occur frequently within a subrange of λ, then the adversary could still confidently infer the subrange in a group. This type of attribute linkage attack is called the *proximity attack* [152]. Consider a *qid* group of 10 data records with 7 different sensitive values, where 9 records have sensitive values between 30 and 35, and 1 record has value 80. As shown in Table 2.6, the group is $(7, 50)$-anonymous because $80 - 30 = 50$. Still, the adversary can infer that a victim inside the group has a sensitive value falling into [30-35] with 90% confidence because 9 out of the 10 records contain values in the sensitive range. Li et al. [152] propose an alternative privacy model, called (ϵ, m)-*anonymity*. Given any numerical sensitive value s in T, this privacy model bounds the probability of inferring $[s - \epsilon, s + \epsilon]$ to be at most $1/m$.

Table 2.6: $(7,50)$-anonymous group

Quasi-identifier		Sensitive	Comment
Job	**Sex**	**Salary**	
Artist	Female	30	*sensitive*
Artist	Female	31	*sensitive*
Artist	Female	30	*sensitive*
Artist	Female	32	*sensitive*
Artist	Female	35	*sensitive*
Artist	Female	34	*sensitive*
Artist	Female	33	*sensitive*
Artist	Female	32	*sensitive*
Artist	Female	35	*sensitive*
Artist	Female	80	*not sensitive*

2.2.8   *t*-Closeness

In a spirit similar to the uninformative principle discussed earlier, Li et al. [153] observe that when the overall distribution of a sensitive attribute is skewed, ℓ-diversity does not prevent attribute linkage attacks. Consider a patient table where 95% of records have *Flu* and 5% of records have *HIV*. Suppose that a *qid* group has 50% of *Flu* and 50% of *HIV* and, therefore, satisfies 2-diversity. However, this group presents a serious privacy threat because any record owner in the group could be inferred as having *HIV* with 50% confidence, compared to 5% in the overall table.

To prevent *skewness attack*, Li et al. [153] propose a privacy model, called *t*-Closeness, which requires the distribution of a sensitive attribute in any group on *QID* to be close to the distribution of the attribute in the overall table. *t*-closeness uses the *Earth Mover Distance* (*EMD*) function to measure the closeness between two distributions of sensitive values, and requires the closeness to be within *t*. *t*-closeness has several limitations and weaknesses. First, it lacks the flexibility of specifying different protection levels for different sensitive values. Second, the *EMD* function is not suitable for preventing attribute linkage on numerical sensitive attributes [152]. Third, enforcing *t*-closeness would greatly degrade the data utility because it requires the distribution of sensitive values to be the same in all *qid* groups. This would significantly damage the correlation between *QID* and sensitive attributes. One way to decrease the damage is to relax the requirement by adjusting the thresholds with the increased risk of skewness attack [66], or to employ the probabilistic privacy models in Chapter 2.4.

2.2.9   Personalized Privacy

Xiao and Tao [250] propose the notion of *personalized privacy* to allow each record owner to specify her own privacy level. This model assumes that each sensitive attribute has a taxonomy tree and that each record owner specifies a guarding node in this tree. The record owner's privacy is violated if an adversary is able to infer any domain sensitive value within the subtree of her guarding node with a probability, called *breach probability*, greater than a certain threshold. For example, suppose HIV and $SARS$ are child nodes of $Infectious\ Disease$ in the taxonomy tree. An HIV patient Alice can set the guarding node to $Infectious\ Disease$, meaning that she allows people to infer that she has some infectious diseases, but not any specific type of infectious disease. Another HIV patient, Bob, does not mind disclosing his medical information, so he does not set any guarding node for this sensitive attribute.

Although both confidence bounding and personalized privacy take an approach to bound the confidence or probability of inferring a sensitive value from a qid group, they have differences. In the confidence bounding approach, the data holder imposes a universal privacy requirement on the entire data set, so the minimum level of privacy protection is the same for every record owner. In the personalized privacy approach, a guarding node is specified for each record by its owner. The advantage is that each record owner may specify a guarding node according to her own tolerance on sensitivity. Experiments show that this personalized privacy requirement could result in lower information loss than the universal privacy requirement [250]. In practice, however, it is unclear how individual record owners would set their guarding node. Often, a reasonable guarding node depends on the distribution of sensitive values in the whole table or in a group. For example, knowing that her disease is very common, a record owner may set a more special (lower privacy protected) guarding node for her record. Nonetheless, the record owners usually have no access to the distribution of sensitive values in their qid group or in the whole table before the data is published. Without such information, the tendency is to play safe by setting a more general (higher privacy protected) guarding node, which may negatively affect the utility of data.

2.2.10 FF-**Anonymity**

Most previously discussed works assume that the data table can be divided into quasi-identifying (QID) attributes and sensitive attributes. Yet, this assumption does not hold when an attribute contains both sensitive values and quasi-identifying values. Wong et al. [238] identify a class of *freeform attacks* of the form $X \rightarrow s$, where s and the values in X can be any values of any attributes in the table T. $X \rightarrow s$ is a privacy breach if any record in T matching X can infer a sensitive value s with a high probability. The privacy model, FF-*anonymity*, bounds the probability of all potential privacy breaches in the form $X \rightarrow s$ to be below a given threshold.

The key idea of FF-anonymity is that it distinguish between observable values and sensitive values at the value level, instead of at the attribute level. Every attribute potentially contains both types of values. For example, some diseases are sensitive and some are not. Thus, non-sensitive diseases become observable to an adversary and may be used in X for linking attacks. There is no notion of a fixed QID as in the other works.

2.3   Table Linkage Model

Both record linkage and attribute linkage assume that the adversary already knows the victim's record is in the released table T. However, in some cases, the presence (or the absence) of the victim's record in T already reveals the victim's sensitive information. Suppose a hospital releases a data table with a particular type of disease. Identifying the presence of the victim's record in the table is already damaging. A *table linkage* occurs if an adversary can confidently infer the presence or the absence of the victim's record in the released table. The following example illustrates the privacy threat of a table linkage.

Example 2.8

Suppose the data holder has released a 3-anonymous patient table T (Table 2.4). To launch a table linkage on a target victim, for instance, Alice, on T, the adversary is presumed to also have access to an external public table E (Table 2.5) where $T \subseteq E$. The probability that Alice is present in T is $\frac{4}{5} = 0.8$ because there are 4 records in T (Table 2.4) and 5 records in E (Table 2.5) containing $\langle Artist, Female, [30\text{-}35] \rangle$. Similarly, the probability that Bob is present in T is $\frac{3}{4} = 0.75$. □

δ-Presence

To prevent table linkage, Ercan Nergiz et al. [176] propose to bound the probability of inferring the presence of any potential victim's record within a specified range $\delta = (\delta_{min}, \delta_{max})$. Formally, given an external public table E and a private table T, where $T \subseteq E$, a generalized table T' satisfies $(\delta_{min}, \delta_{max})$-*presence* if $\delta_{min} \leq P(t \in T | T') \leq \delta_{max}$ for all $t \in E$. δ-presence can indirectly prevent record and attribute linkages because if the adversary has at most $\delta\%$ of confidence that the target victim's record is present in the released table, then the probability of a successful linkage to her record and sensitive attribute is at most $\delta\%$. Though δ-presence is a relatively "safe" privacy model, it assumes that the data holder has access to the same external table E as the adversary does. This may not be a practical assumption in some situations.

2.4   Probabilistic Model

There is another family of privacy models that does not focus on exactly what records, attribute values, and tables the adversary can link to a target victim, but focuses on how the adversary would change his/her probabilistic belief on the sensitive information of a victim after accessing the published data. In general, this group of privacy models aims at achieving the uninformative principle [160], whose goal is to ensure that the difference between the prior and posterior beliefs is small.

2.4.1 (c, t)-Isolation

Chawla et al. [46] suggest that having access to the published anonymous data table should not enhance an adversary's power of isolating any record owner. Consequently, they proposed a privacy model to prevent (c, t)-*isolation* in a statistical database. Suppose p is a data point of a target victim v in a data table, and q is the adversary's inferred data point of v by using the published data and the background information. Let δ_p be the distance between p and q. We say that point q (c, t)-*isolates* point p if $B(q, c\delta_p)$ contains fewer than t points in the table, where $B(q, c\delta_p)$ is a ball of radius $c\delta_p$ centered at point q. Preventing (c, t)-isolation can be viewed as preventing record linkages. Their model considers distances among data records and, therefore, is more suitable for numerical attributes in statistical databases.

2.4.2 ϵ-Differential Privacy

Dwork [74] proposes an insightful privacy notion: the risk to the record owner's privacy should not substantially increase as a result of participating in a statistical database. Instead of comparing the prior probability and the posterior probability before and after accessing the published data, Dwork [74] proposes to compare the risk with and without the record owner's data in the published data. Consequently, the privacy model called ϵ-*differential privacy* ensures that the removal or addition of a single database record does not significantly affect the outcome of any analysis. It follows that no risk is incurred by joining different databases. Based on the same intuition, if a record owner does not provide his/her actual information to the data holder, it will not make much difference in the result of the anonymization algorithm.

The following is a more formal definition of ϵ-differential privacy [74]: A randomized function F ensures ϵ-differential privacy if for all data sets T_1 and T_2 differing on at most one record,

$$|ln\frac{P[F(T_1) = S]}{P[F(T_2) = S]}| \le \epsilon \qquad (2.2)$$

for all $S \in Range(F)$, where $Range(F)$ is the set of possible outputs of the randomized function F. Although ϵ-differential privacy does not prevent record and attribute linkages studied in earlier chapters, it assures record owners that they may submit their personal information to the database securely in the knowledge that nothing, or almost nothing, can be discovered from the database with their information that could not have been discovered without their information. Dwork [74] formally proves that ϵ-differential privacy can provide a guarantee against adversaries with arbitrary background knowledge. This strong guarantee is achieved by comparison with and without the record owner's data in the published data. Dwork [75] proves that if the number of queries is sub-linear in n, the noise to achieve differential privacy is bounded by $o(\sqrt{n})$, where n is the number of records in the database. Dwork [76] further shows that the notion of differential privacy is applicable to both interactive and non-interactive query models, discussed in Chapters 1.2 and 17.1. Refer to [76] for a survey on differential privacy.

2.4.3 (d, γ)-Privacy

Rastogi et al. [193] present a probabilistic privacy definition (d, γ)-*privacy*. Let $P(r)$ and $P(r|T)$ be the prior probability and the posterior probability of the presence of a victim's record in the data table T before and after examining the published table T. (d, γ)-privacy bounds the difference of the prior and posterior probabilities and provides a provable guarantee on privacy and information utility, while most previous work lacks such formal guarantee. Rastogi et al. [193] show that a reasonable trade-off between privacy and utility can be achieved only when the prior belief is small. Nonetheless, (d, γ)-privacy is designed to protect only against attacks that are *d-independent*: an attack is d-independent if the prior belief $P(r)$ satisfies the conditions $P(r) = 1$ or $P(r) \leq d$ for all records r, where $P(r) = 1$ means that the adversary already knows that r is in T and no protection on r is needed. However, this d-independence assumption may not hold in some real-life applications [161]. Differential privacy in comparison does not have to assume that records are independent or that an adversary has a prior belief bounded by a probability distribution.

2.4.4 Distributional Privacy

Motivated by the learning theory, Blum et al. [33] present a privacy model called *distributional privacy* for a non-interactive query model. The key idea is that when a data table is drawn from a distribution, the table should reveal only information about the underlying distribution, and nothing else. Distributional privacy is a strictly stronger privacy notion than differential privacy, and can answer all queries over a discretized domain in a concept class of polynomial VC-dimension, where Vapnik-Chervonenkis (VC) dimension is a measure of the capacity of a statistical classification algorithm. Yet, the algorithm has high computational cost. Blum et al. [33] present an efficient algorithm specifically for simple interval queries with limited constraints. The problems of developing efficient algorithms for more complicated queries remain open.

2.5   Modeling Adversary's Background Knowledge

Most privacy models, such as k-anonymity, ℓ-diversity, confidence bounding, (α, k)-anonymity, and t-closeness, assume the adversary has only very limited background knowledge. Specifically, they assume that the adversary's background knowledge is limited to knowing the quasi-identifier. Yet, recent work has shown the importance of integrating an adversary's background knowledge in privacy quantification. A robust privacy notion has to take background knowledge into consideration. Since an adversary can easily learn background knowledge from various sources, such as common sense, demographic statistic data, social networks, and other individual-level information, a common challenge faced by all research on integrating background knowledge is to determine what and how much knowledge should be considered.

2.5.1   Skyline Privacy

Chen et al. [48] argue that since it is infeasible for a data publisher to anticipate the background knowledge possessed by an adversary, the interesting research direction is to consider only the background knowledge that arises naturally in practice and can be efficiently handled. In particular, three types of background knowledge, known as *three-dimensional knowledge*, are considered in [48]:

- knowledge about the target victim,

- knowledge about other record owners in the published data, and

- knowledge about the group of record owners having the same sensitive value as that of the target victim.

Background knowledge is expressed by conjunctions of *literals* that are in the form of either $s \in t[S]$ or $s \notin t[S]$, denoting that the individual t has a sensitive value s or does not have a sensitive value s respectively. The three-dimensional knowledge is quantified as a (ℓ, k, m) triplet, which indicates that an adversary knows:

1. ℓ sensitive values that the target victim t does not have,

2. the sensitive values of other k individuals, and

3. m individuals having the same sensitive value as that of t.

Then, the authors propose *skyline privacy criterion*, which allows the data publisher to specify a set of *incomparable* (ℓ, k, m) triplets, called a *skyline*, along with a set of confidence thresholds for a sensitive value σ in order to provide more precise and flexible privacy quantification. Under the definition of skyline privacy criterion, an anonymized data set is safe if and only if for all triplets in the skyline, the adversary's maximum confidence of inferring the sensitive value σ is less than the corresponding threshold specified by the data publisher.

2.5.2 Privacy-MaxEnt

The expressive power of background knowledge in [48] is limited. For example, it fails to express probabilistic background knowledge. Du et al. [70] specifically address the background knowledge in the form of probabilities, for example, $P(Ovarian\ Cancer|Male) = 0$. The primary privacy risks in PPDP come from the linkages between the sensitive attributes (S) and the quasi-identifiers (QID). Quantifying privacy is, therefore, to derive $P(S|QID)$ for any instance of S and QID with the probabilistic background knowledge. Du et al. [70] formulate the derivation of $P(S|QID)$ as a non-linear programming problem. $P(s|qid)$ is considered as a variable for each combination of $s \in S$ and $qid \in QID$. To assign probability values to these variables, both background knowledge and the anonymized data set are integrated as constraints guiding the assignment. The meaning of each variable is actually the inference on $P(s|qid)$. The authors deem that such inference should be as unbiased as possible. This thought leads to the utilization of *maximum entropy principle*, which states that when the entropy of these variables is maximized, the inference is the most unbiased [70]. Thus, the problem is re-formulated as finding the maximum-entropy assignment for the variables while satisfying the constraints. Since it is impossible for a data publisher to enumerate all probabilistic background knowledge, a bound of knowledge is used instead. In [70], the bound is specified by both the Top-K *positive association rules* and the Top-K *negative association rules* derived from the published data set. Currently, the paper is limited in handling only equality background knowledge constraints.

2.5.3 Skyline (B, t)-Privacy

Since both [48] and [70] are unaware of exact background knowledge possessed by an adversary, Li and Li [154] propose a generic framework to systematically model different types of background knowledge an adversary may possess. Yet, the paper narrows its scope to background knowledge that is consistent with the original data set T. Modeling background knowledge is to estimate the adversary's prior belief of the sensitive attribute values over all possible QID values. This can be achieved by identifying the underlying prior belief function P_{pri} that best fits T using a *kernel regression estimation method*. One of the components of kernel estimation, the bandwidth B, is used to measure how much background knowledge an adversary has. Based on the background knowledge and the anonymized data set, the paper proposes an approximate inference method called Ω-estimate to efficiently calculate the adversary's posterior belief of the sensitive values. Consequently, the *skyline* (B, t)-*privacy principle* is defined based on the adversary's prior and posterior beliefs. Given a skyline $\{(B_1, t_1), (B_2, t_2), \ldots, (B_n, t_n)\}$, an anonymized data set satisfies the skyline (B, t)-privacy principle if and only if for $i = 1$ to n, the maximum difference between the adversary's prior and posterior beliefs for all tuples in the data set is at most t_i. Li and Li [154] point out that slight changes of B do not incur significant changes of the corresponding privacy risks. Thus, the data publisher only needs to specify a set of well-chosen B values to protect the privacy against all adversaries.

Chapter 3

Anonymization Operations

The raw data table usually does not satisfy a specified privacy requirement and the table must be modified before being published. The modification is done by applying a sequence of anonymization operations to the table. An anonymization operation comes in several flavors: generalization, suppression, anatomization, permutation, and perturbation. Generalization and suppression replace values of specific description, typically the QID attributes, with less specific description. Anatomization and permutation de-associate the correlation between QID and sensitive attributes by grouping and shuffling sensitive values in a qid group. Perturbation distorts the data by adding noise, aggregating values, swapping values, or generating synthetic data based on some statistical properties of the original data. Below, we discuss these anonymization operations in detail.

3.1 Generalization and Suppression

Each generalization or suppression operation hides some details in QID. For a categorical attribute, a specific value can be replaced with a general value according to a given taxonomy. In Figure 3.1, the parent node *Professional* is more general than the child nodes *Engineer* and *Lawyer*. The root node, *ANY_Job*, represents the most general value in *Job*. For a numerical attribute, exact values can be replaced with an interval that covers exact values. If a taxonomy of intervals is given, the situation is similar to categorical attributes. More often, however, no pre-determined taxonomy is given for a numerical attribute. Different classes of anonymization operations have different implications on privacy protection, data utility, and search space. But they all result in a less precise but consistent representation of original data.

A *generalization* replaces some values with a parent value in the taxonomy of an attribute. The reverse operation of generalization is called *specialization*. A *suppression* replaces some values with a special value, indicating that the replaced values are not disclosed. The reverse operation of suppression is called *disclosure*. Below, we summarize five generalization schemes.

Full-domain generalization scheme [148, 201, 217]. In this scheme, all

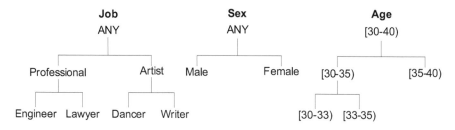

FIGURE 3.1: Taxonomy trees for *Job*, *Sex*, *Age*

values in an attribute are generalized to the same level of the taxonomy
tree. For example, in Figure 3.1, if *Lawyer* and *Engineer* are generalized
to *Professional*, then it also requires generalizing *Dancer* and *Writer*
to *Artist*. The search space for this scheme is much smaller than the
search space for other schemes below, but the data distortion is the
largest because of the same granularity level requirement on all paths of
a taxonomy tree.

Subtree generalization scheme [29, 95, 96, 123, 148]. In this scheme, at
a non-leaf node, either all child values or none are generalized. For example, in Figure 3.1, if *Engineer* is generalized to *Professional*, this
scheme also requires the other child node, *Lawyer*, to be generalized to
Professional, but *Dancer* and *Writer*, which are child nodes of *Artist*,
can remain ungeneralized. Intuitively, a generalized attribute has values
that form a "cut" through its taxonomy tree. A *cut* of a tree is a subset
of values in the tree that contains exactly one value on each root-to-leaf
path.

Sibling generalization scheme [148]. This scheme is similar to the subtree
generalization, except that some siblings may remain ungeneralized. A
parent value is then interpreted as representing all missing child values.
For example, in Figure 3.1, if *Engineer* is generalized to *Professional*,
and *Lawyer* remains ungeneralized, *Professional* is interpreted as all
jobs covered by *Professional* except for *Lawyer*. This scheme produces
less distortion than subtree generalization schemes because it only needs
to generalize the child nodes that violate the specified threshold.

Cell generalization scheme [148, 246, 254]. In all of the above schemes,
if a value is generalized, all its instances are generalized. Such schemes
are called *global recoding*. In cell generalization, also known as *local recoding*, some instances of a value may remain ungeneralized while other
instances are generalized. For example, in Table 2.2 the *Engineer* in the
first record is generalized to *Professional*, while the *Engineer* in the
second record can remain ungeneralized. Compared with global recoding
schemes, this scheme is more flexible; therefore, it produces a smaller

data distortion. Nonetheless, it is important to note that the utility of data is adversely affected by this flexibility, which causes a data exploration problem: most standard data mining methods treat *Engineer* and *Professional* as two independent values, but, in fact, they are not. For example, building a decision tree from such a generalized table may result in two branches, *Professional* → *class*2 and *Engineer* → *class*1. It is unclear which branch should be used to classify a new engineer. Though very important, this aspect of data utility has been ignored by all works that employed the local recoding scheme. Data produced by global recoding does not suffer from this data exploration problem.

Multidimensional generalization [149, 150]. Let D_i be the domain of an attribute A_i. A single-dimensional generalization, such as full-domain generalization and subtree generalization, is defined by a function f_i : $D_{A_i} \rightarrow D'$ for each attribute A_i in QID. In contrast, a multidimensional generalization is defined by a single function $f : D_{A_1} \times \cdots \times D_{A_n} \rightarrow D'$, which is used to generalize $qid = \langle v_1, \ldots, v_n \rangle$ to $qid' = \langle u_1, \ldots, u_n \rangle$ where for every v_i, either $v_i = u_i$ or v_i is a child node of u_i in the taxonomy of A_i. This scheme flexibly allows two qid groups, even having the same value on some v_i and u_i, to be independently generalized into different parent groups. For example $\langle Engineer, Male \rangle$ can be generalized to $\langle Engineer, ANY\_Sex \rangle$ while $\langle Engineer, Female \rangle$ can be generalized to $\langle Professional, Female \rangle$. The generalized table contains both *Engineer* and *Professional*. This scheme produces less distortion than the full-domain and subtree generalization schemes because it needs to generalize only the qid groups that violate the specified threshold. Note, in this multidimensional scheme, *all* records in a qid are generalized to the same qid', but cell generalization does not have such constraint. Both schemes suffer from the data exploration problem discussed above though. Ercan Nergiz and Clifton [177] further evaluate a family of clustering-based algorithms that even attempts to improve data utility by ignoring the restrictions of the given taxonomies.

There are also different suppression schemes. *Record suppression* [29, 123, 148, 201] refers to suppressing an entire record. *Value suppression* [237] refers to suppressing every instance of a given value in a table. *Cell suppression* (or *local suppression*) [52, 168] refers to suppressing *some* instances of a given value in a table.

In summary, the choice of generalization and suppression operations has an implication on the search space of anonymous tables and data distortion. The full-domain generalization has the smallest search space but the largest distortion, and the local recoding scheme has the largest search space but the least distortion. For a categorical attribute with a taxonomy tree H, the number of possible cuts in subtree generalization, denoted by $C(H)$, is equal to $C(H_1) \times \cdots \times C(H_u) + 1$ where $H_1, \ldots, H_u$ are the subtrees rooted at the children of the root of H, and 1 is for the trivial cut at the root of H. The number of potential modified tables is equal to the product of such numbers for all the attributes in QID. The corresponding number is much larger if a local recoding scheme is adopted because any subset of values can be generalized while the rest remains ungeneralized for each attribute in QID.

A table is *minimally anonymous* if it satisfies the given privacy requirement and its sequence of anonymization operations cannot be reduced without violating the requirement. A table is *optimally anonymous* if it satisfies the given privacy requirement and contains most information according to the chosen information metric among all satisfying tables. See Chapter 4 for different types of information metrics. Various works have shown that finding the optimal anonymization is NP-hard: Samarati [201] shows that the optimal k-anonymity by full-domain generalization is very costly. Meyerson and Williams [168] and Aggarwal et al. [12] prove that the optimal k-anonymity by cell suppression, value suppression, and cell generalization is NP-hard. Wong et al. [246] prove that the optimal (α, k)-anonymity by cell generalization is NP-hard. In most cases, finding a minimally anonymous table is a reasonable solution and can be done efficiently.

3.2   Anatomization and Permutation

Unlike generalization and suppression, anatomization (a.k.a. bucketization) [249] does not modify the quasi-identifier or the sensitive attribute, but de-associates the relationship between the two. Precisely, the method releases the data on QID and the data on the sensitive attribute in two separate tables: a *quasi-identifier table* (QIT) contains the QID attributes, a *sensitive table* (ST) contains the sensitive attributes, and both QIT and ST have one common attribute, $GroupID$. All records in the same group will have the same value on $GroupID$ in both tables and, therefore, are linked to the sensitive values in the group in the exact same way. If a group has ℓ distinct sensitive values and each distinct value occurs exactly once in the group, then the probability of linking a record to a sensitive value by $GroupID$ is $1/\ell$. The attribute linkage attack can be distorted by increasing ℓ.

Example 3.1
Suppose that the data holder wants to release the patient data in Table 3.1, where *Disease* is a sensitive attribute and $QID = \{Age, Sex\}$. First, partition (or generalize) the original records into *qid* groups so that, in each group, at most $1/\ell$ of the records contain the same *Disease* value. This intermediate Table 3.2 contains two *qid* groups: $\langle[30\text{-}35), Male\rangle$ and $\langle[35\text{-}40), Female\rangle$. Next, create QIT (Table 3.3) to contain all records from the original Table 3.1,

Table 3.1: Anatomy: original patient data

Age	Sex	Disease (sensitive)
30	Male	Hepatitis
30	Male	Hepatitis
30	Male	HIV
32	Male	Hepatitis
32	Male	HIV
32	Male	HIV
36	Female	Flu
38	Female	Flu
38	Female	Heart
38	Female	Heart

Table 3.2: Anatomy: intermediate QID-grouped table

Age	Sex	Disease (sensitive)
$[30-35)$	Male	Hepatitis
$[30-35)$	Male	Hepatitis
$[30-35)$	Male	HIV
$[30-35)$	Male	Hepatitis
$[30-35)$	Male	HIV
$[30-35)$	Male	HIV
$[35-40)$	Female	Flu
$[35-40)$	Female	Flu
$[35-40)$	Female	Heart
$[35-40)$	Female	Heart

but replace the sensitive values by the *GroupIDs*, and create ST (Table 3.4) to contain the count of each *Disease* for each *qid* group. QIT and ST satisfy the privacy requirement with $\ell \leq 2$ because each *qid* group in QIT infers any associated *Disease* in ST with probability at most $1/\ell = 1/2 = 50\%$. □

The major advantage of *anatomy* is that the data in both QIT and ST are unmodified. Xiao and Tao [249] show that the anatomized tables can more accurately answer aggregate queries involving domain values of the QID and sensitive attributes than the generalization approach. The intuition is that in a generalized table domain values are lost and, without additional knowledge, the uniform distribution assumption is the best that can be used to answer a query about domain values. In contrast, all domain values are retained in the anatomized tables, which give the exact distribution of domain values. For instance, suppose that the data recipient wants to count the number of patients of age 38 having heart disease. The correct count from the origi-

Table 3.3:   Anatomy: quasi-identifier table (QIT) for release

Age	Sex	GroupID
30	Male	1
30	Male	1
30	Male	1
32	Male	1
32	Male	1
32	Male	1
36	Female	2
38	Female	2
38	Female	2
38	Female	2

Table 3.4:   Anatomy: sensitive table (ST) for release

GroupID	Disease (sensitive)	Count
1	Hepatitis	3
1	HIV	3
2	Flu	2
2	Heart	2

nal Table 3.1 is 2. The expected count from the anatomized Table 3.3 and Table 3.4 is $3 \times \frac{2}{4} = 1.5$ since 2 out of the 4 records in *GroupID* = 2 in Table 3.4 have heart disease. This count is more accurate than the expected count $2 \times \frac{1}{5} = 0.4$, from the generalized Table 3.2, where the $\frac{1}{5}$ comes from the fact that the 2 patients with heart disease have an equal chance to be at age $\{35, 36, 37, 38, 39\}$.

Yet, with the data published in two tables, it is unclear how standard data mining tools, such as classification, clustering, and association mining tools, can be applied to the published data, and new tools and algorithms need to be designed. Also, anatomy is not suitable for incremental data publishing, which will be further discussed in Chapter 10. The generalization approach does not suffer from the same problem because all attributes are released in the same table.

Sharing the same spirit of anatomization, Zhang et al. [269] propose an approach called *permutation*. The idea is to de-associate the relationship between a quasi-identifier and a *numerical* sensitive attribute by partitioning a set of data records into groups and shuffling their sensitive values within each group.

3.3 Random Perturbation

Random perturbation has a long history in statistical disclosure control [3, 242, 252] due to its simplicity, efficiency, and ability to preserve statistical information. The general idea is to replace the original data values with some synthetic data values so that the statistical information computed from the perturbed data does not differ significantly from the statistical information computed from the original data. Depending on the degree of randomization, the perturbed data records may or may not correspond to real-world record owners, so the adversary cannot perform the sensitive linkage attacks or recover sensitive information from the published data with high confidence.

Compared to the other anonymization operations discussed earlier, one limitation of the random perturbation approach is that the published records are "synthetic" in that they do not correspond to the real world entities represented by the original data; therefore, individual records in the perturbed data are basically meaningless to the human recipients. Randomized data, however, can still be very useful if aggregate properties (such as frequency distribution of disease) are the target of data analysis. In fact, one can accurately reconstruct such distribution if the prob used for perturbation is known. Yet, the one may argue that, in such a case, the data holder may consider releasing the statistical information or the data mining results rather than the perturbed data [64].

In contrast, generalization and suppression make the data less precise than, but semantically consistent with, the raw data, therefore, preserve the truthfulness of data. For example, after analyzing the statistical properties of a collection of perturbed patient records, a drug company wants to focus on a small number of patients for further analysis. This stage requires the truthful record information instead of perturbed record information. However, the generalized or suppressed data may not be able to preserve the desired statistical information. Below, we discuss several commonly used random perturbation methods, including additive noise, data swapping, and synthetic data generation.

3.3.1 Additive Noise

Additive noise is a widely used privacy protection method in statistical disclosure control [3, 36]. It is often used for hiding sensitive numerical data (e.g., salary). The general idea is to replace the original sensitive value s with $s + r$ where r is a random value drawn from some distribution. Privacy was measured by how closely the original values of a modified attribute can be estimated [16]. Fuller [90] and Kim and Winkler [140] show that some simple statistical information, like means and correlations, can be preserved by adding random noise. Experiments in [19, 72, 84] further suggest that some data mining information can be preserved in the randomized data. However, Kargupta et al. [136] point out that some reasonably close sensitive values can be recovered from the randomized data when the correlation among attributes is high, but the noise is not. Huang et al. [118] present an improved randomization method to limit this type of privacy breach. Some representative privacy models and statistical disclosure control methods that employ additive noise are discussed in Chapters 2.4 and 5.4.

3.3.2   Data Swapping

The general idea of data swapping is to anonymize a data table by exchanging values of sensitive attributes among individual records while the swaps maintain the low-order frequency counts or marginals for statistical analysis. It can be used to protect numerical attributes [196] and categorical attributes [195]. An alternative swapping method is *rank swapping*: First rank the values of an attribute A in ascending order. Then for each value $v \in A$, swap v with another value $u \in A$, where u is randomly chosen within a restricted range $p\%$ of v. Rank swapping can better preserve statistical information than the ordinary data swapping [65].

3.3.3   Synthetic Data Generation

Many statistical disclosure control methods use synthetic data generation to preserve record owners' privacy and retain useful statistical information [200]. The general idea is to build a statistical model from the data and then to sample points from the model. These sampled points form the synthetic data for data publication instead of the original data. An alternative synthetic data generation approach is *condensation* [9, 10]. The idea is to first condense the records into multiple groups. For each group, extract some statistical information, such as sum and covariance, that suffices to preserve the mean and correlations across the different attributes. Then, based on the statistical information, for publication generate points for each group following the statistical characteristics of the group.

Chapter 4

Information Metrics

Privacy preservation is one side of anonymization. The other side is retaining information so that the published data remains practically useful. There are broad categories of information metrics for measuring the data usefulness. A *data metric* measures the data quality in the entire anonymous table with respect to the data quality in the original table. A *search metric* guides each step of an anonymization (search) algorithm to identify an anonymous table with maximum information or minimum distortion. Often, this is achieved by ranking a set of possible anonymization operations and then greedily performing the "best" one at each step in the search. Since the anonymous table produced by a search metric is eventually evaluated by a data metric, the two types of metrics usually share the same principle of measuring data quality.

Alternatively, an information metric can be categorized by their information purposes including *general purpose*, *special purpose*, or *trade-off purpose*. Below, we discuss some commonly used data and search metrics by their purposes.

4.1 General Purpose Metrics

In many cases, the data holder does not know how the published data will be analyzed by the recipient. This is very different from privacy-preserving data mining (PPDM), which assumes that the data mining task is known. In PPDP, for example, the data may be published on the web and a recipient may analyze the data according to her own purpose. An information metric good for one recipient may not be good for another recipient. In such scenarios, a reasonable information metric is to measure "similarity" between the original data and the anonymous data, which underpins the *principle of minimal distortion* [201, 215, 217].

4.1.1 Minimal Distortion

In the minimal distortion metric or MD, a penalty is charged to each instance of a value generalized or suppressed. For example, generalizing 10 instances of *Engineer* to *Professional* causes 10 units of distortion, and further generalizing these instances to ANY_Job causes another 10 units of distortion. This metric is a single attribute measure, and it was previously used in [201, 216, 217, 236] as a data metric and search metric.

4.1.2   *ILoss*

$ILoss$ is a data metric proposed in [250] to capture the information loss of generalizing a specific value to a general value v_g: $ILoss(v_g) = \frac{|v_g|-1}{|D_A|}$ where $|v_g|$ is the number of domain values that are descendants of v_g, and $|D_A|$ is the number of domain values in the attribute A of v_g. This data metric requires all original data values to be at the leaves in the taxonomy. $ILoss(v_g) = 0$ if v_g is an original data value in the table. In words, $ILoss(v_g)$ measures the fraction of domain values generalized by v_g. For example, generalizing one instance of *Dancer* to *Artist* in Figure 3.1 has $ILoss(Artist) = \frac{2-1}{4} = 0.25$. The loss of a generalized record r is given by:

$$ILoss(r) = \sum_{v_g \in r} (w_i \times ILoss(v_g)), \tag{4.1}$$

where w_i is a positive constant specifying the penalty weight of attribute A_i of v_g. The overall loss of a generalized table T is given by:

$$ILoss(T) = \sum_{r \in T} ILoss(r). \tag{4.2}$$

4.1.3   Discernibility Metric

The *discernibility metric* or DM [213] addresses the notion of loss by charging a penalty to each record for being indistinguishable from other records with respect to QID. If a record belongs to a qid group of size $|T[qid]|$, the penalty for the record will be $|T[qid]|$. Thus, the penalty on a group is $|T[qid]|^2$. The overall penalty cost of generalized table T is given by

$$DM(T) = \sum_{qid_i} |T[qid_i]|^2 \tag{4.3}$$

over all qid_i. This data metric, used in [29, 149, 160, 162, 234, 254], works exactly against k-anonymization that seeks to make records indistinguishable with respect to QID.

Another version of DM is to use as a search metric to guide the search of an anonymization algorithm. For example, a bottom-up generalization (or a top-down specialization) anonymization algorithm chooses the generalization $child(v) \to v$ (or the specialization $v \to child(v)$) that minimizes (maximizes) the value of

$$DM(v) = \sum_{qid_v} |T[qid_v]|^2 \tag{4.4}$$

over all qid_v containing v.

Let us compare DM and MD. MD charges a penalty for generalizing a value in a record independently of other records. For example, in MD, generalizing 99 instances of *Engineer* and 1 instance of *Lawyer* to *Professional* has the same penalty as generalizing 50 instances of *Dancer* and 50 instances of *Writer* to *Artist*. In both cases, 100 instances are made indistinguishable; therefore, the costs of both generalizations are the same. The difference is that before the generalization, 99 instances are already indistinguishable in the first case, whereas only 50 instances are indistinguishable in the second case. Therefore, the second case makes more originally distinguishable records become indistinguishable. In contrast, DM can differentiate the two cases:

$$DM(Professional) = 99^2 + 1^2 = 9802$$
$$DM(Artist) = 50^2 + 50^2 = 5000$$

DM can determine that generalizing *Dancer* and *Writer* to *Artist* costs less than generalizing *Engineer* and *Lawyer* to *Professional*.

4.1.4 Distinctive Attribute

A simple search metric, called *distinctive attribute* or DA, was employed in [215] to guide the search for a minimally anonymous table in a full-domain generalization scheme. The heuristic selects the attribute having the most number of distinctive values in the data for generalization. Note, this type of simple heuristic only serves the purpose of guiding the search, but does not quantify the utility of an anonymous table.

4.2 Special Purpose Metrics

If the purpose of the data is known at the time of publication, the purpose can be taken into account during anonymization to better retain information. For example, if the data is published for modeling the classification of a target attribute in the table, then it is important not to generalize the values whose distinctions are essential for discriminating the class labels in the target attribute. A frequently asked question is [177]: if the purpose of data is known, why not extract and publish a data mining result for that purpose (such as a classifier) instead of the data? The answer is that publishing a data mining result is a commitment at the algorithmic level, which is neither practical for the non-expert data holder nor desirable for the data recipient. In practice, there are many ways to mine the data even for a given purpose, and typically it is unknown which one is the best until the data is received and different ways are tried. A real life example is the release of the Netflix data (New York

Times, Oct. 2, 2006) discussed in Chapter 1. Netflix wanted to provide the participants the greatest flexibility to perform their desired analysis, instead of limiting them to a specific type of analysis.

For concreteness, let us consider the classification problem where the goal is to classify *future cases* into some pre-determined classes, drawn from the same underlying population as the *training cases* in the published data. The training cases contain both the useful *classification information* that can improve the classification model, and the useless *noise* that can degrade the classification model. Specifically, the useful classification information is the information that can differentiate the target classes, and holds not only on training cases, but also on future cases. In contrast, the useless noise holds only on training cases. Clearly, only the useful classification information that helps classification should be retained. For example, a patient's birth year is likely to be part of the information for classifying Lung Cancer if the disease occurs more frequently among elderly people, but the exact birth date is likely to be noise. In this case, generalizing birth date to birth year in fact helps classification because it eliminates the noise. This example shows that simply minimizing the distortion to the data, as adopted by all general purpose metrics and optimal k-anonymization, is not addressing the right problem.

To address the classification goal, the distortion should be measured by the classification error on future cases. Since future data is not available in most scenarios, most developed methods [95, 96, 123] measure the accuracy on the training data. Research results in [95, 96] suggest that the useful classification knowledge is captured by different combinations of attributes. Generalization and suppression may destroy some of these useful "classification structures," but other useful structures may emerge to help. In some cases, generalization and suppression may even improve the classification accuracy because some noise has been removed.

Iyengar [123] presents the first work on PPDP for classification. He proposed the *classification metric* or *CM* to measure the classification error on the training data. The idea is to charge a penalty for each record suppressed or generalized to a group in which the record's class is not the majority class. The intuition is that a record having a non-majority class in a group will be classified as the majority class, which is an error because it disagrees with the record's original class. The classification metric CM is defined as follows:

$$CM = \frac{\sum_{r \in T} penalty(r)}{|T|}, \qquad (4.5)$$

where r is a record in data table T, and

$$penalty(r) = \begin{cases} 1 & \text{if } r \text{ is suppressed} \\ 1 & \text{if } class(r) \neq majority(G(r)) \\ 0 & \text{otherwise} \end{cases} \qquad (4.6)$$

where $class(r)$ is the class value of record r, $G(r)$ is the *qid* group containing r, and $majority(G(r))$ is the majority class in $G(r)$.

CM is a data metric and, thus, penalizes modification to the training data. This does not quite address the classification goal, which is actually better off generalizing useless noise into useful classification information. For classification, a more relevant approach is searching for a "good" anonymization according to some heuristics. In other words, instead of optimizing a data metric, this approach employs a search metric to rank anonymization operations at each step in the search. An anonymization operation is ranked high if it retains useful classification information. The search metric could be adopted by different anonymization algorithms. For example, a greedy algorithm or a hill climbing optimization algorithm can be used to identify a minimal sequence of anonymization operations for a given search metric. We will discuss anonymization algorithms in Chapter 5.

Neither a data metric nor a search metric guarantees a good classification on future cases. It is essential to experimentally evaluate the impact of anonymization by building a classifier from the anonymous data and seeing how it performs on testing cases. Few works [95, 96, 123, 150, 239] have actually conducted such experiments, although many such as [29] adopt CM in an attempt to address the classification problem.

4.3 Trade-Off Metrics

The special purpose information metrics aim at preserving data usefulness for a given data mining task. The catch is that the anonymization operation that gains maximum information may also lose so much privacy that no other anonymization operation can be performed. The idea of trade-off metrics is to consider both the privacy and information requirements at every anonymization operation and to determine an optimal trade-off between the two requirements.

Fung et al. [95, 96] propose a search metric based on the principle of *information/privacy trade-off*. Suppose that the anonymous table is searched by iteratively specializing a general value into child values. Each specialization operation splits each group containing the general value into a number of groups, one for each child value. Each specialization operation s gains some information, denoted by $IG(s)$, and loses some privacy, denoted by $PL(s)$. This search metric prefers the specialization s that maximizes the information gained per each loss of privacy:

$$IGPL(s) = \frac{IG(s)}{PL(s) + 1}. \qquad (4.7)$$

The choice of $IG(s)$ and $PL(s)$ depends on the information metric and privacy model. For example in classification analysis, $IG(s)$ could be the information gain $InfoGain(v)$ [191] defined as the decrease of the class entropy [210] after specializing a general group into several specialized groups. $InfoGain(v)$ measures the *goodness* of a specialization on v.

InfoGain(v): Let $T[x]$ denote the set of records in T generalized to the value x. Let $freq(T[x], cls)$ denote the number of records in $T[x]$ having the class cls. Note that $|T[v]| = \sum_c |T[c]|$, where $c \in child(v)$.

$$InfoGain(v) = E(T[v]) - \sum_c \frac{|T[c]|}{|T[v]|} E(T[c]), \qquad (4.8)$$

where $E(T[x])$ is the *entropy* of $T[x]$ [191, 210]:

$$E(T[x]) = -\sum_{cls} \frac{freq(T[x], cls)}{|T[x]|} \times log_2 \frac{freq(T[x], cls)}{|T[x]|}, \qquad (4.9)$$

Intuitively, $E(T[x])$ measures the entropy, or the impurity, of classes for the records in $T[x]$ by estimating the average minimum number of bits required to encode a string of symbols. The more dominating the majority class in $T[x]$ is, the smaller $E(T[x])$ is, due to less entropy in $E(T[x])$). $InfoGain(v)$ is the reduction of the impurity by specializing v into $c \in child(v)$. $InfoGain(v)$ is non-negative.

Alternatively, $IG(s)$ could be the decrease of distortion measured by MD, described in Chapter 4.1, after performing s. For k-anonymity, Fung et al. [95, 96] measure the privacy loss $PL(s)$ by the average decrease of anonymity over all QID_j that contain the attribute of s, that is,

$$PL(s) = avg\{A(QID_j) - A_s(QID_j)\}, \qquad (4.10)$$

where $A(QID_j)$ and $A_s(QID_j)$ denote the anonymity of QID_j before and after the specialization. One variant is to maximize the gain of information by setting $PL(s)$ to zero. The catch is that the specialization that gains maximum information may also lose so much privacy that no other specializations can be performed. Note that the principle of information/privacy trade-off can also be used to select a generalization g, in which case it will minimize

$$ILPG(g) = \frac{IL(g)}{PG(g)} \qquad (4.11)$$

where $IL(g)$ denotes the information loss and $PG(g)$ denotes the privacy gain by performing g.

Chapter 5

Anonymization Algorithms

In this chapter, we examine some representative anonymization algorithms. Refer to Tables 5.1, 5.2, 5.3, and 5.4 for a characterization based on privacy model (Chapter 2), anonymization operation (Chapter 3), and information metric (Chapter 4). Our presentation of algorithms is organized according to linkage models. Finally, we discuss the potential privacy threats even though a data table has been anonymized.

5.1 Algorithms for the Record Linkage Model

We broadly classify record linkage anonymization algorithms into three families: the first two, *optimal anonymization* and *minimal anonymization*, use generalization and suppression methods; the third family uses *perturbation methods*.

5.1.1 Optimal Anonymization

The first family finds an optimal k-anonymization, for a given data metric, by limiting to full-domain generalization and record suppression. Since the search space for the full-domain generalization scheme is much smaller than other schemes, finding an optimal solution is feasible for small data sets. This type of exhaustive search, however, is not scalable to large data sets, especially if a more flexible anonymization scheme is employed.

5.1.1.1 MinGen

Sweeney [217]'s *MinGen* algorithm exhaustively examines all potential full-domain generalizations to identify the optimal generalization, measured in MD. Sweeney acknowledged that this exhaustive search is impractical even for the modest sized data sets, motivating the second family of k-anonymization algorithms to be discussed later. Samarati [201] proposes a *binary search* algorithm that first identifies all minimal generalizations, and then finds the optimal generalization measured in MD. Enumerating all minimal general-

Table 5.1: Anonymization algorithms for record linkage

Algorithm	Operation	Metric	Optimality
Binary Search [201]	FG,RS	MD	yes
MinGen [217]	FG,RS	MD	yes
Incognito [148]	FG,RS	MD	yes
K-Optimize [29]	SG,RS	DM,CM	yes
μ-argus [120]	SG,CS	MD	no
Datafly [215]	FG,RS	DA	no
Genetic Algorithm [123]	SG,RS	CM	no
Bottom-Up Generalization [239]	SG	$ILPG$	no
Top-Down Specialization (TDS) [95, 96]	SG,VS	$IGPL$	no
TDS for Cluster Analysis [94]	SG,VS	$IGPL$	no
Mondrian Multidimensional [149]	MG	DM	no
Bottom-Up & Top-Down Greedy [254]	CG	DM	no
TDS for 2-Party [172]	SG	$IGPL$	no
Condensation [9, 10]	CD	heuristics	no
r-Gather Clustering [13]	CL	heuristics	no

FG=Full-domain Generalization, SG=Subtree Generalization,
CG=Cell Generalization, MG=Multidimensional Generalization,
RS=Record Suppression, VS=Value Suppression, CS=Cell Suppression,
CD=Condensation, CL=Clustering

izations is an expensive operation and, therefore, not scalable for large data sets.

5.1.1.2 Incognito

LeFevre et al. [148] present a suite of optimal bottom-up generalization algorithms, called *Incognito*, to generate all possible k-anonymous full-domain generalizations. The algorithms exploit the rollup property for computing the size of qid groups.

Observation 5.1.1 (Rollup property) If qid is a generalization of $\{qid_1, \ldots, qid_c\}$, then $|qid| = \sum_{i=1}^{c} |qid_i|$. ∎

The rollup property states that the parent group size $|qid|$ can be directly computed from the sum of all child group sizes $|qid_i|$, implying that the group size $|qid|$ of all possible generalizations can be incrementally computed in a bottom-up manner. This property not only allows efficient computation of group sizes, but also provides a terminating condition for further generalizations, leading to the generalization property:

Observation 5.1.2 (Generalization property) Let T' be a table not more specific than table T on all attributes in QID. If T is k-anonymous on QID, then T' is also k-anonymous on QID. ∎

The generalization property provides the basis for effectively pruning the search space of generalized tables. This property is essential for efficiently determining an optimal k-anonymization [148, 201]. Consider a qid in a table T. If qid' is a generalization of qid and $|qid| \geq k$, then $|qid'| \geq k$. Thus, if T is k-anonymous, there is no need to further generalize T because any further generalizations of T must also be k-anonymous but with higher distortion and, therefore, not optimal according to, for example, the minimal distortion metric MD. Although Incognito significantly outperforms the binary search [201] in efficiency, the complexity of all three algorithms, namely MinGen, binary search, and Incognito, increases exponentially with the size of QID.

5.1.1.3 K-Optimize

Another algorithm called *K-Optimize* [29] effectively prunes non-optimal anonymous tables by modeling the search space using a set enumeration tree. Each node represents a k-anonymous solution. The algorithm assumes a totally ordered set of attribute values, and examines the tree in a top-down manner starting from the most general table and prunes a node in the tree when none of its descendants could be a global optimal solution based on discernibility metric DM and classification metric CM. Unlike the above algorithms, K-Optimize employs the subtree generalization and record suppression schemes. It is the only efficient optimal algorithm that uses the flexible subtree generalization.

5.1.2 Locally Minimal Anonymization

The second family of algorithms produces a minimal k-anonymous table by employing a greedy search guided by a search metric. Being heuristic in nature, these algorithms may not find the optimal anonymous solution, but are more scalable than the previous family. Since the privacy guarantee is not compromisable, the algorithms typically preserve the required privacy but may not reach optimal utility in the anonymization. Often local minimality in data distortion is achieved when a greedy search stops at a point within a local search space where no further distortion is required or where any further distortion may compromise the privacy. We sometimes refer to such locally minimal anonymization simply as minimal anonymization.

5.1.2.1 μ-argus

The μ-*argus* algorithm [120] computes the frequency of all 3-value combinations of domain values, then greedily applies subtree generalizations and cell suppressions to achieve k-anonymity. Since the method limits the size of attribute combination, the resulting data may not be k-anonymous when more than 3 attributes are considered.

5.1.2.2 Datafly

Sweeney [215]'s *Datafly* system is the first k-anonymization algorithm scalable to handle real-life large data sets. It achieves k-anonymization by generating an array of qid group sizes and greedily generalizing those combinations with less than k occurrences based on a heuristic search metric DA that selects the attribute having the largest number of distinct values. Datafly employs full-domain generalization and record suppression schemes.

5.1.2.3 Genetic Algorithm

Iyengar [123] is among the first researchers who aims at preserving classification information in k-anonymous data by employing a genetic algorithm with an incomplete stochastic search based on classification metric CM and a subtree generalization scheme. The idea is to encode each state of generalization as a "chromosome" and encode data distortion by a fitness function. The search process is a genetic evolution that converges to the fittest chromosome. Iyengar's experiments suggest that, by considering the classification purpose, a classifier built from the anonymous data generated with a classification purpose produces a lower classification error when compared to a classifier built from anonymous data generated with a general purpose. However, experiments also showed that this genetic algorithm is inefficient for large data sets.

5.1.2.4 Bottom-Up Generalization

To address the efficiency issue in k-anonymization, a bottom-up generalization algorithm was proposed in [239] for finding a minimal k-anonymization for classification. The algorithm starts from the original data that violates k-anonymity, and greedily selects a generalization operation at each step according to a search metric similar to $ILPG$ in Equation 4.11. Each operation increases the group size according to the rollup property in Observation 5.1.1. The generalization process is terminated as soon as all groups have the minimum size k. To select a generalization operation, it first considers those that will increase the minimum group size, called *critical generalizations*, with the intuition that a loss of information should trade for some gain on privacy. When there are no critical generalizations, it considers other generalizations. Wang et al. [239] show that this heuristic significantly reduces the search space. Chapter 6.5 discusses this method in details.

5.1.2.5 Top-Down Specialization

Instead of bottom-up, the *top-down specialization* (*TDS*) method [95, 96] generalizes a table by specializing it from the most general state in which all values are generalized to the most general values of their taxonomy trees. At each step, TDS selects the specialization according to the search metric $IGPL$ in Equation 4.7. The specialization process terminates if no specialization can be performed without violating k-anonymity. The data on termination is a minimal k-anonymization according to the generalization property in Observation 5.1.2. TDS handles both categorical attributes and numerical attributes in a uniform way, except that the taxonomy tree for a numerical attribute is grown on the fly as specializations are searched at each step.

Fung et al. [94] further extend the k-anonymization algorithm to preserve the information for cluster analysis. The major challenge of anonymizing data for cluster analysis is the lack of class labels that could be used to guide the anonymization process. Their solution is to first partition the original data into clusters on the original data, convert the problem into the counterpart problem for classification analysis where class labels encode the cluster information in the data, and then apply TDS to preserve k-anonymity and the encoded cluster information.

In contrast to the bottom-up approach [148, 201, 239], the top-down approach has several advantages. First, the user can stop the specialization process at *any time* and have a k-anonymous table. In fact, every step in the specialization process produces a k-anonymous solution. Second, TDS handles multiple $QIDs$, which is essential for avoiding the excessive distortion suffered by a single high-dimensional QID. Third, the top-down approach is more efficient by going from the most generalized table to a more specific table. Once a group cannot be further specialized, all data records in the group can be discarded. In contrast, the bottom-up approach has to keep all data records until the end of computation. However, data holders employing TDS may encounter the dilemma of choosing (multiple) QID discussed in Chapter 2.1.1.

In terms of efficiency, TDS is an order of magnitude faster than the Genetic Algorithm [123]. For instance, TDS required only 7 seconds to anonymize the benchmark *Adult* data set [179], whereas the genetic algorithm required 18 hours for the same data using the same parameter k. They produce comparable classification quality [95, 96].

5.1.2.6 Mondrian Multidimensional

LeFevre et al. [149] present a greedy top-down specialization algorithm for finding a minimal k-anonymization in the case of the multidimensional generalization scheme. This algorithm is very similar to TDS. Both algorithms perform a specialization on a value v one at a time. The major difference is that TDS specializes in all qid groups containing v. In other words, a specialization is performed only if each specialized qid group contains at least k records. In contrast, Mondrian performs a specialization on *one* qid group if each of its specialized qid groups contains at least k records. Due to such a relaxed constraint, the resulting anonymous data in multidimensional generalization usually has a better quality than in single generalization. The trade-off is that multidimensional generalization is less scalable than other schemes due to the increased search space. Xu et al. [254] show that employing cell generalization could further improve the data quality. Though the multidimensional and cell generalization schemes cause less information loss, they suffer from the data exploration problem discussed in Chapter 3.1.

5.1.3   Perturbation Algorithms

This family of anonymization methods employs perturbation to de-associate the linkages between a target victim and a record while preserving some statistical information.

5.1.3.1   Condensation

Aggarwal and Yu [8, 9, 10] present a condensation method to thwart record linkages. The method first assigns records into multiple non-overlapping groups in which each group has a size of at least k records. For each group, extract some statistical information, such as sum and covariance, that suffices to preserve the mean and correlations across the different attributes. Then, for publishing, based on the statistical information, generate points for each group following the statistical characteristics of the group. This method does not require the use of taxonomy trees and can be effectively used in situations with dynamic data updates as in the case of data streams. As each new data record is received, it is added to the nearest group, as determined by the distance to each group centroid. As soon as the number of data records in the group equals $2k$, the corresponding group needs to be split into two groups of k records each. The statistical information of the new group is then incrementally computed from the original group.

5.1.3.2   *r*-Gather Clustering

In a similar spirit, Aggarwal et al. [13] propose a perturbation method called *r-gather clustering* for anonymizing numerical data. This method partitions records into several clusters such that each cluster contains at least r data points (i.e., records). Instead of generalizing individual records, this approach releases the cluster centers, together with their size, radius, and a set of associated sensitive values. To eliminate the impact of outliers, they relaxed this requirement to (r, ϵ)-*gather clustering* so that at most ϵ fraction of data records in the data set can be treated as outliers for removal from the released data.

5.1.3.3   Cross-Training Round Sanitization

Recall from Chapter 2.4.1 that a point q (c, t)-*isolates* a point p if $B(q, c\delta_p)$ contains fewer than t points in the table, where $B(q, c\delta_p)$ is a ball of radius $c\delta_p$

centered at point q. Chawla et al. [46] propose two sanitization (anonymization) techniques, *recursive histogram sanitization* and *density-based perturbation*, to prevent (c, t)-isolation.

Recursive histogram sanitization recursively divides original data into a set of subcubes according to local data density until all the subcubes have no more than $2t$ data points. The method outputs the boundaries of the subcubes and the number of points in each subcube. However, this method cannot handle high-dimensional spheres and balls. Chawla et al. [47] propose an extension to handle high-dimensionality. Density-based perturbation, a variant of the one proposed by Agrawal and Srikant [19], in which the magnitude of the added noise is relatively fixed, takes into consideration the local data density near the point that needs to be perturbed. Points in dense areas are perturbed much less than points in sparse areas. Although the privacy of the perturbed points are protected, the privacy of the points in the t-neighborhood of the perturbed points could be compromised because the sanitization radius itself could leak information about these points. To prevent such privacy leakage from t-neighborhood points, Chawla et al. [46] further suggest a *cross-training round sanitization* method by combining recursive histogram sanitization and density-based perturbation. In cross-training round sanitization, a data set is randomly divided into two subsets, A and B. B is sanitized using only recursive histogram sanitization, while A is perturbed by adding Gaussian noise generated according to the histogram of B.

5.2 Algorithms for the Attribute Linkage Model

The following algorithms anonymize the data to prevent attribute linkages. They use the privacy models discussed in Chapter 2.2. Though their privacy models are different from those of record linkage, many algorithms for attribute linkage are simple extensions from algorithms for record linkage.

5.2.1 ℓ-Diversity Incognito and ℓ^+-Optimize

Machanavajjhala et al. [160, 162] modify the bottom-up Incognito [148] to identify an optimal ℓ-diverse table. Recall that ℓ-diversity requires every qid group to contain at least ℓ "well-represented" sensitive values. The ℓ-Diversity Incognito operates based on the generalization property, similar to Observation 5.1.2, that ℓ-diversity is non-decreasing with respect to generalization. In other words, generalizations help to achieve ℓ-diversity, just as generalizations help achieve k-anonymity. Therefore, k-anonymization algorithms that employ full-domain and subtree generalization can also be extended into ℓ-diversity algorithms.

Table 5.2:   Anonymization algorithms for attribute linkage

Algorithm	Operation	Metric	Optimality
ℓ-Diversity Incognito [162]	FG,RS	MD,DM	yes
InfoGain Mondrian [150]	MG	IG	no
Top-Down Disclosure [237]	VS	$IGPL$	no
ℓ^+-Optimize [157]	VS	MD,DM,CM	yes
Anatomize [249]	AM	heuristics	no
(k,e)-Anonymity Permutation [269]	PM	min. error	yes
Greedy Personalized [250]	SG,CG	$ILoss$	no
Progressive Local Recoding [246]	CG	MD	no
t-Closeness Incognito [153]	FG,RS	DM	yes

FG=Full-domain Generalization, SG=Subtree Generalization,
CG=Cell Generalization, MG=Multidimensional Generalization,
RS=Record Suppression, VS=Value Suppression, AM=Anatomization

Most works discussed in this Chapter 5.2 employ some heuristic to achieve minimal anonymization. Recently, Liu and Wang [157] present a subtree generalization algorithm, called ℓ^+-*optimize*, to achieve optimal anonymization for ℓ^+-diversity, which is the same as confidence bounding studied in Chapter 2.2.2. ℓ^+-optimize organizes *all* possible cuts into a cut enumeration tree such that the nodes are ranked by a cost function that measures the information loss. Consequently, the optimal solution is obtained by effectively pruning the non-optimal nodes (subtrees) that have higher cost than the currently examined candidate. The efficiency of the optimal algorithm relies on the monotonic property of the cost function. It is a scalable method for finding an optimal ℓ-diversity solution by pruning large search space.

5.2.2   InfoGain Mondrian

LeFevre et al. [150] propose a suite of greedy algorithms to identify a minimally anonymous table satisfying k-anonymity and/or entropy ℓ-diversity with the consideration of a specific data analysis task such as classification modeling multiple target attributes, regression analysis on numerical attributes, and query answering with minimal imprecision. Their top-down algorithms are similar to TDS [95], but LeFevre et al. [150] employ multidimensional generalization.

5.2.3   Top-Down Disclosure

Recall that a privacy template has the form $\langle QID \rightarrow s, h \rangle$ and states that the confidence of inferring the sensitive value s from any group on QID is no more than h. Wang et al. [237] propose an efficient algorithm to minimally suppress a table to satisfy a set of privacy templates. Their algorithm, called *Top-Down Disclosure* (*TDD*), iteratively discloses domain values starting from the table in which all domain values are suppressed. In each iteration, it discloses the suppressed domain value that maximizes the search metric *IGPL* in Equation 4.7, and terminates the iterative process when a further disclosure leads to a violation of some privacy templates. This approach is based on the following key observation.

Observation 5.2.1 (Disclosure property) Consider a privacy template $\langle QID \rightarrow s, h \rangle$. If a table violates the privacy template, so does any table obtained by disclosing a suppressed value. [237] ∎

This property ensures that the algorithm finds a locally minimal suppressed table. This property and, therefore, the algorithm, is extendable to full-domain, subtree, and sibling generalization schemes, with the disclosure operation being replaced with the specialization operation. The basic observation is that the confidence in at least one of the specialized groups will be as large as the confidence in the general group. Based on a similar idea, Wong et al. [246] employ the cell generalization scheme and proposed some greedy top-down and bottom-up methods to identify a locally minimal anonymous solution that satisfies (α, k)-anonymity.

5.2.4 Anatomize

Anatomization (also known as bucketization) provides an alternative way to achieve ℓ-diversity. Refer to Chapter 3.2 for the notion of anatomization. The problem can be described as follows: given a person-specific data table T and a parameter ℓ, we want to obtain a quasi-identifier table (QIT) and a sensitive table (ST) such that an adversary can correctly infer the sensitive value of any individual with probability at most $1/\ell$. The *Anatomize* algorithm [249] first partitions the data table into buckets and then separates the quasi-identifiers with the sensitive attribute by randomly permuting the sensitive attribute values in each bucket. The anonymized data consists of a set of buckets with permuted sensitive attribute values.

Anatomize starts by initiating an empty QIT and ST. Then, it hashes the records of T into buckets by the sensitive values, so that each bucket includes the records with the same sensitive value. The subsequent execution involves a *group-creation* step and a *residue-assignment* step.

The group-creation step iteratively yields a new *qid* group as follows. First, Anatomize obtains a set S consisting of the ℓ hash buckets that currently have the largest number of records. Then, a record is randomly chosen from each bucket in S and is added to the new *qid* group. As a result, the *qid* group contains ℓ records with distinct sensitive values. Repeat this group creation step while there are at least ℓ non-empty buckets. The term *residue record* refers to a record remaining in a bucket, at the end of the group-creation phase. There are at most $\ell - 1$ of residue records. For each residue record r, the residue assignment step collects a set S' of *qid* groups produced from the previous step, where no record has the same sensitive value as r. Then, the record r is assigned to an arbitrary group in S'.

5.2.5 (k, e)-**Anonymity Permutation**

To achieve (k, e)-anonymity, Zhang et al. [269] propose an optimal permutation method to assign data records into groups together so that the sum of error E is minimized, where E, for example, could be measured by the range of sensitive values in each group. The optimal algorithm has time and space complexity in $O(n^2)$ where n is the number of data records. (k, e)-anonymity is also closely related to *range coding* technique, which is used in both process control [199] and statistics [113]. In process control, range coding (also known as coarse coding) permits generalization by allowing the whole numerical area to be mapped to a set of groups defined by a set of boundaries, which is similar to the idea of grouping data records by ranges and keeping boundaries of each group for fast computation in (k, e)-anonymity. Hegland et al. [113] also suggest handling large data sets, as population census data, by dividing them into generalized groups (blocks) and applying a computational model to each group. Any aggregate computation can hence be performed based on manipulation of individual groups. Similarly, (k, e)-anonymity exploits the group boundaries to efficiently answer aggregate queries.

5.2.6 **Personalized Privacy**

Refer to the requirement of personalized privacy discussed in Chapter 2.2.9. Xiao and Tao [250] propose a greedy algorithm to achieve every record owner's privacy requirement in terms of a guarding node as follows: initially, all QID attributes are generalized to the most general values, and the sensitive attributes remain ungeneralized. At each iteration, the algorithm performs a top-down specialization on a QID attribute and, for each *qid* group, performs cell generalization on the sensitive attribute to satisfy the personalized privacy requirement; the breach probability of inferring any domain sensitive values within the subtree of guarding nodes is below certain threshold. Since the breach probability is non-increasing with respect to generalization on the sensitive attribute, and the sensitive values could possibly be generalized to the most general values, the generalized table found at every iteration is publishable without violating the privacy requirement, although a table with lower information loss $ILoss$, measured by Equation 4.2, is preferable. When no better solution with lower $ILoss$ is found, the greedy algorithm terminates and outputs a locally minimal anonymization. Since this approach generalizes the sensitive attribute, $ILoss$ is measured on both QID and sensitive attributes.

Table 5.3: Anonymization algorithms for table linkage

Algorithm	Operation	Metric	Optimality
SPALM [176]	FG	DM	yes
MPALM [176]	MG	heuristics	no

FG=Full-domain Generalization, MG=Multidimensional Generalization

5.3 Algorithms for the Table Linkage Model

The following algorithm aims at preventing table linkages, that is, to prevent adversaries from determining the presence or the absence of a target victim's record in a released table.

5.3.1 δ-Presence Algorithms SPALM and MPALM

Recall that a generalized table T' satisfies $(\delta_{min}, \delta_{max})$-*presence* (or simply δ-presence) with respect to an external table E if $\delta_{min} \leq P(t \in T|T') \leq \delta_{max}$ for all $t \in E$. To achieve δ-presence, Ercan Nergiz et al. [176] present two anonymization algorithms, *SPALM* and *MPALM*. SPALM is an optimal algorithm that employs a full-domain single-dimensional generalization scheme. Ercan Nergiz et al. [176] prove the anti-monotonicity property of δ-presence with respect to full-domain generalization; if table T is δ-present, then a generalized version of T' is also δ-present. SPALM is a top-down specialization approach and exploits the anti-monotonicity property of δ-presence to prune the search space effectively. MPALM is a heuristic algorithm that employs a multi-dimensional generalization scheme, with complexity $O(|C||E|log_2|E|)$, where $|C|$ is the number of attributes in private table T and $|E|$ is the number of records in the external table E. Their experiments showed that MPALM usually results in much lower information loss than SPALM because MPALM employs a more flexible generalization scheme.

5.4 Algorithms for the Probabilistic Attack Model

Many algorithms for achieving the probabilistic privacy models studied in Chapter 2.4 employ random perturbation methods, so they do not suffer from the problem of minimality attacks. The random perturbation algorithms are non-deterministic; therefore, the anonymization operations are non-reversible. The random perturbation algorithms for the probabilistic attack model can be divided into two groups. The first group is local perturbation [21], which

Table 5.4:   Anonymization algorithms for probabilistic attack

Algorithm	Operation	Metric
Cross-Training Round Sanitization [46]	AN	statistical
ϵ-Differential Privacy Additive Noise [74]	AN	statistical
$\alpha\beta$ Algorithm [193]	AN,SP	statistical

AN=Additive Noise, SP=Sampling

assumes that a record owner does not trust anyone except himself and perturbs his own data record by adding noise before submission to the untrusted data holder. The second group is to perturb all records together by a trusted data holder, which is the data publishing scenario studied in this book. Although the methods in the first group are also applicable to the second by adding noise to each individual record, Rastogi et al. [193] and Dwork [75] demonstrate that the information utility can be improved with a stronger lower bounds by assuming a trusted data holder who has the capability to access all records and exploit the overall distribution to perturb the data, rather than perturbing the records individually.

A number of PPDP methods [19, 268] have been proposed for preserving classification information with randomization. Agrawal and Srikant [19] present a randomization method for decision tree classification with the use of the aggregate distributions reconstructed from the randomized distribution. The general idea is to construct the distribution separately from the different classes. Then, a *special* decision tree algorithm is developed to determine the splitting conditions based on the relative presence of the different classes, derived from the aggregate distributions. Zhang et al. [268] present a randomization method for naive Bayes classifier. The major shortcoming of this approach is that *ordinary* classification algorithms will not work on this randomized data. There is a large family of works in randomization perturbation for data mining and data publishing [20, 21, 72, 83, 119, 193, 198].

The statistics community conducts substantial research in the disclosure control of statistical information and aggregate query results [46, 52, 73, 166, 184]. The goal is to prevent adversaries from obtaining sensitive information by correlating different published statistics. Cox [52] propose the $k\%$-dominance rule which suppresses a sensitive cell if the values of two or three entities in the cell contribute more than $k\%$ of the corresponding SUM statistic. The proposed mechanisms include query size and query overlap control, aggregation, data perturbation, and data swapping. Nevertheless, such techniques are often complex and difficult to implement [87], or address privacy threats that are unlikely to occur. There are some decent surveys [3, 63, 173, 267] in the statistics community.

5.4.1 ϵ-Differential Additive Noise

One representative work to thwart probabilistic attack is *differential privacy* [74]; its definition can be found in Chapter 2.4. Dwork [74] proposes an additive noise method to achieve ϵ-differential privacy. The added noise is chosen over a scaled symmetric exponential distribution with variance σ^2 in each component, and $\sigma \geq \epsilon/\Delta f$, where Δf is the maximum difference of outputs of a query f caused by the removal or addition of a single data record. Machanavajjhala et al. [161] propose a revised version of differential privacy called *probabilistic differential privacy* that yields a practical privacy guarantee for synthetic data generation. The idea is to first build a model from the original data, then sample points from the model to substitute original data. The key idea is to filter unrepresentative data and shrink the domain. Other algorithms [32, 62, 77, 78] have been proposed to achieve differential privacy. Refer to [76] for a decent survey on the recent developments in this line of privacy model.

5.4.2 $\alpha\beta$ Algorithm

Recall that (d, γ)-privacy in Chapter 2.4.3 bounds the difference of $P(r)$ and $P(r|T)$, where $P(r)$ and $P(r|T)$ are the prior probability and the posterior probability respectively of the presence of a victim's record in the data table T before and after examining the published table T. To achieve (d, γ)-Privacy, Rastogi et al. [193] propose a perturbation method called $\alpha\beta$ algorithm consisting of two steps. The first step is to select a subset of records from the original table D with probability $\alpha + \beta$ and insert them to the data table T, which is to be published. The second step is to generate some counterfeit records from the domain of all attributes. If the counterfeit records are not in the original table D, then insert them into T with probability β. Hence, the resulting perturbed table T consists of both records randomly selected from the original table and counterfeit records from the domain. The number of records in the perturbed data could be larger than the original data table, in comparison with FRAPP [21] which has a fixed table size. The drawback of inserting counterfeits is that the released data could no longer preserve the truthfulness of the original data at the record level, which is important in some applications, as explained in Chapter 1.1.

5.5 Attacks on Anonymous Data

5.5.1 Minimality Attack

Most privacy models assume that the adversary knows the QID of a target victim and/or the presence of the victim's record in the published data. In addition to this background knowledge, the adversary can possibly determine the privacy requirement (e.g., 10-anonymity or 5-diversity), the anonymization operations (e.g., subtree generalization scheme) to achieve the privacy requirement, and the detailed mechanism of an anonymization algorithm. The adversary can possibly determine the privacy requirement and anonymization operations by examining the published data, or its documentation, and learn the mechanism of the anonymization algorithm by, for example, reading research papers. Wong et al. [245] point out that such additional background knowledge can lead to extra information that facilitates an attack to compromise data privacy. This is called the *minimality attack.*

Many anonymization algorithms discussed in this chapter follow an implicit minimality principle. For example, when a table is generalized from bottom-up to achieve k-anonymity, the table is not further generalized once it minimally meets the k-anonymity requirement. Minimality attack exploits this minimality principle to reverse the anonymization operations and filter out the impossible versions of original table [245]. The following example illustrates minimality attack on confidence bounding [237].

Example 5.1
Consider the original patient Table 5.5, the anonymous Table 5.6, and an external Table 5.7 in which each record has a corresponding original record in Table 5.5. Suppose the adversary knows that the confidence bounding requirement is $\langle\{Job, Sex\} \rightarrow HIV, 60\%\rangle$. With the minimality principle, the adversary can infer that Andy and Bob have HIV based on the following reason: From Table 5.5, $qid = \langle Lawyer, Male\rangle$ has 5 records, and $qid = \langle Engineer, Male\rangle$ has 2 records. Thus, $\langle Lawyer, Male\rangle$ in the original table must already satisfy $\langle\{Job, Sex\} \rightarrow HIV, 60\%\rangle$ because even if both records with HIV have $\langle Lawyer, Male\rangle$, the confidence for inferring HIV is only $2/5 = 40\%$. Since a subtree generalization has been performed, $\langle Engineer, Male\rangle$ must be the qid that has violated the 60% confidence requirement on HIV, and that is possible only if both records with $\langle Engineer, Male\rangle$ have a disease value of HIV.   □

Table 5.5: Minimality attack: original patient data

Job	Sex	Disease
Engineer	Male	HIV
Engineer	Male	HIV
Lawyer	Male	Flu
Lawyer	Male	Flu
Lawyer	Male	Flu
Lawyer	Male	Flu
Lawyer	Male	Flu

Table 5.6: Minimality attack: published anonymous data

Job	Sex	Disease
Professional	Male	HIV
Professional	Male	Flu
Professional	Male	Flu
Professional	Male	Flu
Professional	Male	Flu
Professional	Male	Flu
Professional	Male	HIV

Table 5.7: Minimality attack: external data

Name	Job	Sex
Andy	Engineer	Male
Calvin	Lawyer	Male
Bob	Engineer	Male
Doug	Lawyer	Male
Eddy	Lawyer	Male
Fred	Lawyer	Male
Gabriel	Lawyer	Male

To thwart minimality attack, Wong et al. [245] propose a privacy model called *m-confidentiality* that limits the probability of the linkage from any record owner to any sensitive value set in the sensitive attribute. Minimality attack is applicable to both optimal and minimal anonymization algorithms that employ generalization, suppression, anatomization, or permutation to achieve privacy models including, but not limited to, ℓ-diversity [162], (α, k)-anonymity [246], (k, e)-anonymity [269], personalized privacy [250], anatomy [249], t-closeness [153], m-invariance [251], and (X, Y)-privacy [236]. To avoid minimality attack on ℓ-diversity, Wong et al. [245] propose to first k-anonymize the table. Then, for each *qid* group in the k-anonymous table that violates ℓ-diversity, their method distorts the sensitive values to satisfy ℓ-diversity.

5.5.2 deFinetti Attack

Kifer [138] presents a noble attack on partition-based anonymous data that are obtained by generalization, suppression, or anatomization. Though the general methodology of the attack is applicable to any partition-based algorithm, we illustrate a specific attack against Anatomy (Chapter 3.2), which is one kind of partition-based algorithm. Refer to [138] for details on how this algorithm can be modified to attack other partition-based algorithms such as generalization. We illustrate the attack by the following example.

Table 5.8:   deFinetti attack:
quasi-identifier table (QIT)

Rec#	Smoker?	GroupID
1	Y	1
2	Y	1
3	N	2
4	N	2
5	Y	3
6	N	3
7	Y	4
8	Y	4
9	N	5
10	N	5
11	Y	6
12	N	6

Source: [138] ©2009 Association for Computing
Machinery, Inc. Reprinted by permission.

Example 5.2

Tables 5.8 and 5.9 show a pair of anatomized tables, where the quasi-identifer
(*Smoker?*) and the sensitive attribute (*Disease*) are de-associated by the
GroupID. Each group has size 2. Let's assume an adversary wants to predict
the disease of Rec#11. According to the *random worlds* model (which is the
way the adversary reasons), the probability of Rec#11 to have cancer is 50%
because group 6 contains two records and one of them has cancer disease.
However, Kifer claims that it is appropriate to model the adversary using
random worlds model. By observing the anonymized data, an adversary can
learn that whenever a group contains a smoker (groups 1, 3, 4, and 6), the
group also contains a cancer. Also, a group with no smoker (groups 2 and 5)
has no cancer. Given the correlation between smoker and cancer in the tables,
the probability that Rec#12 has cancer should be less than 0.5, therefore,
Rec#11 is more likely to have cancer. The probability of Rec#12 having cancer and Rec#11 having no disease is approximately 0.16, which is significantly
lower than the random worlds estimate.   □

Kifer calls this class of attack as *deFinetti attack* because the attacking
algorithm is based on the deFinetti's representation theorem to predict the
sensitive attribute of a victim.

5.5.3   Corruption Attack

Many previously discussed privacy models that thwart record linkages and
attribute linkages in Chapters 5.1 and 5.2 assume that the background knowledge of an adversary is limited to the QID attributes, and the adversary uses

Table 5.9: deFinetti attack: sensitive table (ST)

GroupID	Disease
1	Cancer
1	Flu
2	Flu
2	No Disease
3	Cancer
3	No Disease
4	Cancer
4	No Disease
5	Flu
5	No Disease
6	Cancer
6	No Disease

Source: [138] ©2009 Association for Computing Machinery, Inc. Reprinted by permission.

Table 5.10: Corruption attack: 2-diverse table

Job	Sex	Disease
Engineer	Male	HIV
Engineer	Male	Flu
Lawyer	Female	Diabetes
Lawyer	Female	Flu

such background knowledge to link the sensitive attribute of a target victim. What if an adversary has additional background knowledge? For example, an adversary may acquire additional knowledge by colluding with a record owner (a patient) or corrupting a data holder (an employee of a hospital). By using the sensitive values of some records, an adversary may be able to compromise the privacy of other record owners in the anonymous data.

Example 5.3

Suppose an adversary knows that Bob is a male engineer appearing in Table 5.10, therefore, Bob has either *HIV* or *Flu*. We further suppose that the adversary "colludes" with another patient John who is also a male engineer appearing the table, and John discloses to the adversary that he has *Flu*. Due to this additional knowledge, the adversary is now certain that Bob has *HIV*. Note, John has not done anything wrong because he has just disclosed his own disease. □

To guarantee privacy against this kind of additional knowledge of the adversary, Tao et al. [218] propose an anonymization algorithm that integrates generalization with perturbation and stratified sampling. The proposed *per-*

turbed generalization algorithm provides strong privacy guarantee even if the adversary has corrupted an arbitrary number of record owners in the table. In general, the randomization-based approaches are less vulnerable to the above types of attacks due to the random nature, compared to the deterministic partition-based approaches.

Part II

Anonymization for Data Mining

Chapter 6

Anonymization for Classification Analysis: A Case Study on the Red Cross

6.1 Introduction

This chapter uses the Red Cross Blood Transfusion Service (BTS) as a case study to illustrate how the components studied in previous chapters work together to solve a real-life privacy-preserving data publishing problem. Chapter 2 studies the privacy threats caused by data publishing and the privacy models that thwart the privacy threats. Chapter 3 discusses some commonly employed anonymization operations for achieving the privacy models. Chapter 4 studies various types of information metrics that can guide the anonymization operations for preserving the required information depending on the purpose of the data publishing. Chapter 5 provides an overview of different anonymization algorithms for achieving the privacy requirements and preserving the information utility.

Gaining access to high-quality health data is a vital requirement to informed decision making for medical practitioners and pharmaceutical researchers. Driven by mutual benefits and regulations, there is a demand for healthcare institutes to share patient data with various parties for research purposes. However, health data in its raw form often contains sensitive information about individuals, and publishing such data will violate their privacy.

Health Level 7 (HL7) is a not-for-profit organization involved in development of international healthcare standards. Based on an extended data schema from the HL7 framework, this chapter exploits a real-life information sharing scenario in the Hong Kong Red Cross BTS to bring out the challenges of preserving both individual privacy and data mining quality in the context of healthcare information systems. This chapter employs the information system of Red Cross BTS as a use case to motivate the problem and to illustrate the essential steps of the anonymization methods for *classification analysis*. The next chapter presents a unified privacy-preserving data publishing framework for *cluster analysis*.

Figure 6.1 illustrates an overview of different parties in the Red Cross BTS system. After collecting and examining the blood collected from donors, the

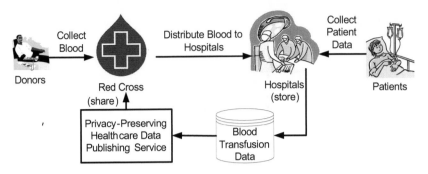

FIGURE 6.1: Overview of the Red Cross BTS ([171] ©2009 Association for
Computing Machinery, Inc. Reprinted by permission.)

BTS distributes the blood to different public hospitals. The hospitals collect
and maintain the health records of their patients and transfuse the blood
to the patients if necessary. The blood transfusion information, such as the
patient data, type of surgery, names of medical practitioners in charge, and
reason for transfusion, is clearly documented and is stored in the database
owned by each individual hospital.

The public hospitals are required to submit the blood usage data, together
with the patient-specific surgery data, to the Government Health Agency.
Periodically, the Government Health Agency submits the data to the BTS
for the purpose of data analysis and auditing. The objectives of the data
mining and auditing procedures are to improve the estimated future blood
consumption in different hospitals and to make recommendation on the blood
usage in future medical cases. In the final step, the BTS submits a report
to the Government Health Agency. Referring to the privacy regulations, such
reports have the property of keeping patients' privacy protected, although
useful patterns and structures have to be preserved. Figure 6.2 provides a
more detailed illustration of the information flow among the hospitals, the
Government Health Agency, and the Red Cross BTS.

The focus of this chapter is to study a data anonymizer in the privacy-
preserving healthcare data publishing service so that both information sharing and privacy protection requirements can be satisfied. This BTS case illustrates a typical dilemma in information sharing and privacy protection faced
by many health institutes. For example, licensed hospitals in California are
also required to submit specific demographic data on every discharged patient [43]. The solution studied in this chapter, designed for the BTS case,
will also benefit other health institutes that face similar challenges in information sharing. We summarize the concerns and challenges of the BTS case
as follows.

Privacy concern: Giving the Red Cross BTS access to blood transfusion
data for data analysis is clearly legitimate. However, it raises some concerns

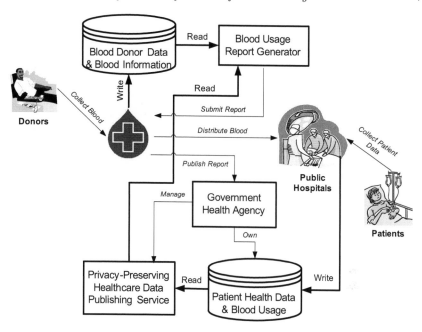

FIGURE 6.2: Data flow in the Red Cross BTS

on patients' privacy. The patients are willing to submit their data to a hospital because they consider the hospital to be a trustworthy entity. Yet, the trust to the hospital may not necessarily be transitive to a third party. Many agencies and institutes consider that the released data is privacy-preserved if explicit identifying information, such as name, social security number, address, and telephone number, is removed. However, as discussed at the beginning of this book, substantial research has shown that simply removing explicit identifying information is insufficient for privacy protection. Sweeney [216] shows that an individual can be re-identified by simply matching other attributes, called *quasi-identifiers* (QID), such as gender, date of birth, and postal code. Below, we illustrate the privacy threats by a simplified Red Cross example.

Example 6.1

Consider the raw patient data in Table 6.1, where each record represents a surgery case with the patient-specific information. *Job*, *Sex*, and *Age* are quasi-identifying attributes. The hospital wants to release Table 6.1 to the Red Cross for the purpose of classification analysis on the class attribute, *Transfuse*, which has two values, Y and N, indicating whether or not the patient has received blood transfusion. Without loss of generality, we assume that the only sensitive value in *Surgery* is *Transgender*. The Government Health Agency and hospitals express concern on the privacy threats

Table 6.1:   Raw patient data

	Quasi-identifier (QID)			Class	Sensitive
ID	**Job**	**Sex**	**Age**	**Transfuse**	**Surgery**
1	Janitor	M	34	Y	Transgender
2	Doctor	M	58	N	Plastic
3	Mover	M	34	Y	Transgender
4	Lawyer	M	24	N	Vascular
5	Mover	M	58	N	Urology
6	Janitor	M	44	Y	Plastic
7	Doctor	M	24	N	Urology
8	Lawyer	F	58	N	Plastic
9	Doctor	F	44	N	Vascular
10	Carpenter	F	63	Y	Vascular
11	Technician	F	63	Y	Plastic

Table 6.2:   Anonymous data ($L = 2$, $K = 2$, $C = 50\%$)

	Quasi-identifier (QID)			Class	Sensitive
ID	**Job**	**Sex**	**Age**	**Transfuse**	**Surgery**
1	Non-Technical	M	$[30-60)$	Y	Transgender
2	Professional	M	$[30-60)$	N	Plastic
3	Non-Technical	M	$[30-60)$	Y	Transgender
4	Professional	M	$[1-30)$	N	Vascular
5	Non-Technical	M	$[30-60)$	N	Urology
6	Non-Technical	M	$[30-60)$	Y	Plastic
7	Professional	M	$[1-30)$	N	Urology
8	Professional	F	$[30-60)$	N	Plastic
9	Professional	F	$[30-60)$	N	Vascular
10	Technical	F	$[60-99)$	Y	Vascular
11	Technical	F	$[60-99)$	Y	Plastic

caused by record linkages and attributes linkages discussed in Chapter 2.1 and Chapter 2.2, respectively. For instance, the hospital wants to avoid record linkage to record #3 via $qid = \langle Mover, 34 \rangle$ and attribute linkage $\langle M, 34 \rangle \rightarrow Transgender$.   □

Patient data is usually high-dimensional, i.e., containing many attributes. Applying traditional privacy models, such as k-anonymity, ℓ-diversity, and confidence bounding, suffers from the curse of high-dimensionality problem and often results in useless data. To overcome this problem, Mohammed et al. [171] employ the LKC-privacy model discussed in Chapter 2.2.6 in this Red Cross BTS problem. Recall that the general intuition of LKC-privacy is to ensure that every combination of values in $QID_j \subseteq QID$ with maximum length L in the data table T is shared by at least K records, and the confidence of inferring any sensitive values in S is not greater than C, where L, K, C are

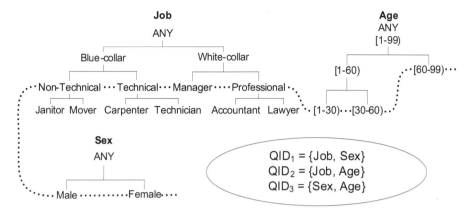

FIGURE 6.3: Taxonomy trees and QIDs

thresholds and S is a set of sensitive values specified by the data holder (the hospital). LKC-privacy bounds the probability of a successful record linkage to be $\leq 1/K$ and the probability of a successful attribute linkage to be $\leq C$, provided that the adversary's prior knowledge does not exceed L values.

Example 6.2

Table 6.2 shows an example of an anonymous table that satisfies $(2, 2, 50\%)$-privacy, where $L = 2$, $K = 2$, and $C = 50\%$, by generalizing all the values from Table 6.1 according to the taxonomies in Figure 6.3 (ignore the dashed curve for now). Every possible value of QID_j with maximum length 2 in Table 6.2 (namely, QID_1, QID_2, and QID_3 in Figure 6.3) is shared by at least 2 records, and the confidence of inferring the sensitive value *Transgender* is not greater than 50%. In contrast, enforcing traditional 2-anonymity will require further generalization. For example, in order to make $\langle Professional, M, [30\text{-}60) \rangle$ to satisfy traditional 2-anonymity, we need to further generalize $[1\text{-}30)$ and $[30\text{-}60)$ to $[1\text{-}60)$, resulting in much higher utility loss. $\square$

Information needs: The Red Cross BTS wants to perform two types of data analysis on the blood transfusion data collected from the hospitals. First, it wants to employ the surgery information as training data for building a classification model on blood transfusion. Second, it wants to obtain some general count statistics.

One frequently raised question is: To avoid the privacy concern, why does not the hospital simply release a classifier or some statistical information to the Red Cross? The Red Cross wants to have access to the blood transfusion data, not only the statistics, from the hospitals for several reasons. First, the practitioners in hospitals and the Government Health Agency have no expertise and interest in doing the data mining. They simply want to share the patient data with the Red Cross, who needs the health data for legitimate reasons. Second, having access to the data, the Red Cross has much better flexibility to perform the required data analysis. It is impractical to continuously request practitioners in a hospital to produce different types of statistical information and fine-tune the data mining results for research purposes.

The rest of the chapter is organized as follows.

- In Chapter 6.2, we present the anonymization problem for classification analysis with the privacy and information requirements.

- In Chapter 6.3, we study an efficient anonymization algorithm, called *High-Dimensional Top-Down Specialization (HDTDS)* [171], for achieving *LKC*-privacy with two different information needs. The first information need maximizes the information preserved for classification analysis; the second information need minimizes the distortion on the anonymous data for general data analysis. Minimizing distortion is useful when the particular information requirement is unknown during information sharing or the shared data is used for various kinds of data mining tasks.

- In Chapters 6.4, 6.5, 6.6, we study three methods that also address the anonymization problem for classification analysis, but with the privacy model of *k*-anonymity instead of *LKC*-privacy. Yet, they can be easily modified to achieve *LKC*-privacy.

- In Chapter 6.7, we present an evaluation methodology for measuring the data quality of the anonymous data with respect to the information needs. Experiments on real-life data suggest that the HDTDS algorithm is flexible and scalable enough to handle large volumes of data that include both categorical and numerical attributes. Scalability is a basic requirement specified by the Red Cross due to the large volume of records.

6.2   Anonymization Problems for Red Cross BTS

We first describe the privacy and information requirements of the Red Cross Blood Transfusion Service (BTS), followed by a problem statement.

6.2.1   Privacy Model

Suppose a health agency wants to publish a health data table

$$T(ID, D_1, \ldots, D_m, Class, Sens) \text{ (e.g., Table 6.1)}$$

to some recipient (e.g., Red Cross) for data analysis. The ID number is an explicit identifier and it should be removed before publication. Each D_i is either a categorical or a numerical attribute. *Sens* is a sensitive attribute. A record has the form $\langle v_1, \ldots, v_m, cls, s \rangle$, where v_i is a domain value of D_i, cls is a class value of *Class*, and s is a sensitive value of *Sens*. The data holder wants to protect against linking an individual to a record or some sensitive value in T through some subset of attributes called a *quasi-identifier* or QID, where $QID \subseteq \{D_1, \ldots, D_m\}$.

One recipient, who is an adversary, seeks to identify the record or sensitive values of some target victim patient V in T. We assume that the adversary knows at most L values of QID attributes of the victim patient. We use qid to denote such prior known values, where $|qid| \leq L$. Based on the prior knowledge qid, the adversary could identify a group of records, denoted by $T[qid]$, that contains qid. $|T[qid]|$ denotes the number of records in $T[qid]$. Suppose $qid = \langle Janitor, M \rangle$. $T[qid] = \{ID\#1, 6\}$ and $|T[qid]| = 2$ in Table 6.1. The adversary could launch two types of privacy attacks, namely record linkages and attribute linkages, based on such prior knowledge.

To thwart the record and attribute linkages on *any* patient in the table T, every qid with a maximum length L in the anonymous table is required to be shared by at least a certain number of records, and the ratio of sensitive value(s) in any group cannot be too high. The LKC-*privacy* model discussed in Chapter 2.2.6 reflects this intuition.

6.2.2 Information Metrics

The measure of data utility varies depending on the data analysis task to be performed on the published data. Based on the information requirements specified by the Red Cross, two information metrics are defined. The first information metric is to preserve the maximal information for classification analysis. The second information metric is to minimize the overall data distortion when the data analysis task is unknown.

In this Red Cross project, a top-down specialization algorithm called HDTDS is proposed to achieve LKC-privacy on high-dimensional data by subtree generalization (Chapter 3.1). The general idea is to anonymize a table by a sequence of specializations starting from the topmost general state in which each attribute has the topmost value of its taxonomy tree [95, 96]. We assume that a *taxonomy tree* is specified for each categorical attribute in QID. A leaf node represents a domain value and a parent node represents a less specific value. For a numerical attribute in QID, a taxonomy tree can be grown at runtime, where each node represents an interval, and each non-leaf node has two child nodes representing some optimal binary split of the parent interval. Figure 6.3 shows a dynamically grown taxonomy tree for *Age*.

Suppose a domain value d has been generalized to a value v in a record. A *specialization* on v, written $v \rightarrow child(v)$, where $child(v)$ denotes the set of child values of v, replaces the parent value v with the child value that gener-

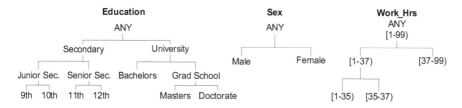

FIGURE 6.4: Taxonomy trees for Tables 6.3-6.7

alizes the domain value d. A specialization is *valid* if the specialization results in a table satisfying the LKC-privacy requirement after the specialization. A specialization is performed only if it is valid. The specialization process can be viewed as pushing the "cut" of each taxonomy tree downwards. A *cut* of the taxonomy tree for an attribute D_i, denoted by Cut_i, contains exactly one value on each root-to-leaf path. Figure 6.3 shows a solution cut indicated by the dashed curve representing the anonymous Table 6.2. The specialization starts from the topmost cut and pushes down the cut iteratively by specializing some value in the current cut until violating the LKC-privacy requirement. In other words, the specialization process pushes the cut downwards until no valid specialization is possible. Each specialization tends to increase data utility and decrease privacy because records are more distinguishable by specific values. Two information metrics are defined depending on the information requirement to evaluate the "goodness" of a specialization.

Case 1: Score for Classification Analysis

For the requirement of classification analysis, information gain, denoted by $InfoGain(v)$, can be used to measure the *goodness* of a specialization on v. One possible information metric, $Score(v)$ is to favor the specialization $v \rightarrow child(v)$ that has the maximum $InfoGain(v)$ [210]:

$$Score(v) = InfoGain(v) = E(T[v]) - \sum_c \frac{|T[c]|}{|T[v]|} E(T[c]), \qquad (6.1)$$

where $E(T[x])$ is the *entropy* of $T[x]$. Refer to Equation 4.8 in Chapter 4.3 for more details on $InfoGain(v)$.

Equation 6.1 uses $InfoGain$ alone, that is, maximizing the information gain produced by a specialization without considering the loss of anonymity. This *Score* function may pick a candidate that has a large reduction in anonymity, which may lead to a quick violation of the anonymity requirement, thereby prohibiting refining the data to a lower granularity. A better information metric is to maximize the information gain per unit of anonymity loss. The next example compares the two *Score* functions and illustrates using $InfoGain$ alone may lead to quick violation.

Table 6.3: Compress raw patient table

Education	Sex	Work_Hrs	Class	# of Recs.
10th	M	40	20Y0N	20
10th	M	30	0Y4N	4
9th	M	30	0Y2N	2
9th	F	30	0Y4N	4
9th	F	40	0Y6N	6
8th	F	30	0Y2N	2
8th	F	40	0Y2N	2
		Total:	20Y20N	40

Table 6.4: Statistics for the most masked table

Candidate	InfoGain	AnonyLoss	Score
ANY_Edu	0.6100	$40 - 4 = 36$	$0.6100/(36 + 1) = 0.0165$
ANY_Sex	0.4934	$40 - 14 = 26$	$0.4934/(26 + 1) = 0.0183$
[1-99)	0.3958	$40 - 12 = 28$	$0.3958/(28 + 1) = 0.0136$

Example 6.3

Consider Table 6.3, the taxonomy trees in Figure 6.4, the 4-anonymity requirement with $QID = \{Education, Sex, Work\_Hrs\}$, the most masked table containing one row $\langle ANY\_Edu, ANY\_Sex, [1\text{-}99) \rangle$ with the class frequency $20Y20N$, and three candidate specialization:

$ANY\_Edu \rightarrow \{8th, 9th, 10th\}$,
$ANY\_Sex \rightarrow \{M, F\}$, and
$[1\text{-}99) \rightarrow \{[1\text{-}40), [40\text{-}99)\}$.

The class frequency is:

Education: $0Y4N$ (*8th*), $0Y12N$ (*9th*), $20Y4N$ (*10th*)
Sex: $20Y6N$ (*M*), $0Y14N$ (*F*)
Work_Hrs: $0Y12N$ ([1-40)), $20Y8N$ ([40-99))

Table 6.4 shows the calculated *InfoGain*, *AnonyLoss*, and *Score* of the three candidate refinements. The following shows the calculations of $InfoGain(ANY\_Edu)$, $InfoGain(ANY\_Sex)$, and $InfoGain([1\text{-}99))$:

$$E(T[ANY\_Edu]) = -\tfrac{20}{40} \times log_2 \tfrac{20}{40} - \tfrac{20}{40} \times log_2 \tfrac{20}{40} = 1$$
$$E(T[8th]) = -\tfrac{0}{4} \times log_2 \tfrac{0}{4} - \tfrac{4}{4} \times log_2 \tfrac{4}{4} = 0$$
$$E(T[9th]) = -\tfrac{0}{12} \times log_2 \tfrac{0}{12} - \tfrac{12}{12} \times log_2 \tfrac{12}{12} = 0$$
$$E(T[10th]) = -\tfrac{20}{24} \times log_2 \tfrac{20}{24} - \tfrac{4}{24} \times log_2 \tfrac{4}{24} = 0.6500$$

$$\textbf{InfoGain(ANY\_Edu)} = E(T[ANY\_Edu]) - (\tfrac{4}{40} \times E(T[8th]) + \tfrac{12}{40} \times E(T[9th])$$
$$+ \tfrac{24}{40} \times E(T[10th])) = 0.6100$$

$$E(T[ANY\_Sex]) = -\tfrac{20}{40} \times log_2 \tfrac{20}{40} - \tfrac{20}{40} \times log_2 \tfrac{20}{40} = 1$$
$$E(T[M]) = -\tfrac{20}{26} \times log_2 \tfrac{20}{26} - \tfrac{6}{26} \times log_2 \tfrac{6}{26} = 0.7793$$

Table 6.5: Final masked table by *InfoGain*

Education	Sex	Work_Hrs	Class	# of Recs.
10th	ANY_Sex	[1-99)	20Y4N	24
9th	ANY_Sex	[1-99)	0Y12N	12
8th	ANY_Sex	[1-99)	0Y4N	4

Table 6.6: Intermediate masked table by *Score*

Education	Sex	Work_Hrs	Class	# of Recs.
ANY_Edu	M	[1-99)	20Y6N	26
ANY_Edu	F	[1-99)	0Y14N	14

$E(T[F]) = -\frac{0}{14} \times log_2 \frac{0}{14} - \frac{14}{14} \times log_2 \frac{14}{14} = 0$
InfoGain(ANY_Sex) $= E(T[ANY\_Sex]) - (\frac{26}{40} \times E(T[M]) + \frac{14}{40} \times E(T[F]))$
$\quad = 0.4934$

$E(T[[1\text{-}99)]) = -\frac{20}{40} \times log_2 \frac{20}{40} - \frac{20}{40} \times log_2 \frac{20}{40} = 1$
$E(T[[1\text{-}40)]) = -\frac{0}{12} \times log_2 \frac{0}{12} - \frac{12}{12} \times log_2 \frac{12}{12} = 0$
$E(T[[40\text{-}99)]) = -\frac{20}{28} \times log_2 \frac{20}{28} - \frac{8}{28} \times log_2 \frac{8}{28} = 0.8631$
InfoGain([1-99)) $= E(T[[1\text{-}99)]) - (\frac{12}{40} \times E(T[[1\text{-}40)]) + \frac{28}{40} \times E(T[[40\text{-}99)]))$
$\quad = 0.3958$

According to the *InfoGain* criterion, *ANY_Edu* will be first specialized because it has the highest *InfoGain*. The result is shown in Table 6.5 with $A(QID) = 4$. After that, there is no further valid specialization because specializing either *ANY_Sex* or *[1-99)* will result in a violation of 4-anonymity. Note that the first 24 records in the table fail to separate the 4N from the other 20Y.

In contrast, according to the *Score* criterion, *ANY_Sex* will be first refined. Below, we show the calculation of *AnonyLoss* of the three candidate refinements:

$AnonyLoss(ANY\_Edu) = A(QID) - A_{ANY\_Edu}(QID)$
$\quad = a(\langle ANY\_Edu, ANY\_Sex, [1\text{-}99)\rangle) - a(\langle 8th, ANY\_Sex, [1\text{-}99)\rangle)$
$\quad = 40 - 4 = 36$, and
$AnonyLoss(ANY\_Sex) = A(QID) - A_{ANY\_Sex}(QID)$
$\quad = a(\langle ANY\_Edu, ANY\_Sex, [1\text{-}99)\rangle) - a(\langle ANY\_Edu, F, [1\text{-}99)\rangle)$
$\quad = 40 - 14 = 26$, and
$AnonyLoss([1\text{-}99)) = A(QID) - A_{[1\text{-}99)}(QID)$
$\quad = a(\langle ANY\_Edu, ANY\_Sex, [1\text{-}99)\rangle) - a(\langle ANY\_Edu, ANY\_Sex, [1\text{-}40)\rangle)$
$\quad = 40 - 12 = 28$.

Table 6.4 shows the calculation of *Score* using *InfoGain* and *AnonyLoss*. The result is shown in Table 6.6, and $A(QID) = 14$. Subsequently, further refinement on *ANY_Edu* is invalid because it will result in $a(\langle 9th, M, [1\text{-}99)\rangle) = 2 < k$, but the refinement on *[1-99)* is valid because it will result in

Table 6.7:   Final masked table by *Score*

Education	Sex	Work_Hrs	Class	# of Recs.
ANY_Edu	M	[40-99)	20Y0N	20
ANY_Edu	M	[1-40)	0Y6N	6
ANY_Edu	F	[40-99)	0Y8N	8
ANY_Edu	F	[1-40)	0Y6N	6

$A(QID) = 6 \geq k$. The final masked table is shown in Table 6.7 where the information for separating the two classes is preserved. Thus by considering the information/anonymity trade-off, the *Score* criterion produces a more desirable sequence of refinements for classification. $\quad\square$

An alternative information metric is to heuristically maximize the information gain, denoted by $InfoGain(v)$, for the classification goal and minimize the anonymity loss, denoted by $AnonyLoss(v)$, for the privacy goal. v is a good candidate for specialization if $InfoGain(v)$ is large and $AnonyLoss(v)$ is small. This alternative information metric, $Score(v)$ is choosing the candidate v, for the next specialization, that has the maximum *information-gain/anonymity-loss trade-off*, defined as

$$Score(v) = IGPL(v), \tag{6.2}$$

where $IGPL(v)$ is defined in Equation 4.7 in Chapter 4.3. Each choice of $InfoGain(v)$ and $AnonyLoss(v)$ gives a trade-off between classification and anonymization.

AnonyLoss(v): This is the average loss of anonymity by specializing v over all QID_j that contain the attribute of v:

$$AnonyLoss(v) = avg\{A(QID_j) - A_v(QID_j)\}, \tag{6.3}$$

where $A(QID_j)$ and $A_v(QID_j)$ represent the anonymity before and after specializing v. Note that $AnonyLoss(v)$ does not just depend on the attribute of v; it depends on all QID_j that contain the attribute of v. Hence, $avg\{A(QID_j) - A_v(QID_j)\}$ is the average loss of all QID_j that contain the attribute of v.

For a numerical attribute, no prior taxonomy tree is given and the taxonomy tree has to be grown dynamically in the process of specialization. The specialization of an interval refers to the optimal binary split that maximizes information gain on the *Class* attribute. Initially, the interval that covers the full range of the attribute forms the root. The specialization on an interval v, written $v \rightarrow child(v)$, refers to the optimal split of v into two child intervals $child(v)$ that maximizes the information gain. The anonymity is not used for finding a split good for classification. This is similar to defining a taxonomy tree where the main consideration is how the taxonomy best describes the application. Due to this extra step of identifying the optimal split of the parent

Table 6.8:   Compressed raw patient table for illustrating optimal split on numerical attribute

Education	Sex	Work_Hrs	Class	# of Recs.
9th	M	30	0Y3N	3
10th	M	32	0Y4N	4
11th	M	35	2Y3N	5
12th	F	37	3Y1N	4
Bachelors	F	42	4Y2N	6
Bachelors	F	44	4Y0N	4
Masters	M	44	4Y0N	4
Masters	F	44	3Y0N	3
Doctorate	F	44	1Y0N	1
		Total:	21Y13N	34

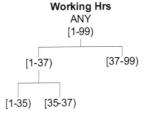

FIGURE 6.5: Taxonomy tree for *Work_Hrs*

interval, numerical attributes have to be treated differently from categorical attributes with taxonomy trees. The following example illustrates how to find an optimal split on a numerical interval.

Example 6.4
Consider the data in Table 6.8. The table has 34 records in total. Each row represents one or more records with the *Class* column containing the class frequency of the records represented, Y for "income $>$50K" and N for "income $\leq$50K." For example, the third row represents 5 records having *Education* = *11th*, *Sex* = *Male* and *Work_Hrs* = *35*. The value $2Y3N$ in the Class column conveys that 2 records have the class Y and 3 records have the class N. Semantically, this compressed table is equivalent to the table containing 34 rows with each row representing one record.

For the numerical attribute *Work_Hrs*, the top most value is the full range interval of domain values, *[1-99]*. To determine the split point of *[1-99]*, we evaluate the information gain for the five possible split points for the values *30, 32, 35, 37, 42,* and *44*. The following is the calculation for the split point at *37*:

$$InfoGain(37) = E(T[[1\text{-}99]]) - (\tfrac{12}{34} \times E(T[[1\text{-}37]]) + \tfrac{22}{34} \times E(T[[37\text{-}99]]))$$
$$= 0.9597 - (\tfrac{12}{34} \times 0.6500 + \tfrac{22}{34} \times 0.5746) = 0.3584.$$

As $InfoGain(37)$ is highest, we grow the taxonomy tree for *Work_Hrs* by adding two child intervals, *[1-37)* and *[37-99)*, under the interval *[1-99)*. The taxonomy tree is illustrated in Figure 6.5. ☐

Case 2: Score for General Data Analysis

Sometimes, the data is shared without a specific task. In this case of general data analysis, we use discernibility cost [213] to measure the data distortion in the anonymous data table. The discernibility cost charges a penalty to each record for being indistinguishable from other records. For each record in an equivalence group qid, the penalty is $|T[qid]|$. Thus, the penalty on a group is $|T[qid]|^2$. To minimize the discernibility cost, we choose the specialization $v \rightarrow child(v)$ that maximizes the value of $Score(v) = \sum_{qid_v} |T[qid_v]|^2$ over all qid_v containing v. The Discernibility Metric (DM) is discussed in Equation 4.4 in Chapter 4.1. Example 6.6 shows the computation of $Score(v)$.

6.2.3 Problem Statement

The goal in this Red Cross problem is to transform a given data set T into an anonymous version T' that satisfies a given LKC-*privacy* requirement and preserves as much information as possible for the intended data analysis task. Based on the information requirements specified by the Red Cross, we define the problems as follows.

DEFINITION 6.1 Anonymization for data analysis   Given a data table T, a LKC-*privacy* requirement, and a taxonomy tree for each categorical attribute contained in QID, the *anonymization problem for classification analysis* is to generalize T on the attributes QID to satisfy the LKC-privacy requirement while preserving as much information as possible for the classification analysis. The *anonymization problem for general analysis* is to generalize T on the attributes QID to satisfy the LKC-privacy requirement while minimizing the overall discernibility cost. ∎

Computing the optimal LKC-privacy solution is NP-hard. Given a QID, there are $\binom{|QID|}{L}$ combinations of decomposed QID_j with maximum size L. For any value of K and C, each combination of QID_j in LKC-privacy is an instance of the (α, k)-anonymity problem with $\alpha = C$ and $k = K$. Wong et al. [246] have proven that computing the optimal (α, k)-anonymous solution is NP-hard; therefore, computing optimal LKC-privacy is also NP-hard. Below, we provide a greedy approach to efficiently identify a sub-optimal solution.

Algorithm 6.3.1 High-Dimensional Top-Down Specialization (HDTDS)

1: Initialize every value in T to the topmost value;
2: Initialize Cut_i to include the topmost value;
3: **while** some candidate $v \in \cup Cut_i$ is valid **do**
4:     Find the *Best* specialization from $\cup Cut_i$;
5:     Perform *Best* on T and update $\cup Cut_i$;
6:     Update $Score(x)$ and validity for $x \in \cup Cut_i$;
7: **end while**;
8: Output T and $\cup Cut_i$.;

6.3 High-Dimensional Top-Down Specialization (HDTDS)

Algorithm 6.3.1 provides an overview of the High-Dimensional Top-Down Specialization (HDTDS) algorithm [171] for achieving LKC-privacy.[1] Initially, all values in QID are generalized to the topmost value in their taxonomy trees, and Cut_i contains the topmost value for each attribute D_i. At each iteration, HDTDS performs the *Best* specialization, which has the highest *Score* among the *candidates* that are valid specializations in $\cup Cut_i$ (Line 4). Then, apply *Best* to T and update $\cup Cut_i$ (Line 5). Finally, update the *Score* of the affected candidates due to the specialization (Line 6). The algorithm terminates when there are no more valid candidates in $\cup Cut_i$. In other words, the algorithm terminates if any further specialization would lead to a violation of the LKC-privacy requirement. An important property of HDTDS is that the LKC-privacy is *anti-monotone* with respect to a specialization: if a generalized table violates LKC-privacy before a specialization, it remains violated after the specialization because a specialization never increases the $|T[qid]|$ and never decreases the maximum $P(s|qid)$. This anti-monotonic property guarantees that the final solution cut is a sub-optimal solution. HDTDS is a modified version of TDS [96].

Example 6.5
Consider Table 6.1 with $L = 2$, $K = 2$, $C = 50\%$, and $QID = \{Job, Sex, Age\}$. The QID_i with maximum size 2 are:

$\langle QID_1 = \{Job\}\rangle,$
$\langle QID_2 = \{Sex\}\rangle,$
$\langle QID_3 = \{Age\}\rangle,$

---

[1]The source code and the executable program is available on the web: http://www.ciise.concordia.ca/~fung/pub/RedCrossKDD09/

$\langle QID_4 = \{Job, Sex\}\rangle,$
$\langle QID_5 = \{Job, Age\}\rangle,$
$\langle QID_6 = \{Sex, Age\}\rangle.$

Initially, all data records are generalized to $\langle ANY\_Job, ANY\_Sex, [1\text{-}99)\rangle$, and $\cup Cut_i = \{ANY\_Job, ANY\_Sex, [1\text{-}99)\}$. To find the *Best* specialization among the candidates in $\cup Cut_i$, we compute $Score\ (ANY\_Job)$, $Score(ANY\_Sex)$, and $Score([1\text{-}99))$. $\quad\Box$

A simple yet inefficient implementation of Lines 4-6 is to scan *all* data records and recompute $Score(x)$ for all candidates in $\cup Cut_i$. The key to the efficiency of the algorithm is having *direct access* to the data records to be specialized, and updating $Score(x)$ based on some statistics maintained for candidates in $\cup Cut_i$, instead of scanning all data records. In the rest of this Chapter 6.3, we explain a scalable implementation and data structures in detail.

6.3.1 Find the Best Specialization

Initially, the algorithm computes the *Score* for all candidates x in $\cup Cut_i$. For each subsequent iteration, information needed to calculate *Score* comes from the update of the previous iteration (Line 7). Finding the best specialization *Best* involves at most $|\cup Cut_i|$ computations of *Score* without accessing data records. The procedure for updating *Score* will be discussed in Chapter 6.3.3.

Example 6.6
Continue from Example 6.5. We show the computation of $Score(ANY\_Job)$ for the specialization

$$ANY\_Job \rightarrow \{Blue\text{-}collar, White\text{-}collar\}.$$

For general data analysis, $Score(ANY\_Job) = 6^2 + 5^2 = 61$. For classification analysis,

$E(T[ANY\_Job]) = -\frac{6}{11} \times log_2\frac{6}{11} - \frac{5}{11} \times log_2\frac{5}{11} = 0.994$
$E(T[Blue\text{-}collar]) = -\frac{1}{6} \times log_2\frac{1}{6} - \frac{5}{6} \times log_2\frac{5}{6} = 0.6499$
$E(T[White\text{-}collar]) = -\frac{5}{5} \times log_2\frac{5}{5} - \frac{0}{5} \times log_2\frac{0}{5} = 0.0$

$InfoGain(ANY\_Job) = E(T[ANY\_Job]) - (\frac{6}{11} \times E(T[Blue\text{-}collar])$
$\qquad\qquad\qquad + \frac{5}{11} \times E(T[White\text{-}collar])) = 0.6396$

$Score(ANY\_Job) = InfoGain(ANY\_Job) = 0.6396.$

$\quad\Box$

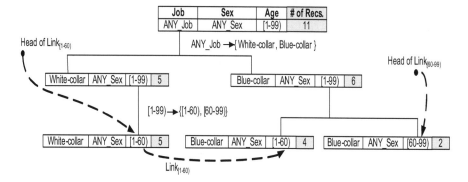

FIGURE 6.6: The TIPS data structure

6.3.2 Perform the Best Specialization

Consider a specialization $Best \rightarrow child(Best)$, where $Best \in D_i$ and $D_i \in QID$. First, we replace $Best$ with $child(Best)$ in $\cup Cut_i$. Then, we need to retrieve $T[Best]$, the set of data records generalized to $Best$, to tell the child value in $child(Best)$ for individual data records. A data structure, called *Taxonomy Indexed PartitionS (TIPS)* [96], is employed to facilitate this operation. This data structure is also crucial for updating $Score(x)$ for candidates x. The general idea is to group data records according to their generalized records on QID.

DEFINITION 6.2 TIPS   Taxonomy Indexed PartitionS (TIPS) is a tree structure with each node representing a generalized record over QID, and each child node representing a specialization of the parent node on exactly one attribute. Stored with each leaf node is the set of data records having the same generalized record, called a *leaf partition*. For each x in $\cup Cut_i$, P_x denotes a leaf partition whose generalized record contains x, and $Link_x$ denotes the link of all P_x, with the head of $Link_x$ stored with x. ∎

At any time, the generalized data is represented by the leaf partitions of TIPS, but the original data records remain unchanged. $Link_x$ provides a direct access to $T[x]$, the set of data records generalized to the value x. Initially, TIPS has only one leaf partition containing all data records, generalized to the topmost value on every attribute in QID. In each iteration, we perform the best specialization $Best$ by refining the leaf partitions on $Link_{Best}$.

Updating TIPS: The algorithm refines each leaf partition P_{Best} found on $Link_{Best}$ as follows. For each value c in $child(Best)$, a child partition P_c is created under P_{Best}, and data records in P_{Best} are split among the child partitions: P_c contains a data record in P_{Best} if c generalizes the correspond-

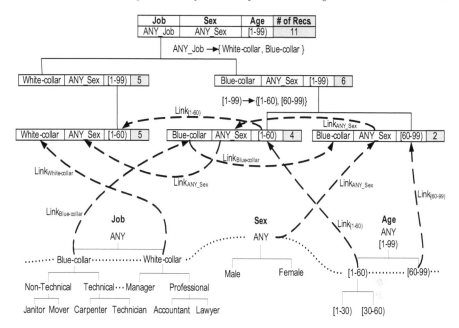

FIGURE 6.7: A complete TIPS data structure

ing domain value in the record. An empty P_c is removed. $Link_c$ is created to link up all P_c's for the same c. Also, link P_c to every $Link_x$ to which P_{Best} was previously linked, except for $Link_{Best}$. This is the only operation in the whole algorithm that requires accessing data records. The overhead of maintaining $Link_x$ is small. For each attribute in $\cup QID_j$ and each leaf partition on $Link_{Best}$, there are at most $|child(Best)|$ "relinkings," or at most $|\cup QID_j| \times |Link_{Best}| \times |child(Best)|$ "relinkings" in total for applying $Best$.

Example 6.7

Initially, TIPS has only one leaf partition containing all data records and representing the generalized record $\langle ANY\_Job, ANY\_Sex, [1\text{-}99)\rangle$. Let the best specialization be $ANY\_Job \rightarrow \{White\text{-}collar, Blue\text{-}collar\}$ on *Job*. Two child partitions

$$\langle White\text{-}collar, ANY\_Sex, [1\text{-}99)\rangle$$
$$\langle Blue\text{-}collar, ANY\_Sex, [1\text{-}99)\rangle$$

are created under the root partition as in Figure 6.6, and split data records between them. Both child partitions are on $Link_{ANY\_Sex}$ and $Link_{[1\text{-}99)}$. $\cup Cut_i$ is updated into $\{White\text{-}collar, Blue\text{-}collar, ANY\_Sex, [1\text{-}99)\}$. Suppose that the next best specialization is $[1\text{-}99) \rightarrow \{[1\text{-}60),[60\text{-}99)\}$, which specializes the two leaf partitions on $Link_{[1\text{-}99)}$, resulting in three child partitions

$\langle$ *White-collar, ANY_Sex, [1-60)* $\rangle$
$\langle$ *Blue-collar, ANY_Sex, [1-60)* $\rangle$
$\langle$ *Blue-collar, ANY_Sex, [60-99)* $\rangle$

as shown in Figure 6.6.

Figure 6.7 shows a complete TIPS data structure with the corresponding

$$\cup Cut_i = \{Blue\text{-}collar, White\text{-}collar, ANY\_Sex, [1\text{-}60), [60\text{-}99)\},$$

where $Link_{Blue\text{-}collar}$ links up

$\langle$ *Blue-collar, ANY_Sex, [1-60)* $\rangle$
$\langle$ *Blue-collar, ANY_Sex, [60-99)* $\rangle$,

and $Link_{White\text{-}collar}$ links up

$\langle$ *White-collar, ANY_Sex, [1-60)* $\rangle$,

and $Link_{ANY\_Sex}$ links up

$\langle$ *White-collar, ANY_Sex, [1-60)* $\rangle$
$\langle$ *Blue-collar, ANY_Sex, [1-60)* $\rangle$
$\langle$ *Blue-collar, ANY_Sex, [60-99)* $\rangle$

and $Link_{[1\text{-}60)}$ links up

$\langle$ *White-collar, ANY_Sex, [1-60)* $\rangle$
$\langle$ *Blue-collar, ANY_Sex, [1-60)* $\rangle$,

and $Link_{[60\text{-}99)}$ links up

$\langle$ *Blue-collar, ANY_Sex, [60-99)* $\rangle$.

$\square$

A scalable feature of the algorithm is maintaining some statistical information for each candidate x in $\cup Cut_i$ for updating $Score(x)$ without accessing data records. For each new value c in $child(Best)$ added to $\cup Cut_i$ in the current iteration, we collect the following *count statistics* of c while scanning data records in P_{Best} for updating TIPS: (1) $|T[c]|$, $|T[d]|$, $freq(T[c], cls)$, and $freq(T[d], cls)$, where $d \in child(c)$ and cls is a class label. (2) $|P_d|$, where P_d is a child partition under P_c *as if* c is specialized, kept together with the leaf node for P_c. This information will be used in Chapter 6.3.3.

TIPS has several useful properties. First, all data records in the same leaf partition have the same generalized record although they may have different raw values. Second, every data record appears in exactly one leaf partition. Third, each leaf partition P_x has exactly one generalized qid on QID and contributes the count $|P_x|$ towards $|T[qid]|$. Later, the algorithm uses the last property to extract $|T[qid]|$ from TIPS.

6.3.3 Update Score and Validity

This step updates $Score(x)$ and validity for candidates x in $\cup Cut_i$ to reflect the impact of the *Best* specialization. The key to the scalability of the algorithm is updating $Score(x)$ using the count statistics maintained in Chapter 6.3.2 without accessing raw records again.

6.3.3.1 Updating Score

The procedure for updating $Score$ is different depending on the information requirement.

Case 1 classification analysis: An observation is that $InfoGain(x)$ is not affected by $Best \rightarrow child(Best)$, except that we need to compute $InfoGain(c)$ for each newly added value c in $child(Best)$. $InfoGain(c)$ can be computed from the count statistics for c collected in Chapter 6.3.2.

Case 2 general data analysis: Each leaf partition P_c keeps the count $|T[qid_c]|$. By following $Link_c$ from TIPS, we can compute $\sum_{qid_c} |T[qid_c]|^2$ for all the qid_c on $Link_c$.

6.3.3.2 Validity Check

A specialization $Best \rightarrow child(Best)$ may change the validity status of other candidates $x \in \cup Cut_i$ if $Best$ and x are contained in the same qid with size not greater than L. Thus, in order to check the validity, we need to keep track of the count of every qid with $|qid| = L$. Note, we can ignore qid with size less than L because if a table satisfies LKC-privacy, then it must also satisfy $L'KC$-privacy where $L' < L$.

We explain an efficient method for checking the validity of a candidate. First, given a QID in T, we identify all $QID_j \subseteq QID$ with size L. Then, for each QID_j, we use a data structure, called $QIDTree_j$, to index all qid_j on QID_j. $QIDTree_j$ is a tree, where each level represents one attribute in QID_j. Each root-to-leaf path represents an existing qid_j on QID_j in the generalized data, with $|T[qid_j]|$ and $|T[qid_j \wedge s]|$ for every $s \in S$ stored at the leaf node. A candidate $x \in \cup Cut_i$ is valid if, for every $c \in child(x)$, every qid_j containing c has $|T[qid_j]| \geq K$ and $P(s|qid_j) \leq C$ for any $s \in S$. If x is invalid, remove it from $\cup Cut_i$.

6.3.4 Discussion

Let $T[Best]$ denote the set of records containing value $Best$ in a generalized table. Each iteration involves two types of work. The first type accesses data records in $T[Best]$ for updating TIPS and count statistics in Chapter 6.3.2. If $Best$ is an interval, an extra step is required for determining the optimal split for each child interval c in $child(Best)$. This requires making a scan on records in $T[c]$, which is a subset of $T[Best]$. To determine a split, $T[c]$ has to be sorted, which can be an expensive operation. Fortunately, resorting $T[c]$ is unnecessary for each iteration because its superset $T[Best]$ is already sorted. Thus, this type of work involves one scan of the records being specialized in each iteration.

The second type computes $Score(x)$ for the candidates x in $\cup Cut_i$ without accessing data records in Chapter 6.3.3. For a table with m attributes and each taxonomy tree with at most p nodes, the number of such x is at most $m \times p$. This computation makes use of the maintained count statistics, rather than accessing data records. In other words, each iteration accesses only the records being specialized. Since $m \times p$ is a small constant, independent of the table size, the HDTDS algorithm is linear in the table size. This feature makes the approach scalable.

The current implementation of HDTDS [171] assumes that the data table fits in memory. Often, this assumption is valid because the qid groups are much smaller than the original table. If qid groups do not fit in the memory, we can store leaf partitions of TIPS on disk if necessary. Favorably, the memory is used to keep only leaf partitions that are smaller than the page size to avoid fragmentation of disk pages. A nice property of HDTDS is that leaf partitions that cannot be further specialized (i.e., on which there is no candidate specialization) can be discarded, and only some statistics for them need to be kept. This likely applies to small partitions in memory and, therefore, the memory demand is unlikely to build up.

Compared to iteratively generalizing the data bottom-up starting from domain values, the top-down specialization is more natural and efficient for handling numerical attributes. To produce a small number of intervals for a numerical attribute, the top-down approach needs only a small number of interval splitting, whereas the bottom-up approach needs many interval merging starting from many domain values. In addition, the top-down approach can discard data records that cannot be further specialized, whereas the bottom-up approach has to keep all data records until the end of computation.

Experimental results on the real-life data sets suggest that HDTDS [171] can effectively preserve both privacy and data utility in the anonymous data for a wide range of LKC-privacy requirements. There is a trade-off between data privacy and data utility with respect to K and L, but the trend is less obvious on C because eliminating record linkages is the primary driving force for generalization. The LKC-privacy model clearly retains more information than the traditional k-anonymity model and provides the flexibility to adjust privacy requirements according to the assumption of the adversary's background knowledge. Finally, HDTDS is highly scalable for large data sets. These characteristics make HDTDS a promising component in the Red Cross blood transfusion information system.

6.4 Workload-Aware Mondrian

LeFevre et al. [150] present a suite of greedy algorithms to address the k-anonymization problem for various data analysis tasks, including classification analysis on single/multiple categorical target attribute(s) and regression analysis on single/multiple numerical target attribute(s). The greedy algorithms recursively partition the QID domain space. The Mondrian method is flexible to adopt the k-anonymity (Chapter 2.1.1), ℓ-diversity (Chapter 2.2.1), and squared-error diversity [150]. The general idea of the anonymization is somewhat similar to the top-down specialization approaches, such as HDTDS (Chapter 6.3). One major difference is that LeFevre et al. [150] employ a multidimensional generalization scheme, which is more flexible than the subtree generalization scheme used in HDTDS. Although Mondrian is designed for achieving k-anonymity, it can be easily modified to adopt the LKC-privacy model in order to accommodate the high-dimensional data.

In the rest of this Chapter 6.4, we briefly discuss Workload-Aware Mondrian on different classification and regression analysis tasks.

6.4.1 Single Categorical Target Attribute

Recall the description of single-dimensional and multidimensional generalization schemes from Chapter 3.1: Let D_i be the domain of an attribute A_i. A *single-dimensional generalization*, such as full-domain generalization and subtree generalization, is defined by a function $f_i : D_{A_i} \to D'$ for each attribute A_i in QID. In contrast, a *multidimensional generalization* is defined by a single function $f : D_{A_1} \times \cdots \times D_{A_n} \to D'$, which is used to generalize $qid = \langle v_1, \ldots, v_n \rangle$ to $qid' = \langle u_1, \ldots, u_n \rangle$ where for every v_i, either $v_i = u_i$ or v_i is a child node of u_i in the taxonomy of A_i. This scheme flexibly allows two qid groups, even having the same value v, to be independently generalized into different parent groups.

Every single-dimensional generalized table can be achieved by a sequence of multidimensional generalization operations. Yet, a multidimensional generalized table cannot be achieved by a sequence of single-dimensional generalization operations because the possible generalization space in the single-dimensional generalization scheme is a subset of the possible generalization space in the multidimensional scheme. Figure 6.8 visualizes this point with respect to classification analysis. Consider a data table with two quasi-identifying attributes, *Age* and *Job* and two classes Y and N. Suppose the data holder wants to release a 3-anonymous table for classification analysis. Using single-dimensional cannot clearly separate the class labels due to the privacy constraint as two Ys are misclassified in the wrong group. In contrast, using multidimensional can clearly separate the classes.

Suppose there is only one categorical target attribute for classification mod-

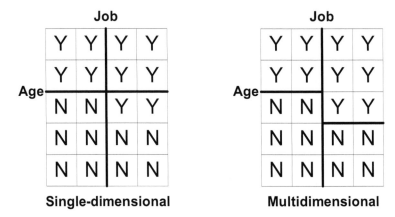

FIGURE 6.8: Illustrate the flexibility of multidimensional generalization scheme

eling. To preserve the information utility for classification analysis, we can employ the *InfoGain Mondrian*, which is a modified version of the Mondrian algorithm [149] but with a different information metric [150]:

$$Entropy(P, C) = \sum_{partitions\ P'} \frac{|P'|}{|P|} \sum_{c \in A_C} -p(c|P')\ log\ p(c|P'), \qquad (6.4)$$

where P and P' denote the partitions before and after the *Best* specialization, $p(c|P')$ is the percentage of records in P' with class label c.

6.4.2   Single Numerical Target Attribute

Most methods that address the anonymization problem for classification analysis, e.g., TDR [95, 96], TDD (Chapter 5.2.3), HDTDS (Chapter 6.3), and Genetic Algorithm (Chapter 5.1.2.3), assume the target attribute is a categorical attribute. What method should be used if the target attribute is a numerical attribute? In other words, the data holder would like to release an anonymous table for regression analysis. Inspired by the CART algorithm for regression trees, which recursively select the split that minimizes the weighted sum of the means *squared errors (MSE)* over the set of resulting partitions, LeFevre et al. [150] propose the *Least Squared Deviance (LSD) Mondrian* algorithm that minimizes the following information metric. The general idea of MSE is to measure the impurity of target numerical attribute Z within a candidate partition P'.

$$Error^2(P, Z) = \sum_{Partitions\ P'} \sum_{i \in P'} (v_i - \bar{v}(P'))^2, \qquad (6.5)$$

where v_i denotes a record value and $\bar{v}(P')$ denotes the mean value of Z in P'.

6.4.3 Multiple Target Attributes

In some privacy-preserving data publisher scenarios, a data holder may want to release an anonymous table for classification and/or regression analysis on multiple target attributes.

For classification analysis on multiple categorical attributes, LeFevre et al. [150] discuss two possible extensions. In the first approach, the data recipient could build a single classifier to predict the combination of class labels $\langle C_1, \ldots, C_m \rangle$, which has domain $D_{C_1} \times \cdots \times D_{C_m}$. The data holder can transform this multi-target attributes problem into a single-target attribute problem and employ the information metric presented in Chapter 6.4.1 to greedily minimize the entropy. The catch is that the domain grows exponentially with the number of target attributes, resulting in a large combination of classes and, thereby, poor classification result.

The second approach is to simplify the problem by assuming independence among target attributes, we can employ a greedy information metric that minimizes the sum of weighted entropies [150]:

$$\sum_{m}^{i=1} Entropy(P, C_i). \tag{6.6}$$

For regression analysis on multiple numerical attributes, we can treat the set of target attributes independently and greedily minimize the sum of squared error [150]:

$$\sum_{m}^{i=1} Error^2(P, Z_i). \tag{6.7}$$

6.4.4 Discussion

The suite of Mondrian algorithms studied above provides a very flexible framework for anonymizing different attributes with respect to multiple and different types of target attributes. Compared to the single-dimensional generalization scheme, the employed multidimensional generalization scheme can help reduce information loss with respect to classification analysis and regression analysis. Yet, multidimensional generalization also implies higher computational cost and suffers from the data exploration problem discussed in Chapter 3.1. The data exploration problem may make the classifier built from the anonymous data become unusable. Furthermore, the Mondrian algorithms do not handle multiple QIDs and they cannot achieve LKC-privacy. Enforcing traditional k-anonymity and ℓ-diversity may result in high information loss due to the curse of high dimensionality [6].

Algorithm 6.5.2 Bottom-Up Generalization

1: **while** T does not satisfy a given k-anonymity requirement **do**
2:     **for all** generalization g **do**
3:         compute $ILPG(g)$;
4:     **end for**
5:     find the *Best* generalization;
6:     generalize T by *Best*;
7: **end while**
8: output T;

6.5   Bottom-Up Generalization

Wang et al. [239] present an effective bottom-up generalization approach to achieve k-anonymity. They employed the subtree generalization scheme (Chapter 3.1). A generalization $g : child(v) \rightarrow v$, replaces all instances of every child value c in $child(v)$ with the parent value v. Although this method is designed for achieving k-anonymity, it can be easily modified to adopt the LKC-privacy model in order to accommodate the high-dimensional data.

6.5.1   The Anonymization Algorithm

Algorithm 6.5.2 presents the general idea of their bottom-up generalization method. It begins the generalization from the raw data table T. At each iteration, the algorithm greedily selects the *Best* generalization g that minimizes the information loss and maximizes the privacy gain. This intuition is captured by the information metric $ILPG(g) = IL(g)/PG(g)$, which has been discussed in Chapter 4.3. Then, the algorithm performs the generalization $child(Best) \rightarrow Best$ on the table T, and repeats the iteration until the table T satisfies the given k-anonymity requirement.

Let $A(QID)$ and $A_g(QID)$ be the minimum anonymity counts in T before and after the generalization g. Given a data table T, there are many possible generalizations that can be performed. Yet, most generalizations g in fact do not affect the minimum anonymity count. In other words, $A(QID) = A_g(QID)$. Thus, to facilitate efficiently choosing a generalization g, there is no need to consider all generalizations. Indeed, we can focus only on the "critical generalizations."

DEFINITION 6.3   A generalization g is *critical* if $A_g(QID) > A(QID)$. ∎

Wang et al. [239] make several observations to optimize the efficiency of Algorithm 6.5.2: A critical generalization g has a positive $PG(g)$ and a finite

---

Algorithm 6.5.3 Bottom-Up Generalization

1: **while** T does not satisfy a given k-anonimity requirement **do**
2:    **for all** critical generalization g **do**
3:       compute $A_g(QID)$;
4:    **end for**
5:    find the *Best* generalization;
6:    generalize T by *Best*;
7: **end while**
8: output T;

$ILPG(g)$, whereas a non-critical generalization g has $PG(g) = 0$ and infinite $ILPG(g)$. Therefore, if at least one generalization is critical, all non-critical generalizations will be ignored by the $ILPG(g)$ information metric. If all generalizations are non-critical, the $ILPG(g)$ metric will select the one with minimum $IL(g)$. In both cases, $A_g(QID)$ is not needed for a non-critical generalization g. Based on this observation, Lines 2-3 in Algorithm 6.5.2 can be optimized as illustrated in Algorithm 6.5.3.

6.5.2   Data Structure

To further improve the efficiency of the generalization operation, Wang et al. [239] propose a data structure, called *Taxonomy Encoded Anonymity (TEA) index* for $QID = D_1, \ldots, D_m$. TEA is a tree of m levels. The ith level represents the current value for D_j. Each root-to-leaf path represents a *qid* value in the current data table, with $a(qid)$ stored at the leaf node. In addition, the TEA index links up the qids according to the generalizations that generalize them. When a generalization g is applied, the TEA index is updated by adjusting the qids linked to the generalization of g. The purpose of this index is to prune the number of candidate generalizations to no more than $|QID|$ at each iteration, where $|QID|$ is the number of attributes in QID. For a generalization $g : child(v) \to v$, a *segment* of g is a maximal set of sibling nodes, $\{s_1, \ldots, s_t\}$, such that $\{s_1, \ldots, s_t\} \subseteq child(v)$, where t is the size of the segment. All segments of g are linked up. A *qid* is generalized by a segment if the *qid* contains a value in the segment.

A segment of g represents a set of sibling nodes in the TEA index that will be merged by applying g. To apply generalization g, we follow the link of the segments of g and merge the nodes in each segment of g. The merging of sibling nodes implies inserting the new node into a proper segment and recursively merging the child nodes having the same value if their parents are merged. The merging of leaf nodes requires adding up $a(qid)$ stored at such leaf nodes. The cost is proportional to the number of qids generalized by g.

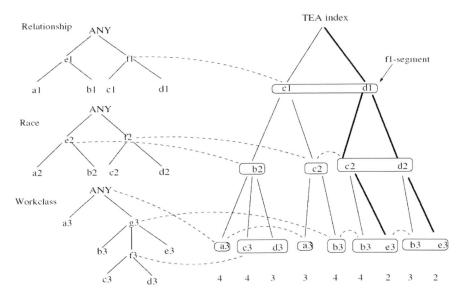

FIGURE 6.9: The TEA structure for QID = {*Relationship, Race, Workclass*} ([239] ©2004 IEEE)

Example 6.8

Figure 6.9 depicts three taxonomy trees for QID attributes {*Relationship, Race, Workclass*} and the TEA index for qids:

$\langle c_1, b_2, a_3 \rangle$
$\langle c_1, b_2, c_3 \rangle$
$\langle c_1, b_2, d_3 \rangle$
$\langle c_1, c_2, a_3 \rangle$
$\langle c_1, c_2, b_3 \rangle$
$\langle d_1, c_2, b_3 \rangle$
$\langle d_1, c_2, e_3 \rangle$
$\langle d_1, d_2, b_3 \rangle$
$\langle d_1, d_2, e_3 \rangle$

A rectangle represents a segment, and a dashed line links up the segments of the same generalization. For example, the left-most path represents the $qid = \langle c_1, b_2, a_3 \rangle$, and $a(\langle c_1, b_2, a_3 \rangle) = 4$. $\{c_1, d_1\}$ at level 1 is a segment of f_1 because it forms a maximal set of siblings that will be merged by f_1. $\{c_1 c_2\}$ and $\{d_1 c_2, d_1 d_2\}$ at level 2 are two segments of f_2. $\{c_1 b_2 c_3, c_1 b_2 d_3\}$ at level 3 is a segment of f_3. $\langle d_1, d_2, e_3 \rangle$ and $\langle d_1, c_2, e_3 \rangle$, in bold face, are the anonymity qids.

Consider applying $\{c_2, d_2\} \rightarrow f_2$. The first segment of f_2 contains only one sibling node $\{c_1 c_2\}$, we simply relabel the sibling by f_2. This creates new qids $\langle c_1, f_2, a_3 \rangle$ and $\langle c_1, f_2, b_3 \rangle$. The second segment of f_2 contains two sibling nodes $\{d_1 c_2, d_1 d_2\}$. We merge them into a new node labeled by f_2, and merge their child nodes having the same label. This creates new qids $\langle d_1, f_2, b_3 \rangle$ and $\langle d_1, f_2, e_3 \rangle$, with $a(\langle d_1, f_2, b_3 \rangle) = 7$ and $a(\langle d_1, f_2, e_3 \rangle) = 4$. $\square$

6.5.3 Discussion

Bottom-Up Generalization is an efficient k-anonymization method. Experimental results [239] suggest that it can effectively identify a k-anonymous solution that preserves information utility for classification analysis. Yet, it has several limitations, making it not applicable to the anonymization problem in the Red Cross BTS.

1. Enforcing traditional k-anonymity on the Red Cross BTS data would result in high utility loss due to the problem of high dimensionality, making the data not useful in practice.

2. The data structure TEA proposed in [239] can handle only a single QID. A new structure is required if the data holder wants to achieve LKC-privacy using the Bottom-Up Generalization method because LKC-privacy in effect is equivalent to breaking a single QID into multiple $QID_i \subseteq QID$, where $|QID_i| \leq L$.

3. Bottom-Up Generalization can handle categorical attributes only. Compared to iteratively masking the data bottom-up starting from domain values, the top-down specialization is more natural and efficient for handling numerical attributes. To produce a small number of intervals for a numerical attribute, the top-down approach needs only a small number of interval splitting, whereas the bottom-up approach needs much interval merging starting from many domain values.

4. The initial step of Bottom-Up Generalization has to identify all combinations of qid values in the raw data table T and keep track of their anonymity counts $a(qid)$. In case T is large, the number of distinct combinations could be huge. Keeping all these combinations and counts in memory may not be feasible. In contrast, the top-down approach can discard data records that cannot be further specialized, whereas the bottom-up approach has to keep all data records until the end of computation.

6.6 Genetic Algorithm

Iyengar [123] is the pioneer to address the anonymization problem for classification analysis and proposed a genetic algorithmic solution to achieve the traditional k-anonymity with the goal of preserving the data utility.

6.6.1 The Anonymization Algorithm

Iyengar [123] modifies the genetic algorithm from [243]. The algorithm has two parts: choosing an attribute for subtree generalization and choosing a record for entire record suppression. The chromosome in the genetic algorithm framework is a bit string that represents the chosen generalizations. The algorithm uses the classification metric CM in Equation 4.5 (Chapter 4.2) to determine the goodness of a k-anonymous solution. Intuitively, the metric charges a penalty for each record suppressed or generalized to a group in which the record's class is not the majority class. It is based on the idea that a record having a non-majority class in a group will be classified as the majority class, which is an error because it disagrees with the record's original class. The general idea is to encode each state of generalization as a "chromosome" and data distortion into the fitness function. Then the algorithm employs the genetic evolution to converge to the fittest chromosome.

6.6.2 Discussion

Iyegnar [123] identifies a new direction for privacy-preserving data publishing. Yet, his proposed solution has several limitations. Similar to Mondrian and Bottom-Up Generalization, the Genetic Algorithm presented in [123] can achieve only k-anonymity. It does not address the privacy threats caused by attribute linkages and does not address the high-dimensionality problem.

The major drawback of the Genetic Algorithm is its inefficiency. It requires 18 hours to transform 30K records [123]. In contrast, the TDD algorithm (Chapter 5.2.3) takes only 7 seconds to produce a comparable accuracy on the same data. The HDTDS algorithm (Chapter 6.3) takes only 30 seconds to produce even better results than the Genetic Algorithm. For large databases, Iyengar suggested running his algorithm on a sample. However, a small sampling error could mean failed protection on the entire data. The other methods presented in this chapter do not suffer from this efficiency and scalability problem.

6.7 Evaluation Methodology

In Part I, we have studied the four major components in privacy-preserving data publishing, namely privacy models, anonymization operations, information metrics, and anonymization algorithms. After choosing the appropriate components to address a specific privacy-preserving data publishing problem, the data holder often would like to know the impact on the data quality. The objective of this section is to present an evaluation methodology for measuring the impact of imposing a privacy requirement on the data quality with respect to some data analysis tasks. Data holders can employ this evaluation methodology to objectively measure the data quality with respect to the privacy protection level before publishing the data. Current or prospective researchers may also find this evaluation methodology beneficial to their future works on privacy-preserving data publishing.

We use the LKC-privacy model (Chapter 6.3) and the anonymization algorithm HDTDS (Chapter 6.3) as examples to illustrate the evaluation methodology. Specifically, we study the impact of enforcing various LKC-privacy requirements on the data quality in terms of classification error and discernibility cost, and to evaluate the efficiency and scalability of HDTDS by varying the thresholds of maximum adversary's knowledge L, minimum anonymity K, and maximum confidence C.

Two real-life data sets, *Blood* and *Adult* are employed. *Blood* is a real-life blood transfusion data set owned by an anonymous health institute. *Blood* contains 10,000 blood transfusion records in 2008. Each record represents one incident of blood transfusion. *Blood* has 62 attributes after removing explicit identifiers; 41 of them are QID attributes. *Blood Group* represents the *Class* attribute with 8 possible values. *Diagnosis Codes*, representing 15 categories of diagnosis, is considered to be the sensitive attribute. The remaining attributes are neither quasi-identifiers nor sensitive.

The publicly available *Adult* data set [179] is a *de facto* benchmark for testing anonymization algorithms [29, 96, 123, 162, 172, 236, 237] in the research area of privacy-preserving data publishing. *Adult* has 45,222 census records on 6 numerical attributes, 8 categorical attributes, and a binary *Class* column representing two income levels, $\leq$50K or >50K. Table 6.9 describes the attributes of *Adult*. *Divorced* and *Separated* in the attribute *Marital-status* are considered as sensitive attribute, and the remaining 13 attributes are considered as QID. All experiments were conducted on an Intel Core2 Quad Q6600 2.4GHz PC with 2GB RAM.

6.7.1 Data Utility

To evaluate the impact on classification quality (Case 1 in Chapter 6.2.2), all records are used for generalization, build a classifier on 2/3 of the generalized records as the training set, and measure the *classification error* (CE) on 1/3 of the generalized records as the testing set. Alternatively, one can employ the 10-fold cross validation method to measure the classification error. For classification models, the experiments use the well-known C4.5 classifier [191]. To better visualize the cost and benefit of the approach, we measure additional errors: *Baseline Error* (BE) is the error measured on the raw data without generalization. $BE - CE$ represents the cost in terms of classification quality for achieving a given LKC-privacy requirement. A naive method to avoid

Table 6.9: Attributes for the *Adult* data set

Attribute	Type	Numerical Range	
		# of Leaves	# of Levels
Age (A)	numerical	17 - 90	
Capital-gain (Cg)	numerical	0 - 99999	
Capital-loss (Cl)	numerical	0 - 4356	
Education-num (En)	numerical	1 - 16	
Final-weight (Fw)	numerical	13492 - 1490400	
Hours-per-week (H)	numerical	1 - 99	
Education (E)	categorical	16	5
Marital-status (M)	categorical	7	4
Native-country (N)	categorical	40	5
Occupation (O)	categorical	14	3
Race (Ra)	categorical	5	3
Relationship (Re)	categorical	6	3
Sex (S)	categorical	2	2
Work-class (W)	categorical	8	5

record and attributes linkages is to simply remove all QID attributes. Thus, we also measure *upper bound error* (UE), which is the error on the raw data with all QID attributes removed. $UE - CE$ represents the benefit of the method over the naive approach.

To evaluate the impact on general analysis quality (Case 2 in Chapter 6.2.2), we use all records for generalization and measure the discernibility ratio (DR) on the final anonymous data.

$$DR = \frac{\sum_{qid} |T[qid]|^2}{|T|^2}. \qquad (6.8)$$

DR is the normalized discernibility cost, with $0 \leq DR \leq 1$. Lower DR means higher data quality.

6.7.1.1 The Blood Data Set

Figure 6.10 depicts the classification error CE with adversary's knowledge $L = 2, 4, 6$, anonymity threshold $20 \leq K \leq 100$, and confidence threshold $C = 20\%$ on the *Blood* data set. This setting allows us to measure the performance of the algorithm against record linkages for a fixed C. CE *generally* increases as K or L increases. However, the increase is not monotonic. For example, the error drops slightly when K increases from 20 to 40 for $L = 4$. This is due to the fact that generalization has removed some noise from the data, resulting in a better classification structure in a more general state. For the same reason, some test cases on $L = 2$ and $L = 4$ have $CE < BE$, implying that generalization not only achieves the given LKC-privacy requirement but sometimes may also improve the classification quality. $BE = 22.1\%$ and $UE =$

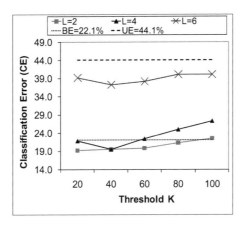

FIGURE 6.10: Classification error on the *Blood* data set ($C = 20\%$)

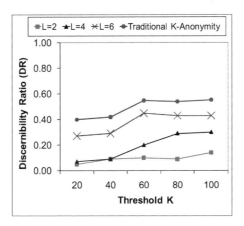

FIGURE 6.11: Discernibility ratio on the *Blood* data set ($C = 20\%$)

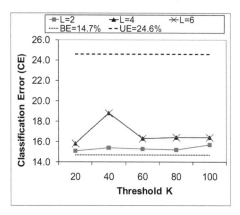

FIGURE 6.12: Classification error on the *Adult* data set $(C = 20\%)$

44.1%. For $L = 2$ and $L = 4$, $CE - BE$ spans from -2.9% to 5.2% and $UE - CE$ spans from 16.8% to 24.9%, suggesting that the cost for achieving LKC-privacy is small, but the benefit is large when L is not large. However, as L increases to 6, CE quickly increases to about 40%, the cost increases to about 17%, and the benefit decreases to 5%. For a greater value of L, the difference between LKC-privacy and k-anonymity is very small in terms of classification error since more generalized data does not necessarily worsen the classification error. This result confirms that the assumption of an adversary's prior knowledge has a significant impact on the classification quality. It also indirectly confirms the curse of high dimensionality [6].

Figure 6.11 depicts the discernibility ratio DR with adversary's knowledge $L = 2, 4, 6$, anonymity threshold $20 \le K \le 100$, and a fixed confidence threshold $C = 20\%$. DR *generally* increases as K increases, so it exhibits some trade-off between data privacy and data utility. As L increases, DR increases quickly because more generalization is required to ensure each equivalence group has at least K records. To illustrate the benefit of the proposed LKC-privacy model over the traditional k-anonymity model, we measure the discernibility ratio, denoted by DR_{TradK}, on traditional K-anonymous solutions produced by the TDR method in [96]. $DR_{TradK} - DR$, representing the benefit of the model, spans from 0.1 to 0.45. This indicates a significant improvement on data quality by making a reasonable assumption on limiting the adversary's knowledge within L known values. Note, the solutions produced by TDR do not prevent attribute linkages although they have higher discernibility ratio.

6.7.1.2   The *Adult* Data set

Figure 6.12 depicts the classification error CE with adversary's knowledge $L = 2, 4, 6$, anonymity threshold $20 \le K \le 100$, and confidence threshold $C = 20\%$ on the *Adult* data set. $BE = 14.7\%$ and $UE = 24.5\%$. For $L = 2$,

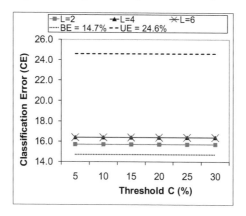

FIGURE 6.13: Classification error on the *Adult* data set ($K = 100$)

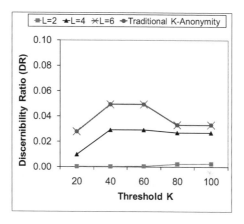

FIGURE 6.14: Discernibility ratio on the *Adult* data set ($C = 20\%$)

$CE - BE$ is less than 1% and $UE - CE$ spans from 8.9% to 9.5%. For $L = 4$ and $L = 6$, $CE - BE$ spans from 1.1% to 4.1%, and $UE - CE$ spans from 5.8% to 8.8%. These results suggest that the cost for achieving LKC-privacy is small, while the benefit of the LKC-privacy anonymization method over the naive method is large.

Figure 6.13 depicts the CE with adversary's knowledge $L = 2, 4, 6$, confidence threshold $5\% \leq C \leq 30\%$, and anonymity threshold $K = 100$. This setting allows us to measure the performance of the algorithm against attribute linkages for a fixed K. The result suggests that CE is insensitive to the change of confidence threshold C. CE slightly increases as the adversary's knowledge L increases.

Figure 6.14 depicts the discernibility ratio DR with adversary's knowledge $L = 2, 4, 6$, anonymity threshold $20 \leq K \leq 100$, and confidence threshold

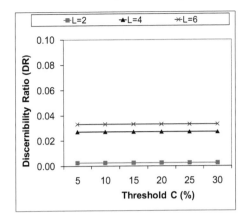

FIGURE 6.15: Discernibility ratio on the *Adult* data set ($K = 100$)

$C = 20\%$. DR sometimes has a drop when K increases. This is due to the fact that the presented greedy algorithm identifies only the sub-optimal solution. DR is insensitive to the increase of K and stays close to 0 for $L = 2$. As L increases to 4, DR increases significantly and finally equals traditional k-anonymity when $L = 6$ because the number of attributes in *Adult* is relatively smaller than in *Blood*. Yet, k-anonymity does not prevent attribute linkages, while LKC-privacy provides this additional privacy guarantee.

Figure 6.15 depicts the DR with adversary's knowledge $L = 2, 4, 6$, confidence threshold $5\% \leq C \leq 30\%$, and anonymity threshold $K = 100$. In general, DR increases as L increases due to a more restrictive privacy requirement. Similar to Figure 6.13, the DR is insensitive to the change of confidence threshold C. It implies that the primary driving forces for generalization are L and K, not C.

6.7.2 Efficiency and Scalability

High-Dimensional Top-Down Specialization (HDTDS) is an efficient and scalable algorithm for achieving LKC-privacy on high-dimensional relational data. Every previous test case can finish the entire anonymization process within 30 seconds. We further evaluate the scalability of HDTDS with respect to data volume by blowing up the size of the *Adult* data set. First, we combined the training and testing sets, giving 45,222 records. For each original record r in the combined set, we created $\alpha - 1$ "variations" of r, where $\alpha > 1$ is the blowup scale. Together with all original records, the enlarged data set has $\alpha \times 45,222$ records. In order to provide a more precise evaluation, the runtime reported below excludes the time for loading data records from disk and the time for writing the generalized data to disk.

Figure 6.16 depicts the runtime from 200,000 to 1 million records for $L = 4$,

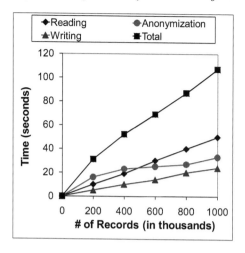

FIGURE 6.16: Scalability ($L = 4, K = 20, C = 100\%$)

$K = 20$, $C = 100\%$. The total runtime for anonymizing 1 million records is 107s, where 50s are spent on reading raw data, 33s are spent on anonymizing, and 24s are spent on writing the anonymous data. The algorithm is scalable due to the fact that the algorithm uses the count statistics to update the *Score*, and thus it only takes one scan of data per iteration to anonymize the data. As the number of records increases, the total runtime increases linearly.

6.8 Summary and Lesson Learned

This chapter uses the Red Cross Blood Transfusion Service (BTS) as a real-life example to motivate the anonymization problem for classification analysis. We have studied the challenge of anonymizing high-dimensional data and presented the *LKC*-privacy model [171] for addressing the challenge. Furthermore, we have studied four privacy-preserving data publishing methods to address the anonymization problem for classification analysis.

The High-Dimensional Top-Down Specialization (HDTDS) algorithm [171] is extended from TDS [95, 96]. HDTDS is flexible to adopt different information metrics in order to accommodate the two different information requirements specified by BTS, namely classification analysis and general counting. The experimental results on the two real-life data sets suggest the followings.

- HDTDS can effectively preserve both privacy and data utility in the anonymous data for a wide range of *LKC*-privacy requirements. There is a trade-off between data privacy and data utility with respect to K

and L, but the trend is less obvious on C.

- The proposed LKC-privacy model retains more information than the traditional k-anonymity model and provides the flexibility to adjust privacy requirements according to the assumption of adversary's background knowledge.

- HDTDS and its predecessor TDS [95, 96] is highly scalable for large data sets.

These characteristics make HDTDS a promising component for anonymizing high-dimensional relational data. The proposed solution could serve as a model for data sharing in the healthcare sector.

We have also studied three other solutions, namely, Workload-Aware Mondrian, Bottom-Up Generalization, and Genetic Algorithm. All these methods aim at achieving traditional k-anonymity and/or ℓ-diversity with an information metric that guides the anonymization to preserve the data utility for classification analysis. Yet, these methods cannot directly apply to the Red Cross BTS problem, which involves high-dimensional data, because applying k-anonymity on high-dimensional data would suffer from high information loss.

The presented solutions in this chapter are very different from privacy-preserving data mining (PPDM), which the goal is to share the *data mining result*. In contrast, the goal of privacy-preserving data publishing (PPDP) is to share the *data*. This is an essential requirement for the Red Cross since they require the flexibility to perform various data analysis tasks.

Health data are complex, often a combination of relational data, transaction data, and textual data. Some recent works [97, 101, 220, 256] that will be discussed in Chapters 13 and 16 are applicable to solve the privacy problem on transaction and textual data in the Red Cross case. Besides the technical issue, it is equally important to educate health institute management and medical practitioners about the latest privacy-preserving technology. When management encounters the problem of privacy-preserving data publishing as presented in this chapter, their initial response is often to set up a traditional role-based secure access model. In fact, alternative techniques, such as privacy-preserving data mining and data publishing [11, 92], are available to them provided that the data mining quality does not significantly degrade.

Chapter 7

Anonymization for Cluster Analysis

7.1 Introduction

Substantial research has been conducted on k-anonymization and its extensions as discussed in Chapter 2, but only few prior works have considered releasing data for some specific purpose of data mining, which is also known as the *workload-aware anonymization* [150]. Chapter 6 presents a practical data publishing framework for generating an anonymized version of data that preserves both individual privacy and information utility for classification analysis. This chapter aims at preserving the information utility for cluster analysis. Experiments on real-life data suggest that by focusing on preserving cluster structure in the anonymization process, the cluster quality is significantly better than the cluster quality of the anonymized data without such focus [94]. The major challenge of anonymizing data for cluster analysis is the lack of class labels that could be used to guide the anonymization process. The approach presented in this chapter converts the problem into the counterpart problem for classification analysis, wherein class labels encode the cluster structure in the data, and presents a framework to evaluate the cluster quality on the anonymized data.

This chapter is organized as follows. Chapter 7.2 presents the anonymization framework that addresses the anonymization problem for cluster analysis. Chapter 7.3 discusses an alternative solution in a different data model. Chapter 7.4 discusses some privacy topics that are orthogonal to the anonymization problem of cluster analysis studied in this chapter. Chapter 7.5 summarizes the chapter.

7.2 Anonymization Framework for Cluster Analysis

Fung et al. [94] define the data publishing scenario as follows. Consider a person-specific data table T with patients' information on *Zip code*, *Birthplace*, *Gender*, and *Disease*. The data holder wants to publish T to some recipient for cluster analysis. However, if a set of attributes, called a *Quasi-Identifier* or a QID, on {*Zip code, Birthplace, Gender*} is so specific that few people match it, publishing the table will lead to linking a unique or small number of individuals with the sensitive information on *Disease*. Even if the currently published table T does not contain sensitive information, individuals in T can be linked to the sensitive information in some external source by a join on the common attributes [201, 216]. These types of privacy attacks are known as record linkage and attribute linkage, which have been extensively discussed in Chapter 2. The problem studied in this chapter is to generate an anonymized version of T that satisfies both the anonymity requirement and the clustering requirement.

Anonymity Requirement: To thwart privacy threats caused by record and attribute linkages, instead of publishing the raw table $T(QID, Sensitive\_attribute)$, the data holder publishes an anonymized table T', where QID is a set of quasi-identifying attributes *masked* to some general concept. Note, we use the term "mask" to refer to the operation of "generalization" or "suppression." In general, the anonymity requirement can be any privacy models that can thwart record linkages (Chapter 2.1) and attribute linkages (Chapter 2.2).

Clustering Requirement: The data holder wants to publish a masked version of T to a recipient for the purpose of cluster analysis. The goal of cluster analysis is to group similar objects into the same cluster and group dissimilar objects into different clusters. We assume that the *Sensitive_attribute* is important for the task of cluster analysis; otherwise, it should be removed. The recipient may or may not be known at the time of data publication.

We study the *anonymization problem for cluster analysis*: For a given anonymity requirement and a raw data table T, a data holder wants to generate an anonymous version of T, denoted by T', that preserves as much of the information as possible for cluster analysis, and then publish T' to a data recipient. The data holder, for example, could be a hospital that wants to share its patients' information with a drug company for pharmaceutical research.

There are many possible masked versions of T' that satisfy the anonymity requirement. The challenge is how to identify the appropriate one for cluster analysis. An inappropriately masked version could put originally dissimilar objects into the same cluster, or put originally similar objects into different clusters because other masked objects become more similar to each other. Therefore, a quality-guided masking process is crucial. Unlike the anonymization problem for classification analysis studied in Chapter 6, the anonymization problem for cluster analysis does not have class labels to guide the masking. Another challenge is that it is not even clear what "information for cluster analysis" means, nor how to evaluate the cluster quality of generalized data. In this chapter, we define the anonymization problem for cluster analysis and present a solution framework to address the challenges in the problem. This chapter answers the following key questions:

1. *Can a masked table simultaneously satisfy both privacy and clustering*

requirements? The insight is that the two requirements are indeed dealing with two types of information: The anonymity requirement aims at masking identifying information that specifically describes individuals; the clustering requirement aims at extracting general structures that capture patterns. Sensitive information tends to be overly specific, thus of less utility, to clustering. Even if masking sensitive information eliminates some useful structures, alternative structures in the data emerge to help. If masking is carefully performed, identifying information can be masked while still preserving the patterns for cluster analysis. Experimental results [94] on real-life data sets support this insight.

2. *What information should be preserved for cluster analysis in the masked data?* This chapter presents a framework to convert the anonymization problem for cluster analysis to the counterpart problem for classification analysis. The idea is to extract the cluster structure from the raw data, encode it in the form of class labels, and preserve such class labels while masking the data. The framework also permits the data holder to evaluate the cluster quality of the anonymized data by comparing the cluster structures before and after the masking. This evaluation process is important for data publishing in practice, but very limited study has been conducted in the context of privacy preservation and cluster analysis.

3. *Can cluster-quality guided anonymization improve the cluster quality in anonymous data?* A naive solution to the studied privacy problem is to ignore the clustering requirement and employ some general purpose anonymization algorithms, e.g., Incognito [148], to mask data for cluster analysis. Extensive experiments [94] suggest that by focusing on preserving cluster structure in the masking process, the cluster quality outperforms the cluster quality on masked data without such focus. In general, the cluster quality on the masked data degrades as the anonymity threshold k increases.

4. *Can the specification of multiple quasi-identifiers improve the cluster quality in anonymous data?* The classic notion of k-anonymity assumes that a single united QID contains all quasi-identifying attributes, but research shows that it often leads to substantial loss of data quality as the QID size increases [6]. The insight is that, in practice, an adversary is unlikely to know all identifying attributes of a target victim (the person being identified), so the data is over-protected by a single QID. The studied method allows the specification of multiple QIDs, each of which has a smaller size, and therefore, avoids over-masking and improves the cluster quality. The idea of having multiple QIDs is similar to the notion of assuming an adversary's background is limited to length L in LKC-privacy studied in Chapter 6

5. *Can we efficiently mask different types of attributes in real-life databases?* Typical relational databases contain both categorical and

numerical attributes. Taxonomy trees like the ones shown in Figure 7.1 are pre-specified for *some* attributes. The taxonomy trees are part of the domain knowledge that allows the data holder to specify a generalization path so that a data value can be masked to a less specific description. However, taxonomy trees may or may not be available in real-life databases. The anonymization algorithm studied in this chapter can effectively mask all these variations of attributes by generalizing categorical attributes with pre-specified taxonomy trees, suppressing categorical attributes without taxonomy trees, and dynamically discretizing numerical attributes.

Given that the clustering task is known in advance, one may ask why not publish the analysis result instead of the data records? Unlike classification trees and association rules, publishing the cluster statistics (e.g., cluster centers, together with their size and radius) usually cannot fulfil the information needs for cluster analysis. Often, data recipients want to browse into the clustered records to gain more knowledge. For example, a medical researcher may browse into some clusters of patients and examine their common characteristics. Publishing data records not only fulfills the vital requirement for cluster analysis, but also increases the availability of information for the recipients.

We first formally define the anonymization problem for cluster analysis, followed by a solution framework.

7.2.1 Anonymization Problem for Cluster Analysis

A *labelled* table discussed in Chapter 6 has the form $T(D_1, \ldots, D_m, Class)$ and contains a set of records of the form $\langle v_1, \ldots, v_m, cls \rangle$, where v_j, for $1 \leq j \leq m$, is a domain value of attribute D_j, and cls is a class label of the *Class* attribute. Each D_j is either a categorical or a numerical attribute. An *unlabelled* table has the same form as a labelled table but without the *Class* attribute.

7.2.1.1 Privacy Model

In order to provide a concrete explanation on the problem and solution of the anonymity for cluster analysis, we specify the privacy model to be the k-anonymity with multiple QIDs in the rest of this chapter. The problem, as well as the solution, can be generalized to achieve other privacy models discussed in Chapter 2.

DEFINITION 7.1 Anonymity requirement   Consider p quasi-identifiers $QID_1, \ldots, QID_p$ on T', where $QID_i \subseteq \{D_1, \ldots, D_m\}$ for $1 \leq i \leq p$. $a(qid_i)$ denotes the number of data records in T' that share the value qid_i on QID_i. The *anonymity* of QID_i, denoted by $A(QID_i)$, is the minimum $a(qid_i)$ for any value qid_i on QID_i. A table T' *satisfies* the *anonymity requirement*

Table 7.1: The labelled table

Rec ID	Education	Gender	Age	...	Class	Count
1-3	9th	M	30		$0C_1$ $3C_2$	3
4-7	10th	M	32		$0C_1$ $4C_2$	4
8-12	11th	M	35		$2C_1$ $3C_2$	5
13-16	12th	F	37		$3C_1$ $1C_2$	4
17-22	Bachelors	F	42		$4C_1$ $2C_2$	6
23-26	Bachelors	F	44		$4C_1$ $0C_2$	4
27-30	Masters	M	44		$4C_1$ $0C_2$	4
31-33	Masters	F	44		$3C_1$ $0C_2$	3
34	Doctorate	F	44		$1C_1$ $0C_2$	1
				Total:	$21C_1$ $13C_2$	34

$\{\langle QID_1, h_1 \rangle, \ldots, \langle QID_p, h_p \rangle\}$ if $A(QID_i) \geq h_i$ for $1 \leq i \leq p$, where QID_i and the *anonymity thresholds* h_i are specified by the data holder. ∎

If some QID_j could be "covered" by another QID_i, then QID_j can be removed from the anonymity requirement. This observation is stated as follows:

Observation 7.2.1 (Cover) Suppose $QID_j \subseteq QID_i$ and $h_j \leq h_i$ where $j \neq i$. If $A(QID_i) \geq h_i$, then $A(QID_j) \geq h_j$. We say that QID_j is *covered by* QID_i; therefore, QID_j is redundant and can be removed. ∎

Example 7.1
Consider the data in Table 7.1 and taxonomy trees in Figure 7.1. Ignore the dashed line in Figure 7.1 for now. The table has 34 records, with each row representing one or more raw records that agree on (*Education, Gender, Age*). The *Class* column stores a count for each class label. The anonymity requirement

$$\{\langle QID_1 = \{Education, Gender\}, 4 \rangle, \langle QID_2 = \{Gender\}, 4 \rangle\}$$

states that every existing qid_1 and qid_2 in the table must be shared by at least 4 records. Therefore, $\langle 9th, M \rangle$, $\langle Masters, F \rangle$, $\langle Doctorate, F \rangle$ violate this requirement. To make the "female doctor" less unique, we can generalize *Masters* and *Doctorate* to *Grad School*. As a result, "she" becomes less identifiable by being one of the four females who have a graduate degree in the masked table T'. Note, QID_2 is covered by QID_1, so QID_2 can be removed. □

Definition 7.1 generalizes the classic notion of k-anonymity [202] by allowing multiple QIDs with different anonymity thresholds. The specification of multiple QIDs is based on an assumption that the data holder knows exactly what external information source is available for sensitive record linkage. The assumption is realistic in some data publishing scenarios. Suppose that the

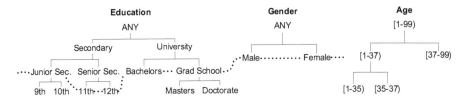

FIGURE 7.1: Taxonomy trees

data holder wants to release a table $T'(A, B, C, D, S)$, where A, B, C, D are identifying attributes and S is a sensitive attribute, and knows that the recipient has access to previously released tables $T1^*(A, B, X)$ and $T2^*(C, D, Y)$, where X and Y are attributes not in T. To prevent linking the records in T to X or Y, the data holder only has to specify the anonymity requirement on $QID_1 = \{A, B\}$ and $QID_2 = \{C, D\}$. In this case, enforcing anonymity on $QID = \{A, B, C, D\}$ will distort the data more than is necessary. The experimental results in [94] confirm that the specification of multiple $QIDs$ can reduce masking and, therefore, improve the data quality.

7.2.1.2   Masking Operations

To transform a table T to satisfy an anonymity requirement, one can apply the following three types of masking operations on every attribute D_j in $\cup QID_i$: If D_j is a categorical attribute with pre-specified taxonomy tree, then we *generalize* D_j. Specifying taxonomy trees, however, requires expert knowledge of the data. In case the data holder lacks such knowledge or, for any reason, does not specify a taxonomy tree for the categorical attribute D_j, then we *suppress* D_j. If D_j is a numerical attribute without a pre-discretized taxonomy tree, then we *discretize* D_j.[1] These three types of masking operations are formally described as follows:

1. *Generalize* D_j if it is a categorical attribute with a taxonomy tree specified by the data holder. Figure 7.1 shows the taxonomy trees for categorical attributes *Education* and *Gender*. A leaf node represents a domain value and a parent node represents a less specific value. A generalized D_j can be viewed as a "cut" through its taxonomy tree. A *cut* of a tree is a subset of values in the tree, denoted by Cut_j, that contains exactly one value on each root-to-leaf path. Figure 7.1 shows a cut on *Education* and *Gender*, indicated by the dash line. If a value v is generalized to its parent, all siblings of v must also be generalized to its parent. This property ensures that a value and its ancestor values will not coexist in

---

[1] A numerical attribute with a pre-discretized taxonomy tree is equivalent to a categorical attribute with a pre-specified taxonomy tree.

the generalized table T'. This subtree generalization scheme is discussed in Chapter 3.1.

2. *Suppress* D_j if it is a categorical attribute without a taxonomy tree. Suppressing a value on D_j means replacing *all* occurrences of the value with the special value $\perp_j$. All suppressed values on D_j are represented by the same value $\perp_j$. We use Sup_j to denote the set of values suppressed by $\perp_j$. This type of suppression is performed at the value level, in that Sup_j in general contains a subset of the values in the attribute D_j. A clustering algorithm treats $\perp_j$ as a new value. Suppression can be viewed as a special case of *sibling generalization* by considering $\perp_j$ to be the root of a taxonomy tree and $child(\perp_j)$ to contain all domain values of D_j. Refer to Chapter 3.1 for a detailed discussion on the sibling generalization scheme. In this suppression scheme, we could selectively suppress some values in $child(\perp_j)$ to $\perp_j$ while some other values in $child(\perp_j)$ remain intact.

3. *Discretize* D_j if it is a numerical attribute. Discretizing a value v on D_j means replacing *all* occurrences of v with an interval containing the value. The presented algorithm dynamically grows a taxonomy tree for intervals at runtime. Each node represents an interval. Each non-leaf node has two child nodes representing some optimal binary split of the parent interval. Figure 7.1 shows such a dynamically grown taxonomy tree for *Age*, where *[1-99)* is split into *[1-37)* and *[37-99)*. More details will be discussed in Chapter 7.2.3.1. A discretized D_j can be represented by the set of intervals, denoted by Int_j, corresponding to the leaf nodes in the dynamically grown taxonomy tree of D_j.

A masked table T can be represented by $\langle \cup Cut_j, \cup Sup_j, \cup Int_j \rangle$, where Cut_j, Sup_j, Int_j are defined above. If the masked table T' satisfies the anonymity requirement, then $\langle \cup Cut_j, \cup Sup_j, \cup Int_j \rangle$ is called a *solution set*. Generalization, suppression, and discretization have their own merits and flexibility; therefore, the unified framework presented in this chapter employs all of them.

7.2.1.3　Problem Statement

What kind of information should be preserved for cluster analysis? Unlike classification analysis, wherein the information utility of attributes can be measured by their power of identifying class labels [29, 95, 123, 150], no class labels are available for cluster analysis. One natural approach is to preserve the cluster structure in the raw data. Any loss of structure due to the anonymization is measured relative to such "raw cluster structure." We define the anonymization problem for cluster analysis as follows to reflect this natural choice of approach.

DEFINITION 7.2 Anonymization problem for cluster analysis
Given an unlabelled table T, an anonymity requirement $\{\langle QID_1, h_1 \rangle, \ldots,$
$\langle QID_p, h_p \rangle\}$, and an optional taxonomy tree for each categorical attribute
in $\cup QID_i$, the *anonymization problem for cluster analysis* is to mask T on
the attributes $\cup QID_i$ such that the masked table T' satisfies the anonymity
requirement and has a cluster structure as similar as possible to the cluster
structure in the raw table T. ∎

Intuitively, two cluster structures, before and after masking, are similar if
the following two conditions are *generally* satisfied:

1. two objects that belong to the same cluster before masking remain in
   the same cluster after masking, and

2. two objects that belong to different clusters before masking remain in
   different clusters after masking.

A formal measure for the similarity of two structures will be discussed in
Chapter 7.2.4.

7.2.2 Overview of Solution Framework

Now we explain an algorithmic framework to generate a masked table T',
represented by a solution set $\langle \cup Cut_j, \cup Sup_j, \cup Int_j \rangle$ that satisfies a given
anonymity requirement and preserves as much as possible the raw cluster
structure.

Figure 7.2 provides an overview of the proposed framework. First, we generate the cluster structure in the raw table T and label each record in T by
a class label. This labelled table, denoted by T_l, has a *Class* attribute that
contains a class label for each record. Essentially, preserving the raw cluster structure is to preserve the power of identifying such class labels during
masking. Masking that diminishes the difference among records belonging to
different clusters (classes) is penalized. As the requirement is the same as
the anonymization problem for classification analysis, one can apply existing
anonymization algorithms for classification analysis (Chapter 6) to achieve
the anonymity, although none of them in practice can perform all of the three
types of masking operations discussed in Chapter 7.2.1. We explain each step
in Figure 7.2 as follows.

1. **Convert T to a labelled table T_l.** Apply a clustering algorithm to T
   to identify the raw cluster structure, and label each record in T by its
   class (cluster) label. The resulting labelled table T_l has a *Class* attribute
   containing the labels.

2. **Mask the labelled table T_l.** Employ an anonymization algorithm for
   classification analysis to mask T_l. The masked T_l^* satisfies the given
   anonymity requirement.

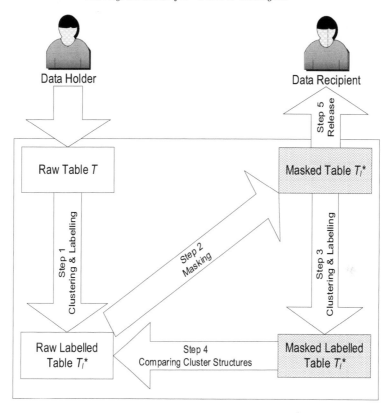

FIGURE 7.2: The framework

3. **Clustering on the masked T_l^*.** Remove the labels from the masked T_l^* and then apply a clustering algorithm to the masked T_l^*, where the number of clusters is the same as in Step 1. By default, the clustering algorithm in this step is the same as the clustering algorithm in Step 1, but can be replaced with the recipient's choice if this information is available. See more discussion below.

4. **Evaluate the masked T_l^*.** Compute the similarity between the cluster structure found in Step 3 and the raw cluster structure found in Step 1. The similarity measures the loss of cluster quality due to masking. If the evaluation is unsatisfactory, the data holder may repeat Steps 1-4 with different specification of taxonomy trees, choice of clustering algorithms, masking operations, number of clusters, and anonymity thresholds if possible.

5. **Release the masked T_l^*.** If the evaluation in Step 4 is satisfactory, the data holder can release the masked T_l^* together with some optional supplementary information: all the taxonomy trees (including those gener-

ated at runtime for numerical attributes), the solution set, the similarity score computed in Step 4, and the class labels generated in Step 1.

In some data publishing scenarios, the data holder does not even know who the prospective recipients are and, therefore, does not know how the recipients will cluster the published data. For example, when the Census Bureau releases data on the World Wide Web, how should the bureau set the parameters, such as the number of clusters, for the clustering algorithm in Step 1? In this case, we suggest releasing one version for each reasonable cluster number so that the recipient can make the choice based on her desired number of clusters, but this will cause a potential privacy breach because an adversary can further narrow down a victim's record by comparing different releases. A remedy is to employ the *multiple views publishing* and *incremental data publishing* methods, which guarantee the privacy even in the presence of multiple releases. Chapters 8 and 10 discuss these extended publishing scenarios in details.

7.2.3   Anonymization for Classification Analysis

To effectively mask both categorical and numerical attributes, we present an anonymization algorithm called *top-down refinement* (*TDR*) [96] that can perform all three types of masking operations in a unified fashion. TDR shares a similar HDTDS discussed in Chapter 6.3, but HDTDS cannot perform suppression and, therefore, cannot handle categorical attributes without taxonomy trees.

TDR takes a labelled table and an anonymity requirement as inputs. The main idea of TDR is to perform maskings that preserve the information for identifying the class labels. The next example illustrates this point.

Example 7.2
Suppose that the raw cluster structure produced by Step 1 has the class (cluster) labels given in the *Class* attribute in Table 7.1. In Example 7.1 we generalize *Masters* and *Doctorate* into *Grad School* to make linking through (*Education, Gender*) more difficult. No information is lost in this generalization because the class label C_1 does not depend on the distinction of *Masters* and *Doctorate*. However, further generalizing *Bachelors* and *Grad School* to *University* makes it harder to separate the two class labels involved.   □

Instead of masking a labelled table T_l^* starting from the most specific domain values, TDR masked T_l^* by a sequence of refinements starting from the most masked state in which each attribute is generalized to the topmost value, suppressed to the special value $\perp$, or represented by a single interval. TDR iteratively refines a masked value selected from the current set of cuts, suppressed values, and intervals, and stops if any further refinement would violate the anonymity requirement. A refinement is *valid* (with respect to T_l^*) if T_l^* satisfies the anonymity requirement after the refinement.

We formally describe different types of refinements in Chapter 7.2.3.1, define the information metric for a single refinement in Chapter 7.2.3.2, and provide the anonymization algorithm TDR in Chapter 7.2.3.3.

7.2.3.1 Refinement

- **Refinement for generalization.** Consider a categorical attribute D_j with a pre-specified taxonomy tree. Let $T_l^*[v]$ denote the set of generalized records that currently contains a generalized value v in the table T_l^*. Let $child(v)$ be the set of child values of v in a pre-specified taxonomy tree of D_j. A refinement, denoted by $v \rightarrow child(v)$, replaces the parent value v in all records in $T_l^*[v]$ with the child value $c \in child(v)$, where c is either a domain value d in the raw record or c is a generalized value of d. For example, a raw data record r contains a value *Masters* and the value has been generalized to *University* in a masked table T_l^*. A refinement *University* $\rightarrow$ {*Bachelors*, *Grad School*} replaces *University* in r by *Grad School* because *Grad School* is a generalized value of *Masters*.

- **Refinement for suppression.** For a categorical attribute D_j without a taxonomy tree, a refinement $\perp_j \rightarrow \{v, \perp_j\}$ refers to disclosing one value v from the set of suppressed values Sup_j. Let $T_l^*[\perp_j]$ denote the set of suppressed records that currently contain $\perp_j$ in the table T_l^*. Disclosing v means replacing $\perp_j$ with v in all records in $T_l^*[\perp_j]$ that originally contain v.

- **Refinement for discretization.** For a numerical attribute, refinement is similar to that for generalization except that no prior taxonomy tree is given and the taxonomy tree has to be grown dynamically in the process of refinement. Initially, the interval that covers the full range of the attribute forms the root. The refinement on an interval v, written $v \rightarrow child(v)$, refers to the optimal split of v into two child intervals $child(v)$, which maximizes the information gain. Suppose there are i distinct values in an interval. Then, there are $i - 1$ number of possible splits. The optimal split can be efficiently identified by computing the information gain of each possible split in one scan of data records containing such an interval of values. See Chapter 7.2.3.2 for the definition of information gain. Due to this extra step of identifying the optimal split of the parent interval, we treat numerical attributes separately from categorical attributes with taxonomy trees.

7.2.3.2 Information Metric

Each refinement increases information utility and decreases anonymity of the table because records are more distinguishable by refined values. The key is selecting the best refinement at each step with both impacts considered. At each iteration, TDR greedily selects the refinement on value v that has the

---

Algorithm 7.2.4 Top-Down Refinement (TDR)

1: initialize every value of D_j to the topmost value or suppress every value of D_j to $\perp_j$ or include every continuous value of D_j into the full range interval, where $D_j \in \cup QID_i$.

2: initialize Cut_j of D_j to include the topmost value, Sup_j of D_j to include all domain values of D_j, and Int_j of D_j to include the full range interval, where $D_j \in \cup QID_i$.

3: **while** some candidate v in $\langle \cup Cut_j, \cup Sup_j, \cup Int_j \rangle$ is valid **do**

4:    find the *Best* refinement from $\langle \cup Cut_j, \cup Sup_j, \cup Int_j \rangle$.

5:    perform *Best* on T_l^* and update $\langle \cup Cut_j, \cup Sup_j, \cup Int_j \rangle$.

6:    update $Score(x)$ and validity for $x \in \langle \cup Cut_j, \cup Sup_j, \cup Int_j \rangle$.

7: **end while**

8: **return** masked T_l^* and $\langle \cup Cut_j, \cup Sup_j, \cup Int_j \rangle$.

---

highest score, in terms of the information gain per unit of anonymity loss:

$$Score(v) = IGPL(v). \tag{7.1}$$

which has been discussed in Chapter 4.1. Refer to Equation 4.7 for a detailed discussion on $InfoGain(v)$, $AnonyLoss(v)$, and $Score(v)$ if D_j is a numerical attribute or a categorical attribute with taxonomy tree.

If D_j is a categorical attribute without taxonomy tree, the refinement $\perp_j \rightarrow \{v, \perp_j\}$ means refining $T'[\perp_j]$ into $T'[v]$ and $T^{*'}[\perp_j]$, where $T'[\perp_j]$ denotes the set of records containing $\perp_j$ before the refinement, $T'[v]$ and $T^{*'}[\perp_j]$ denote the set of records containing v and $\perp_j$ after the refinement, respectively. We employ the same $Score(v)$ function to measure the goodness of the refinement $\perp_j \rightarrow \{v, \perp_j\}$, except that $InfoGain(v)$ is now defined as:

$$InfoGain(v) = E(T'[\perp_j]) - \frac{|T'[v]|}{|T'[\perp_j]|}E(T'[v]) - \frac{|T^{*'}[\perp_j]|}{|T'[\perp_j]|}E(T^{*'}[\perp_j]). \tag{7.2}$$

7.2.3.3   The Anonymization Algorithm (TDR)

Algorithm 7.2.4 summarizes the conceptual algorithm. All attributes not in $\cup QID_i$ are removed from T_l^*, and duplicates are collapsed into a single row with the *Class* column storing the count for each class label. Initially, Cut_j contains only the topmost value for a categorical attribute D_j with a taxonomy tree, Sup_j contains all domain values of a categorical attribute D_j without a taxonomy tree, and Int_j contains the full range interval for a numerical attribute D_j. The valid refinements in $\langle \cup Cut_j, \cup Sup_j, \cup Int_j \rangle$ form the set of *candidates*. At each iteration, we find the candidate of the highest *Score*, denoted by *Best* (Line 4), apply *Best* to T' and update $\langle \cup Cut_j, \cup Sup_j, \cup Int_j \rangle$ (Line 5), and update *Score* and the validity of the candidates in $\langle \cup Cut_j, \cup Sup_j, \cup Int_j \rangle$ (Line 6). The algorithm terminates when there is no more candidate in $\langle \cup Cut_j, \cup Sup_j, \cup Int_j \rangle$, in which case it returns the masked table together with the solution set $\langle \cup Cut_j, \cup Sup_j, \cup Int_j \rangle$.

The following example illustrates how to achieve a given anonymity requirement by performing a sequence of refinements, starting from the most masked table.

Example 7.3

Consider the labelled table in Table 7.1, where *Education* and *Gender* have pre-specified taxonomy trees and the anonymity requirement:

$$\{\langle QID_1 = \{Education, Gender\}, 4\rangle, \langle QID_2 = \{Gender, Age\}, 11\rangle\}.$$

Initially, all data records are masked to

$$\langle ANY\_Edu, ANY\_Gender, [1\text{-}99)\rangle,$$

and

$$\cup Cut_i = \{ANY\_Edu, ANY\_Gender, [1\text{-}99)\}.$$

To find the next refinement, we compute the *Score* for each of *ANY_Edu*, *ANY_Gender*, and *[1-99)*. Table 7.2 shows the masked data after performing the following refinements in order:

$[1\text{-}99) \rightarrow \{[1\text{-}37), [37\text{-}99)\}$
$ANY\_Edu \rightarrow \{Secondary, University\}$
$Secondary \rightarrow \{JuniorSec., Senior\ Sec.\}$
$Senior\ Sec. \rightarrow \{11th, 12th\}$
$University \rightarrow \{Bachelors, Grad\ School\}.$

After performing the refinements, the $a(qid_i)$ counts in the masked table are:

$a(\langle Junior\ Sec., ANY\_Gender\rangle) = 7$
$a(\langle 11th, ANY\_Gender\rangle) = 5$
$a(\langle 12th, ANY\_Gender\rangle) = 4$
$a(\langle Bachelors, ANY\_Gender\rangle) = 10$
$a(\langle Grad\ School, ANY\_Gender\rangle) = 8$
$a(\langle ANY\_Gender, [1\text{-}37)\rangle) = 7 + 5 = 12$
$a(\langle ANY\_Gender, [37\text{-}99)\rangle) = 4 + 10 + 8 = 22$.

The solution set $\cup Cut_i$ is:

$\{JuniorSec., 11th, 12th, Bachelors, GradSchool, ANY\_Gender, [1\text{-}37),$
$[37\text{-}99)\}.$

$\square$

Table 7.2: The masked table, satisfying $\{\langle QID_1, 4\rangle, \langle QID_2, 11\rangle\}$

Rec ID	Education	Gender	Age	...	Count
1-7	Junior Sec.	ANY	[1-37)	...	7
8-12	11th	ANY	[1-37)	...	5
13-16	12th	ANY	[37-99)	...	4
17-26	Bachelors	ANY	[37-99)	...	10
27-34	Grad School	ANY	[37-99)	...	8
			Total:	...	34

7.2.4 Evaluation

This step compares the raw cluster structure found in Step 1 in Chapter 7.2.2, denoted by $\mathcal{C}$, with the cluster structure found in the masked data in Step 3, denoted by $\mathcal{C}_g$. Both $\mathcal{C}$ and $\mathcal{C}_g$ are extracted from the same set of records, so we can evaluate their similarity by comparing their record groupings. We present two evaluation methods: *F-measure* [231] and *match point*.

7.2.4.1 F-measure

F-measure [231] is a well-known evaluation method for cluster analysis with known cluster labels. The idea is to treat each cluster in $\mathcal{C}$ as the relevant set of records for a query, and treat each cluster in $\mathcal{C}_g$ as the result of a query. The clusters in $\mathcal{C}$ are called "natural clusters," and those in $\mathcal{C}_g$ are called "query clusters."

For a natural cluster C_i in $\mathcal{C}$ and a query cluster K_j in $\mathcal{C}_g$, let $|C_i|$ and $|K_j|$ denote the number of records in C_i and K_j respectively, let n_{ij} denote the number of records contained in both C_i and K_j, let $|T|$ denote the total number of records in T'. The *recall, precision*, and *F-measure* for C_i and K_j are calculated as follows:

$$Recall(C_i, K_j) = \frac{n_{ij}}{|C_i|} \tag{7.3}$$

read as the fraction of relevant records retrieved by the query.

$$Precision(C_i, K_j) = \frac{n_{ij}}{|K_j|} \tag{7.4}$$

read as the fraction of relevant records among the records retrieved by the query.

$$F(C_i, K_j) = \frac{2 \times Recall(C_i, K_j) \times Precision(C_i, K_j)}{Recall(C_i, K_j) + Precision(C_i, K_j)}. \tag{7.5}$$

$F(C_i, K_j)$ measures the quality of query cluster K_j in describing the natural cluster C_i, by the harmonic mean of *Recall* and *Precision*.

Table 7.3: The masked labelled table for evaluation

Rec ID	Education	Gender	Age	...	Class	Count
1-7	Junior Sec.	ANY	[1-37)	...	K_1	7
8-12	11th	ANY	[1-37)	...	K_1	5
13-16	12th	ANY	[37-99)	...	K_2	4
17-26	Bachelors	ANY	[37-99)	...	K_2	10
27-34	Grad School	ANY	[37-99)	...	K_2	8
					Total:	34

Table 7.4: The similarity of two cluster structures

Clusters in Table 7.1	Clusters in Table 7.3	
	K_1	K_2
C_1	2	19
C_2	10	3

The success of preserving a natural cluster C_i is measured by the "best" query cluster K_j for C_i, i.e., K_j maximizes $F(C_i, K_j)$. We measure the quality of $\mathcal{C}_g$ using the weighted sum of such maximum F-measures for all natural clusters. This measure is called the *overall F-measure* of $\mathcal{C}_g$, denoted by $F(\mathcal{C}_g)$:

$$F(\mathcal{C}_g) = \sum_{C_i \in \mathcal{C}} \frac{|C_i|}{|T|} max_{K_j \in \mathcal{C}_g}\{F(C_i, K_j)\}. \qquad (7.6)$$

Note that $F(\mathcal{C}_g)$ is in the range [0,1]. A larger value indicates a higher similarity between the two cluster structures generated from the raw data and the masked data, i.e., better preserved cluster quality.

Example 7.4

Table 7.3 shows a cluster structure with $k = 2$ produced from the masked Table 7.2. The first 12 records are grouped into K_1, and the rest are grouped into K_2. By comparing with the raw cluster structure in Table 7.1, we can see that, among the 21 records in C_1, 19 remain in the same cluster K_2 and only 2 are sent to a different cluster. C_2 has a similar pattern. Table 7.4 shows the comparison between the clusters of the two structures. The calculations of $Recall(C_i, K_j)$, $Precision(C_i, K_j)$, and $F(C_i, K_j)$ are illustrated below.

$Recall(C_1, K_1) = 2/21 = 0.10$
$Precision(C_1, K_1) = 2/12 = 0.17$
$F(C_1, K_1) = \frac{2 \times Recall(C_1,K_1) \times Precision(C_1,K_1)}{Recall(C_1,K_1) \times Precision(C_1,K_1)} = \frac{2 \times 0.10 \times 0.17}{0.10 \times 0.17} = 0.12$

$Recall(C_1, K_2) = 19/21 = 0.90$

Table 7.5: The F-measure computed from Table 7.4

$F(C_i, K_j)$	K_1	K_2
C_1	0.12	0.88
C_2	0.8	0.17

$Precision(C_1, K_2) = 19/22 = 0.86$

$F(C_1, K_2) = \frac{2 \times Recall(C_1,K_2) \times Precision(C_1,K_2)}{Recall(C_1,K_2) \times Precision(C_1,K_2)} = \frac{2 \times 0.90 \times 0.86}{0.90 \times 0.86} = 0.88$

$Recall(C_2, K_1) = 10/13 = 0.77$

$Precision(C_2, K_1) = 10/12 = 0.83$

$F(C_2, K_1) = \frac{2 \times Recall(C_1,K_1) \times Precision(C_2,K_1)}{Recall(C_2,K_1) \times Precision(C_2,K_1)} = \frac{2 \times 0.77 \times 0.83}{0.77 \times 0.83} = 0.8$

$Recall(C_2, K_2) = 3/13 = 0.23$

$Precision(C_2, K_2) = 3/22 = 0.14$

$F(C_2, K_2) = \frac{2 \times Recall(C_2,K_2) \times Precision(C_2,K_2)}{Recall(C_2,K_2) \times Precision(C_2,K_2)} = \frac{2 \times 0.23 \times 0.14}{0.23 \times 0.14} = 0.17$

Table 7.5 shows the F-measure. The overall F-measure is:

$$F(C_g) = \frac{|C_1|}{|T|} \times F(C_1, K_2) + \frac{|C_2|}{|T|} \times F(C_2, K_1)$$
$$= \frac{21}{34} \times 0.88 + \frac{13}{34} \times 0.8 = 0.85.$$

$\square$

F-measure is an efficient evaluation method, but it considers *only* the best query cluster K_j for each natural cluster C_i; therefore, it does not capture the quality of other query clusters and may not provide a full picture of the similarity between two cluster structures. An alternative evaluation method, called *match point*, can directly measure the preserved cluster structure.

7.2.4.2   Match Point

Intuitively, two cluster structures C and C_g are similar if two objects that belong to the same cluster in C remain in the same cluster in C_g, and if two objects that belong to different clusters in C remain in different clusters in C_g. To reflect the intuition, the method builds two square matrices $Matrix(C)$ and $Matrix(C_g)$ to represent the grouping of records in cluster structures C and C_g, respectively. The square matrices are $|T|$-by-$|T|$, where $|T|$ is the total number of records in table T. The $(i, j)^{th}$ element in $Matrix(C)$ (or $Matrix(C_g)$) has value 1 if the ith record and the jth record in the raw table T (or the masked table T') are in the same cluster; 0 otherwise. Then, *match point* is the percentage of matched values between $Matrix(C)$ and $Matrix(C_g)$:

$$Match\ Point(Matrix(C), Matrix(C_g)) = \frac{\sum_{1 \leq i,j \leq |T|} M_{ij}}{|T|^2}, \qquad (7.7)$$

Table 7.6: *Matrix*($\mathcal{C}$) of clusters $\{1, 2, 3\}$ and $\{4, 5\}$

	1	2	3	4	5
1	1	1	1	0	0
2	1	1	1	0	0
3	1	1	1	0	0
4	0	0	0	1	1
5	0	0	0	1	1

Table 7.7: *Matrix*($\mathcal{C}_g$) of clusters $\{1, 2\}$ and $\{3, 4, 5\}$

	1	2	3	4	5
1	1	1	0	0	0
2	1	1	0	0	0
3	0	0	1	1	1
4	0	0	1	1	1
5	0	0	1	1	1

Table 7.8: *Match Point* table for *Matrix*($\mathcal{C}$) and *Matrix*($\mathcal{C}_g$)

	1	2	3	4	5
1	1	1	0	1	1
2	1	1	0	1	1
3	0	0	1	0	0
4	1	1	0	1	1
5	1	1	0	1	1

where M_{ij} is 1 if the $(i, j)^{th}$ element in *Matrix*($\mathcal{C}$) and *Matrix*($\mathcal{C}_g$) have the same value; 0 otherwise. Note that match point is in the range of [0,1]. A larger value indicates a higher similarity between the two cluster structures generated from the raw data and the masked data, i.e., better preserved cluster quality.

Example 7.5

Let $\mathcal{C} = \{\{1, 2, 3\}, \{4, 5\}\}$ be the clusters before anonymization. Let $\mathcal{C}_g = \{\{1, 2\}, \{3, 4, 5\}\}$ be the clusters after anonymization. $\mathcal{C}$ and $\mathcal{C}_g$ are plotted in Table 7.6 and Table 7.7, respectively. Table 7.8 is the *Match Point* table, which has a value 1 in a cell if the corresponding cells in Table 7.6 and Table 7.7 have the same value. *Match Point* $= 17/5^2 = 0.68$. ☐

7.2.5 Discussion

We discuss some open issues and possible improvements in the studied privacy framework for cluster analysis.

7.2.5.1   Recipient Oriented vs. Structure Oriented

Refer to Figure 7.2. One open issue is the choice of clustering algorithms employed by the data holder in Step 1. Each clustering algorithm has its own search bias or preference. Experimental results in [94] suggest that if the same clustering algorithm is employed in Step 1 and Step 3, then the cluster structure from the masked data is very similar to the raw cluster structure; otherwise, the cluster structure in the masked data could not even be extracted. There are two methods for choosing clustering algorithms.

Recipient oriented. This approach minimizes the difference generated if the recipient had applied her clustering algorithm to both the raw data and the masked data. It requires the clustering algorithm in Step 1 to be the same, or to use the same bias, as the recipient's algorithm. One can implement this approach in a similar way as for determining the cluster number: either the recipient provides her clustering algorithm information, or the data holder releases one version of masked data for each popular clustering algorithm, leaving the choice to the recipient. Refer to Chapter 10 for handling potential privacy breaches caused by multiple releases.

Structure oriented. This approach focuses on preserving the "true" cluster structure in the data instead of matching the recipient's choice of algorithms. Indeed, if the recipient chooses a bad clustering algorithm, matching her choice may minimize the difference but is not helpful for cluster analysis. This approach aims at preserving the "truthful" cluster structure by employing a *robust* clustering algorithm in Step 1 and Step 3. Dave and Krishnapuram [57] specify a list of requirements in order for a clustering algorithm to be robust. The principle is that "the performance of a robust clustering algorithm should not be affected significantly by small deviations from the assumed model and it should not deteriorate drastically due to noise and outliers." If the recipient employs a less robust clustering algorithm, it may not find the "true" cluster structure. This approach is suitable for the case in which the recipient's preference is unknown at the time of data release, and the data holder wants to publish only one or a small number of versions. Optionally, the data holder may release the class labels in Step 1 as a sample clustering solution.

7.2.5.2   Summary of Empirical Study

Experiments on real-life data [94] have verified the claim that the proposed approach of converting the anonymity problem for cluster analysis to the counterpart problem for classification analysis is effective. This is demonstrated by the preservation of most of the cluster structure in the raw data after masking identifying information for a broad range of anonymity requirements. The experimental results also suggest that the cluster quality-guided anonymization can preserve better cluster structure than the general purpose anonymization.

The experiments demonstrate the cluster quality with respect to the variation of anonymity thresholds, QID size, and number of clusters. In general, the cluster quality degrades as the anonymity threshold increases. This trend is more obvious if the data set size is small or if anonymity threshold is large. The cluster quality degrades as the QID size increases. The cluster quality exhibits no obvious trend with respect to the number of clusters, as the natural number of clusters is data dependent.

The experiments confirm that the specification of the multi-QID anonymity requirement helps avoid unnecessary masking and, therefore, preserves more of the cluster structure. However, if the data recipient and the data holder employ different clustering algorithms, then there is no guarantee that the encoded raw cluster structure can be extracted. Thus, in practice, it is important for the data holder to validate the cluster quality, using the evaluation methods proposed in the framework, before releasing the data. Finally, experiments suggest that the proposed anonymization approach is highly efficient and scalable for single QID, but less efficient for multi-QID.

7.2.5.3 Extensions

Chapter 7.2 presents a flexible framework that makes use of existing solutions as "plug-in" components. These include the cluster analysis in Steps 1 and 3, the anonymization in Step 2, and the evaluation in Step 4. For example, instead of using the proposed TDR algorithm, the data holder has the option to perform the anonymization by employing any one of the anonymization methods discussed in Chapter 6 with some modification.

The solution presented above focuses on preventing the privacy threats caused by record linkages, but the framework is extendable to thwart attribute linkages by adopting different anonymization algorithms and achieving other privacy models, such as ℓ-diversity and confidence bounding, discussed in Chapter 2. The extension requires modification of the *Score* or cost functions in these algorithms to bias on refinements or maskings that can distinguish class labels. The framework can also adopt other evaluation methods, such as entropy [210], or any ad-hoc methods defined by the data holder.

The study in TDR focuses mainly on single-dimensional global recoding. Alternative masking operations, such as local recoding and multidimensional recoding, for achieving k-anonymity and its extended privacy notions are also applicable to the problem. Nonetheless, it is important to note that local recoding and multidimensional recoding may suffer from the data exploration problem discussed in Chapter 3.1.

One useful extension of privacy-preserving data publishing for cluster analysis is to building a visualization tool to allow the data holder to adjust the parameters, such as the number of clusters and anonymity thresholds, and visualize their influence on the clusters interactively.

7.3   Dimensionality Reduction-Based Transformation

Oliveira and Zaiane [182] introduce an alternative data anonymization approach, called *Dimensionality Reduction-Based Transformation (DRBT)*, to address the problem of *privacy-preserving clustering (PPC)* defined as follows.

DEFINITION 7.3 Problem of privacy-preserving clustering (PPC)
Let T be a relational database and C be a set of clusters generated from T. The goal is to transform T into T' so that the following restrictions hold:

- The transformed T' conceals the values of the sensitive attributes.

- The similarity between records in T' has to be approximately the same as that one in T. The clusters in T and T' should be as close as possible.

The general principle of the PPC problem [182] is similar to the anonymization problem for cluster analysis discussed in Definition 7.2. The major differences are on the privacy model. First, the problem of PPC aim at anonymizing the sensitive attributes while most of the k-anonymization related methods aim at anonymizing the quasi-identifying attributes. Second, PPC assumes that all the attributes to be transformed are numerical. The general idea of DRBT is to transform m-dimensional objects into r-dimensional objects, where r is much smaller than m. The privacy is guaranteed by ensuring that the transformation is non-invertible.

7.3.1   Dimensionality Reduction

DRBT assumes that the data records are represented as points (vectors) in a multidimensional space. Each dimension represents a distinct attribute of the individual. The database is represented as an $n \times m$ matrix with n records and m columns. The goal of the methods for dimensionality reduction is to map n-dimensional records into r-dimensional records, where $r \ll m$ [145]. Dimensionality reduction methods map each object to a point a r-dimensional space with the goal of minimizing the *stress* function, which measures the average relative error that the distances in $r - n$ space suffer from:

$$stress = \frac{\sum_{i,j}(\hat{d}_{ij} - d_{ij})^2}{\sum_{i,j} d_{ij}^2} \qquad (7.8)$$

where d_{ij} is the dissimilarity measure between records i and j in a r-dimensional space, and $\hat{d}_{ij}$ is the dissimilarity measure between records i and j in a m-dimensional space [182].

Random projection is a linear transformation represented by a $m \times r$ matrix R. The transformation is achieved by first setting each entry of the matrix to a value drawn from an independent and identically distributed $N(0, 1)$ distribution with 0 mean and 1 unit of variance, and then normalizing the columns to unit length. Given a m-dimensional data set represented as an $n \times m$ matrix T, the mapping $T \times R$ results in reduced-dimension data set:

$$T'_{n \times r} = T_{n \times m} R_{m \times r}. \tag{7.9}$$

In the reduced space, the distance between two m-dimensional records X_i and X_j can be approximated by the scaled down Euclidean distance of these records as down in Equation

$$\sqrt{\frac{m}{r}} \|X_i - X_j\|. \tag{7.10}$$

where the scaling term $\sqrt{\frac{m}{r}}$ takes the decrease in the dimensionality of the data into consideration [182]. The key point in this method is to choose a random matrix R. DRBT employs the following simple distribution [2] for each element e_{ij} in R:

$$e_{ij} = \sqrt{3} \times \begin{cases} +1 & \text{with probability } 1/6 \\ 0 & \text{with probability } 2/3 \\ -1 & \text{with probability } 1/6 \end{cases} \tag{7.11}$$

7.3.2 The DRBT Method

The DRBT method addresses the problem privacy-preserving clustering in three steps [182].

1. *Attributes suppression*: Suppress the attributes that are irrelevant to the clustering task.

2. *Dimensions reduction*: Transform the original data set T into the anonymized data set T' using random projection. We apply Equation 7.9 to reduce the dimension of T with m dimensions to T' with r dimensions. The random matrix R is computed by first setting each entry of the matrix to a value drawn from an independent and identically distributed $N(0, 1)$ distribution and then normalizing the columns to unit length. Alternatively, each element e_{ij} in matrix R can be computed by using Equation 7.11.

3. *Cluster evaluation*: Evaluate the cluster quality of the anonymized data set T' with respect to the original data set T using the *stress* function in 7.8.

7.4   Related Topics

We discuss some privacy works that are orthogonal to the anonymization problem of cluster analysis studied in this chapter. There is a family of anonymization methods [8, 9, 10, 13] that achieves privacy *by* clustering similar data records together. Their objective is very different from the studied problem in this chapter, which is publishing data *for* cluster analysis. Aggarwal and Yu [8] propose an anonymization approach, called *condensation*, to first condense the records into multiple non-overlapping groups in which each group has a size of at least h records. Then, for each group, the method extracts some statistical information, such as sum and covariance, that suffices to preserve the mean and correlation across different attributes. Finally, based on the statistical information, the method generates synthetic data records for each group. Refer to Chapter 5.1.3.1 for more details on condensation.

In a similar spirit, *r-gather clustering* [13] partitions records into several clusters such that each cluster contains at least r data points. Then the cluster centers, together with their size, radius, and a set of associated sensitive values, are released. Compared to the masking approach, one limitation of the clustering approach is that the published records are "synthetic" in that they may not correspond to the real world entities represented by the raw data. As a result, the analysis result is difficult to justify if, for example, a police officer wants to determine the common characteristics of some criminals from the data records. Refer to Chapter 5.1.3.2 for more details on r-gather clustering.

Many secure protocols have been proposed for distributed computation among multiple parties. For example, Vaidya and Clifton [229] and Inan et al. [121] present secure protocols to generate a clustering solution from vertically and horizontally partitioned data owned by multiple parties. In their model, accessing data held by other parties is prohibited, and only the final cluster solution is shared among participating parties. We consider a completely different problem, of which the goal is to share data that is immunized against privacy attacks.

7.5   Summary

We have studied the problem of releasing person-specific data for cluster analysis while protecting privacy. The top-down-specialization solution discussed in Chapter 7.2 is to mask unnecessarily specific information into a less specific but semantically consistent version, so that person-specific identifying information is masked but essential cluster structure remains [94]. The major challenge is the lack of class labels that could be used to guide the masking process. This chapter illustrates a general framework for converting this problem into the counterpart problem for classification analysis so that the masking process can be properly guided. The key idea is to encode the original cluster structure into the class label of data records and subsequently preserve the class labels for the corresponding classification problem. The experimental results verified the effectiveness of this approach.

We also studied several practical issues arising from applying this approach in a real-life data publishing scenario. These include how the choices of clustering algorithms, number of clusters, anonymity threshold, and size and type of quasi-identifiers can affect the effectiveness of this approach, and how to evaluate the effectiveness in terms of cluster quality. These studies lead to the recommendation of two strategies for choosing the clustering algorithm in the masking process, each having a different focus. The materials provide a useful framework of secure data sharing for the purpose of cluster analysis.

In Chapter 7.3, we have studied an efficient anonymization algorithm called Dimensionality Reduction-Based Transformation (DRBT) [182]. The general idea is to consider the raw data table as a m dimensional matrix and reduce it to a r dimensional matrix by using random projection. The data model considered in DRBT has several limitations. First, the distortion is applied on the sensitive attribute, which could be important for the task of cluster analysis. If the sensitive attributes are not important for cluster analysis, they should be removed first. Second, the DRBT method is applicable only on numerical attributes. Yet, real-life databases often contain both categorical and numerical attributes.

Part III

Extended Data Publishing Scenarios

Chapter 8

Multiple Views Publishing

8.1 Introduction

So far, we have considered the simplest case where the data is published to a single recipient. In practice, the data is often published to multiple recipients and different data recipients may be interested in different attributes. Suppose there is a person-specific data table $T(Job, Sex, Age, Race, Disease, Salary)$. A data recipient (for example, a pharmaceutical company) is interested in classification modeling the target attribute $Disease$ with attributes $\{Job, Sex, Age\}$. Another data recipient (such as a social service department) is interested in clustering analysis on $\{Job, Age, Race\}$.

One approach is to publish a single view on $\{Job, Sex, Age, Race\}$ for both purposes. A drawback is that information is unnecessarily released in that neither of the two purposes needs all four attributes; it is more vulnerable to attacks. Moreover, if the information needed in the two cases is different, the data anonymized in a single view may not be good for either of the two cases. A better approach is to anonymize and publish a tailored view for each data mining purpose; each view is anonymized to best address the specific need of that purpose.

Suppose a data holder has released multiple views of the same underlying raw data data. Even if the data holder releases one view to each data recipient based on their information needs, it is difficult to prevent them from colluding with each other behind the scene. Thus, some recipient may have access to multiple or even all views. In particular, an adversary can combine attributes from the two views to form a sharper QID that contains attributes from both views. The following example illustrates the *join attack* in multiple views.

Example 8.1
Consider the data in Table 8.1 and Table 8.2. Suppose that the data holder releases one projection view T_1 to one data recipient and releases another projection view T_2 to another data recipient. Both views are from the same underlying patient table. Further suppose that the data holder does not want $\{Age, Birthplace\}$ to be linked to $Disease$. When T_1 and T_2 are examined separately, the $Age = 40$ group and the $Birthplace = France$ group have

Table 8.1: Multiple views publishing: T_1

Age	Job	Class
30	Lawyer	c1
30	Lawyer	c1
40	Carpenter	c2
40	Electrician	c3
50	Engineer	c4
50	Clerk	c4

Table 8.2: Multiple views publishing: T_2

Job	Birthplace	Disease
Lawyer	US	Cancer
Lawyer	US	Cancer
Carpenter	France	HIV
Electrician	UK	Cancer
Engineer	France	HIV
Clerk	US	HIV

Table 8.3: Multiple views publishing: the join of T_1 and T_2

Age	Job	Birthplace	Disease	Class
30	Lawyer	US	Cancer	c1
30	Lawyer	US	Cancer	c1
40	Carpenter	France	HIV	c2
40	Electrician	UK	Cancer	c3
50	Engineer	France	HIV	c4
50	Clerk	US	HIV	c4
30	Lawyer	US	Cancer	c1
30	Lawyer	US	Cancer	c1

size 2. However, by joining T_1 and T_2 using $T_1.Job = T_2.Job$ (see Table 8.3), an adversary can uniquely identify the record owner in the $\{40, France\}$ group, thus linking $\{Age, Birthplace\}$ to $Disease$ without difficulty. Moreover, the join reveals the inference $\{30, US\} \rightarrow Cancer$ with 100% confidence for the record owners in the $\{30, US\}$ group. Such inference cannot be made when T_1 and T_2 are examined separately [236]. □

In this chapter, we study several works that measure information disclosure arising from linking two or more views. Chapter 8.2 studies Yao et al. [262]'s method for detecting k-anonymity violation on a set of views, each view obtained from a projection and selection query. Kifer and Gehrke [139] propose to increase the utility of published data by releasing additional *marginals* that are essentially duplicate preserving projection views. Chapter 8.3 studies the privacy threats caused by the marginals and a detection method to check the violations of some given k-anonymity and ℓ-diversity requirements.

8.2 Checking Violations of k-Anonymity on Multiple Views

We first illustrate violations of k-anonymity in the data publishing scenario where data in a raw data table T are being released in the form of a view set. A *view set* is a pair (V, v), where V is a list of selection-projection queries $(q_1, \ldots, q_n)$ on T, and v is a list of relations $(r_1, \ldots, r_n)$ without duplicate records [262]. Then, we also consider the privacy threats caused by functional dependency as prior knowledge, followed by a discussion on the violations detection methods. For a data table T, $\Pi(T)$ and $\sigma(T)$ denote the projection and selection over T.

8.2.1 Violations by Multiple Selection-Project Views

Yao et al. [262] assume that privacy violation takes the form of linkages, that is, pairs of values appearing in the same data record. For example, neither *Calvin* nor *HIV* in Table 8.4 alone is sensitive, but the linkage of the two values is. Instead of publishing the raw data table that contains sensitive linkages, Yao et al. consider publishing the materialized views. For example, given raw data table T in Table 8.4, sensitive linkages can be defined by $\Pi_{Name,Disease}(T)$, while the published data are two views, $V_1 = \Pi_{Name,Job}(T)$ and $V_2 = \Pi_{Job,Disease}(T)$. Given V_1 and V_2 as shown in Table 8.5 and Table 8.6, an adversary can easily deduce that *Calvin* has *HIV* because *Calvin* is a lawyer in V_1 and *the* lawyer in V_2 has *HIV*, assuming that the adversary has the knowledge that V_1 and V_2 are projects of the same underlying raw data table.

Checking k-anonymity on multiple views could be a complicated task if the views are generated based on some selection conditions. The following example illustrates this point.

Example 8.2
Tables 8.7-8.9 show three views that are generated based on different projection and selection conditions of Table 8.4. By performing an intersection between V_3 and V_4, an adversary knows that *Bob* is the only person in the raw table T who has an age between 45 and 55. By further observing V_5, the adversary can induce that *Bob* has *Diabetes* because the selection condition of V_5 satisfies the selection condition of the intersection of V_3 and V_4. □

Table 8.4:   Raw data table T

Name	Job	Age	Disease
Alice	Cook	40	Flu
Bob	Cook	50	Diabetes
Calvin	Lawyer	60	HIV

Table 8.5:   View $V_1 = \Pi_{Name,Job}(T)$

Name	Job
Alice	Cook
Bob	Cook
Calvin	Lawyer

Table 8.6:   View $V_2 = \Pi_{Job,Disease}(T)$

Job	Disease
Cook	SARS
Cook	Diabetes
Lawyer	HIV

Example 8.2 illustrates that an adversary may be able to infer the sensitive value of a target victim from multiple selection-project views. Yao et al. [262] present a comprehensive study to detect violations of k-anonymity on multiple views. The following example shows the intuition of the detection method. Refer to [262] for details of the violations detection algorithm.

Example 8.3
Consider views V_3, V_4, and V_5 in Table 8.7, Table 8.8, and Table 8.9, respectively. We use

Table 8.7:   View $V_3 = \Pi_{Name}\sigma_{Age>45}(T)$

Name
Bob
Calvin

Table 8.8:   View $V_4 = \Pi_{Name}\sigma_{Age<55}(T)$

Name
Alice
Bob

Table 8.9:   View $V_5 = \Pi_{Name}\sigma_{40<Age<55}(T)$

Disease
Diabetes

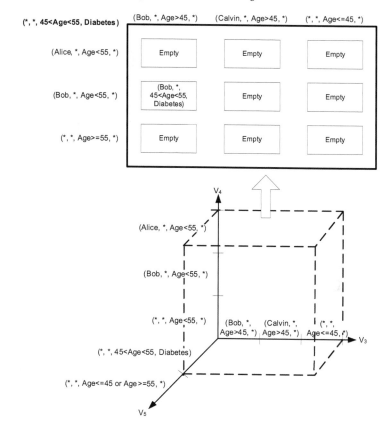

FIGURE 8.1: Views V_3, V_4, and V_5

$$(Name, Job, Age, Disease)$$

to denote the set of records matching the selection conditions. For example, $(Alice, *, Age < 55, *)$ denotes the set of records that have $Name = Alice$, $Age < 55$, Job and $Disease$ can be any values. A complement record sets of $(Alice, *, Age < 55, *)$ is $(*, *, Age \geq 55, *)$.

The general idea of the k-anonymity violation detection algorithm is to intersect the views that are generated based on the selection conditions, and to check whether or not every non-empty intersection contains at least k records. In Figure 8.1, we plot the three sets of record sets of V_3, V_4, and V_5, and the complement record sets. In the upper portion of Figure 8.1, we illustrate a record set for the projection fact of $Diabetes$ in V_5, which is $(Bob, *, 45 < Age < 55, Diabetes)$. Since the record set represented by the intersection contains only one record, the three views violate 2-anonymity. Figure 8.2 further illustrates the intersection of two sets of record sets of V_3 and V_4. □

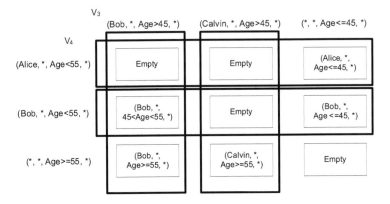

FIGURE 8.2: Views V_3 and V_4

8.2.2   Violations by Functional Dependencies

Another type of violation is caused by the presence of functional dependencies as adversary's background knowledge. A functional dependency (FD) is a constraint between two sets of attributes in a table from a database. Given a data table T, a set of attributes X in T is said to *functionally determine* another attribute Y, also in T, denoted by $(X \rightarrow Y)$, if and only if each X value is associated with precisely one Y value. Even though the data holder does not release such functional dependencies to the data recipients, the data recipients often can obtain such knowledge by interpreting the semantics of the attributes. For example, the functional dependency $Name \rightarrow Age$ can be derived by common sense. Thus, it is quite possible that the adversary could use functional dependencies as background knowledge. The following examples illustrate the privacy threats caused by functional dependency.

Example 8.4
Consider the raw data R in Table 8.10, and two projection views V_6 and V_7 in Table 8.11 and Table 8.12, respectively. Every record in V_6 has a corresponding record in V_7. Suppose an adversary knows there is a functional dependency $Name \rightarrow Disease$, meaning that every patient has only one disease. The adversary then can infer that *Alice* has *Cancer* because *Alice* has two records in V_6 and HIV is the only value appearing twice in V_7.   □

8.2.3   Discussion

Yao et al. [262] present a comprehensive study on k-anonymity with multiple views. First, they proposed a violation detection algorithm for k-anonymity without functional dependencies. The data complexity of the detection algorithm is polynomial, $O((max(|V_i|)^N)$, where $|V_i|$ is the size of the view V_i and

Table 8.10: Raw data table R for illustrating privacy threats caused by functional dependency

Name	Doctor	Disease
Alice	Smith	Cancer
Alice	Thomson	Cancer
Brian	Smith	Flu
Cathy	Thomson	Diabetes

Table 8.11: View $V_6 = \Pi_{Name,Doctor}(R)$

Name	Doctor
Alice	Smith
Alice	Thomson
Brian	Smith
Cathy	Thomson

Table 8.12: View $V_7 = \Pi_{Doctor,Disease}(R)$

Doctor	Disease
Smith	Cancer
Thomson	Cancer
Smith	Flu
Thomson	Diabetes

N is the number of dimensions. Second, the knowledge of functional dependency is available to the adversary. Yao et al. [262] suggest a conservative checking algorithm that always catches k-anonymity violation, but it may make mistakes when a view set actually does not violate k-anonymity.

In summary, the k-anonymity violation detection algorithm presented in [262] has several limitations. First, it does not consider the case that different views could have been generalized to different levels according to some taxonomy trees, which is very common in multiple views publishing. Second, it does not consider attribute linkages with confidence as discussed in Chapter 2.2. Third, Yao et al. [262] present algorithms only for *detecting* violations, not anonymizing the views for achieving k-anonymity. Subsequent chapters in Part III address these limitations.

8.3 Checking Violations with Marginals

In addition to the anonymous base table, Kifer and Gehrke [139] propose to increase the utility of published data by releasing several anonymous *marginals* that are essentially duplicate preserving projection views. For example,

Table 8.13:   Raw patient table

quasi-identifier		sensitive
Zip Code	**Salary**	**Disease**
25961	43K	HIV
25964	36K	Anthrax
25964	32K	Giardiasis
25964	42K	Cholera
25961	58K	Flu
25961	57K	Heart
25961	56K	Flu
25964	63K	Cholera
25964	61K	Heart
24174	34K	Flu
24174	48K	Cholera
24179	48K	Cholera
24179	40K	Heart

Table 8.15 is the *Salary* marginal, Table 8.16 is the *Zip/Disease* marginal, and Table 8.17 is the *Zip/Salary* marginal for the $(2,3)$-diverse base Table 8.14. The availability of additional marginals (views) provides additional information for data mining, but also poses new privacy threats. For example, if an adversary knows that a patient who lives in 25961 and has salary under 50K is in the raw patient Table 8.13, then the adversary can join Table 8.14 and Table 8.16 to infer that the patient has *HIV* because $\{Anthrax, Cholera, Giardiasis, HIV\} \cap \{Flu, Heart, HIV\} = HIV$. Kifer and Gehrke [139] extend k-anonymity and ℓ-diversity for marginals and pre-

Table 8.14: $(2,3)$-diverse patient table

quasi-identifier		sensitive
Zip Code	**Salary**	**Disease**
2596*	≤50K	Anthrax
2596*	≤50K	Cholera
2596*	≤50K	Giardiasis
2596*	≤50K	HIV
2596*	>50K	Cholera
2596*	>50K	Flu
2596*	>50K	Flu
2596*	>50K	Heart
2596*	>50K	Heart
2417*	≤50K	Cholera
2417*	≤50K	Cholera
2417*	≤50K	Flu
2417*	≤50K	Heart

Table 8.15: Salary marginal

Salary	Count
[31K-35K]	2
[36K-40K]	2
[41K-45K]	2
[46K-50K]	2
[51K-55K]	0
[56K-60K]	3
[61K-65K]	2

Table 8.16: Zip code/disease marginal

Zip Code	Disease	Count
25961	Flu	2
25961	Heart	1
25961	HIV	1
25964	Cholera	2
25964	Heart	1
25964	Anthrax	1
25964	Giardiasis	1
24174	Flu	1
24174	Cholera	1
24179	Cholera	1
24179	Heart	1

sented a method to check whether published marginals violate the privacy requirement on the anonymous base table.

Barak et al. [26] also study the privacy threats caused by marginals along the line of differential privacy [74] studied in Chapter 2.4.2. Their primary contribution is to provide a formal guarantee to preserve *all* of privacy, accuracy, and consistency in the published marginals. Accuracy bounds the difference between the original marginals and published marginals. Consistency ensures that there exists a contingency table whose marginals equal to the published marginals. Instead of adding noise to the original data records at the cost of accuracy, or adding noise to the published marginals at the cost of consistency, they have proposed to transform the original data into the *Fourier* domain, apply differential privacy to the transformed data by perturbation, and employ linear programming to obtain a non-negative contingency table based on the given Fourier coefficients.

Table 8.17:   Zip code/salary marginal

Zip Code	Salary	Count
25961	[41K-50K]	1
25961	[51K-60K]	3
25964	[31K-40K]	2
25964	[41K-50K]	1
25964	[61K-70K]	2
24174	[31K-40K]	1
24174	[41K-50K]	1
24179	[31K-40K]	1
24179	[41K-50K]	1

8.4   MultiRelational k-Anonymity

Most works on k-anonymity focus on anonymizing a single data table. Ercan Nergiz et al. [178] propose a privacy model called *MultiR k-anonymity* to ensure k-anonymity on multiple relational tables. Their model assumes that a relational database contains a person-specific table PT and a set of tables $T_1, \ldots, T_n$, where PT contains a person identifier Pid and some sensitive attributes, and T_i, for $1 \le i \le n$, contains some foreign keys, some attributes in QID, and sensitive attributes. The general privacy notion is to ensure that for each record owner o contained in the join of all tables $PT \Join T_1 \Join \cdots \Join T_n$, there exists at least $k-1$ other record owners who share the same QID with o. It is important to emphasize that the k-anonymization is applied at the *record owner* level, not at the *record* level in traditional k-anonymity. This idea is similar to (X, Y)-anonymity discussed in Chapter 2.1.2, where $X = QID$ and $Y = \{Pid\}$.

8.5   Multi-Level Perturbation

Recently, Xiao et al. [252] study the problem of *multi-level perturbation* whose objective is to publish multiple anonymous versions of the same underlying raw data set. Each version can be anonymized at different privacy levels depending on the trustability levels of the data recipients. The major challenge is that data recipients may collude and share their data to infer sensitive information beyond their permitted levels. Xiao et al.'s randomization method overcomes the challenge by ensuring that the colluding data recipients cannot learn any information that is more than the information known by the most trustworthy data recipient alone. Another major strength of the randomization approach is that each data recipient can utilize the received data for privacy-preserving data mining as the output of conventional uniform randomization. Similar to other randomization approaches, this method does not preserve the data truthfulness at the record level.

8.6   Summary

In this chapter, we have studied several methods for detecting violations of privacy requirements on multiple views. These detection methods are applicable for detecting violations on data views publishing and database queries that violate privacy requirements. What can we do if some combinations of views or database queries violate the privacy requirement? A simple yet non-user friendly solution is to reject the queries, or not to release the views. Obviously, this approach defeats the goal of data publishing and answering database queries. Thus, simply detecting violations is insufficient. The recent work on MultiR k-anonymity (Chapter 8.4) and multi-level perturbation (Chapter 8.5) present effective methods for anonymizing multiple relational databases and views at different privacy protection levels for different recipients.

The works on multiple views publishing share a common assumption: the entire raw data set is static and is available to the data provider at time of anonymization and publication. Yet, in practice, this assumption may not hold as new data arrive and a new release has to be published subsequently together with some previously published data. The adversary may combine multiple releases to sharpen the identification of a record owner and his sensitive information. In Chapters 9 and 10, we study several methods that anonymize multiple data releases and views without compromising the desirable property of preserving data truthfulness.

Chapter 9

Anonymizing Sequential Releases with New Attributes

9.1 Introduction

An organization makes a new release as new information becomes available, releases a tailored view for each data request, or releases sensitive information and identifying information separately. The availability of related releases sharpens the identification of individuals by a global quasi-identifier consisting of attributes from related releases. Since it is not an option to anonymize previously released data, the current release must be anonymized to ensure that a global quasi-identifier is not effective for identification.

In multiple views publishing studied in Chapter 8, several tables, for different purposes, are published at one time. In other words, a data holder already has *all* the raw data when the views are published. Since all the data are known, the data holder has the flexibility to anonymize different views in order to achieve the given privacy and information requirements on the views. In this chapter, we will study a more general data publishing scenario called *sequential anonymization* [236], in which the data holder knows only part of the raw data when a release is published, and has to ensure that subsequent releases do not violate a privacy requirement even an adversary has access to all releases. A key question is how to anonymize the current release so that it cannot be linked to previous releases yet remains useful for its own release purpose. We will study an anonymization method [236] for this sequential releases scenario. The general idea is to employ the *lossy join*, a negative property in relational database design, as a way to hide the join relationship among releases.

9.1.1 Motivations

k-anonymity addresses the problem of reducing the risk of record linkages in a person-specific table. Refer to Chapter 2.1.1 for details of k-anonymity and the notion of quasi-identifier. In case of single release, the notion of QID is restricted to the current table, and *the database is made anonymous to itself*. In many scenarios, however, related data were released previously: an orga-

Table 9.1:   Raw data table T_1

Pid	Job	Disease
\multicolumn{3}{c}{T_1}		
1	Banker	Cancer
2	Banker	Cancer
3	Clerk	HIV
4	Driver	Cancer
5	Engineer	HIV

Table 9.2:   Raw data table T_2

Pid	Name	Job	Class
1	Alice	Banker	c1
2	Alice	Banker	c1
3	Bob	Clerk	c2
4	Bob	Driver	c3
5	Cathy	Engineer	c4

nization makes a new release as new information becomes available, releases a separate view for each data sharing purpose (such as classifying a different target variable as studied in the Red Cross case in Chapter 6), or makes separate releases for personally-identifiable data (e.g., names) and sensitive data (e.g., DNA sequences) [164]. In such scenarios, the QID can be a combination of attributes from several releases, and *the database must be made anonymous to the combination of all releases thus far.*

The next example illustrates a scenario of *sequential release*: T_2 was unknown when T_1 was released, and T_1, once released, cannot be modified when T_2 is considered for release. This scenario is different from the scenario multiple views publishing studied in Chapter 8, where both T_1 and T_2 are parts of a view and can be modified before the release, which means more "rooms" to satisfy a privacy and information requirement. In the sequential release, each release has its own information need and the join that enables a global identifier should be prevented. In the view release, however, all data in the views may serve the information need collectively, possibly through the join of all tables.

Example 9.1
Consider the data in Tables 9.1-9.3. *Pid* is the person identifier and is included only for discussion, not for release. Suppose the data holder has *previously* released T_1 and *now* wants to release T_2 for classification analysis of the *Class* column. Essentially T_1 and T_2 are two projection views of the patient records. $T_2.Job$ is a discriminator of *Class* but this may not be known to the data holder. The data holder does not want *Name* to be linked to *Disease* in the

Table 9.3:   The join of T_1 and T_2

| | | The join on $T_1.Job = T_2.Job$ | | |
Pid	Name	Job	Disease	Class
1	Alice	Banker	Cancer	c1
2	Alice	Banker	Cancer	c1
3	Bob	Clerk	HIV	c2
4	Bob	Driver	Cancer	c3
5	Cathy	Engineer	HIV	c4
-	Alice	Banker	Cancer	c1
-	Alice	Banker	Cancer	c1

join of the two releases; in other words, the join should be k-anonymous on $\{Name, Disease\}$. Below are several observations that motivate the approach presented in this chapter.

1. **Join sharpens identification**: after the natural join (based on equality on all common attributes), the adversary can uniquely identify the individuals in the $\{Bob, HIV\}$ group through the combination $\{Name, Disease\}$ because this group has size 1. When T_1 and T_2 are examined separately, both Bob group and HIV group have size 2. Thus, the join may increase the risk of record linkages.

2. **Join weakens identification**: after the natural join, the $\{Alice, Cancer\}$ group has size 4 because the records for different persons are matched (i.e., the last two records in the join table). When T_1 and T_2 are examined separately, both $Alice$ group and $Cancer$ group have smaller size. In the database terminology, the join is *lossy*. Since the join attack depends on matching the records for the *same* person, a lossy join can be used to combat the join attack. Thus, the join may decrease the risk of record linkages. Note, the ambiguity caused by the lossy join is not considered information loss here because the problem is to weaken the linkages of records among the releases.

3. **Join enables inferences across tables**: the natural join reveals the inference $Alice \rightarrow Cancer$ with 100% confidence for the individuals in the $Alice$ group. Thus, the join may increase the risk of attribute linkages.

□

This sequential anonymization problem was briefly discussed in some pioneering works on k-anonymity, but they did not provide a practical solution. For example, Samarati and Sweeney [203] suggest to k-anonymize all potential join attributes as the QID in the next release T_p. Sweeney [216] suggests to generalize T_p based on the previous releases $T_1, \ldots, T_{p-1}$ to ensure that all values in T_p are not more specific than in any $T_1, \ldots, T_{p-1}$. Both solutions suffer from *monotonically distorting* the data in a later release: as more and more releases are published, a later release is more and more constrained due to the previous releases, thus are more and more distorted. The third solution is to release a "complete" cohort in which all potential releases are anonymized at one time, after which no additional mechanism is required. This requires predicting future releases. The "under-prediction" means no room for additional releases and the "over-prediction" means unnecessary data distortion. Also, this solution does not accommodate the new data added at a later time.

The problem of *sequential anonymization* considers three motivating scenarios:

1. make new release when new attributes arrive,

2. release some selected attributes for each data request, and

3. make separate releases for personally-identifiable attributes and sensitive attributes.

The objective is to anonymize the current release T_2 in the presence of a previous release T_1, assuming that T_1 and T_2 are projections of the same underlying table. The release of T_2 must satisfy a given information requirement and privacy requirement. The information requirement could include such criteria as minimum classification error (Chapter 4.3) and minimum data distortion (Chapter 4.1). The privacy requirement states that, even if the adversary joins T_1 with T_2, he/she will not succeed in linking individuals to sensitive properties. This requirement is formalized to be limiting the linking between two attribute sets X and Y over the join of T_1 and T_2. The privacy notion (X, Y)-*privacy* (Chapter 2.2.4) generalizes k-anonymity (Chapter 2.1.1) and confidence bounding (Chapter 2.2.2).

The basic idea is generalizing the current release T_2 so that the join with the previous release T_1 becomes lossy enough to disorient the adversary. Essentially, a lossy join hides the true join relationship to cripple a global quasi-identifier. In Chapter 9.1.2, we first formally define the problem, and show that the sequential anonymization subsumes the k-anonymization, thus the optimal solution is NP-hard. Then, we study a greedy method for finding a minimally generalized T_1. To ensure the minimal generalization, the lossy join responds dynamically to each generalization step. Therefore, one challenge is checking the privacy violation over such dynamic join because a lossy join can be extremely large. Another challenge is pruning, as early as possible, unpromising generalization steps that lead to privacy violation. To address these challenges, we will study a top-down approach, introduced by Wang and Fung [236], to progressively specialize T_1 starting from the most generalized state in Chapter 9.3. It checks the privacy violation without executing the join and prunes unpromising specialization based on a proven monotonicity of (X, Y)-privacy in Chapter 9.2. Finally, the extension to more than one previous release is discussed in Chapter 9.4.

9.1.2   Anonymization Problem for Sequential Releases

For a table T, $\Pi(T)$ and $\sigma(T)$ denote the projection and selection over T, $att(T)$ denotes the set of attributes in T, and $|T|$ denotes the number of distinct records in T.

9.1.2.1   Privacy Model

In this problem, X and Y are assumed to be disjoint sets of attributes that describe individuals and sensitive properties in any order. An example is $X = \{Name, Job\}$ and $Y = \{Disease\}$. There are two ways to limit the linking between X and Y: record linkage and attribute linkage.

To thwart record linkages, sequential anonymization employs the notion of (X, Y)-anonymity. Recall from Chapter 2.1.2, (X, Y)-anonymity states that each value on X is linked to at least k distinct values on Y. k-anonymity is the special case where X serves QID and Y is a key in T. The next example shows the usefulness of (X, Y)-anonymity where Y is not a key in T and k-anonymity fails to provide the required anonymity.

Example 9.2

Consider the data table

$$Inpatient(Pid, Job, Zip, PoB, Test).$$

A record in the table represents that a patient identified by Pid has Job, Zip, PoB (place of birth), and $Test$. In general, a patient can have several tests, thus several records. Since $QID = \{Job, Zip, PoB\}$ is not a key in the table, the k-anonymity on QID fails to ensure that each value on QID is linked to at least k (*distinct*) patients. For example, if each patient has at least 3 tests, it is possible that the k records matching a value on QID may involve no more than $k/3$ patients. With (X, Y)-anonymity, we can specify the anonymity with respect to *patients* by letting $X = \{Job, Zip, PoB\}$ and $Y = Pid$, that is, each X group must be linked to at least k distinct values on Pid. If $X = \{Job, Zip, PoB\}$ and $Y = Test$, each X group is required to be linked to at least k distinct tests. $\square$

Being linked to k persons or tests does not imply that the probability of being linked to any of them is $1/k$ if some person or test occurs more frequently than others. Thus, a large k does not necessarily limit the linking probability. The (X, Y)-*linkability* addresses this issue. Recall from Chapter 2.2.3, (X, Y)-linkability limits the confidence of inferring a value on Y from a value on X. With X and Y describing individuals and sensitive properties, any such inference with a high confidence is a privacy breach.

Example 9.3

Suppose that (j, z, p) on $X = \{Job, Zip, PoB\}$ occurs with the HIV test in

Table 9.4: The
patient data (T_1)

PoB	Sex	Zip
UK	M	Z3
UK	M	Z3
UK	F	Z5
FR	F	Z5
FR	M	Z3
FR	M	Z3
US	M	Z3

9 records and occurs with the *Diabetes* test in 1 record. The confidence of $(j, z, p) \rightarrow HIV$ is 90%. With $Y = Test$, the (X, Y)-linkability states that no test can be inferred from a value on X with a confidence higher than a given threshold. $\qquad\square$

Often, not all but some values y on Y are sensitive, in which case Y can be replaced with a subset of y_i values on Y, written $Y = \{y_1, \ldots, y_p\}$, and a different threshold k can be specified for each y_i. More generally, the problem of sequential anonymization allows multiple Y_i, each representing a subset of values on a different set of attributes, with Y being the union of all Y_i. For example, $Y_1 = \{HIV\}$ on *Test* and $Y_2 = \{Banker\}$ on *Job*. Such a "value-level" specification provides a great flexibility essential for minimizing the data distortion.

Example 9.4
Consider the medical test data and the patient data in Table 9.5 and Table 9.4. Suppose the data holder wants to release Table 9.5 for classification analysis on the *Class* attribute. Europeans (i.e., UK and FR) have the class label Yes and US has the class label No. Suppose that the data holder has previously released the patient data (T_1) and now wants to release the medical test data (T_2) for classification analysis on *Class*, but wants to prevent any inference of the value HIV in T_1 using the combination $\{Job, PoB, Zip\}$ in the join of T_1 and T_2. This requirement is specified as the (X, Y)-linkability, where

$$X = \{Job, PoB, Zip\} \text{ and } Y = \{y = HIV\}.$$

Here *PoB* in X refers to $\{T_1.PoB, T_2.PoB\}$ since *PoB* is a common attribute. In the join, the linkability from X to HIV is $L_y(X) = 100\%$ because all 4 joined records containing $\{Banker, UK, Z3\}$ contain the value HIV. If the data holder can tolerate at most 90% linkability, Table 9.5 (T_2) without modification is not safe for release. $\qquad\square$

Table 9.5:   The medical test data (T_2)

The medical test data				
Test	Job	PoB	Sex	Class
HIV	Banker	UK	M	Yes
HIV	Banker	UK	M	Yes
Eye	Banker	UK	F	Yes
Eye	Clerk	FR	F	Yes
Allergy	Driver	US	M	No
Allergy	Engineer	US	M	No
Allergy	Engineer	FR	M	Yes
Allergy	Engineer	FR	M	Yes

When no distinction is necessary, we use the term (X, Y)-*privacy* to refer to either (X, Y)-anonymity or (X, Y)-linkability. The following corollary can be easily verified.

COROLLARY 9.1
Assume that $X \subseteq X'$ and $Y' \subseteq Y$. For the same threshold k, if (X', Y')-privacy is satisfied, (X, Y)-privacy is satisfied. ■

9.1.2.2   Generalization and Specialization

One way to look at a (X, Y)-privacy is that Y serves the "reference point" with respect to which the privacy is measured and X is a set of "grouping attributes." For example, with $Y = Test$ each test in Y serves a reference point, and $A_Y(X)$ measures the minimum number of tests associated with a group value on X, and $L_Y(X)$ measures the maximum confidence of inferring a test from X. To satisfy a (X, Y)-privacy, Wang and Fung [236] employ the subtree generalization scheme to generalize X while fixing the reference point Y. The purpose is to increase $A_Y(X)$ or decrease $L_Y(X)$ as a test from X becomes more general. Such subtree generalization scheme is more general than the full-domain generalization where all generalized values must be on the same level of the taxonomy tree. Refer to Chapter 3.1 for different generalization schemes.

A generalized table can be obtained by a sequence of specializations starting from the *most generalized table*. Each *specialization* is denoted by $v \rightarrow \{v_1, \ldots, v_c\}$, where v is the parent value and $v_1, \ldots, v_c$ are the child values of v. It replaces the value v in every record containing v with the child value v_i that is consistent with the original domain value in the record. A specialization for a numerical attribute has the form $v \rightarrow \{v_1, v_2\}$, where v_1 and v_2 are two sub-intervals of the larger interval v. Instead of being predetermined, the splitting point of the two sub-intervals is chosen on-the-fly to maximize information utility. Refer to Example 6.4 in Chapter 6.2.2 for the technique on dynamically growing a taxonomy tree for a numerical attribute.

9.1.2.3   Sequential Releases

Consider a previously released table T_1 and the current table T_2, where T_1 and T_2 are projections of the same underlying table and contain some common attributes. T_1 may have been generalized. The problem is to generalize T_2 to satisfy a given (X, Y)-privacy. To preserve information, T_2's generalization is not necessarily based on T_1, that is, T_2 may contain values more specific than in T_1. Given T_1 and T_2, the adversary may apply prior knowledge to match the records in T_1 and T_2. Entity matching has been studied in database, data mining, AI and web communities for information integration, natural language processing, and Semantic Web. See [211] for a list of works. We cannot consider a priori every possible way of matching. Thus, the problem of sequential anonymization primarily considers the matching based on the following prior knowledge available to both the data holder and the adversary: the schema information of T_1 and T_2, the taxonomies for categorical attributes, and the following inclusion-exclusion principle for matching the records. Assume that $t_1 \in T_1$ and $t_2 \in T_2$.

- *Consistency Predicate*: for every common categorical attribute A, $t_1.A$ matches $t_2.A$ if they are on the same generalization path in the taxonomy tree for A. Intuitively, this says that $t_1.A$ and $t_2.A$ can possibly be generalized from the same domain value. For example, *Male* matches *Single_Male*. This predicate is implicit in the taxonomies for categorical attributes.

- *Inconsistency Predicate*: for two distinct categorical attributes $T_1.A$ and $T_2.B$, $t_1.A$ matches $t_2.B$ only if $t_1.A$ and $t_2.B$ are not semantically inconsistent according to the "common sense." This predicate excludes impossible matches. If not specified, "not semantically inconsistent" is assumed. If two values are semantically inconsistent, so are their specialized values. For example, *Male* and *Pregnant* are semantically inconsistent, so are *Married_Male* and *6_Month_Pregnant*.

Numerical attributes are not considered in the predicates of the join attributes because their taxonomies may be generated differently for T_1 and T_2. Both the data holder and the adversary use these predicates to match records from T_1 and T_2. The data holder can "catch up with" the adversary by incorporating the adversary's knowledge into such "common sense." We assume that a *match function* tests whether (t_1, t_2) is a match. (t_1, t_2) is a *match* if both consistency predicate and inconsistency predicate hold. The *join* of T_1 and T_2 is a table on $att(T_1) \cup att(T_2)$ that contains all matches (t_1, t_2). The *join attributes* refer to all attributes that occur in either predicates. Note that every common attribute A has two columns $T_1.A$ and $T_2.A$ in the join. The following observation says that generalizing the join attributes produces more matches, thereby making the join more lossy. The approach presented in this chapter exploits this property to hide the original matches.

Observation 9.1.1 (*Join preserving*) If (t_1, t_2) is a match and if t_1' is a generalization of t_1, (t_1', t_2) is a match. (*Join relaxing*) If (t_1, t_2) is not a match and if t_1' is a generalization of t_1 on some join attribute A, (t_1', t_2) is a match if and only if $t_1'.A$ and $t_2.A$ are on the same generalization path and $t_1'.A$ is not semantically inconsistent with any value in t_2. ∎

Consider a (X, Y)-privacy. We generalize T_2 on the attributes $X \cap att(T_2)$, called the *generalization attributes*. Corollary 9.1 implies that including more attributes in X makes the privacy requirement stronger. Observation 9.1.1 implies that including more join attributes in X (for generalization) makes the join more lossy. Therefore, from the privacy point of view it is a good practice to include all join attributes in X for generalization. Moreover, if X contains a common attribute A from T_1 and T_2, under the matching predicate, one of $T_1.A$ and $T_2.A$ could be more specific (so reveal more information) than the other. To ensure privacy, X should contain both $T_1.A$ and $T_2.A$ in the (X, Y)-privacy specification, so that they can be generalized.

DEFINITION 9.1 Sequential anonymization   The data holder has previously released a table T_1 and wants to release the next table T_2, where T_1 and T_2 are projections of the same underlying table and contain some common attributes. The data holder wants to ensure a (X, Y)-privacy on the join of T_1 and T_2. The *sequential anonymization* is to generalize T_2 on $X \cap att(T_2)$ so that the join of T_1 and T_2 satisfies the (X, Y)-privacy requirement and T_2 remains as useful as possible. ∎

THEOREM 9.1
The sequential anonymization is at least as hard as the k-anonymization problem.

PROOF   The k-anonymization of T_1 on QID is the special case of sequential anonymization with (X, Y)-anonymity, where X is QID and Y is a common key of T_1 and T_2 and the only join attribute. In this case, the join trivially appends the attributes of T_1 to T_2 according to the common key, after which the appended attributes are ignored. □

9.2   Monotonicity of Privacy

To generalize T_2, the anonymization algorithm presented in [236] specializes T_2 starting from the most generalized state. A main reason for this approach is the following *anti-monotonicity* of (X, Y)-privacy with respect to specialization: if (X, Y)-privacy is violated, it remains violated after a specialization. Therefore, the anonymization algorithm can stop further specialization whenever the (X, Y)-privacy is violated for the first time. This is a highly desirable property for pruning unpromising specialization. We first show this property for a single table.

THEOREM 9.2
On a single table, the (X, Y)-privacy is anti-monotone with respect to specialization on X.

PROOF   See [236]   □

However, on the join of T_1 and T_2, in general, (X, Y)-anonymity is not anti-monotone with respect to a specialization on $X \cap att(T_2)$. To see this, let $T_1(D, Y) = \{d_3 y_3, d_3 y_2, d_1 y_1\}$ and $T_2(C, D) = \{c_1 d_3, c_2 d\}$, where c_i, d_i, y_i are domain values and d is a generalized value of d_1 and d_2. $A_Y(X)$ is the minimum number of value Y associated with a group value on X. The join based on D contains 3 matches $(c_1 d_3, d_3 y_2)$, $(c_1 d_3, d_3 y_3)$, $(c_2 d, d_1 y_1)$, and $A_Y(X) = A_Y(c_2 d d_1) = 1$, where $X = \{C, T_1.D, T_2.D\}$. After specializing the record $c_2 d$ in T_1 into $c_2 d_2$, the join contains only two matches $(c_1 d_3, d_3 y_2)$ and $(c_1 d_3, d_3 y_3)$, and $A_Y(X) = a_Y(c_1 d_3 d_3) = 2$. Thus, $A_Y(X)$ increases after the specialization.

The above situation arises because the specialized record $c_2 d_2$ matches no record in T_2 or becomes dangling. However, this situation does not arise for the T_1 and T_2 encountered in the sequential anonymization. Two tables are *population-related* if every record in each table has at least one matching record in the other table. Essentially, this property says that T_1 and T_2 are about the same "population" and there is no dangling record. Clearly, if T_1 and T_2 are projections of the same underlying table, as assumed in the problem setting of sequential anonymization, T_1 and T_2 are population-related. Observation 9.1.1 implies that generalizing T_2 preserves the population-relatedness.

Observation 9.2.1 If T_1 and T_2 are population-related, so are they after generalizing T_2. ■

LEMMA 9.1
If T_1 and T_2 are population-related, $A_Y(X)$ does not increase after a specialization of T_2 on $X \cap att(T_2)$.

Now, we consider (X, Y)-linkability on the join of T_1 and T_2. It is not immediately clear how a specialization on $X \cap att(T_2)$ will affect $L_Y(X)$ because the specialization will reduce the matches, therefore, both $a(y, x)$ and $a(x)$ in

$l_y(x) = a(y,x)/a(x)$. The next lemma shows that $L_Y(X)$ does not decrease after a specialization on $X \cap att(T_2)$.

LEMMA 9.2

If Y contains attributes from T_1 or T_2, but not from both, $L_Y(X)$ does not decrease after a specialization of T_2 on the attributes $X \cap att(T_2)$.

COROLLARY 9.2

The (X, Y)-anonymity on the join of T_1 and T_2 is anti-monotone with respect to a specialization of T_2 on $X \cap att(T_2)$. Assume that Y contains attributes from either T_1 or T_2, but not both. The (X, Y)-linkability on the join of T_1 and T_2 is anti-monotone with respect to a specialization of T_2 on $X \cap att(T_2)$.
■

COROLLARY 9.3

Let T_1, T_2 and (X, Y)-privacy be as in Corollary 9.2. There exists a generalized T_2 that satisfies the (X, Y)-privacy if and only if the most generalized T_2 does.
■

Remarks. Lemma 9.1 and Lemma 9.2 can be extended to multiple previous releases. Thus, the anti-monotonicity of (X, Y)-privacy holds for one or more previous releases. The extension in Chapter 9.4 makes use of this observation.

9.3 Anonymization Algorithm for Sequential Releases

We explain the algorithm for generalizing T_2 to satisfy the given (X, Y)-privacy on the join of T_1 and T_2. Corollary 9.3 is first applied to test if there exists a solution. In the rest of Chapter 9.3, we assume a solution exists. Let X_i denote $X \cap att(T_i)$, Y_i denote $Y \cap att(T_i)$, and J_i denote the join attributes in T_i, where $i = 1, 2$.

9.3.1 Overview of the Anonymization Algorithm

The algorithm, called *Top-Down Specialization for Sequential Anonymization (TDS4SA)*, is given in Algorithm 9.3.5. The input consists of T_1, T_2, the (X, Y)-privacy requirement, and the taxonomy tree for each categorical attribute in X_2. Starting from the most generalized T_2, the algorithm iteratively specializes the attributes A_j in X_2. T_2 contains the current set of *generalized records* and Cut_j contains the current set of *generalized values* for A_j. In each iteration, if some Cut_j contains a "valid" candidate for specialization, it

---

Algorithm 9.3.5 Top-Down Specialization for Sequential Anonymization (TDS4SA)

Input: T_1, T_2, a (X,Y)-privacy requirement, a taxonomy tree for each categorical attribute in X_1.
Output: a generalized T_2 satisfying the privacy requirement.

1: generalize every value of A_j to ANY_j where $A_j \in X_2$;
2: **while** there is a valid candidate in $\cup Cut_j$ **do**
3: find the winner w of highest $Score(w)$ from $\cup Cut_j$;
4: specialize w on T_2 and remove w from $\cup Cut_j$;
5: update $Score(v)$ and the valid status for all v in $\cup Cut_j$;
6: **end while**
7: output the generalized T_2 and $\cup Cut_j$;

---

chooses the winner w that maximizes *Score*. A candidate is *valid* if the join specialized by the candidate does not violate the privacy requirement. The algorithm then updates $Score(v)$ and status for the candidates v in $\cup Cut_j$. This process is repeated until there is no more valid candidate. On termination, Corollary 9.2 implies that a further specialization produces no solution, so T_2 is a maximally specialized state satisfying the given privacy requirement.

Below, we focus on the three key steps in Lines 3 to 5.

9.3.2 Information Metrics

TDS4SA employs the information metric $Score(v) = IGPL(v)$ presented in Chapter 4.2 to evaluate the "goodness" of a specialization v for preserving privacy and information. Each specialization gains some "information," $InfoGain(v)$, and loses some "privacy," $PrivLoss(v)$. TDS4SA chooses the specialization that maximizes the trade-off between the gain of information and the loss of privacy, which has been studied in Chapter 6.2.2.

$InfoGain(v)$ is measured on T_2 whereas $PrivLoss(v)$ is measured on the join of T_1 and T_2. Consider a specialization $v \rightarrow \{v_1, \ldots, v_c\}$. For a numerical attribute, $c = 2$, and v_1 and v_2 represent the binary split of the interval v that maximizes $InfoGain(v)$. Before the specialization, $T_2[v]$ denotes the set of generalized records in T_2 that contain v. After the specialization, $T_2[v_i]$ denotes the set of records in T_2 that contain v_i, $1 \le i \le c$.

The choice of $InfoGain(v)$ and $PrivLoss(v)$ depends on the information requirement and privacy requirement. If T_2 is released for classification on a specified class column, $InfoGain(v)$ could be the reduction of the class entropy defined by Equation 4.8 in Chapter 4.3. The computation depends only on the class frequency and some count statistics of v and v_i in $T_2[v]$ and $T_2[v_1] \cup \cdots \cup T_2[v_c]$. Another choice of $InfoGain(v)$ could be the notion of minimal distortion MD or $ILoss$ discussed in Chapter 4.1. If generalizing a child value v_i to the parent value v costs one unit of distortion, the information gained by the specialization: $InfoGain(v) = |T_2[v]|$. The third choice can be the discernibility (DM) in Chapter 4.1.

The above choices are by no means exhaustive. As far as TDS4SA is concerned, what is important is that $InfoGain(v)$ depends on the single column $att(v)$, and its class frequency, and the specialization of v only affects the records in $T_2[v]$ and the column $att(v)$. We will exploit this property to maintain $Score(v)$ efficiently for all candidates.

For (X, Y)-privacy, $PrivLoss(v)$ is measured by the decrease of $A_Y(X)$ or the increase of $L_Y(X)$ due to the specialization of v: $A_Y(X) - A_Y(X_v)$ for (X, Y)-anonymity, and $L_Y(X_v) - L_Y(X)$ for (X, Y)-linkability, where X and X_v represent the attributes before and after specializing v respectively. Computing $PrivLoss(v)$ involves the count statistics about X and Y over the join of T_1 and T_2, before and after the specialization of v, which can be expensive. The data holder may choose to ignore the privacy aspect by letting $PrivLoss(v) = 0$ in $Score(v)$.

Challenges. Though Algorithm 9.3.5 has a simple high level structure, several computational challenges must be resolved for an efficient implementation. First, each specialization of the winner w affects the matching of join, hence, the checking of the privacy requirement (i.e., the status on Line 5). It is extremely expensive to rejoin the two tables for each specialization performed. Second, it is inefficient to "perform" every candidate specialization v just to update $Score(v)$ on Line 5 (note that $A_Y(X_v)$ and $L_Y(X_v)$ are defined for the join assuming the specialization of v is performed). Moreover, materializing the join is impractical because a lossy join can be very large. A key contribution of Wang and Fung's work [236] is an efficient solution that incrementally maintains some count statistics without executing the join. We consider the two types of privacy separately.

9.3.3 (X, Y)-**Linkability**

Two expensive operations on performing the winner specialization w are accessing the records in T_2 containing w and matching the records in T_2 with the records in T_1. To support these operations efficiently, we organize the records in T_1 and T_2 into two tree structures. Recall that $X_1 = X \cap att(T_1)$ and $X_2 = X \cap att(T_2)$, and J_1 and J_2 denote the join attributes in T_1 and T_2.

Tree1 and Tree2. In *Tree2*, we partition the T_2 records by the attributes X_2 and $J_2 - X_2$ in that order, one level per attribute. Each root-to-leaf path represents a generalized record on $X_2 \cup J_2$, with the partition of the original records generalized being stored at the leaf node. For each generalized value v in Cut_j, $Link[v]$ links up all nodes for v at the attribute level of v. Therefore, $Link[v]$ provides a direct access to all T_2 partitions generalized to v. Tree2 is updated upon performing the winner specialization w in each iteration. In *Tree1*, we partition the T_1 records by the attributes J_1 and $X_1 - J_1$ in that order. No specialization is performed on T_1, so Tree1 is static. Some *count*

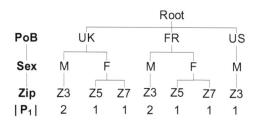

FIGURE 9.1: The static Tree1

statistics are stored for each partition in Tree1 and Tree2 to facilitate efficient computation of $Score(v)$.

Specialize w (Line 4). This step performs the winner specialization $w \to \{w_1, \ldots, w_c\}$, similar to the TDS algorithm for a single release in Chapter 6.3. It follows $Link[w]$ to specialize the partitions containing w. For each partition P_2 on the link, TDS4SA performs two steps:

1. Refine P_2 into the specialized partitions for w_i, link them into $Link[w_i]$. The specialized partitions remain on the other links of P_2. The step will scan the raw records in P_2 and collect some count statistics to facilitate the computation of $Score(v)$ in subsequent iterations.

2. Probe the matching partitions in Tree1. Match the last $|J_2|$ attributes in P_2 with the first $|J_1|$ attributes in Tree1. For each matching node at the level $|J_1|$ in Tree1, scan all partitions P_1 below the node. If x is the value on X represented by the pair (P_1, P_2), increment $a(x)$ by $|P_1| \times |P_2|$, increment $a(x, y)$ by $|P_1[y]| \times |P_2|$ if Y is in T_2, or by $|P_2| \times |P_1[y]|$ if Y is in T_1, where y is a value on Y. We employ an "X-tree" to keep $a(x)$ and $a(x, y)$ for the values x on X. In the X-*tree*, the x values are partitioned by the attributes X, one level per attribute, and are represented by leaf nodes. $a(x)$ and $a(x, y)$ are kept at the leaf node for x. Note that $l_y(x) = a(x, y)/a(x)$ and $L_y(X) = max\{l_y(x)\}$ over all the leaf nodes x in the X-tree.

Remarks. This step (Line 4) is the only time that raw records are accessed in the algorithm.

Update Score(v) (Line 5). After specializing w, for each candidate v in $\cup Cut_j$, the new $InfoGain(v)$ is obtained from the count statistics stored together with the partitions on $Link[v]$. $L_Y(X)$ is updated to $L_Y(X_w)$ that was computed in the previous iteration. If $L_Y(X_v) \leq k$, mark v as *valid*.

Refer to [236] for the details of each step.

Example 9.5

Continue with Example 9.4. Recall that T_1 denotes the patient data, T_2 denotes the medical test data, $X = \{Job, PoB, Zip\}$, $Y = \{y = HIV\}$ and the

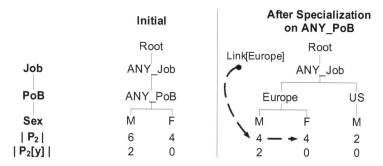

FIGURE 9.2: Evolution of Tree2 ($y = HIV$)

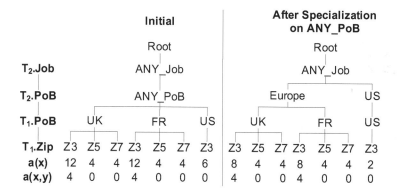

FIGURE 9.3: Evolution of X-tree

join attributes $J = \{PoB, Sex\}$. $X_1 = \{PoB, Zip\}$ and $X_2 = \{Job, PoB\}$. Initially, all values for X_2 are generalized to ANY_{Job} and ANY_{PoB}, and $\cup Cut_j$ contains these values. To find the winner w, we compute $Score(v)$ for every v in $\cup Cut_j$. Figure 9.2 shows (static) Tree1 for T_1, grouped by $X_1 \cup J$, and Figure 9.2 shows on the left the initial Tree2 for the most generalized T_2, grouped by $X_2 \cup J$. For example, in Tree2 the partition generalized to $\{ANY_{Job}, ANY_{PoB}, M\}$ on X_1 has 6 records, and 2 of them have the value HIV.

Figure 9.3 shows the initial X-tree on the left. $a(x)$ and $a(x, y)$ in the X-tree are computed from Tree1 and Tree2. For example,

$$a(ANY_{Job}, ANY_{PoB}, UK, Z3) = 6 \times 2 = 12,$$
$$a(ANY_{Job}, ANY_{PoB}, UK, Z3, HIV) = 2 \times 2 = 4,$$

where the $\times 2$ comes from matching the left-most path in Tree2 with the left-most path in Tree1 on the join attribute J. In this initial X-tree, $L_y(X) = 4/12 = 33\%$.

On specializing $ANY_{PoB} \rightarrow \{Europe, US\}$, three partitions are created in Tree2 as depicted in Figure 9.2 on the right. The X-tree is updated accordingly as depicted in Figure 9.3 on the right. To compute $a(x)$ and $a(x, y)$ for these updated x's, we access all partitions in one scan of $Link[Europe]$ and $Link[US]$ in Tree2 and match with the partitions in Tree1 , e.g.,

$a(ANY_{Job}, Europe, UK, Z3) = 4 \times 2 = 8,$
$a(ANY_{Job}, Europe, UK, Z3, HIV) = 2 \times 2 = 4.$

In the updated X-tree, $L_y(X) = 4/8 = 50\%.$ ☐

We provide an analysis on this algorithm:

1. The records in T_1 and T_2 are stored only once in Tree1 and Tree2. For the static Tree1, once it is created, data records can be discarded.

2. On specializing the winner w, $Link[w]$ provides a direct access to the records involved in T_2 and Tree1 provides a direct access to the matching partitions in T_1. Since the matching is performed at the partition level, not the record level, it scales up with the size of tables.

3. The cost of each iteration has two parts. The first part involves scanning the affected partitions on $Link[w]$ for specializing w in Tree2 and maintaining the count statistics. This is the only operation that accesses records. The second part involves using the count statistics to update the score and status of candidates.

4. In the whole computation, each record in T_2 is accessed at most $|X \cap att(T_2)| \times h$ times because a record is accessed only if it is specialized on some attribute from $X \cap att(T_2)$, where h is the maximum height of the taxonomies for the attributes in $X \cap att(T_2)$.

5. The algorithm can be terminated any time with a generalized T_2 satisfying the given privacy requirement.

9.3.4 (X, Y)-Anonymity

Like for (X, Y)-linkability, we use Tree1 and Tree2 to find the matching partitions (P_1, P_2), and performing the winner specialization and updating $Score(v)$ is similar to Chapter 9.3.3. But now, we use the X-tree to update $a_Y(x)$ for the values x on X, and there is one important difference in the update of $a_Y(x)$. Recall that $a_Y(x)$ is the number of *distinct* values y on Y associated with the value x. Since the same (x, y) value may be found in more than one matching (P_1, P_2) pair, we cannot simply sum up the count extracted from all pairs. Instead, we need to keep track of distinct Y values for each x value to update $a_Y(x)$. In general, this is a time-consuming operation, e.g., requiring sorting/hashing/scanning. Refer to [236] for the cases in which $a_Y(x)$ can be updated efficiently.

9.4 Extensions

TDS4SA can be extended to anonymize the current release T_p with the presence of multiple previous releases $T_1, \ldots, T_{p-1}$. One solution is first joining all previous releases $T_1, \ldots, T_{p-1}$ into one "history table" and then applying the proposed method for two releases. This history table is likely extremely large because all $T_1, \ldots, T_{p-1}$ are some generalized versions and there may be no join attributes between them. A preferred solution should deal with all releases at their original size. As remarked at the end of Chapter 9.2, Lemma 9.1-9.2 can be extended to this general case. Below, we briefly describe the modified problem definition. Refer to [236] for the modification required for the TDS4SA in Chapter 9.3.

Let t_i be a record in T_i. The *Consistency Predicate* states that, for all releases T_i that have a common attribute A, $t_i.A$'s are on the same generalization path in the taxonomy tree for A. The *Inconsistency Predicate* states that for distinct attributes $T_i.A$ and $T_j.B$, $t_i.A$ and $t_j.B$ are not semantically inconsistent according the "common sense." $(t_1, t_2, \ldots, t_p)$ is a *match* if it satisfies both predicates. The *join* of $T_1, T_2, \ldots, T_p$ is a table that contains all matches $(t_1, t_2, \ldots, t_p)$. For a (X, Y)-privacy on the join, X and Y are disjoint subsets of $att(T_1) \cup att(T_2) \cup \cdots \cup att(T_p)$ and if X contains a common attribute A, X contains all $T_i.A$ such that T_i contains A.

DEFINITION 9.2 Sequential anonymization   Suppose that tables $T_1, \ldots, T_{p-1}$ were previously released. The data holder wants to release a table T_p, but wants to ensure a (X, Y)-privacy on the join of $T_1, T_2, \ldots, T_p$. The *sequential anonymization* is to generalize T_p on the attributes in $X \cap att(T_p)$ such that the join satisfies the privacy requirement and T_p remains as useful as possible. ∎

9.5 Summary

Previous discussions on k-anonymization focused on a single release of data. In reality, data is not released in one-shot, but released continuously to serve various information purposes. The availability of related releases enables sharper identification attacks through a global quasi-identifier made up of the attributes across releases. In this chapter, we have studied the anonymization problem of the current release under this assumption, called *sequential anonymization* [236]. The privacy notion, (X, Y)-privacy has been extended to address the privacy issues in this case. We have also studied the notion of lossy join as a way to hide the join relationship among releases and a scalable anonymization solution to the sequential anonymization problem.

There is an empirical study in [236] thats shows extensive experiments on TDS4SA to evaluate the impact of achieving (X, Y)-privacy on the data quality in terms of classification error and distortion per record. Experimental results on real-life data suggest that it requires only a small data penalty to achieve a wide range of (X, Y)-privacy requirements in the scenario of sequential releases. The method is superior to several obvious solution candidates, such as k-anonymizing the current release, removing the join attributes, and removing the sensitive attributes. All these alternative solutions do not respond dynamically to the (X, Y)-privacy specification and the generalization of join. The experiments show that the dynamical response to the generalization of join helps achieve the specified privacy with less data distortion. The index structure presented in Figures 9.1-9.3 is highly scalable for anonymizing large data sets.

Chapter 10

Anonymizing Incrementally Updated Data Records

10.1 Introduction

k-anonymization has been primarily studied for a single static release of data in Parts I and II. In practice, however, new data arrives continuously and up-to-date data has to be published to researchers in a timely manner. In the model of *incremental data publishing*, the data holder has previously published $T_1, \ldots, T_{p-1}$ and now wants to publish T_p, where T_i is an updated release of T_{i-1} with record insertions and/or deletions. The problem assumes that all records for the same individual remain the same in all releases. Unlike the sequential anonymization problem studied in Chapter 9 which assumes all releases are projections of the same underlying data table, this problem assumes all releases share the same database schema.

The problem of incremental data publishing has two challenges. (1) Even though each release $T_1, \ldots, T_p$ is individually anonymous, the privacy requirement could be compromised by comparing different releases and eliminating some possible sensitive values for a victim. (2) One approach to solve the problem of incremental data publishing is to anonymize and publish new records *separately* each time they arrive. This naive approach suffers from severe data distortion because small increments are anonymized independently. Moreover, it is difficult to analyze a collection of independently anonymized data sets. For example, if the country name (e.g., Canada) is used in the release for first month records and if the city name (e.g., Toronto) is used in the release for second month records, counting the total number of persons born in Toronto is not possible. Another approach is to enforce the later release to be no more specialized than the previous releases [217]. The major drawback is that each subsequent release gets increasingly distorted, even if more new data are available.

The incremental data anonymization problem assumes that the adversary knows the timestamp and QID of the victim, so the adversary knows exactly which releases contain the victim's data record. The following example shows the privacy threats caused by record insertions and deletions.

Table 10.1: Continuous data publishing: 2-diverse T_1

Job	Sex	Disease
Professional	Female	Cancer
Professional	Female	Diabetes
Artist	Male	Fever
Artist	Male	Cancer

Table 10.2: Continuous data publishing: 2-diverse T_2 after an insertion to T_1

Job	Sex	Disease
Professional	Female	Cancer
Professional	Female	Diabetes
Professional	Female	HIV
Artist	Male	Fever
Artist	Male	Cancer

Example 10.1

Let Table 10.1 be the first release T_1. Let Table 10.2 be the second release T_2 after inserting a new record to T_1. Both T_1 and T_2 satisfy 2-diversity independently. Suppose the adversary knows that a female lawyer, Alice, has a record in T_2 but not in T_1, based on the timestamp that Alice was admitted to a hospital. From T_2, the adversary can infer that Alice must have contracted either *Cancer*, *Diabetes*, or *HIV*. By comparing T_2 with T_1, the adversary can identify that the first two records in T_2 must be old records from T_1 and, thus, infer that Alice must have contracted *HIV*. □

Example 10.2

Let Table 10.1 be the first release T_1. Let Table 10.3 be the second release T_2 after deleting the record ⟨*Professional, Female, Diabetes*⟩ from and inserting a new record ⟨*Professional, Female, Fever*⟩ to T_1. Both T_1 and T_2 satisfy 2-diversity independently. Suppose the adversary knows that a female engineer, Beth, must be in both T_1 and T_2. From T_1, the adversary can infer that Beth must have contracted either *Cancer* or *Diabetes*. Since T_2 contains no *Diabetes*, the adversary can infer that Beth must have contracted *Cancer*. □

Byun et al. [42] are the pioneers who propose an anonymization technique that enables privacy-preserving incremental data publishing after new records have been inserted. Specifically, it guarantees every release to satisfy ℓ-diversity, which requires each qid group to contain at least ℓ distinct sensitive values. Since this instantiation of ℓ-diversity does not consider the frequencies of sensitive values, an adversary could still confidently infer a sensitive value of

Table 10.3: Continuous data publishing: 2-diverse T_2 after a deletion from and an insertion to T_1

Job	Sex	Disease
Professional	Female	Cancer
Professional	Female	Fever
Artist	Male	Fever
Artist	Male	Cancer

a victim if the value occurs frequently in a *qid* group. Thus, the instantiation employed by Byun et al. [42] cannot prevent attribute linkage attacks.

Byun et al. [42] attempt to address the privacy threats caused by record insertions but not deletions, so the current release T_p contains all records in previous releases. The algorithm inserts new records into the current release T_p only if two privacy requirements remain satisfied after the insertion: (1) T_p is ℓ-diverse. (2) Given any previous release T_i and the current release T_p together, there are at least ℓ distinct sensitive values in the remaining records that could potentially be the victim's record. This requirement can be verified by comparing the difference and intersection of the sensitive values in any two "comparable" *qid* groups in T_i and T_p. The algorithm prefers to specialize T_p as much as possible to improve the data quality, provided that the two privacy requirements are satisfied. If the insertion of some new records would violate any of the privacy requirements, even after generalization, the insertions are delayed until later releases. Nonetheless, this strategy sometimes may run into a situation in which no new data could be released. Also, it requires a very large memory buffer to store the delayed data records.

In this chapter, we study two scenarios of privacy-preserving incremental data publishing: *continuous data publishing* [93] in Chapter 10.2 and *dynamic data republishing* [251] in Chapter 10.3. In continuous data publishing, every release is an "accumulated" version of data at each time instance, which contains all records collected so far. Thus, every data release publishes the "history," i.e., the events that happened up to time of the new release. The model captures the scenario that once a record is collected, it cannot be deleted. In contrast, dynamic data republishing assumes the raw data of any previously records can be inserted, deleted, and updated. A new release contains some new records and some updated records. Every release is the data collected at each time instance. In both cases, the adversary has access to all releases published at each time instance.

Some works misinterpret that Fung et al.'s work [93] allows only records insertion but not records deletion. In fact, T_1 and T_2 can be arbitrary sets of records, not necessarily the result of inserting or deleting records from the other table. The difference is that the work in [93] anonymizes $(T_1 \cup T_2)$ as one release to allow the data analysis on the *whole* data set. In contrast, all other works [251] anonymize each T_i independently, so the publishing model in [251] does not benefit from new data because each T_i is small, resulting in large distortion.

10.2 Continuous Data Publishing

k-anonymization is an important privacy protection mechanism in data publishing. While there has been a great deal of work in recent years, almost all considered a single static release. Such mechanisms only protect the data up to the first release or first recipient. In practical applications, data is published continuously as new data arrive; the same data may be anonymized differently for a different purpose or a different recipient. In such scenarios, even when all releases are properly k-anonymized, the anonymity of an individual may be unintentionally compromised if the recipient cross-examines all the releases received or colludes with other recipients. Preventing such attacks, called *correspondence attacks*, faces major challenges.

Fung et al. [93] show a method to systematically quantify the exact number of records that can be "cracked" by comparing all k-anonymous releases. A record in a k-anonymous release is "cracked" if it is impossible to be a candidate record of the target victim. After excluding the cracked records from a release, a table may no longer be k-anonymous. In some cases, data records, with sensitive information of some victims, can even be uniquely identified from the releases. Fung et al. [93] propose a privacy requirement, called *BCF-anonymity*, to measure the true anonymity in a release after excluding the cracked records, and present a generalization method to achieve BCF-anonymity without delaying record publication or inserting counterfeit records. Note, the traditional k-anonymity does not consider the sensitive values, but BCF-anonymity relies on the sensitive values to determine the cracked records. In Chapter 10.2, we study the correspondence attacks and the BCF-anonymity in details.

10.2.1 Data Model

Suppose that the data holder previously collected a set of records T_1 timestamped t_1, and published a k-anonymized version of T_1, denoted by release R_1. Then the data holder collects a new set of records T_2 timestamped t_2 and wants to publish a k-anonymized version of all records collected so far, $T_1 \cup T_2$, denoted by release R_2. Note, T_i contains the "events" that happened at time t_i. An event, once occurred, becomes part of the history, therefore, cannot be deleted. This *publishing scenario* is different from *update scenario* in standard data management where deletion of records can occur. R_i simply publishes the "history," i.e., the events that happened up to time t_i. A real-life example can be found in California where the hospitals are required to submit specific demographic data of all discharged patients every six months.[1] The above publishing model directly serves the following scenarios.

Continuous data publishing. Publishing the release R_2 for $T_1 \cup T_2$ would permit an analysis on the data over the combined time period of t_1 and t_2. It also takes the advantage of data abundance over a longer period of time to reduce data distortion required by anonymization.

Multi-purpose publishing. With T_2 being empty, R_1 and R_2 can be two releases of T_1 anonymized differently to serve different information needs, such as correlation analysis vs. clustering analysis, or different recipients, such as a medical research team vs. a health insurance company. These recipients may collude together by sharing their received data.

We first describe the publishing model with two releases and then show the extension beyond two releases and beyond k-anonymity in Chapter 10.2.6. Following the convention of k-anonymity [201, 217], we assume that each individual has at most one record in $T_1 \cup T_2$. This assumption holds in many real-life databases. For example, in a normalized customer data table, each customer has only one profile. In the case that an individual has a record in both T_1 and T_2, there will be two duplicates in $T_1 \cup T_2$ and one of them can be removed in a preprocessing.

10.2.2   Correspondence Attacks

We use the following example to illustrate the idea of correspondence attack and show that the traditional k-anonymization is insufficient for preventing correspondence attacks.

Example 10.3
Consider Tables 10.4-10.5 with taxonomy trees in Figure 10.1, where QID is [Birthplace,Job] and the sensitive attribute is Disease. The data holder (e.g., a hospital) published the 5-anonymized R_1 for 5 records a_1-a_5 collected in the previous month (i.e., timestamp t_1). The anonymization was done by generalizing UK and France into Europe; the original values in the brackets are not released. In the current month (i.e., timestamp t_2), the data holder collects 5 new records (i.e., b_6-b_{10}) and publishes the 5-anonymized R_2 for all 10 records collected so far. Records are shuffled to prevent mapping between R_1 and R_2 by their order. The recipients know that every record in R_1 has a "corresponding record" in R_2 because R_2 is a release for $T_1 \cup T_2$. Suppose that one recipient, the *adversary*, tries to identify his neighbor Alice's record from R_1 or R_2, knowing that Alice was admitted to the hospital, as well as Alice's QID and timestamp. Consider the following scenarios with Figure 10.2.

---
[1]http://www.oshpd.ca.gov/HQAD/PatientLevel/

Table 10.4: 5-anonymized R_1

RID	Birthplace	Job	Disease
(a_1)	Europe (UK)	Lawyer	Flu
(a_2)	Europe (UK)	Lawyer	Flu
(a_3)	Europe (UK)	Lawyer	Flu
(a_4)	Europe (France)	Lawyer	HIV
(a_5)	Europe (France)	Lawyer	HIV

Table 10.5: 5-anonymized R_2

RID	Birthplace	Job	Disease
(b_1)	UK	Professional (Lawyer)	Flu
(b_2)	UK	Professional (Lawyer)	Flu
(b_3)	UK	Professional (Lawyer)	Flu
(b_4)	France	Professional (Lawyer)	HIV
(b_5)	France	Professional (Lawyer)	HIV
(b_6)	France	Professional (Lawyer)	HIV
(b_7)	France	Professional (Doctor)	Flu
(b_8)	France	Professional (Doctor)	Flu
(b_9)	UK	Professional (Doctor)	HIV
(b_{10})	UK	Professional (Lawyer)	HIV

Scenario I. Alice has QID=[France, Lawyer] and timestamp t_1. The adversary seeks to identify Alice's record in R_1. Examining R_1 alone, Alice's QID matches all 5 records in R_1. However, examining R_1 and R_2 *together*, the adversary learns that the records a_1,a_2,a_3 cannot all originate from Alice's QID; otherwise R_2 would have contained at least 3 records of [France, Professional, Flu] since every record in R_1 has a corresponding record in R_2. Consequently, the adversary excludes one of a_1,a_2,a_3 as possibility; the choice among a_1,a_2,a_3 does not matter as they are identical. The crossed out record a_2 in Figure 10.2 represents the excluded record.

Scenario II. Alice has QID=[France, Lawyer] and timestamp t_1. Knowing that R_2 contains all records at t_1 and t_2, the adversary seeks to identify Alice's record in R_2. The adversary infers that, among the matching records b_4-b_8 in R_2, at least one of b_4,b_5,b_6 must have timestamp t_2; otherwise b_4,b_5,b_6 would have timestamp t_1, in which case there would have been at least 3 (corresponding) records of the form [Europe, Lawyer, HIV] in R_1. In this case, the adversary excludes at least one of b_4,b_5,b_6 since Alice has timestamp t_1.

FIGURE 10.1: Taxonomy trees for *Birthplace* and *Job*

Scenario I: F-attack Exclude a_2		Scenario II: C-attack Exclude b_6		Scenario III: B-attack Exclude b_2	
(a_1) Flu	HIV (b_4)	(a_1) Flu	HIV (b_4)	(a_1) Flu	Flu (b_1)
~~(a_2) Flu~~	HIV (b_5)	(a_2) Flu	HIV (b_5)	(a_2) Flu	~~Flu (b_2)~~
(a_3) Flu	HIV (b_6)	(a_3) Flu	~~HIV (b_6)~~	(a_3) Flu	Flu (b_3)
(a_4) HIV	Flu (b_7)	(a_4) HIV	Flu (b_7)	(a_4) HIV	Flu (b_7)
(a_5) HIV	Flu (b_8)	(a_5) HIV	Flu (b_8)	(a_5) HIV	Flu (b_8)
					HIV (b_9)
					HIV (b_{10})

FIGURE 10.2: Correspondence attacks

The crossed out record b_6 in Figure 10.2 represents the excluded record.

Scenario III. Alice has QID=[UK, Lawyer] and timestamp t_2 and the adversary seeks to identify Alice's record in R_2. The adversary infers that, among the matching records $b_1, b_2, b_3, b_9, b_{10}$ in R_2, at least one of b_1, b_2, b_3 must have timestamp t_1; otherwise one of a_1, a_2, a_3 would have no corresponding record in R_2. In this case, at least one of b_1, b_2, b_3 is excluded since Alice has timestamp t_2. The crossed out record b_2 in Figure 10.2 represents the excluded record.

In each scenario, at least one matching record is excluded, so the 5-anonymity of Alice is compromised. □

All these attacks "crack" some matching records in R_1 or R_2 by inferring that they either do not originate from Alice's QID or do not have Alice's timestamp. Such cracked records are not related to Alice, thus, excluding them allows the adversary to focus on a smaller set of candidates. Since cracked records are identified by cross-examining R_1 and R_2 and by exploiting the knowledge that every record in R_1 has a "corresponding record" in R_2, such attacks are called *correspondence attacks*.

Having access to only R_1 and R_2, not T_1 and T_2, cracking a record is not straightforward. For example, to crack a record in R_1 for Alice having QID=[France, Lawyer], the adversary must show that the *original* birthplace in the record is not France, whereas the published Europe may or may not originate from France. Similarly, it is not straightforward to infer the timestamp of a record in R_2. For example, any three of b_1, b_2, b_3, b_7, b_8 can be the corresponding records of a_1, a_2, a_3, so none of them must have timestamp t_1. In fact, observing only the published records, there are many possible assignments of corresponding records between R_1 and R_2. For example, one assignment is

(a_1, b_1), (a_2, b_2), (a_3, b_3), (a_4, b_4), (a_5, b_5),

where the original record represented by (a_1, b_1) is [UK, Lawyer, Flu]. Another assignment is

(a_1, b_7), (a_2, b_2), (a_3, b_8), (a_4, b_6), (a_5, b_9).
In this assignment, the original record represented by (a_1, b_7) is [France, Lawyer, Flu]. All such assignments are possible to the adversary because they all produce the same "view," i.e., R_1 and R_2. Detecting correspondence attacks assuming this view of the adversary is non-trivial.

In Chapter 10.2, we formalize the notion of correspondence attacks and present an approach to prevent such attacks. We focus on answering several key questions:

- *Given that there are many possible ways of assigning corresponding pairs, and each may lead to a different inference, what should the adversary assume while cracking a record?* We present a model of correspondence attacks to address this issue and show that the continuous data publishing problem subsumes the case with multiple colluding recipients (Chapter 10.2.3).

- *What are exactly the records that can be cracked based on R_1 and R_2?* We systematically characterize the set of cracked records by correspondence attacks and propose the notion of *BCF-anonymity* to measure anonymity assuming this power of the adversary (Chapter 10.2.4).

- *Can R_2 be anonymized such that R_2 satisfies BCF-anonymity yet remains useful?* We show that the optimal BCF-anonymization is NP-hard. Then, we develop a practically efficient algorithm to determine a BCF-anonymized R_2 (Chapter 10.2.5), and extend the proposed approach to deal with more than two releases (Chapter 10.2.6).

10.2.3 Anonymization Problem for Continuous Publishing

To generalize a table, Fung et al. [93] employ the subtree generalization scheme discussed in Chapter 3.1. A generalized attribute A_j can be represented by a "cut" through its taxonomy tree. R_1 and R_2 in Tables 10.4-10.5 are examples. There are some other generalization schemes, such as multi-dimensional and local recoding, that cause less data distortion, but these schemes make data analysis difficult and suffer from the data exploration problem discussed in Chapter 3.1.

In a *k-anonymized* table, records are partitioned into equivalence classes of size (i.e., the number of records) at least k. Each equivalence class contains all records having the same value on QID. qid denotes both a value on QID and the corresponding equivalence class. $|qid|$ denotes the size of the equivalence class. A *group g* in an equivalence class qid consists of the records in qid that have the same value on the sensitive attribute. In other words, a group contains all records in the table that are indistinguishable with respect to QID and the sensitive attribute. Note that this group notion is different from that of QID groups in the literature, which require only being identical on

QID. A person *matches* a (generalized) record in a table if her QID is either equal to or more specific than the record on every attribute in QID.

The data holder previously collected some data T_1 timestamped t_1 and published a k-anonymized version of T_1, called release R_1. Then the data holder collects new data T_2 timestamped t_2 and publishes a k-anonymized version of $T_1 \cup T_2$, called release R_2. An *adversary*, one of the recipients of R_1 and R_2, attempts to identify the record of some *target* person, denoted by P, from R_1 or R_2. The problem assumes that the adversary is aware of P's QID and timestamp. In addition, the adversary has the following *correspondence knowledge*:

1. Every record timestamped t_1 (i.e., from T_1) has a record in R_1 and a record in R_2, called *corresponding records*.

2. Every record timestamped t_2 (i.e., from T_2) has a record in R_2, but not in R_1. Below is an intuition of the three possible attacks based on such knowledge.

Forward-attack, denoted by F-attack(R_1, R_2). P has timestamp t_1 and the adversary tries to identify P's record in the *cracking release* R_1 using the *background release* R_2. Since P has a record in R_1 and a record in R_2, if a matching record r_1 in R_1 represents P, there must be a corresponding record in R_2 that matches P's QID and agrees with r_1 on the sensitive attribute. If r_1 fails to have such a corresponding record in R_2, then r_1 does not originate from P's QID, and therefore, r_1 can be excluded from the possibility of P's record. Scenario I is an example.

Cross-attack, denoted by C-attack(R_1, R_2). P has timestamp t_1 and the adversary tries to identify P's record in the *cracking release* R_2 using the *background release* R_1. Similar to F-attack, if a matching record r_2 in R_2 represents P, there must be a corresponding record in R_1 that matches P's QID and agrees with r_2 on the sensitive attribute. If r_2 fails to have such a corresponding record in R_1, then r_2 either has timestamp t_2 or does not originate from P's QID, and therefore, r_2 can be excluded from the possibility of P's record. Scenario II is an example.

Backward-attack, denoted by B-attack(R_1, R_2). P has timestamp t_2 and the adversary tries to identify P's record in the *cracking release* R_2 using the *background release* R_1. In this case, P has a record in R_2, but not in R_1. Therefore, if a matching record r_2 in R_2 has to be the corresponding record of some record in R_1, then r_2 has timestamp t_1, and therefore, r_2 can be excluded from the possibility of P's record. Scenario III is an example. Note that it is impossible to single out the matching records in R_2 that have timestamp t_2 but do not originate from P's QID since all records at t_2 have no corresponding record in R_1.

Table 10.6 summarizes all four possible combinations of cracking release (R_1 or R_2) and target P's timestamp (t_1 or t_2). Note that if a target P has

Table 10.6:   Types of correspondence attacks

	Target P's timestamp	Cracking release	Background release
F-attack	t_1	R_1	R_2
C-attack	t_1	R_2	R_1
B-attack	t_2	R_2	R_1
No attack	t_2	R_1	R_2

timestamp t_2, P does not have a record in R_1, so it is impossible to crack P's record in R_1 in such a case and there are only three types of attacks.

All these attacks are based on making some inferences about corresponding records. There are many possible assignments of corresponding records that are consistent with the published view R_1 and R_2, and the adversary's knowledge. Each assignment implies a possibly different underlying data (D'_1, D'_2), not necessarily the *actual* underlying data (T_1, T_2) collected by the data holder. Since all such underlying data (D'_1, D'_2) generate the same published R_1 and R_2, they are all possible to the adversary who knows about the data only through the published R_1 and R_2. This observation suggests that we should consider only the inferences that do not depend on a particular choice of a candidate (D'_1, D'_2). First, let us define the space of such candidates underlying data for the published R_1 and R_2.

Consider a record r in R_1 or R_2. An *instantiation* of r is a raw record that agrees with r on the sensitive attribute and specializes r or agrees with r on QID. A *generator* of (R_1, R_2) is an assignment, denoted by I, from the records in $R_1 \cup R_2$ to their instantiations such that: for each record r_1 in R_1, there is a distinct record r_2 in R_2 such that $I(r_1) = I(r_2)$; (r_1, r_2) is called *buddies* under I. Duplicate records are treated as distinct records. The buddy relationship is *injective*: no two records have the same buddy. Every record in R_1 has a buddy in R_2 and exactly $|R_1|$ records in R_2 have a buddy in R_1. If r_2 in R_2 has a buddy in R_1, $I(r_2)$ has timestamp t_1; otherwise $I(r_2)$ has timestamp t_2. Intuitively, a generator represents an underlying data for (R_1, R_2) and each pair of buddies represent corresponding records in the generator.

Example 10.4
Refer to R_1 and R_2 in Table 10.4 and Table 10.5. One generator has the buddies:

(a_1, b_1), assigned to [UK, Lawyer, Flu]
(a_2, b_2), assigned to [UK, Lawyer, Flu]
(a_3, b_3), assigned to [UK, Lawyer, Flu]
(a_4, b_4), assigned to [France, Lawyer, HIV]
(a_5, b_5), assigned to [France, Lawyer, HIV]

$I(b_1)$-$I(b_5)$ have timestamp t_1. b_6-b_{10} can be assigned to any instantiation.

Another generator has the buddies:

(a_1, b_7), assigned to [France, Lawyer, Flu]
(a_2, b_2), assigned to [UK, Lawyer, Flu]
(a_3, b_8), assigned to [France, Lawyer, Flu]
(a_4, b_9), assigned to [UK, Lawyer, HIV]
(a_5, b_{10}), assigned to [UK, Lawyer, HIV]

$I(b_2)$, $I(b_7)$-$I(b_{10})$ have timestamp t_1.

Another generator has the buddies:

(a_1, b_7), assigned to [France, Lawyer, Flu]
(a_2, b_2), assigned to [UK, Lawyer, Flu]
(a_3, b_8), assigned to [France, Lawyer, Flu]
(a_4, b_6), assigned to [France, Lawyer, HIV]
(a_5, b_9), assigned to [UK, Lawyer, HIV]

$I(b_2)$, $I(b_6)$-$I(b_9)$ have timestamp t_1. Note that these generators give different underlying data. □

Consider a record r in R_1 or R_2. Suppose that for *some* generator I, the instantiation $I(r)$ matches P's QID and timestamp. In this case, excluding r means information loss for the purpose of attack because there is some underlying data for (R_1, R_2) (given by I) in which r is P's record. On the other hand, suppose that for *no* generator I the instantiation $I(r)$ can match P's QID and timestamp. Then r *definitely* cannot be P's record, so excluding r losses no information to the adversary. The attack model presented in [93] is based on excluding such non-representing records.

For a target P with timestamp t_1, if P has a record in R_1, P must match some qid_1 in R_1 and some qid_2 in R_2. Therefore, we assume such a matching pair (qid_1, qid_2) for P. Recall that a group g_i in an equivalence class qid_i consists of the records in qid_i that agree on the sensitive attribute. For a generator I, $I(g_i)$ denotes the set of records $\{I(r_i) \mid r_i \in g_i\}$. Below, we present the formal definition for each type of attacks. r_i, g_i, qid_i refer to records, groups, and equivalence classes from R_i, $i = 1, 2$.

10.2.3.1   F-attack

The F-attack seeks to identify as many as possible records in an equivalence class qid_1 that do not represent P in *any* choice of the generator. Such *cracked records* definitely cannot be P's record, and therefore can be excluded. Since all records in a group are identical, the choice of cracked records in a group does not make a difference and determining the number of cracked records (i.e., the crack size) is sufficient to define the attack.

DEFINITION 10.1 Crack size   Assume that a target P has timestamp t_1 and matches (qid_1, qid_2). A group g_1 in qid_1 has *crack size* c with respect to P if c is maximal such that for every generator I, at least c records in $I(g_1)$ do not match P's QID. ∎

If g_1 has crack size c, at least c records in g_1 can be excluded from the possibility of P's record. On the other hand, with c being maximal, excluding more than c records will result in excluding some record that can possibly be P's record. Therefore, the crack size is both the minimum and the maximum number of records that can be excluded from g_1 without any information loss for the purpose of attack.

Example 10.5
Consider Scenario I in Example 10.3. Alice has QID=[France, Lawyer] and matches (qid_1, qid_2), where

$$qid_1 = [\text{Europe, Lawyer}] = \{a_1, a_2, a_3, a_4, a_5\}$$
$$qid_2 = [\text{France, Professional}] = \{b_4, b_5, b_6, b_7, b_8\}.$$

qid_1 has two groups: $g_1 = \{a_1, a_2, a_3\}$ for Flu and $g_1' = \{a_4, a_5\}$ for HIV. g_1 has crack size 1 with respect to Alice because, for any generator I, at least one of $I(a_1), I(a_2), I(a_3)$ does not match Alice's QID: if all of $I(a_1), I(a_2), I(a_3)$ match Alice's QID, R_2 would have contained three buddies of the form [France, Professional, Flu]. The crack size is maximal since the second generator I in Example 10.4 shows that only one of $I(a_1), I(a_2), I(a_3)$ (e.g., $I(a_2)$ in Figure 10.2) does not match Alice's QID. □

Definition 10.1 does not explain *how* to effectively determine the crack size, which is the topic in Chapter 10.2.4. For now, assuming that the crack size is known, we want to measure the anonymity after excluding the cracked records from each equivalence class. The F-anonymity below measures the minimum size of an equivalence class in R_1 after excluding all records cracked by F-attack.

DEFINITION 10.2 F-anonymity   Let $F(P, qid_1, qid_2)$ be the sum of the crack sizes for all groups in qid_1 with respect to P. $F(qid_1, qid_2)$ denotes the maximum $F(P, qid_1, qid_2)$ for any target P that matches (qid_1, qid_2). $F(qid_1)$ denotes the maximum $F(qid_1, qid_2)$ for all qid_2 in R_2. The *F-anonymity* of (R_1, R_2), denoted by $FA(R_1, R_2)$ or FA, is the minimum $(|qid_1| - F(qid_1))$ for all qid_1 in R_1. ∎

10.2.3.2 C-attack

DEFINITION 10.3 Crack size   Assume that a target P has timestamp t_1 and matches (qid_1, qid_2). A group g_2 in qid_2 has *crack size* c with respect to P if c is maximal such that for every generator I, at least c records in $I(g_2)$ do not match either P's timestamp or P's QID. ∎

Example 10.6
Consider Scenario II in Example 10.3. Alice has $QID=$[France, Lawyer] and matches (qid_1, qid_2) where

$$qid_1 = [\text{Europe, Lawyer}] = \{a_1, a_2, a_3, a_4, a_5\}$$
$$qid_2 = [\text{France, Professional}] = \{b_4, b_5, b_6, b_7, b_8\}.$$

qid_2 has two groups: $g_2 = \{b_7, b_8\}$ for Flu, and $g_2' = \{b_4, b_5, b_6\}$ for HIV. g_2' has crack size 1 with respect to Alice since, for any generator I at least one of $I(b_4), I(b_5), I(b_6)$ does not match Alice's timestamp or QID; otherwise, R_1 would have contained three buddies of the form [Europe, Lawyer, HIV]. The crack size is maximal since the first generator I in Example 10.4 shows that $I(b_4)$ and $I(b_5)$ match Alice's timestamp and QID. b_6 is excluded in Figure 10.2. □

DEFINITION 10.4 C-anonymity   Let $C(P, qid_1, qid_2)$ be the sum of crack sizes of all groups in qid_2 with respect to P. $C(qid_1, qid_2)$ denotes the maximum $C(P, qid_1, qid_2)$ for any target P that matches (qid_1, qid_2). $C(qid_2)$ denotes the maximum $C(qid_1, qid_2)$ for all qid_1 in R_1. The *C-anonymity of* (R_1, R_2), denoted by $CA(R_1, R_2)$ or CA, is the minimum $(|qid_2| - C(qid_2))$ for all qid_2 in R_2. ∎

10.2.3.3 B-attack

A target P for B-attack has timestamp t_2, thus, does not have to match any qid_1 in R_1.

DEFINITION 10.5 Crack size   Assume that a target P has timestamp t_2 and matches qid_2 in R_2. A group g_2 in qid_2 has *crack size* c with respect to P if c is maximal such that for every generator I, at least c records in $I(g_2)$ have timestamp t_1.

Example 10.7
Consider Scenario III in Example 10.3. Alice has timestamp t_2 and $QID=$[UK, Lawyer]. $qid_2=$[UK, Professional] consists of $g_2 = \{b_1, b_2, b_3\}$ for Flu and $g_2' = \{b_9, b_{10}\}$ for HIV. g_2 has crack size 1 with respect to Alice. For every

generator I, at least one of $I(b_1),I(b_2),I(b_3)$ has timestamp t_1; otherwise, one of a_1,a_2,a_3 would have no buddy in R_2. The crack size is maximal since the second generator I in Example 10.4 shows that only $I(b_2)$ in Figure 10.2, among $I(b_1),I(b_2),I(b_3)$, has timestamp t_1. □

DEFINITION 10.6 B-anonymity   Let $B(P,qid_2)$ be the sum of the crack sizes of all groups in qid_2 with respect to P. $B(qid_2)$ denotes the maximum $B(P,qid_2)$ for any target P that matches qid_2. The *B-anonymity* of (R_1,R_2), denoted by $BA(R_1,R_2)$ or BA, is the minimum $(|qid_2| - B(qid_2))$ for all qid_2 in R_2.

10.2.3.4   Detection and Anonymization Problems

A *BCF-anonymity requirement* states that *all* of BA, CA and FA are equal to or larger than some data-holder-specified threshold. We study two problems. The first problem checks whether a BCF-anonymity requirement is satisfied, assuming the input (i.e., R_1 and R_2) as viewed by the adversary.

DEFINITION 10.7 Detection   Given R_1 and R_2, as described above, the *BCF-detection problem* is to determine whether a BCF-anonymity requirement is satisfied. ∎

The second problem is to produce a generalized R_2 that satisfies a given BCF-anonymity requirement and remains useful. This problem assumes the input as viewed by the data holder, that is, R_1, T_1 and T_2, and uses an information metric to measure the usefulness of the generalized R_2. Examples are *discernibility cost* [213] and *data distortion* [203].

DEFINITION 10.8 Anonymization   Given R_1, T_1 and T_2, as described above, the *BCF-anonymization problem* is to generalize $R_2 = T_1 \cup T_2$ so that R_2 satisfies a given BCF-anonymity requirement and remains as useful as possible with respect to a specified information metric. ∎

In the special case of empty T_1, F-attack and C-attack do not happen and B-anonymity coincides with k-anonymity of R_2 for T_2. Since the optimal k-anonymization is NP-hard [168], the optimal BCF-anonymization is NP-hard.

So far, the problem assumes that both R_1 and R_2 are received by one recipient. In the special case of empty T_2, R_1 and R_2 are two different generalized versions of the same data T_1 to serve different information requirements or different recipients. In this case, there are potentially multiple adversaries. What happens if the adversaries collude together? The collusion problem may seem to be very different. Indeed, Definitions 10.7-10.8 subsume the collusion problem. Consider the worst-case collusion scenario in which *all* recipients collude together by sharing *all* of their received data. This scenario is equivalent to publishing all releases to one adversary.

10.2.4 Detection of Correspondence Attacks

The key to the BCF-detection problem is computing the crack size in Definitions 10.1, 10.3, 10.5. Fung et al. [93] present a method for computing the crack size of a group. Their insight is that if a record r represents the target P for some generator, its buddy in the other release (i.e., the corresponding record) must satisfy some conditions. If such conditions fail, r does not represent P for that generator. One of the conditions is the following "comparable" relationship.

DEFINITION 10.9   For qid_1 in R_1 and qid_2 in R_2, (qid_1, qid_2) are *comparable* if for every attribute A in QID, $qid_1[A]$ and $qid_2[A]$ are on the same path in the taxonomy of A. For a record in r_1 (or a group) in qid_1 and a record r_2 (or a group) in qid_2, (r_1, r_2) are *comparable* if they agree on the sensitive attribute and (qid_1, qid_2) are comparable. For comparable (qid_1, qid_2), $CG(qid_1, qid_2)$ denotes the set of group pairs $\{(g_1, g_2)\}$, where g_1 and g_2 are groups in qid_1 and qid_2 for the same sensitive value and there is one pair (g_1, g_2) for each sensitive value (unless both g_1 and g_2 are empty). ∎

Essentially, being comparable means sharing a common instantiation. For example, $qid_1 = $ [Europe, Lawyer] and $qid_2 = $ [UK, Professional] are comparable, but $qid_1 = $ [Europe, Lawyer] and $qid_2 = $ [Canada, Professional] are not. It is easy to see that if a target P matches (qid_1, qid_2), (qid_1, qid_2) are comparable; if (r_1, r_2) are buddies (for some generator), (r_1, r_2) are comparable; comparable (r_1, r_2) can be assigned to be buddies (because of sharing a common instantiation). The following fact can be verified:

THEOREM 10.1
Suppose that P matches (qid_1, qid_2) and that (r_1, r_2) are buddies for a generator I. If $I(r_1)$ and $I(r_2)$ match P's QID, then r_1 is in g_1 if and only if r_2 is in g_2, where (g_1, g_2) is in $CG(qid_1, qid_2)$. ∎

Theorem 10.1 follows because buddies agree on the sensitive attribute and $I(r_1)$ and $I(r_2)$ matching P's QID implies that r_1 is in qid_1 and r_2 is in qid_2. The next two lemmas are used to derive an upper bound on crack size. The first states some transitivity of the "comparable" relationship, which will be used to construct a required generator in the upper bound proof.

LEMMA 10.1 3-hop transitivity
Let r_1, r_1' be in R_1 and r_2, r_2' be in R_2. If each of (r_1', r_2), (r_2, r_1), and (r_1, r_2')

is comparable, (r_1', r_2') is comparable.

PROOF   See [93].   □

The following is the key lemma for proving the upper bound of crack size.

LEMMA 10.2
Let (g_1, g_2) be in $CG(qid_1, qid_2)$. There exists a generator in which exactly $min(|g_1|, |g_2|)$ records in g_1 have a buddy in g_2.

PROOF   See [93].   □

Below, we show how to determine the crack size for F-attack. For C-attack and B-attack, we use examples to illustrate the general. Refer to [93] for the details for determining the crack sizes of C-attack and B-attack.

10.2.4.1   F-attack

Assume that P matches (qid_1, qid_2). Consider a group pair (g_1, g_2) in $CG(qid_1, qid_2)$. Since the buddy relationship is injective, if g_1 contains more records than g_2, i.e., $|g_1| > min(|g_1|, |g_2|)$, at least $|g_1| - min(|g_1|, |g_2|)$ records in g_1 do not have a buddy in g_2 for *any* generator. According to Theorem 10.1, these records do not originate from P's QID for any generator. Thus the crack size of g_1 is at least $|g_1| - min(|g_1|, |g_2|)$ (i.e., a lower bound). On the other hand, according to Lemma 10.2, there exists *some* generator in which *exactly* $|g_1| - min(|g_1|, |g_2|)$ records in g_1 do not have a buddy in g_2; according to Theorem 10.1, these records do not originate from P's QID for any generator. By Definition 10.1, $|g_1| - min(|g_1|, |g_2|)$ is the crack size of g_1.

THEOREM 10.2
Suppose that a target P matches (qid_1, qid_2). Let (g_1, g_2) be in $CG(qid_1, qid_2)$. (1) g_1 has crack size c with respect to P, where $c = |g_1| - min(|g_1|, |g_2|)$. (2) $F(qid_1, qid_2) = \sum c$, where $\sum$ is over (g_1, g_2) in $CG(qid_1, qid_2)$ and g_1 has the crack size c determined in (1).

Remarks. $F(P, qid_1, qid_2)$ is the same for all targets P that match (qid_1, qid_2), i.e., $F(qid_1, qid_2)$ computed by Theorem 10.2. To compute FA, we compute $F(qid_1, qid_2)$ for all comparable (qid_1, qid_2). This requires partitioning the records into equivalence classes and groups, which can be done by sorting the records on all attributes. The F-attack happens when $|g_1| > min(|g_1|, |g_2|)$, that is, g_1 contains too many records for their buddies to be contained in g_2. This could be the case if R_2 has less generalization due to additional records at timestamp t_2.

Example 10.8

Continue with Example 10.5. Alice matches qid_1=[Europe, Lawyer] and qid_2=[France, Professional]. qid_1 consists of $g_1 = \{a_1, a_2, a_3\}$ for Flu and $g_1' = \{a_4, a_5\}$ for HIV. qid_2 consists of $g_2 = \{b_7, b_8\}$ for Flu and $g_2' = \{b_4, b_5, b_6\}$ for HIV. $CG(qid_1, qid_2) = \{(g_1, g_2), (g_1', g_2')\}$. $|g_1| = 3$, $|g_2| = 2$, $|g_1'| = 2$ and $|g_2'| = 3$. So, g_1 has crack size 1 and g_1' has crack size 0. $\qquad\square$

10.2.4.2 C-attack

By a similar argument, at least $|g_2| - min(|g_1|, |g_2|)$ records in g_2 do not have a buddy in g_1 in *any* generator, so the crack size of g_2 is at least $|g_2| - min(|g_1|, |g_2|)$.

THEOREM 10.3

Suppose that a target P matches (qid_1, qid_2). Let (g_1, g_2) be in $CG(qid_1, qid_2)$. (1) g_2 has crack size c with respect to P, where $c = |g_2| - min(|g_1|, |g_2|)$. (2) $C(qid_1, qid_2) = \sum c$, where $\sum$ is over (g_1, g_2) in $CG(qid_1, qid_2)$ and g_2 has the crack size c determined in (1).

Example 10.9

Continue with Example 10.6. Alice matches qid_1=[Europe, Lawyer] and qid_2=[France, Professional]. qid_1 consists of $g_1 = \{a_1, a_2, a_3\}$ and $g_1' = \{a_4, a_5\}$. qid_2 consists of $g_2 = \{b_7, b_8\}$ and $g_2' = \{b_4, b_5, b_6\}$. $CG(qid_1, qid_2) = \{(g_1, g_2), (g_1', g_2')\}$. $|g_2| = 2$, $|g_1| = 3$, $|g_2'| = 3$ and $|g_1'| = 2$. Thus g_2 has crack size 0 and g_2' has crack size 1. $\qquad\square$

10.2.4.3 B-attack

Suppose that P matches some qid_2 in R_2. Let g_2 be a group in qid_2. The crack size of g_2 is related to the number of records in g_2 that have a buddy in R_1 (thus timestamp t_1). Let G_1 denote the set of records in R_1 comparable to g_2. So G_1 contains all the records in R_1 that *can* have a buddy in g_2. Let G_2 denote the set of records in R_2 comparable to some record in G_1. The next lemma implies that all records in G_1 *can* have a buddy in $G_2 - g_2$.

LEMMA 10.3

Every record in G_2 is comparable to all records in G_1 and only those records in G_1.

From Lemma 10.3, all records in G_1 and only those records in G_1 can have a buddy in G_2. Each record in G_1 has its buddy either in g_2 or in $G_2 - g_2$, but not in both. If $|G_1| > |G_2| - |g_2|$, the remaining $c = |G_1| - (|G_2| - |g_2|)$ records in G_1 must have their buddies in g_2, or equivalently, c records in g_2

must have their buddies in R_1 (therefore, timestamp t_1). The next theorem follows from this observation.

THEOREM 10.4

Suppose that a target P has timestamp t_2 and matches qid_2 in R_2. Let g_2 in qid_2. (1) If $|G_2| < |g_2|$, g_2 has crack size 0 with respect to P. (2) If $|G_2| \geq |g_2|$, g_2 has crack size c, where $c = max(0, |G_1| - (|G_2| - |g_2|))$. (3) $B(qid_2) = \sum c$, where $\sum$ is over g_2 in qid_2 and g_2 has the crack size c determined in (1) and (2).

Example 10.10

Continue with Example 10.7. Alice has [UK, Lawyer] and timestamp t_2. $qid_2 =$ [UK, Professional] has g_2 for Flu and g_2' for HIV:

$$g_2 = \{b_1, b_2, b_3\}$$
$$G_1 = \{a_1, a_2, a_3\}$$
$$G_2 = \{b_1, b_2, b_3, b_7, b_8\}$$
$$|G_1| - (|G_2| - |g_2|) = 3 - (5 - 3) = 1$$

$$g_2' = \{b_9, b_{10}\}$$
$$G_1 = \{a_4, a_5\}$$
$$G_2 = \{b_4, b_5, b_6, b_9, b_{10}\}$$
$$|G_1| - (|G_2| - |g_2'|) = 2 - (5 - 2) = -1$$

Thus g_2 has crack size 1 and g_2' has crack size 0.   □

10.2.4.4   Equivalence of F-attack and C-attack

F-attack and C-attack are motivated under different scenarios and have a different characterization of crack size. Despite such differences, we show that these attacks are not independent of each other at all; in fact, $FA = CA$. Refer to [93] for a formal proof.

10.2.5   Anonymization Algorithm for Correspondence Attacks

An algorithm called *BCF-anonymizer* for anonymizing R_2 to satisfy all of $FA \geq k, CA \geq k, BA \geq k$ can be found in [93]. BCF-anonymizer iteratively specializes R_2 starting from the *most generalized state* of R_2. In the most generalized state, all values for each attribute $A_j \in QID$ are generalized to the top most value in the taxonomy. Each *specialization*, for some attribute in QID, replaces a parent value with an appropriate child value in every record containing the parent value. The top-down specialization approach relies on the *anti-monotonicity* property of BCF-anonymity: FA, CA, and BA are non-

---

Algorithm 10.2.6 BCF-Anonymizer

Input: R_1, $R_2 = T_1 \cup T_2$, k, taxonomy for each $A_j \in QID$.
Output: a BCF-anonymized R_2.

1: generalize every value for $A_j \in QID$ in R_2 to ANY_j;
2: let candidate list $= \cup Cut2_j$ containing all ANY_j;
3: sort candidate list by *Score* in descending order;
4: **while** the candidate list is not empty **do**
5:    **if** the first candidate w in candidate list is valid **then**
6:       specialize w into $w_1, \ldots, w_z$ in R_2;
7:       compute *Score* for all w_i;
8:       remove w from $\cup Cut2_j$ and the candidate list;
9:       add $w_1, \ldots, w_z$ to $\cup Cut2_j$ and the candidate list;
10:       sort the candidate list by *Score* in descending order;
11:    **else**
12:       remove w from the candidate list;
13:    **end if**
14: **end while**
15: output R_2 and $\cup Cut2_j$;

---

increasing in this specialization process. Therefore, all further specializations can be pruned once any of the above requirements are violated.

THEOREM 10.5

Each of FA, CA and BA is non-increasing with respect to a specialization on R_2.

According to Theorem 10.5, if the most generalized R_2 does not satisfy $FA \geq k$, $CA \geq k$, and $BA \geq k$, no generalized R_2 does. Therefore, we can first check if the most generalized R_2 satisfies this requirement before searching for a less generalized R_2 satisfying the requirement.

COROLLARY 10.1

For a given requirement on BCF-anonymity, there exists a generalized R_2 that satisfies the requirement if and only if the most generalized R_2 does. ■

Below, we study the general idea of an efficient algorithm for producing a locally maximal specialized R_2.

Finding an optimal BCF-anonymized R_2 is NP-hard. BCF-anonymizer, summarized in Algorithm 10.2.6, aims at producing a maximally specialized (suboptimal) BCF-anonymized R_2 which any further specialization leads to a violation. It starts with the most generalized R_2. At any time, R_2 contains the generalized records of $T_1 \cup T_2$ and $Cut2_j$ gives the generalization cut for

$A_j \in QID$. Each equivalence class qid_2 in R_2 is associated with a set of groups g_2 with stored $|g_2|$. Each group g_2 is associated with the set of raw records in $T_1 \cup T_2$ generalized to the group. R_1 is represented similarly with $|qid_1|$ and $|g_1|$ stored, except that no raw record is kept for g_1. $Cut1_j$ contains the generalization cut $A_j \in QID$ in R_1. $Cut1_j$ never change once created.

Initially, $\cup Cut2_j$ and the candidate list contain the most general value ANY_j for every $A_j \in QID$ (Lines 1-3). In each iteration, BCF-anonymizer examines the first valid candidate specialization ranked by a criterion *Score*. If the candidate w is *valid*, that is, not violating the BCF-anonymity after its specialization, we specialize w on R_2 (Lines 6-10); otherwise, we remove w from the candidate list (Line 12). This iteration is repeated until there is no more candidate. From Theorem 10.5, the returned R_2 is maximal (suboptimal). Similar to the top-down specialization approaches studied in previous chapters, *Score* ranks the candidates by their "information worth." We employ the discernibility cost DM (Chapter 4.1) which charges a penalty to each record for being indistinguishable from other records.

In general, Lines 5-7 require scanning all pairs (qid_1, qid_2) and all records in R_2, which is highly inefficient for a large data set. Fung et al. [93] present an incremental computation of FA, CA, and BA that examines only comparable pairs (qid_1, qid_2) and raw records in R_2 that are *involved* in the current specialization.

10.2.6 Beyond Two Releases

Fung et al. [93] also extend the two-release case to the general case involving more than two releases. Consider the raw data $T_1, \ldots, T_n$ collected at timestamp $t_1, \ldots, t_n$. Let R_i denote the release for $T_1 \cup \cdots \cup T_i$, $1 \leq i \leq n$. All records in R_i have the special timestamp, denoted by T_i^*, that matches *any* timestamp from $t_1, \ldots, t_i$. The correspondence knowledge now has the form that every record in R_i (except the last one) has a corresponding record in all releases R_j such that $j > i$. The notion of "generators" can take this into account. Given more releases, the adversary can conduct two additional types of correspondence attacks described below.

Optimal micro attacks: The general idea is to choose the "best" background release, yielding the largest possible crack size, *individually* to crack each group.

Composition of micro attacks: Another type of attack is to "compose" multiple micro attacks together (apply *one after another*) in order to increase the crack size of a group. Composition is possible *only if* all the micro attacks in the composition assume the same timestamp for the target and the correspondence knowledge required for the next attack holds after applying previous attacks.

The anonymization algorithm can be extended as follows to handle multiple releases.

1. The notion of BCF-anonymity should be defined based on the optimal crack size of a group with respect to micro attacks as well as composed attacks on the group.

2. Each time we anonymize the next release R_n for $T_1 \cup \cdots \cup T_n$, we assume that $R_1, \ldots, R_{n-1}$ satisfy BCF-anonymity. Hence, the anonymization of R_n only needs to ensure that BCF-anonymity is not violated by any attack that *involves* R_n.

3. The anti-monotonicity of BCF-anonymity, in the spirit of Theorem 10.5, remains valid in this general case. These observations are crucial for maintaining the efficiency.

As the number of releases increases, the constraints imposed on the next release R_n become increasingly restrictive. However, this does not necessarily require more distortion because the new records T_n may help reduce the need of distortion. In case the distortion becomes too severe, the data holder may consider starting a new chain of releases without including previously published records.

10.2.7 Beyond Anonymity

The presented detection and anonymization methods can be extended to thwart attribute linkages by incorporating with other privacy models, such as entropy ℓ-diversity and (c,ℓ)-diversity in Chapter 2.2.1, confidence bounding in Chapter 2.2.2, and (α,k)-anonymity in Chapter 2.2.5. The first modification is to take the privacy requirements into account to the exclusion of cracked records. In this case, the crack size of each group gives all the information needed to exclude sensitive values from an equivalence class. For the extension of the anonymization algorithm, anonymity is a *necessary* privacy property because identifying the exact record of an individual from a small set of records is too easy. Thus, BCF-anonymity is required even if other privacy requirements are desired. Under this assumption, the proposed approach is still applicable to prune unpromising specializations based on the anti-monotonicity of BCF-anonymity.

10.3 Dynamic Data Republishing

Xiao and Tao [251] study the privacy issues in the *dynamic data republishing model*, in which both record insertions and deletions may be performed before every release. They also present a privacy model and an anonymization method for the dynamic data republishing model. The following example [251] illustrates the privacy threats in this scenario.

Table 10.7:   Raw data T_1

Not release	Quasi-identifier (QID)		Sensitive
Rec ID	**Age**	**Salary**	**Surgery**
1	31	22K	Transgender
2	32	24K	Plastic
3	34	28K	Vascular
4	33	35K	Urology
5	51	30K	Vascular
6	46	37K	Urology
7	47	43K	Transgender
8	50	45K	Vascular
9	53	36K	Urology
10	62	43K	Transgender
11	66	44K	Urology

Table 10.8:   2-anonymous and 2-diverse R_1

Not release	Quasi-identifier (QID)		Sensitive
Rec ID	**Age**	**Salary**	**Surgery**
1	[31-32]	[22K-24K]	Transgender
2	[31-32]	[22K-24K]	Plastic
3	[33-34]	[28K-35K]	Vascular
4	[33-34]	[28K-35K]	Urology
5	[46-51]	[30K-37K]	Vascular
6	[46-51]	[30K-37K]	Urology
7	[47-53]	[36K-45K]	Transgender
8	[47-53]	[36K-45K]	Vascular
9	[47-53]	[36K-45K]	Urology
10	[62-66]	[43K-44K]	Transgender
11	[62-66]	[43K-44K]	Urology

10.3.1   Privacy Threats

Example 10.11

A hospital wants to periodically, say every three months, publish the *current* patient's records. Let T_1 (Table 10.7) be the raw data of the first release. *Rec ID* is for discussion only, not for release. $QID = \{Age, Salary\}$ and *Surgery* is sensitive. The hospital generalizes T_1 and publishes R_1 (Table 10.8). Then, during the next three months, records # 2, 3, 6, 8, and 10 are deleted, and new records # 12-16 are added. The updated raw data table T_2 is shown in Table 10.9, where the new records are bolded. The hospital then generalizes T_2 and publishes a new release R_2 (Table 10.10). Though both R_1 and R_2 are individually 2-anonymous and 2-diverse, an adversary can still identify the sensitive value of some patients.

Suppose an adversary has targeted a victim, Annie, and knows that Annie is 31 years old and has salary 22K as background knowledge. Based on generalized R_1, the adversary can determine that Annie's received surgery is either *Transgender* or *Plastic* because records # 1 and 2 are the only records matching the background knowledge. Based on the generalized R_2, the adversary can determine that Annie's received surgery is either *Transgender* or *Urology*. Thus, by combining the aforementioned knowledge, the adversary can correctly infer that Annie's received surgery is *Transgender*. $\qquad\Box$

The above illustrated privacy threats cannot be resolved by generalizations because the value *Plastic* is absent in T_2; therefore, the adversary can infer that Annie's received surgery is *Transgender* no matter how T_2 is generalized. This problem is called *critical absence* [251].

One naive solution to tackle the problem of critical absence is to let the deleted records remain in the subsequent releases and use them to disorient the inferences by the adversary. Yet, this strategy implies that the number of records increases monotonically in every release while many records are no longer relevant for that period of time. Also, keeping the deleted records may not necessarily provide the privacy guarantee as expected if an adversary is aware of the records' deletion timestamps [251].

10.3.2   *m*-invariance

To address both record insertions and deletions in this dynamic data republishing model, Xiao and Tao [251] propose a privacy model called *m-invariance*. A sequence of releases $R_1, \ldots, R_p$ is *m*-invariant if (1) every *qid* group in any R_i contains at least *m* records and all records in *qid* have different sensitive values, and (2) for any record r with published lifespan $[x, y]$ where $1 \leq x, y \leq p$, $qid_x, \ldots, qid_y$ have the same set of sensitive values where $qid_x, \ldots, qid_y$ are the generalized *qid* groups containing r in $R_x, \ldots, R_y$. The rationale of *m*-invariance is that, if a record r has been published in $R_x, \ldots, R_y$, then all *qid* groups containing r must have the same set of sensitive values. This will ensure that the intersection of sensitive values over all such *qid* groups does not reduce the set of sensitive values compared to each *qid* group. Thus, the above mentioned critical absence does not occur.

Note, (2) does not guarantee the privacy if the life span is "broken," not continuous. In this case, the two broken lifespan is never checked for privacy guarantee. In other words, the model assumes that a record cannot reappear after its first lifespan; however, this assumption may not be realistic. For example, a patient got some diseases over several releases and recovered, and later on got other diseases again. Consequently, his records will appear in multiple, broken time intervals.

Given a sequence of *m*-invariant $R_1, \ldots, R_{p-1}$, Xiao and Tao [251] maintain a sequence of *m*-invariant $R_1, \ldots, R_p$ by minimally adding counterfeit

Table 10.9: Raw data T_2

Not release	Quasi-identifier (QID)		Sensitive
Rec ID	**Age**	**Salary**	**Surgery**
1	31	22K	Transgender
4	33	35K	Urology
12	**25**	**31K**	**Vascular**
7	47	43K	Transgender
9	53	36K	Urology
5	51	30K	Vascular
13	**56**	**40K**	**Urology**
14	**64**	**41K**	**Transgender**
11	66	44K	Urology
15	**70**	**54K**	**Urology**
16	**75**	**46K**	**Vascular**

Table 10.10: 2-anonymous and 2-diverse R_2

Not release	Quasi-identifier (QID)		Sensitive
Rec ID	**Age**	**Salary**	**Surgery**
1	[31-33]	[22K-35K]	Transgender
4	[31-33]	[22K-35K]	Urology
12	[35-53]	[31K-43K]	Vascular
7	[35-53]	[31K-43K]	Transgender
9	[35-53]	[31K-43K]	Urology
5	[51-56]	[30K-40K]	Vascular
13	[51-56]	[30K-40K]	Urology
14	[64-66]	[41K-44K]	Transgender
11	[64-66]	[41K-44K]	Urology
15	[70-75]	[46K-54K]	Urology
16	[70-75]	[46K-54K]	Vascular

data records and generalizing the current release R_p. The following example illustrates the general idea of counterfeited generalization.

Example 10.12
Let us revisit Example 10.11, where the hospital has published R_1 (Table 10.8) and wants to anonymize T_2 for the second release R_2. Following the method of counterfeited generalization [251], R_2 contains two tables:

1. The generalized data table (Table 10.11) with 2 counterfeits c_1 and c_2. An adversary cannot tell whether a record is counterfeit or real.

2. The auxiliary table (Table 10.12), indicating the *qid* group $\langle$ *[31-32], [22K-24K]* $\rangle$ contains 1 counterfeit, and the *qid* group $\langle$ *[47-53], [36K-43K]* $\rangle$ contains 1 counterfeit. The objective of providing such additional information is to improve the effectiveness of data analysis.

Table 10.11: R_2 by counterfeited generalization

Not release	*Quasi-identifier (QID)*		*Sensitive*
Rec ID	**Age**	**Salary**	**Surgery**
1	[31-32]	[22K-24K]	Transgender
c_1	[31-32]	[22K-24K]	Plastic
4	[33-35]	[31K-35K]	Urology
12	[33-35]	[31K-35K]	Vascular
7	[47-53]	[36K-43K]	Transgender
c_2	[47-53]	[36K-43K]	Vascular
9	[47-53]	[36K-43K]	Urology
5	[51-56]	[30K-40K]	Vascular
13	[51-56]	[30K-40K]	Urology
14	[64-66]	[41K-44K]	Transgender
11	[64-66]	[41K-44K]	Urology
15	[70-75]	[46K-54K]	Urology
16	[70-75]	[46K-54K]	Vascular

Table 10.12: Auxiliary table

qid **group**	**Number of counterfeits**
⟨[31-32], [22K-24K]⟩	1
⟨[47-53], [36K-43K]⟩	1

Now, suppose the adversary has a target victim, Annie, with background knowledge $Age = 31$ and $Salary = 22K$. By observing R_1 in Table 10.8 and R_2 with counterfeits in Table 10.11, the adversary can use the background knowledge to identify the *qid* groups ⟨ *[31-32], [22K-24K]* ⟩ in both releases. Since the *qid* groups in both releases share the same set of sensitive values {*Transgender, Plastic*}, the adversary can only conclude that Annie's received surgery is either *Transgender* or *Plastic*, with 50% of chance on each. Note, the auxiliary information in Table 10.12 does not provide any additional information to the adversary to crack Annie's sensitive value. □

From the above example, we notice that the key to privacy-preserving dynamic data re-publication is to ensure certain "invariance" in all *qid* groups that record is generalized to in different releases [251]. The privacy model m-invariance captures this notion.

10.4 HD-Composition

With m-invariance, we assume that the QID attribute values and the sensitive attribute values of each individual does not change over time. However, in

Table 10.13: Voter registration list ($\mathcal{RL}$)

PID	Age	Zip
p_1	23	16355
p_2	22	15500
p_3	21	12900
p_4	26	18310
p_5	25	25000
p_6	20	29000
p_7	24	33000
...	...	...
$p_{|RL|}$	31	31000

$\mathcal{RL}_1$

PID	Age	Zip
p_1	23	16355
p_2	22	15500
p_3	21	12900
p_4	26	18310
p_5	25	25000
p_6	20	29000
p_7	24	33000
...	...	...
$p_{|RL|}$	31	31000

$\mathcal{RL}_2$

PID	Age	Zip
p_1	23	16355
p_2	22	15500
p_3	21	12900
p_4	26	18310
p_5	25	*15000*
p_6	20	29000
p_7	24	33000
...	...	...
$p_{|RL|}$	31	31000

$\mathcal{RL}_3$

realistic applications, both the QID value and sensitive value of an individual can change over time, while some special sensitive values should remain unchanged. For example, after a move, the postal code of an individual changes. That is, the external table such as a voter registration list can have multiple releases and changes from time to time. Also, a patient may recover from one disease but develop another disease, meaning that the sensitive value can change over time. Bu et al. [42] propose a method called *HD-composition* to deal with this scenario.

The motivating example described by [42] and [251] is that the adversary may notice a neighbor being sent to hospital, from which s/he knows that a record for the neighbor must exist in two or more consecutive releases. They further assume that the disease attribute of the neighbor must remain the same in these releases. However, the presence of the neighbor in multiple data releases does not imply that the records for the neighbor will remain the same in terms of the sensitive value.

At the same time, some sensitive values that once linked to a record owner can never be unlinked. For instance, in medical records, sensitive diseases such as HIV, diabetes, and cancers are to this date incurable, and therefore they are expected to persist. These are the *permanent sensitive values*. Permanent sensitive values can be found in many domains of interest. Some examples are "having a pilot's qualification" and "having a criminal record."

Let us illustrate the problem with an example. In Table 10.13, $\mathcal{RL}_1$, $\mathcal{RL}_2$, and $\mathcal{RL}_3$ are snapshots of a voter registration list at times 1, 2, and 3, respectively. The raw data in Tables 10.14 T_1, T_2, and T_3 are to be anonymized at times 1, 2, and 3, respectively. In Table 10.15, three tables T_1^*, T_2^*, and T_3^* are published serially at times 1, 2, and 3, respectively. It is easy to see that T_1^*, T_2^*, and T_3^* satisfy 3-invariance. This is because in any release, for each individual, the set of 3 distinct sensitive values that the individual is linked to in the corresponding *qid* group remains unchanged. Note that HIV is a *permanent* disease but Flu and Fever are *transient* diseases. Furthermore, assume that from the registration lists, one can determine that $p_1, p_2, \ldots, p_6$ are the only individuals who satisfy the QID conditions for the groups with GID $= 1$ and GID $= 2$ in all the three tables of T_1^*, T_2^*, and T_3^*. Then surprisingly, the adversary can determine that p_4 has HIV with 100% probability. The reason is based on *possible world exclusion* from all published releases.

It can be shown that p_1 and p_6 cannot be linked to HIV. Suppose that p_1 suffers from HIV. In T_1^*, since p_1, p_2, and p_3 form a *qid* group containing one HIV value, we deduce that both p_2 and p_3 are not linked to HIV. Similarly, in T_2^*, since p_1, p_4, and p_5 form a *qid* group containing one HIV value, p_4 and p_5 are non-HIV carriers. Similarly, from T_3^*, we deduce that p_4 and p_6 are not linked to HIV. Then, we conclude that p_2, p_3, p_4, p_5, and p_6 do not contract HIV. However, in each of the releases T_1^*, T_2^*, and T_3^*, we know that there are two HIV values. This leads to a contradiction. Thus, p_1 cannot be linked to HIV. Similarly, by the same inductions, p_6 cannot be an HIV carrier. Finally, from the *qid* group with GID $= 2$ in T_3^*, we figure out that p_4 must be an

Table 10.14:

Raw data (T)

PID	Disease
p_1	Flu
p_2	HIV
p_3	Fever
p_4	HIV
p_5	Flu
p_6	Fever

T_1

PID	Disease
p_1	Flu
p_2	HIV
p_3	*Flu*
p_4	HIV
p_5	*Fever*
p_6	Fever

T_2

PID	Disease
p_1	Flu
p_2	HIV
p_3	Flu
p_4	HIV
p_5	Fever
p_6	Fever

T_3

HIV carrier!

No matter how large m is, this kind of possible world exclusion can appear after several publishing rounds. Note that even if the registration list remains unchanged, the same problem can occur since the six individuals can be grouped in the same way as in T_1^*, T_2^*, and T_3^* at 3 different times, according to the algorithm proposed by [251].

The anonymization mechanism for serial publishing should provide *individual-based protection*. Yet, Byun et al. [42] and Xiao and Tao [251] focus on *record-based protection*. In m-invariance, each record is associated with a lifespan of contiguous releases and a signature which is an *invariant* set of sensitive values linking to r_j in the published table. If a record r_j for individual p_i appears at time j, disappears at time $j + 1$ (e.g., p_i may discontinue treatment or may switch to another hospital), and reappears at time $j + 2$,

Table 10.15: Published tables T^* satisfying 3-invariance

PID	GID	Age	Zip	Disease
p_1	1	[21, 23]	[12k, 17k]	Flu
p_2	1	[21, 23]	[12k, 17k]	HIV
p_3	1	[21, 23]	[12k, 17k]	Fever
p_4	2	[20, 26]	[18k, 29k]	HIV
p_5	2	[20, 26]	[18k, 29k]	Flu
p_6	2	[20, 26]	[18k, 29k]	Fever

First Publication T_1^*

PID	GID	Age	Zip	Disease
p_2	1	[20, 22]	[12k, 29k]	HIV
p_3	1	[20, 22]	[12k, 29k]	Flu
p_6	1	[20, 22]	[12k, 29k]	Fever
p_1	2	[23, 26]	[16k, 25k]	Flu
p_4	2	[23, 26]	[16k, 25k]	HIV
p_5	2	[23, 26]	[16k, 25k]	Fever

Second Publication T_2^*

PID	GID	Age	Zip	Disease
p_2	1	[21, 25]	[12k, 16k]	HIV
p_3	1	[21, 25]	[12k, 16k]	Flu
p_5	1	[21, 25]	[12k, 16k]	Fever
p_1	2	[20, 26]	[16k, 29k]	Flu
p_4	2	[20, 26]	[16k, 29k]	HIV
p_6	2	[20, 26]	[16k, 29k]	Fever

Third Publication T_3^*

the appearance at $j + 2$ is treated as a new record r_{j+2} in the anonymization process adopted by [251]. There is no memory of the previous signature for r_j, and a new signature is created for r_{j+2}. Let us take a look at T_1^* in Table 10.15. From T_1^*, we can find that by 3-invariance, the signature of the records for p_1 and p_3 in T_1^* is {Flu, HIV, Fever}. If p_1 and p_3 recover from Flu and Fever at time 2 (not in T_2), and reappears due to other disease at time 3(in T_3), the reappearance of p_1 and p_3 in T_3 is treated as new records r_1', r_3' and by m-invariance, there is no constraint for their signature. Thus, at time 3, if the signatures for r_1' and r_3' do not contain HIV, p_1 and p_3 will be excluded from HIV. Consequently, p_2 will be found to have HIV!

To handle the above challenges, Bu et al. [38] propose an anonymization method called *HD-composition* which protects individual privacy for permanent sensitive values. The method involves two major roles, namely *holder* and *decoy*. The objective is to bound the probability of linkage between any individual and any permanent sensitive value by a given threshold, e.g., $1/\ell$. Suppose an individual p_i has a permanent sensitive value s in the microdata. One major technique used for anonymizing static data is to form a *qid* group mixing p_i and other individuals whose sensitive values are not s. Merely having the published *qid* groups, the adversary cannot establish strong linkage from p_i to s. The anonymization also follows this basic principle, where the individual to be protected is named as a holder and some other individuals for protection are named as decoys.

There are two major principles for partitioning: *role-based partition* and *cohort-based partition*. By role-based partition, in every *qid* group of the published data, for each holder of a permanent sensitive value s, $\ell - 1$ decoys which are not linked to s can be found. Thus, each holder is masked by $\ell - 1$ decoys. By cohort-based partition, for each permanent sensitive value s, the proposed method constructs ℓ cohorts, one for holders and the other $\ell - 1$ for decoys, and disallows decoys from the same cohort to be placed in the same partition. The objective is to imitate the properties of the true holders.

10.5   Summary

In this chapter, we have studied two scenarios of incremental data publishing. In Chapter 10.2, we have discussed the anonymization problem for a scenario where the data are continuously collected and published. Each release contains the new data as well as previously collected data. Even if each release is k-anonymized, the anonymity of an individual can be compromised by cross-examining multiple releases. We formalized this notion of attacks and presented a detection method and an anonymization algorithm to prevent such attacks. Finally, we showed that both the detection and the anonymization methods are extendable to deal with multiple releases and other privacy requirements.

Recall that the anatomy approach discussed in Chapter 3.2 publishes the exact QID and the sensitive attribute in two separate tables, QIT and ST, linked by a common *GroupID*. In this continuous data publishing scenario, however, publishing the exact QID allows the adversary to isolate the new records added in later release by comparing the difference between the old (QIT,ST) and the new (QIT,ST). Once new records are isolated, the attack can focus on the usually small increment, which increases the re-identification risk. Thus, anatomy is not suitable for continuous data publishing.

In Chapter 10.3, we have studied the privacy threats caused by dynamic data republishing, in which both record insertions and deletions may be performed before every release, and discussed a privacy model called m-invariance to ensure the invariance of sensitive values in the intersection of *qid* groups across all releases. m-invariance is achieved by adding counterfeit records and generalizations. Adding counterfeits is necessary in order to address the problem of critical absence. However, a table with counterfeit records could no longer preserve the data truthfulness at the record level, which is important in some applications, as explained in Chapter 1.1. Bu et al. [38] further relax the PPDP scenario and assume that the QID and sensitive values of a record owner could change in subsequent releases.

With m-invariance, we assume that the QID attribute values and the sensitive attribute values of each individual does not change over time. This assumption, however, may not hold in real-life data publishing. In Chapter 10.4, we have studied another approach that addresses these issues. Pei et al. [186] also consider privacy threats in the incremental data publishing scenario that the Case-ID of records must be published. Case-ID are unique identifiers associated with an entity, e.g., a patient. Most works on incremental data publishing consider the scenario that the data holder has removed the Case-ID of records, so the attack based on Case-ID does not occur. Publishing Case-ID gives the adversary the very powerful knowledge of locating the corresponding published records in two releases. This additional threat can be removed by not publishing Case-ID. In fact, most aggregate data analysis (such as count queries) does not depend on the Case-ID. Iwuchukwu and Naughton [122] propose an efficient index structure to incrementally k-anonymize each individual release, but it does not address the attack models studied in this chapter.

Chapter 11

Collaborative Anonymization for Vertically Partitioned Data

11.1   Introduction

Nowadays, one-stop service has been a trend followed by many competitive business sectors, where a single location provides multiple related services. For example, financial institutions often provide all of daily banking, mortgage, investment, insurance in one location. Behind the scene, this usually involves information sharing among multiple companies. However, a company cannot indiscriminately open up the database to other companies because privacy policies [221] place a limit on information sharing. Consequently, there is a dual demand on information sharing and information protection, driven by trends such as one-stop service, end-to-end integration, outsourcing, simultaneous competition and cooperation, privacy and security.

A typical scenario is that two parties wish to integrate their private databases to achieve a common goal beneficial to both, provided that their privacy requirements are satisfied. In this chapter, we consider the goal of achieving some common data mining tasks over the integrated data while satisfying the k-anonymity privacy requirement. The k-anonymity requirement states that domain values are generalized so that each value of some specified attributes identifies at least k records. The generalization process must not leak more specific information other than the final integrated data. In this chapter, we study some solutions to this problem.

So far, we have considered only a single data holder. In real-life data publishing, a single organization often does not hold the complete data. Organizations need to share data for mutual benefits or for publishing to a third party. For example, two credit card companies want to integrate their customer data for developing a fraud detection system, or for publishing to a bank. However, the credit card companies do not want to indiscriminately disclose their data to each other or to the bank for reasons such as privacy protection and business competitiveness. Figure 11.1 depicts this scenario, called *collaborative anonymization for vertically partitioned data* [172]: several data holders own different sets of attributes on the same set of records and want to publish the integrated data on all at-

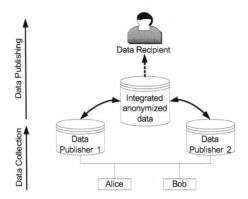

FIGURE 11.1: Collaborative anonymization for vertically partitioned data

tributes. Say, publisher 1 owns $\{RecID, Job, Sex, Age\}$ and publisher 2 owns $\{RecID, Salary, Disease\}$, where $RecID$, such as the SSN, is the record identifier shared by all data holders. They want to publish an integrated k-anonymous table on all attributes. Also, no data holder should learn more specific information, owned by the other data holders, than the information appears in the final integrated table.

In Chapter 11.2, we study the problem of collaborative anonymization for vertically partitioned data in the context of a data mashup application and use a real-life scenario to motivate the information and privacy requirements as well as the solution. In Chapter 11.3, we study the cryptographic approaches to the collaborative anonymization problem.

11.2   Privacy-Preserving Data Mashup

The problem of collaborative anonymization for vertically partitioned data has been applied to the scenario of a distributed data mashup application [172]. In this Chapter 11.2, we use this real-life data mashup application to illustrate the problem and the solution.

Mashup is a web technology that combines information and services from more than one source into a single web application. It was first discussed in a 2005 issue of Business Week [117] on the topic of integrating real estate information into Google Maps. Since then, web giants like Amazon, Yahoo!, and Google have been actively developing mashup applications. Mashup has created a new horizon for service providers to integrate their data and expertise to deliver highly customizable services to their customers.

Data mashup is a special type of mashup application that aims at integrating data from multiple data holders depending on the user's service request.

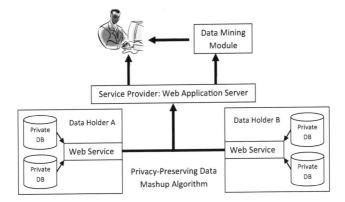

FIGURE 11.2: Architecture of privacy-preserving data mashup

Figure 11.2 illustrates a typical architecture of the data mashup technology. A service request could be a general data exploration or a sophisticated data mining task such as classification analysis. Upon receiving a service request, the data mashup web application dynamically determines the data holders, collects information from them through their web service application programming interface (API),[1] and then integrates the collected information to fulfill the service request. Further computation and visualization can be performed at the user's site (e.g., a browser or an applet). This is very different from the traditional web portal which simply divides a web page or a website into independent sections for displaying information from different sources.

A typical application of data mashup is to implement the concept of one-stop service. For example, a single health mashup application could provide a patient all of her health history, doctor's information, test results, appointment bookings, insurance, and health reports. This concept involves information sharing among multiple parties, e.g., hospital, drug store, and insurance company.

To service providers, data mashup provides a low-cost solution to integrate their services with their partners and broaden their market. To users, data mashup provides a flexible interface to obtain information from different service providers. However, to adversaries, data mashup could be a valuable tool for identifying sensitive information. A data mashup application can help ordinary users explore new knowledge. Nevertheless, it could also be misused by adversaries to reveal sensitive information that was not available before the data integration.

In this chapter, we study the privacy threats caused by data mashup and discuss a privacy-preserving data mashup (PPMashup) algorithm to securely

---

[1]Authentication may be required to ensure that the user has access rights to the requested data.

integrate person-specific sensitive data from different data holders, whereas the integrated data still retains the essential information for supporting general data exploration or a specific data mining task, such as classification analysis. The following *real-life* scenario illustrates the simultaneous need of information sharing and privacy preservation in the financial industry.

This data mashup problem was discovered in a collaborative project [172] with a provider of unsecured loans in Sweden. Their problem can be generalized as follows: A loan company A and a bank B observe different sets of attributes about the same set of individuals identified by the common key SSN,[2] e.g., $T_A(SSN, Age, Balance)$ and $T_B(SSN, Job, Salary)$. These companies want to implement a data mashup application that integrates their data to support better decision making such as loan or credit limit approval, which is basically a data mining task on classification analysis. In addition to companies A and B, their partnered credit card company C also have access to the data mashup application, so all three companies A, B, and C are data recipients of the final integrated data. Companies A and B have two privacy concerns. First, simply joining T_A and T_B would reveal the sensitive information to the other party. Second, even if T_A and T_B individually do not contain person specific or sensitive information, the integrated data can increase the possibility of identifying the record of an individual. Their privacy concerns are reasonable because Sweden has a population of only 9 million people. Thus, it is possible to identify the record of an individual by collecting information from other data sources. The next example illustrates this point.

Example 11.1
Consider the data in Table 11.1 and taxonomy trees in Figure 11.3. Party A (the loan company) and Party B (the bank) own $T_A(SSN, Sex, \dots, Class)$ and $T_B(SSN, Job, Salary, \dots, Class)$, respectively. Each row represents one or more raw records and *Class* contains the distribution of class labels Y and N, representing whether or not the loan has been approved. After integrating the two tables (by matching the SSN field), the female lawyer on (Sex, Job) becomes unique, therefore, vulnerable to be linked to sensitive information such as *Salary*. In other words, record linkage is possible on the fields *Sex* and *Job*. To prevent such linkage, we can generalize *Accountant* and *Lawyer* to *Professional* so that this individual becomes one of many female professionals. No information is lost as far as classification is concerned because *Class* does not depend on the distinction of *Accountant* and *Lawyer*.   □

The *privacy-preserving data mashup* problem is defined as follows. Given multiple private tables for the same set of records on different sets of attributes (i.e., vertically partitioned tables), we want to efficiently produce an integrated table on all attributes for releasing it to to both parties or even to a third

---

[2]SSN is called "personnummer" in Sweden.

Table 11.1: Raw tables

Shared		Party A		Party B		
SSN	**Class**	**Sex**	...	**Job**	**Salary**	...
1-3	0Y3N	Male		Janitor	30K	
4-7	0Y4N	Male		Mover	32K	
8-12	2Y3N	Male		Carpenter	35K	
13-16	3Y1N	Female		Technician	37K	
17-22	4Y2N	Female		Manager	42K	
23-25	3Y0N	Female		Manager	44K	
26-28	3Y0N	Male		Accountant	44K	
29-31	3Y0N	Female		Accountant	44K	
32-33	2Y0N	Male		Lawyer	44K	
34	1Y0N	Female		Lawyer	44K	

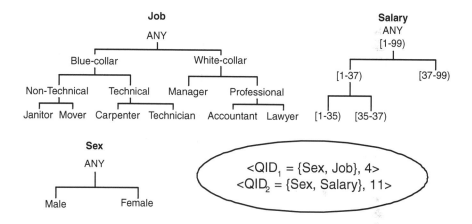

FIGURE 11.3: Taxonomy trees and QIDs

party. The integrated table must satisfy both the following anonymity and information requirements:

Anonymity Requirement: The integrated table has to satisfy k-anonymity as discussed in previous chapters: A data table T satisfies k-anonymity if every combination of values on QID is shared by at least k records in T, where the *quasi-identifier* (QID) is a set of attributes in T that could potentially identify an individual in T, and k is a user-specified threshold. k-anonymity can be satisfied by generalizing domain values into higher level concepts. In addition, at any time in the procedure of generalization, no party should learn more detailed information about the other party other than those in the final integrated table. For example, *Lawyer* is more detailed than *Professional*. In other words, the generalization process must not leak more specific information other than the final integrated data.

Information Requirement: The generalized data should be as useful as possible to classification analysis. Generally speaking, the privacy goal requires masking sensitive information that is *specific* enough to identify individuals, whereas the classification goal requires extracting trends and patterns that are *general* enough to predict new cases. If generalization is *carefully* performed, it is possible to mask identifying information while preserving patterns useful for classification.

In addition to the privacy and information requirements, the data mashup application is an online web application. The user dynamically specifies their requirement and the system is expected to be efficient and scalable to handle high volumes of data.

There are two obvious yet incorrect approaches. The first one is "integrate-then-generalize": first integrate the two tables and then generalize the integrated table using some single table anonymization methods discussed in Chapters 5 and 6, such as K-Optimize [29], Top-Down Specialization (TDS) [95, 96], HDTDS [171], Genetic Algorithm [123], and InfoGain Mondrian [150]. Unfortunately, these approaches do not preserve privacy in the studied scenario because any party holding the integrated table will immediately know all private information of both parties. The second approach is "generalize-then-integrate": first generalize each table locally and then integrate the generalized tables. This approach does not work for a quasi-identifier that spans multiple tables. In the above example, the k-anonymity on (Sex, Job) cannot be achieved by the k-anonymity on each of Sex and Job separately.

The rest of this Chapter 11.2 is organized as follows. In Chapter 11.2.1, we illustrate a real-life privacy problem in the financial industry and generalize their requirements to formulate the privacy-preserving data mashup problem. The goal is to allow data sharing for classification analysis in the presence of privacy concern. This problem is very different from cryptographic approach [128, 259], which will be discussed in Chapter 11.3, that allows "result sharing" (e.g., the classifier in this case) but completely prohibits data sharing. In some applications, data sharing gives greater flexibility than result sharing because data recipients can perform their required analysis and data exploration, such as, mine patterns in a specific group of records, visualize the transactions containing a specific pattern, try different modeling methods and parameters.

In Chapter 11.2.3, we illustrate a service-oriented architecture for the problem privacy-preserving data mashup. The architecture defines communication paths of all participating parties, and defines the role of the *mashup coordinator* who is responsible to initialize the protocol execution and present the final integrated data set to the user. The architecture does *not* require the mashup coordinator to be a trusted entity.

In Chapters 11.2.4-11.2.5, we discuss two algorithms to securely integrate private data from multiple parties for two different adversary models. The first algorithm assumes that parties are *semi-honest*. In the semi-honest adversarial model, it is assumed that parties do follow protocol but may try to deduce additional information. This is the common security definition adopted in the Secure Multiparty Computation (SMC) literature [128]. The second algorithm further addresses the data integration model with *malicious* parties. We show that a party may deviate from the protocol for its own benefit. To overcome the malicious problem, we discuss a game-theoretic approach to combine incentive compatible strategies with the anonymization technique.

The studied algorithm, PPMashup, can effectively achieve an anonymity requirement without compromising the useful data for classification, and the methods are scalable to handle large data sets. The algorithm for the semi-honest model produces the same final anonymous table as the integrate-then-generalize approach, and only reveals local data that has satisfied a given k-anonymity requirement. Moreover, the algorithm for the malicious model provides additional security by ensuring fair participation of the data holders.

In Chapter 11.2.4.4, we discuss the possible extensions to thwart attribute linkages by achieving other privacy requirements, such as ℓ-diversity [162], (α,k)-anonymity [246], and confidence bounding [237].

11.2.1 Anonymization Problem for Data Mashup

To ease explanation, we assume the privacy requirement to be the anonymity requirement, $QID_1, \ldots, QID_p$, discussed in Definition 7.1, which is in effect k-anonymity with multiple QIDs. Yet, the privacy requirement is not limited to k-anonymity and can be other privacy models in practice.

Example 11.2

$\langle QID_1 = \{Sex, Job\}, 4 \rangle$ states that every qid on QID_1 in T must be shared by at least 4 records in T. In Table 11.1, the following qids violate this requirement:

⟨*Male, Janitor*⟩,
⟨*Male, Accountant*⟩,
⟨*Female, Accountant*⟩,
⟨*Male, Lawyer*⟩,
⟨*Female, Lawyer*⟩.

The example in Figure 11.3 specifies the anonymity requirement with two QIDs. □

Consider n data holders {Party 1,…,,Party n}, where each Party y owns a private table $T_y(ID, Attribs_y, Class)$ over the same set of records. ID and $Class$ are shared attributes among all parties. $Attribs_y$ is a set of private attributes. $Attribs_y \cap Attribs_z = \emptyset$ for any $1 \leq y, z \leq n$. These parties agree to release "minimal information" to form an integrated table T (by matching the ID) for conducting a joint classification analysis. The notion of minimal information is specified by the *joint anonymity requirement*

$\{\langle QID_1, k_1\rangle, \ldots, \langle QID_p, k_p\rangle\}$ on the integrated table. QID_j is *local* if it contains only attributes from one party, and *global* otherwise.

DEFINITION 11.1 Privacy-preserving data mashup   Given multiple private tables $T_1, \ldots, T_n$, a joint anonymity requirement $\{\langle QID_1, k_1\rangle, \ldots, \langle QID_p, k_p\rangle\}$, and a taxonomy tree for each categorical attribute in $\cup QID_j$, the problem of *privacy-preserving data mashup* is to efficiently produce a generalized integrated table T such that

1. T satisfies the joint anonymity requirement,

2. contains as much information as possible for classification, and

3. each party learns nothing about the other party more specific than what is in the final generalized T. We assume that the data holders are semi-honest, meaning that they will follow the protocol but may attempt to derive sensitive information from the received data. ∎

The problem requires achieving anonymity in the final integrated table as well as in any intermediate table. For example, if a record in the final T has values *Female* and *Professional* on *Sex* and *Job*, and if Party A learns that *Professional* in this record comes from *Lawyer*, condition (3) is violated.

11.2.1.1   Challenges

In case all QIDs are locals, we can generalize each table T_A and T_B independently, and join the generalized tables to produce the integrated data. However, if there are global QIDs, global QIDs are ignored in this approach. Further generalizing the integrated table using global QIDs does not work because the requirement (3) is violated by the intermediate table that contains more specific information than the final table.

It may seem that local QIDs can be generalized beforehand. However, if a local QID_l shares some attributes with a global QID_g, the local generalization ignores the chance of getting a better result by generalizing QID_g first, which leads to a sub-optimal solution. A better strategy is generalizing shared attributes in the presence of both QID_l and QID_g. Similarly, the generalization of shared attributes will affect the generalization of other attributes in QID_l, thus, affect other local QIDs that share an attribute with QID_l. As a result, all local QIDs reachable by a path of shared attributes from a global QID should be considered in the presence of the global QID.

11.2.1.2   General Join

So far, we have assumed that the join between T_A and T_B is through the common key ID. If the join attributes are not keys in T_A or T_B, a preprocessing step is required to convert the problem to that defined in Definition 11.1.

The two parties first perform a join on their join attributes, but not the person-specific data, then assign a unique ID to each joint record, and use these joint records to join the local table T_A or T_B. Both T_A and T_B now contain the common key column ID. In the rest of this chapter, we consider only join of T_A and T_B through the common key ID. Note, this model assumes that the join attributes are not sensitive.

In this case, we have $T_A(ID_A, J_A, D_1, \ldots, D_t)$ and $T_B(ID_B, J_B, D_{t+1}, \ldots, D_m)$, where ID_A and ID_B are the record identifier in T_A and T_B, and J_A and J_B are join columns in T_A and T_B. The two parties first compute equijoin of $\Pi_{ID_A, J_A}(T_A)$ and $\Pi_{ID_B, J_B}(T_B)$ based on $J_A = J_B$. Let Π_{ID, ID_A, ID_B} be the projection of the join onto ID_A, ID_B, where ID is a new identifier for the records on ID_A, ID_B. Each party replaces ID_A and ID_B with ID.

11.2.2 Information Metrics

To generalize T, a *taxonomy tree* is specified for each categorical attribute in $\cup QID_j$. For a numerical attribute in $\cup QID_j$, a taxonomy tree can be grown at runtime, where each node represents an interval, and each non-leaf node has two child nodes representing some optimal binary split of the parent interval. The algorithm generalizes a table T by a sequence of specializations starting from the top most general state in which each attribute has the top most value of its taxonomy tree. A *specialization*, written $v \rightarrow child(v)$, where $child(v)$ denotes the set of child values of v, replaces the parent value v with the child value that generalizes the domain value in a record. In other words, the algorithms employ the subtree generalization scheme. Refer to Chapter 3.1 for the details of generalization and specialization.

A specialization is *valid* if the specialization results in a table satisfying the anonymity requirement after the specialization. A specialization is *beneficial* if more than one class are involved in the records containing v. If not then that specialization does not provide any helpful information for classification. Thus, a specialization is performed only if it is both valid and beneficial. The notions of specialization, $InfoGain(v)$, $AnonyLoss(v)$, $Score(v)$, and the procedure of dynamically growing a taxonomy tree on numerical attributes have been studied in Chapter 6.2.2.

Example 11.3
The specialization ANY_Job refines the 34 records into 16 records for *Blue-collar* and 18 records for *White-collar*. $Score(ANY\_Job)$ is calculated as follows.

$$E(T[ANY\_Job]) = -\tfrac{21}{34} \times log_2 \tfrac{21}{34} - \tfrac{13}{34} \times log_2 \tfrac{13}{34} = 0.9597$$
$$E(T[Blue\text{-}collar]) = -\tfrac{5}{16} \times log_2 \tfrac{5}{16} - \tfrac{11}{16} \times log_2 \tfrac{11}{16} = 0.8960$$
$$E(T[White\text{-}collar]) = -\tfrac{16}{18} \times log_2 \tfrac{16}{18} - \tfrac{2}{18} \times log_2 \tfrac{2}{18} = 0.5033$$
$$InfoGain(ANY\_Job) = E(T[ANY\_Job]) - (\tfrac{16}{34} \times E(T[Blue\text{-}collar])$$
$$+ \tfrac{18}{34} \times E(T[White\text{-}collar])) = 0.2716$$

$$AnonyLoss(ANY\_Job) = avg\{A(QID_1) - A_{ANY\_Job}(QID_1)\}$$
$$= (34 - 16)/1 = 18$$
$$Score(ANY\_Job) = \frac{0.2716}{18+1} = 0.0143.$$

□

In practice, the data holders can define their information metrics. The methods studied in this chapter are also applicable to achieve other information requirements, not limited to classification analysis. Here, we assume the goal of classification analysis in order to illustrate a concrete scenario.

11.2.3 Architecture and Protocol

In this Chapter 11.2.3, we discuss the technical architecture [225] shown in Figure 11.4 with the communication paths of all participating parties followed by a privacy-preserving data mashup protocol in Chapter 11.2.4. Referring to the architecture, the *mashup coordinator* plays the central role in initializing the protocol execution and presenting the final integrated data set to the user. The architecture does *not* require the mashup coordinator to be a trusted entity. This makes the architecture practical because a trusted party is often not available in real-life scenarios.

The mashup coordinator of the communication protocol separates the architecture into two phases. In Phase I, the mashup coordinator receives requests from users, establishes connections with the data holders who contribute their data in a privacy-preserving manner. In Phase II, the mashup coordinator manages the privacy-preserving data mashup algorithm (PPMashup) among the data holders for a particular client request.

11.2.3.1 Phase I: Session Establishment

The objective of Phase I is to establish a common session context among the contributing data holders and the user. An operational context is successfully established by proceeding through the steps of *user authentication, contributing data holders identification, session initialization,* and *common requirements negotiation*.

Authenticate user: The mashup coordinator first authenticates a user to the requested service, generates a session token for the current user interaction, and then identifies the data holders *accessible* by the user. Some data holders are public and are accessible by any users.

Identify contributing data holders: Next, the mashup coordinator queries the data schema of the accessible data holders to identify the data holders that can contribute data for the requested service. To facilitate more efficient queries, the mashup coordinator could pre-fetch data schema from the data holders (i.e., the pull model), or the data holders could update their data schema periodically (i.e., the push model).

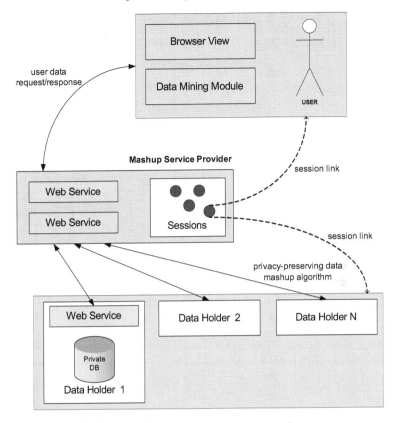

FIGURE 11.4: Service-oriented architecture for privacy-preserving data mashup

Initializing session context: Then, the mashup coordinator notifies all contributing data holders with the session identifier. All prospective data holders share a common session context, which represents a stateful presentation of information related to a specific execution of privacy-preserving data mashup algorithm *PPMashup*, which will be discussed in Chapter 11.2.3.2. Due to the fact that multiple parties are involved and the flow of multiple protocol messages is needed in order to fulfill the data mashup, we can use a Web Service Resource Framework (WSRF) to keep stateful information along an initial service request. An established session context stored as a single web service resource contains several attributes to identify a PPMashup process, which are an unique session identifier (making use of end-point reference (EPR), which is built from service address and identifiers of the resource in use), the client address, the data holder addresses and their certificates, an authentication token (containing the user certificate), as well as additional status information.

Negotiating privacy and information requirements: The mashup coordinator is responsible to communicate the negotiation of privacy and information requirements among the data holders and the user. Specifically, this step involves negotiating the price, the anonymity requirement, and the expected information quality. For example, in the case of classification analysis, information quality can be estimated by classification error on some testing data.

11.2.3.2 Phase II: Initiating Privacy-Preserving Protocol

After a common session has been established among the data holders, the mashup coordinator initiates PPMashup and stays back. Upon the completion of the protocol, the mashup coordinator will receive an integrated table that satisfies both the information and anonymity requirements. There are two advantages that the mashup coordinator does not have to participate in the PPMashup protocol. First, the architecture does not require the mashup coordinator to be a trusted entity. The mashup coordinator only has access to the final integrated k-anonymous data. Second, this setup removes the computation burden from the mashup coordinator, and frees up the coordinator to handle other requests. Chapter 11.2.4 and Chapter 11.2.5 discuss anonymization algorithms for semi-honest model and for malicious model, respectively.

11.2.4 Anonymization Algorithm for Semi-Honest Model

In Chapter 6.3, we have studied a *top-down specialization (TDS)* [95, 96] approach to generalize a **single table** T. One non-privacy-preserving approach to the problem of data mashup is to first join the multiple private tables into a single table T and then generalize T to satisfy a k-anonymity requirement using TDS. Though this approach does not satisfy the privacy requirement (3) in Definition 11.1 (because the party that generalizes the joint table knows all the details of the other parties), the integrated table produced satisfies requirements (1) and (2). Therefore, it is helpful to first have an overview of TDS: Initially, all values are generalized to the top most value in its taxonomy tree, and Cut_i contains the top most value for each attribute D_i. At each iteration, TDS performs the best specialization, which has the highest $Score$ among the *candidates* that are valid, beneficial specializations in $\cup Cut_i$, and then updates the $Score$ of the affected candidates. The algorithm terminates when there is no more valid and beneficial candidate in $\cup Cut_i$. In other words, the algorithm terminates if any further specialization would lead to a violation of the anonymity requirement. An important property of TDS is that the anonymity requirement is *anti-monotone* with respect to a specialization: If it is violated before a specialization, it remains violated after the specialization. This is because a specialization never increases the anonymity count $a(qid)$.

Now, we consider that the table T is given by two tables ($n = 2$) T_A and T_B with a common key ID, where Party A holds T_A and Party B holds T_B. At first glance, it seems that the change from one party to two parties is trivial

---

Algorithm 11.2.7 PPMashup for Party A (Same as Party B) in Semi-Honest Model

---

1: initialize T_g to include one record containing top most values;
2: initialize $\cup Cut_i$ to include only top most values;
3: **while** some candidate $v \in \cup Cut_i$ is valid **do**
4:     find the local candidate x of highest $Score(x)$;
5:     communicate $Score(x)$ with Party B to find the winner;
6:     **if** the winner w is local **then**
7:         specialize w on T_g;
8:         instruct Party B to specialize w;
9:     **else**
10:         wait for the instruction from Party B;
11:         specialize w on T_g using the instruction;
12:     **end if**
13:     replace w with $child(w)$ in the local copy of $\cup Cut_i$;
14:     update $Score(x)$ and beneficial/validity status for candidates $x \in \cup Cut_i$;
15: **end while**
16: **return** T_g and $\cup Cut_i$;

---

because the change of *Score* due to specializing a single attribute depends only on that attribute and *Class*, and each party knows about *Class* and the attributes they have. This observation is wrong because the change of *Score* involves the change of $A(QID_j)$ that depends on the combination of the attributes in QID_j. In PPMashup, each party keeps a copy of the current $\cup Cut_i$ and generalized T, denoted by T_g, in addition to the private T_A or T_B. The nature of the top-down approach implies that T_g is more general than the final answer, therefore, does not violate the requirement (3) in Definition 11.1. At each iteration, the two parties cooperate to perform the same specialization as identified in TDS by communicating certain information in a way that satisfies the requirement (3) in Definition 11.1. Algorithm 11.2.7 describes the procedure at Party A (same for Party B).

First, Party A finds the local best candidate using the specialization criteria presented in Chapter 11.2.2 and communicates with Party B to identify the overall global winner candidate, say w. To protect the input score, the secure multiparty maximum protocol [260] can be used. Suppose that w is local to Party A (otherwise, the discussion below applies to Party B). Party A performs $w \rightarrow child(w)$ on its copy of $\cup Cut_i$ and T_g. This means specializing each record $t \in T_g$ containing w into those $t'_1, \ldots, t'_z$ containing child values in $child(w)$. Similarly, Party B updates its $\cup Cut_i$ and T_g, and partitions $T_B[t]$ into $T_B[t'_1], \ldots, T_B[t'_z]$. Since Party B does not have the attribute for w, Party A needs to instruct Party B how to partition these records in terms of IDs.

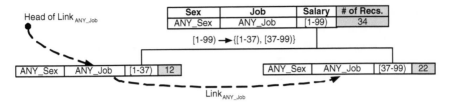

FIGURE 11.5: The TIPS after the first specialization

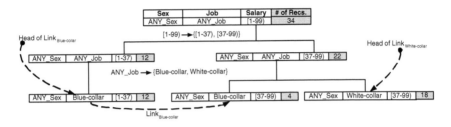

FIGURE 11.6: The TIPS after the second specialization

Example 11.4

Consider Table 11.1 and the joint anonymity requirement:

$\{\langle QID_1 = \{Sex, Job\}, 4 \rangle, \ \langle QID_2 = \{Sex, Salary\}, 11 \rangle \}$.

Initially,

$T_g = \{\langle ANY\_Sex, ANY\_Job, [1\text{-}99) \rangle\}$

and

$\cup Cut_i = \{ANY\_Sex, ANY\_Job, [1\text{-}99) \}$,

and all specializations in $\cup Cut_i$ are candidates. To find the candidate, Party A computes $Score(ANY\_Sex)$, and Party B computes $Score(ANY\_Job)$ and $Score([1\text{-}99))$. □

Algorithm 11.2.7 makes no claim on efficiency. In a straightforward method, Lines 4, 7, and 11 require scanning all data records and recomputing *Score* for all candidates in $\cup Cut_i$. The key to the efficiency of the algorithm is *directly* accessing the data records to be specialized, and updating *Score* based on some statistics maintained for candidates in $\cup Cut_i$, instead of accessing data records. Below, we briefly describe the key steps: find the winner candidate (Lines 4-5), perform the winning specialization (Lines 7-11), and update the score and status of candidates (Line 14). For Party A (or Party B), a *local attribute* refers to an attribute from T_A (or T_B), and a *local specialization* refers to that of a local attribute. Refer to [172] for details.

11.2.4.1 Find the Winner Candidate

Party A first finds the local candidate x of highest $Score(x)$, by making use of computed $InfoGain(x)$, $A_x(QID_j)$ and $A(QID_j)$, and then communicates with Party B (using secure multiparty max algorithm in [260]) to find the winner candidate. $InfoGain(x)$, $A_x(QID_j)$ and $A(QID_j)$ come from the update done in the previous iteration or the initialization prior to the first iteration. This step does not access data records. Updating $InfoGain(x)$, $A_x(QID_j)$ and $A(QID_j)$ is considered in Chapter 11.2.4.3.

11.2.4.2 Perform the Winner Candidate

Suppose that the winner candidate w is local at Party A (otherwise, replace Party A with Party B). For each record t in T_g containing w, Party A accesses the raw records in $T_A[t]$ to tell how to specialize t. To facilitate this operation, we represent T_g by the data structure called *Taxonomy Indexed PartitionS (TIPS)*, which has been discussed in Chapter 6.3.2.

With the TIPS, we can find all raw records generalized to x by following $Link_x$ for a candidate x in $\cup Cut_i$. To ensure that each party has only access to its own raw records, a leaf partition at Party A contains only raw records from T_A and a leaf partition at Party B contains only raw records from T_B. Initially, the TIPS has only the root node representing the most generalized record and all raw records. In each iteration, the two parties cooperate to perform the specialization w by refining the leaf partitions P_w on $Link_w$ in their own TIPS.

Example 11.5
Continue with Example 11.4. Initially, TIPS has the root representing the most generalized record $\langle ANY\_Sex, ANY\_Job, [1\text{-}99) \rangle$, $T_A[root] = T_A$ and $T_B[root] = T_B$. The root is on $Link_{ANY\_Sex}$, $Link_{ANY\_Job}$, and $Link_{[1-99)}$. See the root in Figure 11.5. The shaded field contains the number of raw records generalized by a node. Suppose that the winning candidate w is

$$[1\text{-}99) \rightarrow \{[1\text{-}37), [37\text{-}99)\} \text{ (on } Salary).$$

Party B first creates two child nodes under the root and partitions $T_B[root]$ between them. The root is deleted from all the $Link_x$, the child nodes are added to $Link_{[1-37)}$ and $Link_{[37-99)}$, respectively, and both are added to $Link_{ANY\_Job}$ and $Link_{ANY\_Sex}$. Party B then sends the following instruction to Party A:

IDs 1-12 go to the node for *[1-37)*.
IDs 13-34 go to the node for *[37-99)*.

On receiving this instruction, Party A creates the two child nodes under the root in its copy of TIPS and partitions $T_A[root]$ similarly. Suppose that the next winning candidate is

$$ANY\_Job \rightarrow \{Blue\text{-}collar, White\text{-}collar\}.$$

Similarly the two parties cooperate to specialize each leaf node on $Link_{ANY\_Job}$, resulting in the TIPS in Figure 11.6.   □

We summarize the operations at the two parties, assuming that the winner w is local at Party A.

Party A. Refine each leaf partition P_w on $Link_w$ into child partitions P_c. $Link_c$ is created to link up the new P_c's for the same c. Mark c as *beneficial* if the records on $Link_c$ has more than one class. Also, add P_c to every $Link_x$ other than $Link_w$ to which P_w was previously linked. While scanning the records in P_w, Party A also collects the following information.

- *Instruction for Party B*. If a record in P_w is specialized to a child value c, collect the pair (id,c), where id is the ID of the record. This information will be sent to B to refine the corresponding leaf partitions there.

- *Count statistics*. Some count statistics for computing the updating the *Score*. See [172] for details.

Party B. On receiving the instruction from Party A, Party B creates child partitions P_c in its own TIPS. At Party B, P_c's contain raw records from T_B. P_c's are obtained by splitting P_w among P_c's according to the (id, c) pairs received.

Note, updating TIPS is the only operation that accesses raw records. Subsequently, updating $Score(x)$ makes use of the count statistics without accessing raw records anymore. The overhead of maintaining $Link_x$ is small. For each attribute in $\cup QID_j$ and each leaf partition on $Link_w$, there are at most $|child(w)|$ "relinkings." Therefore, there are at most $|\cup QID_j| \times |Link_w| \times |child(w)|$ "relinkings" for performing w.

11.2.4.3   Update the Score

The key to the scalability of PPMashup algorithm is updating $Score(x)$ using the maintained count statistics without accessing raw records again. $Score(x)$ depends on $InfoGain(x)$, $A_x(QID_j)$ and $A(QID_j)$. The updated $A(QID_j)$ is obtained from $A_w(QID_j)$, where w is the specialization just performed.

11.2.4.4   Beyond k-Anonymity

k-anonymity is an effective privacy requirement that prevents record linkages. However, if some sensitive values occur very frequently within a qid group, the adversary could still confidently infer the sensitive value of an individual by his/her qid value. This type of attribute linkage attacks was studied in Chapter 2.2. The proposed approach in this chapter can be extended to incorporate with other privacy models, such as ℓ-diversity [162], confidence bounding [237], and (α,k)-anonymity [246], to thwart attribute linkages.

To adopt these privacy requirements, we make three changes.

1. The notion of valid specialization has to be redefined depending on the privacy requirement. The PPMashup algorithm guarantees that the identified solution is local optimal if the privacy measure holds the (anti-)monotonicity property with respect to specialization. ℓ-diversity (Chapter 2.2.1), confidence bounding (Chapter 2.2.2), and (α,k)-anonymity (Chapter 2.2.5) hold such (anti-)monotonicity property.

2. The *AnonyLoss(v)* function in Chapter 11.2.2 has to be modified in order to reflect the loss of privacy with respect to a specialization on value v. We can, for example, adopt the *PrivLoss(v)* function in [237] to capture the increase of confidence on inferring a sensitive value by a qid.

3. To check the validity of a candidate, the party holding the sensitive attributes has to first check the distribution of sensitive values in a qid group *before* actually performing the specialization. Suppose Party B holds a sensitive attribute S_B. Upon receiving a specialization instruction on value v from Party A, Party B has to first verify whether specializing v would violate the privacy requirement. If there is a violation, Party B rejects the specialization request and both parties have to redetermine the next candidate; otherwise, the algorithm proceeds the specialization as in Algorithm 11.2.7.

11.2.4.5 Analysis

PPMashup in Algorithm 11.2.7 produces the same integrated table as the single party algorithm TDS in Chapter 6.3 on a joint table, and ensures that no party learns more detailed information about the other party other than what they agree to share. This claim follows from the fact that PPMashup performs exactly the same sequence of specializations as in TDS in a distributed manner where T_A and T_B are kept locally at the sources. The only information revealed to each other is those in $\cup Cut_j$ and T_g at each iteration. However, such information is more general than the final integrated table that the two parties agree to share.

PPMashup is extendable for multiple parties with minor changes: In Line 5, each party should communicate with all the other parties for determining the winner. Similarly, in Line 8, the party holding the winner candidate should instruct all the other parties and in Line 10, a party should wait for instruction from the winner party.

The cost of PPMashup can be summarized as follows. Each iteration involves the following work:

1. Scan the records in $T_A[w]$ and $T_B[w]$ for updating TIPS and maintaining count statistics (Chapter 11.2.4.2).

2. Update $QIDTree_j$, $InfoGain(x)$ and $A_x(QID_j)$ for affected candidates x (Chapter 11.2.4.3).

3. Send "instruction" to the remote party. The instruction contains only IDs of the records in $T_A[w]$ or $T_B[w]$ and child values c in $child(w)$, therefore, is compact.

Only the work in (1) involves accessing data records; the work in (2) makes use of the count statistics without accessing data records and is restricted to only affected candidates. For the communication cost (3), each party communicates (Line 5 of Algorithm 11.2.7) with others to determine the global best candidate. Thus, each party sends $n - 1$ messages, where n is the number of parties. Then, the winner party (Line 8) sends instruction to other parties. This communication process continues for at most s times, where s is the number of valid specializations which is bounded by the number of distinct values in $\cup QID_j$. Hence, for a given data set, the total communication cost is $s\{n(n-1) + (n-1)\} = s(n^2 - 1) \approx O(n^2)$. If $n = 2$, then the total communication cost is $3s$.

In the special case that the anonymity requirement contains only local QIDs, one can shrink down the TIPS to include only local attributes. Parties do not have to pass around the specialization array because each party specializes only local attributes. A party only has to keep track of $QIDTree_j$ only if QID_j is a local QID. The memory requirement and network traffic can be further reduced and the efficiency can be further improved. In the special case that there is only a single QID, each root-to-leaf path in TIPS has represented a qid. One can store $a(qid)$ directly at the leaf partitions in TIPS without QIDTrees. A single QID is considered in where the QID contains all potentially identifying attributes to be used for linking the table to an external source. PPMashup can be more efficient in this special case.

PPMashup presented in Algorithm 11.2.7 is based on the assumption that all the parties are semi-honest. An interesting extension is to consider the presence of malicious and selfish parties [180]. In such scenario, the algorithm has to be not only secure, but also incentive compatible to ensure fair contributions. We study this scenario next.

11.2.5 Anonymization Algorithm for Malicious Model

The PPMashup algorithm presented in Algorithm 11.2.7 satisfies all the conditions of Definition 11.1 only if all the parties follow the defined protocol. However, a malicious party can easily cheat others by under declaring its *Score* value, thus avoiding to share its data with others. Suppose Party A is malicious. During the anonymization process, Party A can always send 0 as its *Score* value to Party B (Line 5 of Algorithm 11.2.7) for determining

Table 11.2: Anonymous tables, illustrating a selfish Party A

Shared		Party A		Party B		
SSN	Class	Sex	...	Job	Salary	...
1-7	0Y7N	ANY		Non-Technical	[1-35)	
8-16	5Y4N	ANY		Technical	[35-37)	
17-25	7Y2N	ANY		Manager	[37-99)	
26-34	9Y0N	ANY		Professional	[37-99)	

the global winner candidate. Hence, Party A indirectly forces Party B to specialize its attributes in every round. This can continue as long as Party B has a valid candidate. Thus, the malicious Party A successfully obtains the locally anonymized data of Party B while sharing no data of its own. Table 11.2 is an example of an integrated anonymous table, where Party A does not participate in the anonymization process. Moreover, this gives Party A a global data set, which is less anonymous than if it has cooperated with Party B.

Next, we provide a solution to prevent parties from reporting fake *Score* values. We assume that a party exhibits its malicious behavior only by reporting a fake *Score* value. It however does not provide wrong data to other parties (Line 8 of Algorithm 11.2.7). Preventing malicious parties from sharing fake data is difficult since data is a private information of a party, which is not verifiable. Further investigation is needed to thwart this kind of misbehavior. In this regard, mechanism design theory [180] could be a potential tool to motivate parties to share their real data.

11.2.5.1 Rational Participation

To generate the integrated anonymous table, each party specializes its own attributes, which can be considered as a contribution. The contribution can be measured by the attribute's *Score* value. Thus, the total contribution of Party A, denoted by μ_A, is the summation of all the *Score* values from its attribute specializations. We use φ_A to denote the contributions of all other parties excluding Party A. This is the ultimate value that each party wants to maximize from the integrated anonymous table.

The *Score* function in Equation 6.1 uses information gain (*InfoGain*) to identify the next candidate for specialization. Yet, *InfoGain* favors the candidate value that has a larger number of child values in the taxonomy tree [191]. If we compare μ_i across different parties, parties having values with a larger number of child values tend to high *Score*, and thereby, resulting in unfair contributions. To avoid this problem, a better *Score* function is to use *GainRatio*, which normalizes the *InfoGain* by *SplitInfo*.

$$Score(v) = GainRatio(v) = \frac{InfoGain(v)}{SplitInfo(v)}. \tag{11.1}$$

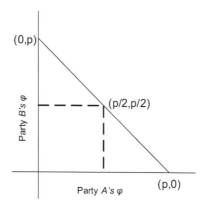

FIGURE 11.7: Rational participation

where

$$SplitInfo(v) = -\sum_{c} \frac{|T[c]|}{|T[v]|} \times log_2 \frac{|T[c]|}{|T[v]|}. \qquad (11.2)$$

Example 11.6

Consider the raw data in 11.1. Initially, $\cup Cut_i = \{ANY\_Sex, ANY\_Job, [1\text{-}99)\}$. The specialization ANY_Job refines the 34 records into 16 records for *Blue-collar* and 18 records for *White-collar*. $Score(ANY\_Job)$ is calculated as follows.

$E(ANY\_Job) = -\frac{21}{34} \times log_2 \frac{21}{34} - \frac{13}{34} \times log_2 \frac{13}{34} = 0.960$

$E(Blue\text{-}collar) = -\frac{5}{16} \times log_2 \frac{5}{16} - \frac{11}{16} \times log_2 \frac{11}{16} = 0.896$

$E(White\text{-}collar) = -\frac{16}{18} \times log_2 \frac{16}{18} - \frac{2}{18} \times log_2 \frac{2}{18} = 0.503$

$InfoGain(ANY\_Job) = E(ANY\_Job) - (\frac{16}{34} \times E(Blue\text{-}collar)$
$\qquad\qquad + \frac{18}{34} \times E(White\text{-}collar)) = 0.272$

$SplitInfo(ANY\_Job) = -\frac{16}{34} \times log_2 \frac{16}{34} - \frac{18}{34} \times log_2 \frac{18}{34} = 0.998$

$GainRatio(ANY\_Job) = \frac{0.272}{0.998} = 0.272.$

□

The value of φ for each party is a function of the anonymization process participated by the different parties. Since all the parties are rational, their actions are driven by self interest. Hence, they may want to deviate from the algorithm to maximize their φ while minimizing μ as much as possible. To overcome this problem, the presented algorithm has to be such that

1. following the algorithm parties will reach a fair distribution of φ

2. deviating from the algorithm will eventually decrease the value of φ.

An anonymous integrated table can be achieved in two ways. Firstly, both the parties ($n = 2$) can specialize their attributes. Certainly, there can be many different choices for attribute selection. The heuristic function presented in Equation 11.1 is one of them. The data holder may apply other heuristic functions. Secondly, only one party can specialize its attributes (based on only local QIDs), while the other party's attributes are generalized to the top most values. In this case, part of the table is locally anonymized and part of the table is completely generalized to the top most values. As an example, consider Party A and B, having the same number of local attributes and being equally capable of contributing to the anonymization process. Let's assume that the integrated table cannot be more specialized after any s number of attribute specializations. Each specialization has the same *Score* value and the sum of the *Score* value is p. Figure 11.7 shows the possible values of φ for both the parties. The line joining points $(0, p)$ and $(p, 0)$ shows different choices of φ values. Both the extreme points represent the participation of one party, while the points in between are the different levels of contributions from the parties. Each party cannot increase its φ value without decreasing the other party's φ. It is now easy to find the unique operating point from these possible alternatives. Rationality suggests that the only point that can be accepted by both the parties is $(p/2, p/2)$. The proposed algorithm ensures that following the algorithm parties will reach this rational participation point.

In reality, each party holds different attributes and some attributes are more informative than others for classification analysis. Thus, all the parties are not equally capable of contributing to the anonymization process. Based on the contribution capability, we assume that parties are divided into y different classes, where parties belonging to class 1 are able to contribute the most and parties belonging to class y are the least capable ones. If there are different numbers of parties from different classes then extending the concept of rationality, we can conclude that the interaction between them will be dominated by the party of the least capable class. For example, if one party of class 1 and two parties of class 2 participate to form an integrated anonymous table, then the party of class 1 will behave as if it belongs to class 2. It is because by contributing more than the class 2 parties, the party of class 1 will not receive any additional contribution from them.

The problem of ensuring honest participation falls into the framework of *non-cooperative game theory*. To make the chapter self-contained, we provide some background information on game theory below. A more general overview of game theory can be found in [24, 183].

11.2.5.2 Game Theory

A game can be defined as an interaction model among players,[3] where each player has its own strategies and possible payoffs. Game theory is the tool

---

[3]We use the word player to refer a party

Player 2 / Player 1	Cooperate	Defect
Cooperate	(5, 5)	(-5, 10)
Defect	(10, - 5)	(0, 0)

FIGURE 11.8: Payoff matrix for prisoner's dilemma

that studies this interaction which is established and broken in the course of cooperation and competition between the players. Game theory can be classified into two categories: *cooperative game theory* and *non-cooperative game theory*. Below we introduce a well known non-cooperative game with an example and illustrate how this model can be used to derive a solution for the aforementioned problem.

Basic Definitions

A normal game consists of a finite set of players $P = \{1, 2, \ldots, n\}$, a strategy set s_1, for each player and a set of outcomes, O. Figure 11.8 shows different elements of a game where two players have two strategies each. The columns represent the strategies of player 2 and the rows represent the strategies of player 1. The intersections between the row and the column represent the payoff of player 1 and 2. For example, the payoff of both the players are 5 when they both choose to "cooperate."

Strategy: Each player can select his strategy from a strategy set s_i. For example, the strategy set for each player is $S_1 = S_2 = \{Cooperate, Defect\}$. A strategy profile $s = \{s_1, s_2, \ldots, s_n\}$ is the vector of strategies. It is the set of all the strategies chosen by the players, whereas $s_{-i} = \{s_1, \ldots, s_{i-1}, s_{i+1}, \ldots, s_n\}$ denotes the strategies of all the players except player i. Strategy profile is the outcome, $o(s) \epsilon O$, of the game. For example, the possible outcomes of the game are (Cooperate, Cooperate), (Cooperate, Defect), (Defect, Cooperate), and (Defect, Defect). Each player chooses its strategy in such a way that its preferred outcome occurs and the preference over the outcome of the game is expressed by the utility function.

Utility Function: Each player has preferences over the outcomes of the game. Preferences over outcomes are represented through a utility function, u_i. Utility function of a player i can be considered as a transformation of the outcome to a real number. It is expressed formally as:

$$u_i : O \rightarrow \Re \qquad (11.3)$$

A player prefers outcome o_1 over outcome o_2 if $u_i(o_1) > u_i(o_2)$. A rational player always wants to maximize its utility. Thus, it chooses a strategy which will increase its expected utility given the preferences of the outcomes, the structure of the game and the belief of others' strategies.

Solution Concepts: Game theory uses different techniques to determine the outcome of the game. These outcomes are the stable or the equilibrium points of the game. The most well known equilibrium concept is known as the *Nash equilibrium*. It states that each player plays its best strategy to maximize the utility, given the strategies of the other players.

DEFINITION 11.2 Nash Equilibrium   A strategy profile

$$s^* = \{s_1^*, s_2^*, \ldots, s_n^*\}$$

is a Nash equilibrium if this strategy profile maximizes the utility of every player, i. Formally

$$\forall i \; u_i(o(s_i^*, s_{-i}^*)) \geq u_i(o(\acute{s}_i, s_{-i}^*)), \forall \acute{s}_i \qquad (11.4)$$

Nash equilibrium is the point where no player can take advantage of the other player's strategy to improve his own position. ∎

For the given example, both the players will play the strategy "defect" since that ensures better payoff regardless of what another player chooses.

Iterated Prisoner's Dilemma

Prisoner's Dilemma (PD) is a classical example of a non-cooperative game, which can be used to describe the decision making process regarding contribution of the rational parties. In PD, two players can choose to cooperate or defect one another. If both the players cooperate, they receive some benefits. If both defect, they receive punishments. If only exactly one cooperates, then the cooperator gets the punishment while the other player receives benefit. The payoff matrix of Figure 11.8 is a canonical example of the prisoner's dilemma.

Certainly, the mutual benefit of both the players is to cooperate. However, from each player's perspective, defect is the best strategy. For example, Player 1 notices that it always gets higher payoff by choosing defect than cooperate irrespective of the strategy of Player 2. Thus, the Nash equilibrium of PD given in Figure 11.8 is to defect for both the players. However, cooperation can emerge as the Nash equilibrium, if this one shot game is played repeatedly. Such a repeated game is known as iterative prisoner's dilemma. In an iterated PD game, each player selects its strategy based on the strategy of the other player in the previous games. This allows players to cooperate with each other. *Generous Tit for Tit (GTFT)* is a well known strategy that enables cooperation to emerge as the Nash equilibrium. In GTFT strategy, each player behaves as the other player does. However, occasionally a player is generous by cooperating even if its opponent defects. It has been proven that GTFT strategy enforces all the players to cooperate in an iterative prisoner's dilemma [24].

11.2.5.3 Participation Strategy

The privacy-preserving data mashup problem can be modeled as an iterative prisoner's dilemma game. If both (n=2) parties cooperate, then they can form a joint integrated table and, thus, both receive benefits. If both choose defect, then it is not possible to form an integrated table, which can be considered as a loss or punishment. However, if one cooperates (the party that contributes), the cooperator gets no benefit, while the other receives more benefit.

To ensure that both the parties will contribute to form the joint integrated table, we can employ a GTFT strategy and adopt it in the context of the privacy-preserving data mashup problem. GTFT helps the parties to reach towards the rational participating point and therefore rationality dictates to follow the strategy. In the revised version of the PPMashup algorithm, each party keeps track of μ and φ values. These values indicate the contributions of the parties. In each iteration, each party decides whether or not to contribute based on these two variables. For two parties, the decision strategy works as follows:

$$\textbf{If } (\mu > \varphi + \epsilon) \textbf{ then } \textit{Not-contribute} \textbf{ else } \textit{Contribute} \qquad (11.5)$$

where ϵ is a small positive number. The general intuition is that each party participates in the anonymization process if it has not contributed more than the other party. However, each party is a bit generous in a sense that it contributes as long as the difference is small. In the case of multiple parties, we can generalize decision strategy as follows:

$$\textbf{If } (\mu > \frac{\varphi}{n-1} + \epsilon) \textbf{ then } \textit{Not-contribute} \textbf{ else } \textit{Contribute} \qquad (11.6)$$

where n is the number of parties.

We incorporate the decision strategy in Algorithm 11.2.7 and present Algorithm 11.2.8 for integrating private tables from multiple malicious parties. The extended algorithm has the following key differences. First, in Lines 5-6, a party does not further contribute if its contributions are larger than the contributions of other parties plus some generosity. Second, in Lines 7-9, the algorithm terminates and returns the current generalized table if all other parties also do not contribute. Finally, in Lines 16 and 20, every party keeps track of its own contributions and other parties' contributions.

11.2.5.4 Analysis

Algorithm 11.2.8 has some nice properties. First, each party only requires to keep two extra variables disregarding the number of participating parties. This makes the decision algorithm scalable. Second, each party decides whether or not to contribute based on the locally generated information. Thus, a party cannot be exploited by others in the decision making process. Third, although the values of μ are not exactly the same for all the parties when the algorithm

---

Algorithm 11.2.8 PPMashup for Every Party in Malicious Model

1: initialize T_g to include one record containing top most values;
2: initialize $\cup Cut_i$ to include only top most values;
3: **while** some candidate $v \in \cup Cut_i$ is valid **do**
4:     find the local candidate x of highest $Score(x)$;
5:     **if** $\mu > \frac{\varphi}{n-1} + \epsilon$ or the party has no valid candidate **then**
6:         send *Not-contribute*;
7:         **if** receive *Not-contribute* from every other party **then**
8:             break;
9:         **end if**
10:     **else**
11:         communicate $Score(x)$ with all other parties to find the winner;
12:     **end if**
13:     **if** the winner w is local **then**
14:         specialize w on T_g;
15:         instruct all other to specialize w;
16:         $\mu := \mu + Score(w)$;
17:     **else**
18:         wait for the instruction from the party who owns w;
19:         specialize w on T_g using the instruction;
20:         $\varphi := \varphi + Score(w)$;
21:     **end if**
22:     replace w with $child(w)$ in the local copy of $\cup Cut_i$;
23:     update $Score(x)$ and beneficial/validity status for candidates $x \in \cup Cut_i$;
24: **end while**
25: **return** T_g and $\cup Cut_i$;

---

terminates, the algorithm progresses by ensuring an almost even contribution from all the parties with a maximum different ϵ. Since parties are unable to determine the last iteration of the algorithm, they will cooperate until the anonymization finishes. Finally, the computational and communication cost of the algorithm remains to be the same as Algorithm 11.2.7 discussed in Chapter 11.2.4.5.

11.2.6 Discussion

We have presented a service-oriented architecture for the privacy-preserving data mashup algorithm. The architecture clearly separates the requesting consumer of the mashup application from the backend process. Due to issues of convenience and control, a mashup coordinator represents a static point of connection between clients and providers with a high rate of availability. A mashup coordinator would also be able to cache frequently requested data tables during a period where they are valid. Requests are attached to a session token identifying a kind of contract between a user and several data holders and are maintained by the mashup coordinator, who can also be a generic service provider. Another benefit is that the mashup coordinator is able to handle and unify several service level agreements among different data holders and queues service requests according to the workload of individual data holders.

In real-life collaborative anonymization problems, different parties agree to share their data when they have mutual trust and benefits. However, if the parties do not want to share their data more than others, then Algorithm 11.2.8 provides an appropriate solution. The participating data holders can decide whether to employ Algorithm 11.2.7 or Algorithm 11.2.8.

Experiments on real-life data verified several claims about the PPMashup algorithms [94]. First, data integration does lead to improved data analysis. Second, PPMashup achieves a broad range of anonymity requirements without sacrificing significantly the usefulness of data to classification. The data quality is identical or comparable to the result produced by the single party anonymization methods [95, 96, 123]. This study suggests that classification analysis has a high tolerance towards data generalization, thereby, enabling data mashup across multiple data holders even in a broad range of anonymity requirements. Third, PPMashup is scalable for large data sets and different single QID anonymity requirements. It provides a practical solution to data mashup where there is the dual need for information sharing and privacy protection.

11.3 Cryptographic Approach

11.3.1 Secure Multiparty Computation

Information integration has been an active area of database research [58, 244]. This literature typically assumes that all information in each database can be freely shared [17]. Secure multiparty computation (SMC), on the other hand, allows sharing of the computed result (e.g., a classifier), but completely prohibits sharing of data [260], which is a primary goal of the problem studied in this chapter. An example is the secure multiparty computation of classifiers [50, 69, 71, 259].

Yang et al. [258] propose several cryptographic solutions to collect information from a large number for data owners. Yang et al. [259] develop a cryptographic approach to learn classification rules from a large number of data owners while their sensitive attributes are protected. The problem can be viewed as a horizontally partitioned data table in which each transaction is owned by a different data owner. The model studied in this chapter can be viewed as a vertically partitioned data table, which is completely different from [258, 259]. More importantly, the output of their method is a classifier, but the output of PPMashup is an integrated anonymous data that supports classification analysis. Having accessed the data, the data recipient has the freedom to apply her own classifier and parameters.

Vaidya and Clifton [228, 229] propose techniques to mine association rules and to compute k-means clustering in a distributed setting without sharing data. Comparing to data mining results sharing, data sharing offers more freedom to the data recipients to apply her own classifiers and parameters. Refer to [227, 230] for more details on privacy-preserving distributed data mining (PPDDM).

Jiang and Clifton [127, 128] propose a cryptographic approach. First, each data holder determines a locally k-anonymous table. Then, the intersection of *RecID*'s for the *qid* groups in the two locally k-anonymous tables is determined. If the intersection size of each pair of *qid* group is at least k, then the algorithm returns the join of the two locally k-anonymous tables that is globally k-anonymous; otherwise, further generalization is performed on both tables and the *RecID* comparison procedure repeated. To prevent the other data holder from learning more specific information than that appearing in the final integrated table through *RecID*, a commutative encryption scheme [189] is employed to encrypt the *RecID*'s for comparison. This scheme ensures the equality of two values encrypted in different order on the same set of keys, i.e., $E_{Key1}(E_{Key2}(RecID)) = E_{Key2}(E_{Key1}(RecID))$.

Their methods, however, have several limitations. This model is limited to only two parties, whereas the technique presented in this chapter is applicable for multiple parties. This data model [128] assumes the participating parties are *semi-honest*, meaning that the data holders follow the secure protocol but may attempt to derive additional (sensitive) information from their collected data. Their solution cannot guarantee the security and fair contributions in the presence of malicious participants as discussed in Chapter 11.2.5. While determining a locally k-anonymous table, each party does not communicate with other parties. As a result, each generalizes the data according to a different set of QID attributes. The locally optimized anonymization may lead to very different *qid* groups. Consequently, the second phase tends to produce very small intersection of record IDs; therefore, the data will be excessively generalized locally in order to have minimal intersection size k. In contrast, the PPMashup always builds the same grouping across all parties by sharing the grouping information. Thus, PPMashup does not generalize the data excessively because of inconsistent groupings at different parties.

11.3.2 Minimal Information Sharing

Agrawal et al. [17] propose the notion of minimal information sharing for computing queries spanning private databases. They considered computing intersection, intersection size, equijoin and equijoin size, assuming that certain metadata such as the cardinality of databases can be shared to both parties. Besides, there exists an extensive literature on inference control in multilevel secure databases [87, 104, 115, 116, 125]. All these works prohibit the sharing of databases.

11.4   Summary and Lesson Learned

We have studied the problem of collaborative anonymization for vertically partitioned data, motivated the problem with a real-life scenario, and generalized the privacy and information requirements from the financial industry to the problem of privacy-preserving data mashup for the purpose of joint classification analysis. This problem has been formalized as achieving the k-anonymity on the integrated data without revealing more detailed information in this process. We have studied several secure protocols for the semi-honest and malicious models. Compared to classic secure multiparty computation, a unique feature in collaborative anonymization is to allow data sharing instead of only result sharing. This feature is especially important for data analysis where the process is hardly performing an input/output black-box mapping and user interaction and knowledge about the data often lead to superior results. Being able to share data records would permit such exploratory data analysis and explanation of results.

In general, the financial sector prefers simple privacy requirement. Despite some criticisms on k-anonymity as we have discussed in previous chapters, the financial sector (and probably some other sectors) finds that k-anonymity is an ideal privacy requirement due to its intuitiveness. Their primary concern is whether they can still effectively perform the task of data analysis on the anonymous data. Therefore, solutions that solely satisfy some privacy requirements are insufficient for them. They demand anonymization methods that can preserve information for various data analysis tasks.

Chapter 12

Collaborative Anonymization for Horizontally Partitioned Data

12.1 Introduction

In the previous chapter, we have studied the data publishing model where multiple data holders want to collaboratively anonymize their vertically partitioned data. In this chapter, we study the problem of *collaborative anonymization for horizontally partitioned data*, where multiple data holders own sets of person-specific data records on the same set of attributes. The model assumes that the sets of records are *disjoint*, meaning that a record owner appears in at most one record set. Often there is a strong urge to integrate scattered data owned by different parties for greater benefits [131]. A good example is the Shared Pathology Informatics Network (SPIN) initiated by National Cancer Institute.[1] The objective is to create a virtual database combining data from different healthcare institutions to facilitate research investigations. Though the virtual database is an integration of different databases, however in reality the data should remain physically in different locations under the complete control of the local healthcare institutions.

There are several practical challenges in such a scenario. First, according to the Health Insurance Portability and Accountability Act (HIPAA), it is not allowed to share the patient's records directly without de-identification. Second, the institutions cannot share their patients' record among themselves due to the confidentiality of the data. Hence, similar to the problem of privacy-preserving data mashup studied in Chapter 11.2, the data integration should take place in such a way that the final integrated table should satisfy some jointly agreed privacy requirements, such as k-anonymity and ℓ-diversity, and every data holder should not learn more detailed information other than those in the final integrated table. This particular scenario can be generalized to the problem of collaborative anonymization for horizontally partitioned data.

Different approaches can be taken to enable data anonymization for distributed databases. Let's first try the same two naive approaches mentioned in the previous chapter: "generalize-then-integrate" and "integrate-

---

[1]Shared Pathology Informatics Network. http://www.cancerdiagnosis.nci.nih.gov/spin/

then-generalize." In the "generalize-then-integrate" approach, each party first locally anonymizes the data and then integrates. Unlike privacy-preserving data mashup, this solution is correct since all the parties own the same set of attributes. However, it suffers from over generalization because each party has a smaller data set, therefore, losing data utility. On the other hand, "integrate-then-generalize" approach is incorrect since the party holding the integrated table has access to all the private data, therefore, violating the privacy requirement. An easy solution is to assume the existence of a trusted third party, where all the data can be integrated before anonymization. Needless to mention, this assumption is not practical since it is not always feasible to find such a trusted third party. Moreover, a third party-based solution is risky because any failure in the trusted third party will comprise the complete privacy of all the participating parties.

In this chapter, we will describe a fully distributed solution proposed by Jurczyk and Xiong in [131] for horizontally partitioned data. The privacy model and proposed solution will be presented briefly followed by discussion.

12.2   Privacy Model

There are two different privacy requirements: privacy for record owners and privacy for data holders.

1. Privacy for record owners requires that the integrated data should not contain any identifiable information of any record owners. To protect the privacy of the record owners, the final integrated table should satisfy both k-anonymity (Chapter 2.1.1) and ℓ-diversity (Chapter 2.2.1) privacy models.

2. Privacy for data holders imposes that the data holder should not reveal any extra information to others in the process of anonymization, nor the ownership of the data.

The second goal of the privacy model is to protect the privacy of the data holders. This requires that each data holder should not reveal any additional information to other data holders than what is in the final integrated table. This requirement is similar to the secure multiparty computation (SMC) protocols, where no participant learns more information than the outcome of the function. To achieve this privacy, the data holders are considered to be *semi-honest*. Refer to Chapter 11.2 for the definition of semi-honest.

The privacy model further requires that the ownership of a particular record in the integrated table should also be concealed. For example, given a particular record, an adversary with some background knowledge should not identify that this record is from a particular hospital. To overcome this problem, ℓ-diversity privacy principle can be used considering location as sensitive information. Thus, for each equivalent class, the records should be from ℓ different locations. This privacy requirement is known as the ℓ-site diversity.

12.3   Overview of the Solution

Initially, the data is located in L different locations, where $L > 2$. Thus, the minimum number of data holders is three. Each data holder $Party_i$ owns a private database d_i over the same set of attributes. The integrated database is the anonymous union of the local databases, denoted by $d = \cup_{1 \leq i \leq L} d_i$. Note that the quasi-identifiers are uniform across all the local databases. Data holders participate in the distributed protocol and produce a local anonymous database which itself may not be k-anonymous and ℓ-diverse, however, the union of the local anonymous databases is guaranteed to be k-anonymous and ℓ-diverse. Note, the solution is not applicable to two parties ($L = 2$) because the secure sum protocol, which will be discussed later, only works for $L > 2$.

The distributed anonymization algorithm is based on the top-down Mondrian algorithm [149]. It is worth mentioning that for distributed anonymization, top-down approach is better than bottom-up anonymization algorithms since anything revealed during the protocol execution has a more general view than the final result. The original Mondrian algorithm was designed for single party, however now it has to be decomposed and SMC protocols have to be used to make a secure distributed algorithm. Refer to Chapter 5.1.2.6 for more details on the Mondrian algorithm.

The distributed anonymization algorithm executes these three phases among different parties securely with the help of SMC protocols. Initially, the data holders are divided into leading and non-leading nodes. One node among all the parties acts as a leading node and guides the anonymization process. The leading node first determines the attribute to specialize. To do this, it needs to calculate the range of all the candidates in $d = \cup_{1 \leq i \leq L} d_i$. A secure k^{th} element protocol can be used to securely compute the minimum ($k = 1$) and maximum values of each attribute across the databases [14].

Once it determines the split attribute, it instructs other data holders to do the specialization. After the partitioning, the leading node recursively checks whether or not further specialization will violate the specified privacy requirements. In order to determine validity of a specialization, a secure sum protocol [207] is used to determine the number of tuples across the whole database. This secure sum protocol is secure when there are more than two data holders with a leading node. The leading node is the only node that is able to

Table 12.1:　Node 0

Original data			Generalized data		
Rec ID	Age	Salary	Rec ID	Age	Salary
1	30	41K	1	30-36	41K-42K
2	33	42K	2	30-36	41K-42K

Table 12.2:　Node 1

Original data			Generalized data		
Rec ID	Age	Salary	Rec ID	Age	Salary
3	45	55K	3	37-56	42K-55K
4	56	42K	4	37-56	42K-55K

Table 12.3:　Node 2

Original data			Generalized data		
Rec ID	Age	Salary	Rec ID	Age	Salary
5	30	32K	5	30-36	32K-40K
6	53	32K	6	37-56	32K-41K

Table 12.4:　Node 3

Original data			Generalized data		
Rec ID	Age	Salary	Rec ID	Age	Salary
7	38	41K	7	37-56	32K-41K
8	33	40K	8	30-36	32K-40K

determine the value of the summation. This imposes some limitations on the proposed distributed algorithm which will be discussed in Chapter 12.4.

Example 12.1
Tables 12.1-12.4 show an example scenario of distribute anonymization. The union of the generalized data in Table 12.5 satisfies 2-anonymity and 1-site-diversity. Note that although the local anonymous data at nodes 2 and 3 are not 2-anonymous individually, the union of all the local generalized data satisfies the 2-anonymity requirement. The union satisfies only 1-site-diversity because the two records in $qid = \langle 30 - 36, 41K - 42K \rangle$ come from the same node.　□

12.4　Discussion

The aforementioned distributed anonymization algorithm is simple, secure, and privacy preserved. One of the advantages of the proposed model is its

Table 12.5: Union of the generalized data

Node ID	Rec ID	Age	Salary
0	1	30-36	41K-42K
0	2	30-36	41K-42K
1	3	37-56	42K-55K
1	4	37-56	42K-55K
2	5	30-36	32K-40K
2	6	37-56	32K-41K
3	7	37-56	32K-41K
3	8	30-36	32K-40K

flexibility to adapt different anonymization algorithms. Though it is built on the multi-dimensional top-down Mondrian algorithm, alternative top-down anonymization algorithms, such as TDS, can also be used with little modification. The overall complexity of the distributed algorithm is $O(nlog^2 n)$, where n is the number of records of the integrated data table.

One weakness of the proposed method is that the distributed anonymization algorithm can only be applied when there are more than two data holders. It is due to the limitation of the secure sum protocol that is used to determine whether any further split of a particular subgroup is possible or not. Besides, though the proposed architecture is distributed, one node acts as a leading node. This leading node controls the entire anonymization process and decides which subgroup to split and when to stop the anonymization process. This architecture works perfectly under the assumption of the semi-honest adversary model; however, if the leading node turns out to be malicious, then the privacy of both the data holders and the record owners are jeopardized. Thus, further investigation is needed to devise an alternative technique of secure sum protocol so that the architecture can be used for two data holders without the need of a leading node.

The method guarantees the privacy of the integrated data to be k-anonymous. However, a data holder can always identify its own data records and remove them from the integrated data. The remaining data records are no longer k-anonymous. This remains to be an issue for open discussion.

Part IV

Anonymizing Complex Data

Chapter 13

Anonymizing Transaction Data

13.1 Introduction

So far, we have considered relational data where all records have a fixed set of attributes. In real life scenarios, there is often a need to publish unstructured data. In this chapter, we examine anonymization techniques for one type of unstructured data, *transaction data*. Like relational data, transaction data D consists of a set of records, $t_1, \ldots, t_n$. Unlike relational data, each record t_i, called a *transaction*, is an arbitrary set of *items* drawn from a universe I. For example, a transaction can be a web query containing several query terms, a basket of purchased items in a shopping transaction, a click stream in an online session, an email or a text document containing several text terms. Transaction data is a rich source for data mining [108]. Examples are association rule mining [18], user behavior prediction [5], recommender systems (www.amazon.com), information retrieval [53] and personalized web search [68], and many other web based applications [253].

13.1.1 Motivations

Detailed transaction data concerning individuals often contain sensitive personal information and publishing such data could lead to serious privacy breaches. America Online (AOL) recently released a database of query logs to the public for research purposes [28]. For privacy protection, all explicit identifiers of searchers have been removed from the query logs. However, by examining the query terms contained in a query, the searcher No. 4417749 was traced back to Thelma Arnold, a 62-year-old widow who lives in Lilburn. Essentially, the re-identification of the searcher is made possible by matching certain "background knowledge" about a searcher with query terms in a query. According to [108], this scandal leads to not only the disclosure of private information for AOL users, but also damages to data publishers' enthusiasm on offering anonymized data to researchers.

The retailer example. To have a closer look at how background knowledge is used in such attacks, let us consider a toy example. Suppose that a web-based retailer released online shopping data to a marketing company for customer behavior analysis. Albert, who works in the marketing company, learned that Jane, a colleague, purchased "printer," "frame," and "camera" from this web site some days ago. Such background knowledge could be acquired from an office conversion, for instance. Having the access to the transaction data, Albert matched these items against all transaction records and surprisingly found only three transactions matched. Furthermore, out of these three transactions, two contain "adult toy." Albert then concluded, with 67% certainty, that Jane bought "adult toy," an item that Jane does not intend to reveal to anybody.

13.1.2   The Transaction Publishing Problem

The problem we consider here, called *privacy-preserving transaction publishing*, can be described as follows. We assume that a set of original transactions D can be collected by a publisher, where each transaction corresponds to an individual (a searcher, a patient, a customer, etc.). The publisher wants to produce and publish an anonymized version D' of D, such that (i) an adversary with background knowledge on an individual cannot link the individual to his transaction in D' or to a sensitive item in his transaction, with a high certainty, (ii) D' retains as much information of D as possible for research. A *record linkage attack* refers to linking an individual to a specific transaction, and an *attribute linkage attack* refers to linking an individual to a specific item. This problem has two emphases that distinguish it from previous works on privacy-preserving data mining.

First, it emphasizes publishing the data, instead of data mining results. There are several reasons why the researcher must receive the actual data, instead of data mining results. First, the researcher wants to have the control over how to mine the data. Indeed, there are many ways that the data can be analyzed and the researcher may want to try more than one of them. Second, data mining is exploratory in nature in that often it is hard to know exactly what patterns will be searched in advance. Instead, the goal of search is refined during the mining process as the data miner gets more and more knowledge about the data. In such cases, publishing the data is essential.

Another emphasis is dealing with background knowledge of an adversary. Background knowledge, also called external knowledge, refers to knowledge that comes from a source other than the published data. In the above retailer example, from an office conversion Albert acquired the background knowledge that Jane purchased "printer," "frame," and "camera." Typical background knowledge includes geographical and demographic information and other not so sensitive information such as items purchased and query terms in a web query. Such knowledge may be acquired either from public sources (such as voter registration lists) or from close interaction with the target individual. Modeling such background knowledge and preventing linking it to a transaction is the key.

13.1.3   Previous Works on Privacy-Preserving Data Mining

Similar to the data publishing problem, privacy-preserving data mining considers hiding certain sensitive information in transactions. Unlike the data publishing problem, however, these works either do not consider publishing the data, or do not consider background knowledge for linking attacks. In this sense, these works are only loosely related to our data publishing problem, therefore, we only briefly review these works. The details can be found in the given references.

Several early works consider publishing data mining results, instead of publishing data, e.g., [233, 206, 35, 22]. As we discussed above, we consider the scenario where publishing data is essential. Therefore, these works are not directly applicable to our problem. The synthetic data approach [241] advocates publishing synthetic data that has similar statistical characteristics but no real semantics associated. A drawback of this approach is that the lack of data semantics disables the use of human's domain knowledge to guide the search in the data mining process. There is a similar problem with the encryption approach [146]. Verykios et al. [233] consider hiding a set of sensitive association rules in a data set of transactions. The original transactions are altered by adding or removing items, in such a way that the sensitive rules do not have the minimum support or the minimum confidence. Note that this approach uses a small support as a means of protection. The exact opposite is true in our problem: a small support means that an individual will be linked to a small number of transactions, which is a privacy breach.

Randomization [84] is another approach to control breaches that arise from the published transactions. However, this approach does not attempt to control breaches that arise from background knowledge besides the transactions. In addition, this approach considers the data collection scenario (instead of the data publishing scenario). In the data collection scenario, there is one server and many clients. Each client has a set of items. The clients want the server to gather statistical information about associations among items. However, the clients do not want the server to know with certainty who has got which items. When a client sends its set of items to the server, it modifies the set according to some specific randomization operators. The server then gathers statistical information from the modified sets of items (transactions) and recovers from it the actual associations. For example, the server wants to learn itemsets that occur frequently within transactions.

The intuition of randomization is that, in addition to replacing some of the items, we shall insert so many "false" items into a transaction that one is as likely to see a "false" itemset as a "true" one [84]. Take the *select-a-size* randomization operator as an example. This operator has parameters $0 \leq \rho \leq 1$ and probabilities $\{p[j]\}_{j=0}^{m}$. Given a transaction t, the operator generates another transaction t' in three steps:

1. The operator selects an integer j at random from the set $\{0, 1, \ldots, m\}$ so that $P[j \text{ is chosen}] = p[j]$;

2. It selects j items from t, uniformly at random (without replacement). These items, and no other items of t, are placed into t';

3. It considers each item $a \notin t$ in turn and tosses a coin with probability ρ of "heads" and $1 - \rho$ of "tails." All those items for which the coin faces "heads" are added to t'.

ρ determines the amount of new items added, and $\{p[j]\}_{j=0}^{m}$ determines the amount of original items deleted. Given ρ, one heuristic is to set the $p[j]$'s so that many original items are made to the randomized transaction, i.e., to maximize $\sum_{j=0}^{m} j \times p[j]$. In [83], the authors consider ρ_1-to-ρ_2 privacy: there is a $\rho_1 - to - \rho_2$ privacy breach with respect to property $Q(t)$ if for some randomized transaction t', $P[t] \leq \rho_1$ and $P[t|t'] \geq \rho_2$, where $0 < \rho_1 < \rho_2 < 1$. In other words, a privacy breach occurs if the posterior $P[t|t']$ has significantly increased (compared to the prior $P[t]$). Evfimievski et al. [83] present a method for finding the $p[j]$'s that maximizes the utility objective $\sum_{j=0}^{m} j \times p[j]$ while eliminating all ρ_1-to-ρ_2 privacy breaches.

13.1.4 Challenges and Requirements

At first glance, the transaction publishing problem is similar to the publishing problem for relational data. However, the unstructured nature of transaction data presents some unique challenges in modeling and eliminating the attacks. Below is a summary of these challenges.

High dimensionality. Since each transaction is an arbitrary set of items, transaction data does not have a natural notion of "attributes," thus, the notion of quasi-identifier (QID), as found on relational data. Typically, the item universe I is very large and a transaction contains a small fraction of the items in I. In the above retailer example, I may have 10,000 items and a transaction typically contains a tiny fraction (say 1% or less) of all items. In the relational presentation, QID would contain one binary attribute for each item in I, thus, has an extremely high dimensionality. Forming an equivalence class on this QID means suppressing or generalizing mostly all items [6].

Itemset based background knowledge. Another implication of the high dimensionality of transaction data is that it is hard to know in advance what sets of items might be used as background knowledge. In the above retailer example, the subset $\{printer, frame, camera\}$ is used as background knowledge. In principle, any subset of items from I can be background knowledge provided that it can be acquired by the adversary on an individual. On the other hand, a "realistic" adversary is frequently limited by the effort required to observe an item on an individual. For example, to find that Jane purchased "printer," "frame," and "camera" from a particular place, Albert has to conduct some investigation. This requires effort and time on the adversary side and is not always successful.

Itemset based utility. Though it is often unknown exactly what data mining tasks the data will be used for, certain elements in the data are generally useful for a wide range of data mining tasks, thus, should be preserved as much as possible. One type of such elements is *frequent itemsets* [18], i.e., the items that co-occur frequently in transactions. Co-occurrences of items potentially represent interesting relationships among items, thus, are excellent candidates for many data mining applications, including association rules mining [18], classification or predication [156], correlation analysis [37], emerging patterns [67], recommender systems (www.amazon.com), and many web based applications [253]. Existing utility metrics designed for relational data fail to capture such itemset based utilities because they measure information loss for each attribute independently.

Besides addressing the above challenges, several other considerations are important for ensuring the practical usefulness of the anonymized data.

Limitation on background knowledge. An adversary uses her background knowledge on the individual to extract relevant transactions. More background knowledge implies more accurate extraction. From the privacy perspective, it is always safer to assume an adversary with as much background knowledge as possible. However, this assumption renders the data less useful. In practice, a "realistic" adversary is often bounded by the amount of background knowledge that can be acquired. Therefore, it makes sense to consider a *bounded* adversary that is limited by the maximum number of items that can be acquired as background knowledge in an attack. An *unbounded* adversary does not have this restriction and can obtain background knowledge on any subset of items.

Truthfulness of results. When the original data is modified to satisfy the privacy constraint, it is essential that the analysis results obtained from the modified data holds on the original data. For example, in the original data, all customers who bought cream and meat have also bought a pregnancy test with 100% certainty, but in the modified data only half of all customers who bought cream and meat have bought a pregnancy test. In this sense, the results derived from the modified data do not hold on the original data. Such results can be misleading and hard to use because the analyst cannot tell whether the 50% is the original certainty or the modified one.

Permitting inferences. The ℓ-diversity principle prevents linking attacks by enforcing the certainty of sensitive inferences $\alpha \to s$ (s being a sensitive item) to no more than $1/l$, where l is typically 4-10. On the other hand, with all inferences being modified to have a certainty below $1/l$, the data becomes less useful, because in most cases, such as prediction and classification, it is the inferences with a high certainty that are most interesting. For a bounded adversary, it is possible to retain all inferences that require background knowledge beyond the power of a bounded adversary. For example, if a bounded adversary can only acquire background knowledge on no more than 10 items, then an inference $\alpha \rightarrow s$ with β containing more than 10 items cannot be exploited by such adversaries. On the other hand, this inference can be used by the researcher for predicting the disease s.

Value exclusiveness. A largely ignored utility aspect is value exclusiveness, that is, the items retained in the modified data are exclusive of each other. This property has a significant impact on data usefulness in practice. Unfortunately, the local recoding transformation [149] does not have this property. Suppose that "Canada" and "USA" are two child items of "North America." Local recoding would allows to generalize x out of y ($x < y$) occurrences of "Canada" and x' out of y' ($x' < y'$) occurrences of "USA," leaving $y - x$ "Canada," $y' - x'$ "USA," and $x + y$ "North America" in the modified data. Now the published count $y - x$ on "Canada" and $y' - x'$ on "USA" are misleading about the original data. In fact, it is not possible to count the number of transactions containing "Canada" (or "USA") from the modified data. Although local recoding has the flexibility of generalizing fewer occurrences of detailed items than global recoding, this example shows that the retained detailed items have little utility. In addition, most data mining algorithms assume value exclusiveness and rely on counting queries. Global recoding scores better in this aspect because it provides value exclusiveness, which enables standard algorithms on the anonymized data.

The rest of this chapter focuses on several recent works on privacy-preserving transaction publishing and query log publishing. The organization is as follows. Chapters 13.2 and 13.3 present two approaches to preventing attribute linkage attacks, i.e., the coherence approach [256, 255] and the band matrix approach [101]. Chapters 13.4 and 13.5 discuss two approaches to preventing record linkage attacks, i.e., the k^m-anonymity approach [220] and the transactional k-anonymity approach [112]. Chapter 13.6 studies the anonymization problem for query log. Chapter 13.7 summarizes the chapter.

13.2 Cohesion Approach

Xu et al. [256] present an approach called *coherence* for eliminating both record linkage attacks and attribute linkage attacks. For any background knowledge on a subset of items, this approach guarantees some minimum number of transactions in the anonymized data such that (i) these transactions match the subset and (ii) no sensitive information in the matching transactions can be inferred with a high certainty. (i) ensures that no specific transaction can be linked and (ii) ensures that no specific sensitive information can be linked. In this Chapter 13.2, we examine this approach in more details.

One assumption in this approach is that the items in I are classified into public items and private items. Public items correspond to potential information on which background knowledge may be acquired by an adversary. Private items correspond to sensitive information that should be protected. For specialized applications such as health care, financial sectors, and insurance industry, well defined guidelines for classifying public/private items often exist.

To launch an attack on a target individual who has a transaction in D, the adversary has the background knowledge that the transaction contains some public items denoted by β (called a public itemset below). An attack is described by $\beta \rightarrow e$, where e is a private item the adversary tries to infer about the target individual. The adversary applies the background knowledge β to focus on the transactions that contain all the items in β. $Sup(\beta)$, called the support of β, denotes the number of such transactions.

$$P(\beta \rightarrow e) = \frac{Sup(\beta \cup \{e\})}{Sup(\beta)}$$

is the probability that a transaction contains e given that it contains β. The *breach probability* of β, denoted by $P_{breach}(\beta)$, is defined by the maximum $P(\beta \rightarrow e)$ for any private item e, i.e., $max_e\{P(\beta \rightarrow e)|e$ is a private item$\}$.

In the retailer example, the adversary has the background knowledge $\beta = \{$"*printer*," "*frame*," "*camera*"$\}$, and finds that, out of the three transactions that contain β, two contains "adult toy." So $Sup(\beta) = 3, Sup(\beta \rightarrow adult\_toy) = 2, P(\beta \rightarrow adult\_toy) = 2/3$. The adversary then infers that Jane bought "adult toy" with the probability $P(\beta \rightarrow adult\_toy) = 2/3 = 67\%$.

13.2.1 Coherence

Given the large size of I, a realistic adversary is limited by a maximum size $|\beta|$ (the number of items in β) of background knowledge β. An adversary has the *power* p if he/she can only acquire background knowledge of up to p public items, i.e., $|\beta| \leq p$. For such β, if $Sup(\beta) < k$, the adversary is able to link a target individual to a transaction with more than $1/k$ probability; if $P_{breach}(\beta) > h$, the adversary is able to link a target individual to a private item with more than h probability. This motivates the following privacy notion.

DEFINITION 13.1 Coherence   A public itemset β with $|\beta| \leq p$ and $Sup(\beta) > 0$ is called a *mole* with respect to (h, k, p) if either $Sup(\beta) < k$ or $P_{breach}(\beta) > h$. The data D is (h, k, p)-*coherent* if D contains no moles with respect to (h, k, p), that is, for all public itemsets β with $|\beta| \leq p$ and $Sup(\beta) > 0$, $Sup(\beta) \geq k$ and $P_{breach}(\beta) \leq h$. ∎

Table 13.1: $D, k = 2, p = 2, h = 0.8$

TID	Activities	Medical History
T_1	a,c,d,f,g	Diabetes
T_2	a,b,c,d	Hepatitis
T_3	b,d,f,x	Hepatitis
T_4	b,c,g,y,z	HIV
T_5	a,c,f,g	HIV

$Sup(\beta) < k$ and $P_{breach}(\beta) > h$ correspond to record linkage attacks and attribute linkage attacks. A mole is any background knowledge (constrained by the maximum size p) that can lead to a linking attack. The goal of coherence is to eliminate all moles.

Example 13.1
Suppose that a healthcare provider publishes the data D in Table 13.1 for research on life styles and illnesses. "Activities" refer to the activities a person engages in (e.g., drinking, smoking) and are public. "Medical History" refers to the person's major illness and is considered private. Each person can have a number of activities and illness chosen from a universe I. Consider $k = 2, p = 2, h = 80\%$. D violates (h, k, p)-coherence because only one transaction T_2 contains ab (we use ab for $\{a, b\}$). So an adversary acquiring the background knowledge ab can uniquely identify T_2 as the transaction of the target individual. For the background knowledge bf, transactions T_2 and T_3 contain bf. However, both transactions also contain "Hepatitis." Therefore, an adversary with the background knowledge bf can infer "Hepatitis" with 100% probability. $\qquad\square$

13.2.2   Item Suppression

A mole can be removed by suppressing any item in the mole. *Global suppression* of an item refers to deleting the item from *all* transactions containing it. *Local suppression* of an item refers to deleting the item from *some* transactions containing it. Global suppression has two nice properties. First, it guarantees to eliminate all moles containing the suppressed item. Second, it leaves any remaining itemset with the support equal to the support in the original data. The second property implies that any result derived from the modified data also holds on the original data. Local suppression does not have these properties. For this reason, we shall consider global suppression of items.

Example 13.2
Consider three transactions $\{a, b, HIV\}$, $\{a, b, d, f, HIV\}$, and $\{b, d, f, Diabetes\}$. The global suppression of a and f transforms these transactions into $\{b, HIV\}$,

$\{b, d, HIV\}$, and $\{b, d, Diabetes\}$. After the suppression, the remaining item-sets bd and $bdHIV$ have the support of 2 and 1, which is the same as in the original data. Instead, the local suppression of b from only the transaction $\{a, b, d, f, HIV\}$ leaves the itemsets bd and $bdHIV$ with the support of 1 and 0, which is different from the support in the original data. □

Let $IL(e)$ denote the information loss caused by suppressing an item e. There are many metrics for information loss. A simple metric is a constant penalty associated with each item e. Another metric is the number of occur-rences of e suppressed, which is equal to $Sup(e)$ under global suppression. More sophisticatedly, $IL(e)$ can be defined by the number of patterns, such as frequent itemsets, eliminated by the suppression of e. We will consider this metrics in Chapter 13.2.4. We assume that private items are important and will not be suppressed. Suppose that D is transformed to D' by suppress-ing zero or more public items. We define $IL(D, D') = \sum_e IL(e)$ to be the information loss of the transformation, where e is an item suppressed.

DEFINITION 13.2 Let D' be a transformation of D by suppressing public items. D' is a (h, k, p)-*cohesion* of D if D' is (h, k, p)-coherent. D' is an *optimal* (h, k, p)-cohesion of D if D' is a (h, k, p)-cohesion of D and for every other (h, k, p)-cohesion D'' of D, $IL(D, D'') \geq IL(D, D')$. The optimal cohesion problem is to find an optimal (h, k, p)-cohesion of D. ∎

It can be shown that D has no (h, k, p)-cohesion if and only if the empty itemset is a mole with respect to (h, k, p). We assume that the empty set is not a mole. Xu et al. [256] show, by a reduction from the vertex cover problem, that the optimal cohesion problem is NP-hard, even for the special case of $k = 2, p = 2, IL(e) = 1$.

13.2.3 A Heuristic Suppression Algorithm

Since the optimal cohesion problem is NP-hard, a heuristic solution was proposed in [256]. The algorithm greedily suppresses the next item e with the maximum $Score(e)$ until all moles are removed. The algorithm focuses on *minimal moles*, i.e., those moles that contain no proper subset as a mole, as removing all such moles is sufficient for removing all moles. Let $MM(e)$ denote the set of minimal moles containing the public item e and $|MM(e)|$ denote the number of minimal moles in $MM(e)$. The score

$$Score(e) = \frac{|MM(e)|}{IL(e)} \tag{13.1}$$

measures the number of minimal moles eliminated per unit of information loss. Algorithm 13.2.9 shows this greedy algorithm.

Algorithm 13.2.9 The Greedy Algorithm

1: suppress all size-1 moles from D;
2: **while** there are minimal moles in D **do**
3:     suppress a remaining public item e with the maximum $Score(e)$ from D;
4: **end while**;

Two questions remain. The first question is how to tell whether there are minimal moles in D at line 2. The second question is how to identify the public item e with the maximum $Score(e)$ at line 3. Recomputing all minimal moles in each iteration is not scalable because the number of minimal moles is large. Another approach is finding all minimal moles in a preprocessing step and maintaining minimal moles in each iteration. Below, we describe the detail of finding minimal moles and maintaining minimal moles.

13.2.3.1   Finding Minimal Moles

A minimal mole contains no subset as a minimal mole. Thus one strategy for finding all minimal moles is examining i-itemsets in the increasing size i until an itemset becomes a mole *for the first time*, at which time it must be a minimal mole. If an examined i-itemset β is not a mole, we then extend β by one more item; such β is called an *extendible non-mole*. The benefit of this strategy is that all examined candidates of size $i + 1$ can be constructed from extendible non-moles of size i, so that we can limit the search to extendible non-moles in each iteration.

Let M_i denote the set of minimal moles of size i and let F_i denote the set of extendible non-moles of size i. For every $\beta = \langle e_1, \ldots, e_{i-1}, e_i, e_{i+1} \rangle$ in M_{i+1} or in F_{i+1}, by definition, no i-subset of β should be in M_i and both of $\langle e_1, \ldots, e_{i-1}, e_i \rangle$ and $\langle e_1, \ldots, e_{i-1}, e_{i+1} \rangle$ should be in F_i. In other words, each $\beta = \langle e_1, \ldots, e_{i-1}, e_i, e_{i+1} \rangle$ in M_{i+1} and F_{i+1} can be constructed from a pair of $\langle e_1, \ldots, e_{i-1}, e_i \rangle$ and $\langle e_1, \ldots, e_{i-1}, e_{i+1} \rangle$ in F_i. This computation is given in Algorithm 13.2.10.

This algorithm shares some similarity with Apriori [18] for mining frequent itemsets. Apriori exploits the subset property that every proper subset of a frequent itemset is a frequent itemset. A minimal mole has the property that every proper subset of a minimal mole (and an extendible non-mole) is an extendible non-mole. To exploit the subset property, we have to construct M_{i+1} and F_{i+1} in parallel.

13.2.3.2   Maintaining Minimal Moles

After suppressing an item e in the current iteration in Algorithm 13.2.9, we shall maintain the set of remaining minimal moles, M^*, and $Score(e')$ for each remaining public item e'. Note that $IL(e')$ defined by $Sup(e')$ is unaffected by

Algorithm 13.2.10 Identifying Minimal Moles
1: find M_1 and F_1 in one scan of D;
2: **while** $i < p$ and F_i is not empty **do**
3:      generate the candidate set C_{i+1} from F_i as described above;
4:      scan D to count $Sup(\beta)$ and $P_{breach}(\beta)$ for all β in C_{i+1};
5:      **for all** β in C_{i+1} **do**
6:        **if** $Sup(\beta) < k$ or $P_{breach}(\beta) > h$ **then**
7:          add β to M_{i+1};
8:        **else**
9:          add β to F_{i+1};
10:        **end if**
11:      **end for**
12:      $i + +$;
13: **end while**

the suppression of e. $|MM(e')|$ will be decreased by the number of minimal moles that contain $e'e$. To compute this number, we can store all minimal moles in M^* in the following MOLE-tree. The *MOLE-tree* contains the root labeled "null" and a root-to-leaf path for each minimal mole in M^*. Each non-root node has three fields: *label* - the item at this node; *mole-num* - the number of minimal moles that pass this node; *node-link* - the link pointing to the next node with the same label. In addition, the *Score* table contains three fields for each remaining public item e: $|MM(e)|$, $IL(e)$, *head-of-link(e)* that points to the first node on the node-link for e. On suppressing e, all minimal moles containing e can be found and deleted by following the node-link for e. The next example illustrates this update.

Example 13.3

Figure 13.1 shows the MOLE-tree for seven minimal moles

$$M^* = \{db, da, dg, dc, ba, bg, bf\},$$

where items are arranged in the descending order of $|MM(e)|$. Assume $IL(e) = Sup(e)$. The node $< b : 3 >$ indicates that 3 minimal moles pass the node, i.e., ba, bg, bf. The entry $< b : 4, 3 >$ in the *Score* table indicates that $|MM(b)| = 4, IL(b) = 3$. Since the item d has the maximum $Score = |MM|/IL$, we first suppress d by deleting all minimal moles passing the (only) node for d. This is done by traversing the subtree at the node for d and decreasing $|MM|$ for b, a, g, and c by 1, and decreasing $|MM|$ for d by 4. Now $|MM(d)|$ and $|MM(c)|$ become 0, so the entries for d and c are deleted from the *Score* table. The new MOLE-tree and *Score* table are shown in Figure 13.2. Next, the item b has the maximum $|MM|/IL$ and is suppressed. At this point, all remaining moles are deleted and now the Score table becomes empty. $\square$

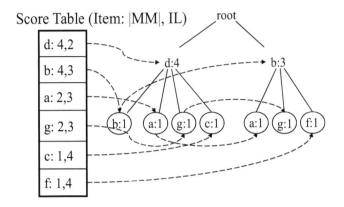

FIGURE 13.1: MOLE-tree: $k = 2, p = 2, h = 80\%$

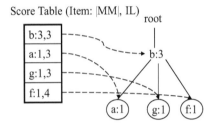

FIGURE 13.2: MOLE-tree: $k = 2, p = 2, h = 80\%$

The above approach has been evaluated on a variety of data sets in [256]. The main findings are that, for a dense data, it suffices to suppress a small number of low support items and distortion is low (usually less than 10%). For a sparse data, distortion is larger (usually 15%) because of the large number of moles to eliminate. Also, the study shows that more public items and a larger adversary's power lead to more distortion.

13.2.4 Itemset-Based Utility

The aforementioned information loss $IL(e)$ is measured by considering only the item e itself (e.g., $Sup(e)$). In some applications, certain co-occurrences of items are the source of utility. For example, frequent itemset mining [18] is looking for the itemsets that have support no less than some threshold. If an item e occurs in no frequent itemset, suppressing the item incurs no information loss. On the other hand, if an item e occurs in many frequent itemsets, suppressing the item incurs a large information loss because all frequent itemsets containing e are removed from the data.

To model the above itemset based utility, Xu et al. [255] consider an itemset α to be a *nugget* with respect to (k', p') if $|\alpha| \leq p'$ and $Sup(\alpha) \geq k'$, where k' and p' are user-specified parameters. In other words, a nugget is an itemset that has a large support and a size bounded by a maximum length. Let $N(D)$ denote the set of nuggets in D with respect to (k', p') and $|N(D)|$ denote the number of nuggets in D. Note that, for any D' obtained from D by global suppression of items, $N(D') \subseteq N(D)$.

The goal is to find a (h, k, p)-cohesion D' with the maximum $|N(D')|$. Let $M(e)$ and $N(e)$ denote the set of moles and nuggets containing the item e. To retain nuggets, we can suppress a remaining public item e with the maximum $Score(e) = |M(e)|/|N(e)|$, which maximizes the number of moles eliminated per nugget lost. For each remaining public item e', $|M(e')|$ and $|N(e')|$ will be decreased by the number of moles and nuggets containing ee'. In Chapter 13.2.3.2, we maintain all minimal moles because eliminating minimal moles is sufficient for eliminating all moles. This approach is not applicable to nuggets because we must compute the actual count $|N(e)|$ for preserving nuggets. However, maintaining all nuggets is not an option because the number of nuggets grows exponentially.

Xu et al. [255] propose a border approach for updating $|M(e')|$ and $|N(e')|$. The observation is that $M(D)$ can be represented by a border $[U, L]$: U is the collection of minimal itemsets in $M(D)$ (i.e., those that have no subset in $M(D)$) and L is the collection of maximal itemsets in $M(D)$ (i.e., those that have no superset in $M(D)$). Similarly, $N(D)$ can be represented by a border. Xu et al. [255] present an algorithm for maintaining these borders and a method for computing $|M(e')|$ and $|N(e')|$ using these borders. Since borders are much smaller than the full sets of all itemsets that they represent, maintaining borders requires much less space and time.

13.2.5 Discussion

Terrovitis et al. [220] propose the notion of k^m-anonymity to prevent record linkage attacks: D satisfies k^m-*anonymity* if for any itemset β with $|\beta| \leq m$, at least k transactions in D contain all the items in β. We can show that k^m-anonymity is a special case of (h, k, p)-coherence. To model k^m-anonymity, we consider all the items in I as public items and a new item universe $I' = I \bigcup \{e\}$, where e is a new item and is the only private item. We add the new item e to every transaction in D. Now each attack under the coherence model has the form $\beta \rightarrow e$, where β is an itemset with items drawn from I and e is the new item. By setting $h = 100\%$, the condition $P_{breach}(\beta) \leq h$ always holds and the (h, k, p)-coherence degenerates into the requirement that, for all itemsets β drawn from I with $|\beta| \leq p$ and $Sup(\beta) > 0$, $Sup(\beta) \geq k$. This requirement is exactly the k^m-anonymity with $m = p$.

PROPOSITION 13.1
Let D and D' be the transaction data defined above. D is k^m-anonymous if and only if D' is (h, k, p)-coherent with $h = 100\%$ and $p = m$. ∎

Another interesting property of (h, k, p)-coherence is that it *permits* data mining rules $\beta \rightarrow s$ for a private item s with $|\beta| > p$. In 13.1, for $p = 1, k = 2, h = 80\%$, D is (h, k, p)-coherent, though $bf \rightarrow Hepatitis$ has 100% probability. This means that, for a data recipient with the power $p = 1$, she will be able to extract this rule for research purposes, but is not able to link this rule to an individual. This property is particularly interesting as the research in [156] shows that accurate rules $\beta \rightarrow s$ usually involve a long antecedent β. A long antecedent sets up a high bar for the adversary under our model but enables data mining for a genuine researcher. In contrast, ℓ-diversity forces all rules $\beta \rightarrow s$ for a private item s to no more than $1/l$ certainty, where l is usually 4 or larger, as required by privacy protection. Such rules are less useful for data mining because the certainty is too low.

In Chapter 13.2.2, we discussed that total item suppression retains the original support of remaining itemsets. This property guarantees that rules extracted from the modified data hold on the original data. For example, the usefulness of the association rule $bd \rightarrow HIV$ depends on the confidence $Sup(bdHIV)/Sup(bd)$. A small change in the support $Sup(bdHIV)$ or $Sup(bd)$ could lead to a significant difference in the confidence, thus, unexpected or even invalid data mining results. In Example 13.2, the global suppression a and f leaves the rule $bd \rightarrow HIV$ with the same confidence as in the original data, i.e., 50%, but the local suppression yields the confidence of 0%, which does not hold on the original data. Unfortunately, this issue has not received much attention in the literature. For example, local recoding has a similar problem to local suppression, thus, does not retain the original occurrence count of attribute/value combinations.

13.3   Band Matrix Method

Ghinita et al. [101] present another method called *band matrix method* below for preventing attribute linkage attacks. Given a set of transactions D containing items from I, this method determines a partitioning P of D into anonymized groups with "privacy degree" at least p, such that the "reconstruction error" using such groups is minimized. Like the coherence approach, this method classifies the items in I into sensitive items (i.e., private items), S, and non-sensitive items (i.e., public items), $Q = I - S$. We call such items S-items and Q-items, respectively. A transaction containing no S-item is a non-sensitive transaction, otherwise, a sensitive transaction. We explain the notion of privacy degree, reconstruction error, and the algorithm for grouping transactions.

A transformation of transaction data D has *privacy degree* p if the probability of associating any transaction $t \in D$ with a particular sensitive item does not exceed $1/p$. To enforce this privacy requirement, D is partitioned into disjoint sets of transactions, called *anonymized groups*. Like Anatomy [249], for each group G, it publishes the exact Q-items, together with a summary of the frequencies of S-items contained in G. Let $f_1, \ldots, f_m$ be the number of occurrences for sensitive items $s_1, \ldots, s_m$ in G. Then group G offers privacy degree $p^G = min_{i=1..m} |G|/f_i$. The privacy degree of an entire partitioning P of D is defined by the minimum p^G for all groups G.

13.3.1 Band Matrix Representation

Another criterion for grouping transactions is to preserve the correlation between items as much as possible. In other words, transactions that share many items in common should be assigned to the same group. To identify such transactions, D is represented by a *band matrix* [103, 194]. In a band matrix, rows correspond to transactions t and columns correspond to Q-items i, with the 0/1 value in each entry (t, i) indicating whether t contains i. A band matrix has the general form shown in Figure 13.3, where all entries of the matrix are 0, except for the main diagonal d_0, a number of U upper diagonals $(d_1, \ldots, d_U)$, and L lower diagonals $(d_{-1}, \ldots, d_{-L})$. The objective of band matrix is to minimize the total bandwidth $B = U + L + 1$, by rearranging the order of rows and columns in the matrix, thus, bringing transactions that share items in common close to each other. Finding an optimal band matrix, i.e. with minimum B, is NP-complete. Multiple heuristics have been proposed to obtain band matrices with low bandwidth. The most prominent is the Reverse Cuthill-McKee algorithm, a variation of the Cuthill-McKee algorithm [54].

13.3.2 Constructing Anonymized Groups

Once the data is transformed to a band matrix with a narrow bandwidth, the next step is to create anonymized groups of transactions. To satisfy the privacy requirement, each sensitive transaction is grouped with non-sensitive transactions or sensitive ones with different sensitive items. A greedy algorithm called *Correlation-aware Anonymization of High-dimensional Data* (*CAHD*) is presented in [101]. This algorithm adopts the "one-occurrence-per-group" heuristic that allows only one occurrence of each sensitive item in a group. It is shown that if solution to the anonymization problem with privacy degree p exists, then such an heuristic will always find a solution.

CAHD works as follows: given a sensitive transaction t_0, it forms a candidate list (CL) by including all the non-conflicting transactions in a window centered at t_0. A transaction is non-conflicting with t_0 if either it is non-sensitive or it has a different sensitive S-item. The window contains $2\alpha p - 1$ non-conflicting

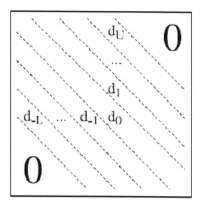

FIGURE 13.3: A band matrix ([101] ©2008 IEEE)

transactions, where α is a system parameter. Then, out of the transactions in $CL(t_0)$, the $p-1$ of them that have the largest number of Q-items in common with t_0 are chosen to form the anonymized group with t_0. The intuition is that, the more transactions share the same Q-items, the smaller the reconstruction error is (see the discussion below shortly). All selected transactions are then removed from D, and the process continues with the next sensitive transaction in the order.

It is important that at any time, forming a group will not yield a remaining set of transactions that can not be anonymized (for instance, if all remaining transactions share one common sensitive item). To ensure this, a histogram with the number of remaining occurrences for each sensitive item is maintained every time a new group is formed. If forming a group yields a remaining set of transactions that violates the privacy requirement, the current group is rolled back and a new group formation is attempted starting from the next sensitive transaction in the sequence.

Example 13.4
Table 13.2 shows the original matrix with the sensitive items. Table 13.3 shows the matrix after the rearrangement of rows and columns, where non-sensitive items are more closely clustered around the main diagonal. Table 13.4 shows two groups that have privacy degree 2. From the original data in Table 13.2, we can infer that all customers who bought cream but not meat have also bought a pregnancy test (with 100% certainty). From the anonymized data in Table 13.4, the adversary can only infer that half of such customers have bought a pregnancy test. This example is borrowed from [101]. □

Table 13.2: Example of band matrix: original data

Name	Wine	Meat	Cream	Strawberries	Sensitive Items Pregnancy Test	Viagra
Bob	X		X			X
David	X		X			
Claire		X		X	X	
Andrea		X	X			
Ellen	X		X	X		

Source: [101] ©2008 IEEE

Table 13.3: Example of band matrix: re-organized data

Name	Wine	Meat	Cream	Strawberries	Sensitive Items Pregnancy Test	Viagra
Bob	X	X				X
David	X	X				
Ellen	X	X	X			
Andrea		X		X		
Claire			X	X	X	

Source: [101] ©2008 IEEE

Table 13.4: Example of band matrix: anonymized data

Name	Wine	Meat	Cream	Strawberries	Sensitive Items
Bob	X	X			
David	X	X			Viagra: 1
Ellen	X	X	X		
Andrea		X		X	Pregnancy
Claire			X	X	Test: 1

Source: [101] ©2008 IEEE

13.3.3 Reconstruction Error

The information loss of anonymized groups is measured by the reconstruction error in terms of the KL-divergence of the distribution of S-items in the result for answering a query. A query has the form

SELECT COUNT(*)
FROM D
WHERE (Sensitive Item s is present) AND Cell

Cell is a condition on Q-items $q_1, \ldots, q_r$ of the form $q_1 = val_1 \wedge \cdots \wedge q_r = val_r$. Such queries can be modeled using a probability distribution function (pdf) of a S-item s over the space defined by all cells for $q_1, \ldots, q_r$. The total number of such cells is 2^r, corresponding to all combinations of presence and absence of these Q-items in a transaction. The actual pdf value of a S-item s for a cell C is

$$Act_C^s = \frac{\text{Occurrences of } s \text{ in } C}{\text{Total occurrences of } s \text{ in } D} \tag{13.2}$$

In other words, Act_C^s is the proportion of s in C.

When the query is applied to a group G, the query result for the cell C on G is estimated as follows. Denote the number of occurrences of S-item s in G by a, and the number of transactions that match the Q-items selection predicate in Cell of the query by b. Then the estimated result of the query for G is $a\Delta b/|G|$. Intuitively, $b/|G|$ is the probability that a transaction matches the Q-item selection predicate Cell for G. For the estimated pdf Est_C^s, we replace the numerator "Occurrences of s in C" of Equation 13.2 with $a\Delta b/|G|$ summed over all groups G that intersect C. Then the utility of the anonymized data is measured as the distance between Act_C^s and Est_C^s over all cells C, measured by the KL-divergence:

$$\sum_C Act_C^s log \frac{Act_C^s}{Est_C^s}. \tag{13.3}$$

13.3.4 Discussion

Since exact Q-items are published, the band matrix method cannot be used to prevent record linkage attacks. Indeed, in this case, each anonymized group is a set of original transactions, and publishing such groups leads to publishing the exact original database.

Like ℓ-diversity [160] and Anatomy [249], the anonymized data produced by the band matrix method could yield untruthful analysis results, i.e., results that do not hold on the original data. Example 13.4 illustrates this point. In the original data, all customers who bought cream but not meat have also bought a pregnancy test with 100% certainty; whereas in the anonymized data, only half of all customers who bought cream but not meat have bought a pregnancy test. The 50% certainty derived from the modified data does not hold on the original data. Since the analyst cannot tell whether the 50% certainty is the original certainty or the modified one, it is hard to use such analysis results because it may or may not hold on the original data.

As dictated by the privacy degree p, all correlations involving S-items have a low certainty, i.e., no more than $1/p$. Typically, p is 4 or larger. With the certainty being so low, such correlations are less useful for data mining. On the other hand, this method loses no information on correlations involving only Q-items because exact Q-items are published.

13.4 k^m-**Anonymization**

Now we turn to two methods that focus on record linkage attacks (note that the coherence approach also handles record linkage attacks). We discuss the k^m-anonymity method proposed in [220], and in Chapter 13.5, we discuss the k-anonymity method for transaction data proposed in [112]. Both methods assume that any subset of items can be used as background knowledge and that an item taxonomy is available. Both remove record linkage attacks by generalizing detailed items to general items according to the given item taxonomy. They differ mainly in the notion of privacy.

13.4.1 k^m-**Anonymity**

Like the coherence approach, the k^m-anonymity approach assumes that an adversary is limited by the maximum number m of items that can be acquired as background knowledge in an attack.

DEFINITION 13.3 k^m-*anonymity*   A transaction database D is said to be k^m-*anonymous* if no adversary that has background knowledge of up to m items of a transaction $t \in D$ can use these items to identify less than k transactions from D. The k^m-anonymization problem is to find a k^m-anonymous transformation D' for D with minimum information loss. ∎

In other words, k^m-anonymity means that for any subset of up to m items, there are at least k transactions that contain all the items in the subset. As discussed in Chapter 13.2, this privacy notion coincides with the special case of (h, k, p)-coherence with $h = 100\%$ and $p = m$. In this case, a subset of items that causes violation of k^m-anonymity is exactly a mole under the (h, k, p)-coherence model.

To transform D to a k^m-anonymous D', Terrovitis et al. [220] employ an item taxonomy to generalize precise items to general items, in contrast to the suppression operation for coherence. Terrovitis et al. [220] adopt the global recoding scheme: if any child node is generalized to the parent node, all its sibling nodes are generalized to the parent node, and the generalization always applies to all transactions. Figure 13.4 shows a sample database and the transformation using the generalization rule $\{a_1, a_2 \rightarrow A\}$. Each possible transformation under the global recoding scheme corresponds to a possible horizontal cut of the taxonomy tree. The set of possible cuts also forms a hierarchy lattice, based on the generalization relationship among cuts. A set of possible cuts is shown in Figure 13.5 for the small taxonomy and the hierarchy lattice for these cuts is shown in Figure 13.6.

The information loss of a cut can be measured in various ways. For con-

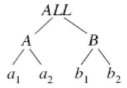

id	contents
t_1	$\{a_1, b_1, b_2\}$
t_2	$\{a_2, b_1\}$
t_3	$\{a_2, b_1, b_2\}$
t_4	$\{a_1, a_2, b_2\}$

(a) original database (D)

id	contents
t_1'	$\{A, b_1, b_2\}$
t_2'	$\{A, b_1\}$
t_3'	$\{A, b_1, b_2\}$
t_4'	$\{A, b_2\}$

(b) transformed database (D')

FIGURE 13.4: Transformation using generalization rule $\{a_1, a_2\} \rightarrow A$ ([220])

creteness, consider the *loss metric* proposed in [123]. For each generalized item i, this metric charges an information loss that is proportional to (i) the percentage of leaf nodes under i in the item taxonomy and (ii) the occurrences of i in the generalized data. Therefore, if the cut c_0 is more general than the cut c, both (i) and (ii) of c_0 will be larger than those of c, so c_0 has a higher cost (information loss) than c.

The set of possible cuts satisfies the following *monotonicity property*. If the hierarchy cut c results in a k^m-anonymous database, then all cuts c_0, such that c_0 is more general than c, also result in a k^m-anonymous database. Under the above cost metric for information loss, based on this monotonicity property, as soon as we find a cut c that satisfies the k^m-anonymity constraint, we do not have to seek for a better cut in c's ancestors.

13.4.2   Apriori Anonymization

Enumerating the entire cut lattice is not scalable. In addition, validating a cut requires checking if any subset of up to m items causes a violation of the anonymity requirement. The number of such subsets can be very large. A greedy algorithm called Apriori anonymization (AA) is proposed in [220] to find a good cut. This algorithm is based on the apriori principle: if a i-itemset α causes anonymity violation, so does each superset of α. Thus it explores the space of itemsets in an apriori, bottom-up fashion. It first identifies and eliminates anonymity violations caused by $(l-1)$-itemsets, before checking l-itemsets, $l = 2, \ldots, m$. By operating in such a bottom-up fashion, the number of itemsets that have to be checked at a higher level are greatly reduced, as detailed items could have been generalized to more generalized ones. This algorithm is given in Algorithm 13.4.11.

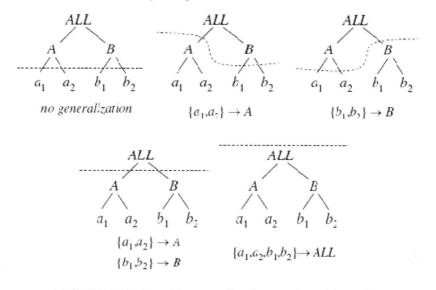

FIGURE 13.5: Possible generalizations and cut hierarchy

Algorithm 13.4.11 Apriori-Based Anonymization

$AA(D, k, m)$

1: initialize *GenRules* to the empty set;
2: **for all** $i := 1$ to m **do**
3:    initialize a new count-tree;
4:    **for all** $t \in D$ **do**
5:      extend t according to *GenRules*;
6:      add all i-subsets of extended t to count-tree;
7:      run DA on count-tree for $m = i$ and update *GenRules*;
8:    **end for**;
9: **end for**;

First, the algorithm initializes the set of generalization rules *GenRules* to the empty set. In the ith iteration, a count-tree data structure is constructed to keep track of all i-itemsets and their support. This structure is very similar to the MOLE-tree used for counting moles in Chapter 13.2. Each root-to-leaf path in the count-tree represents a i-itemset. Line 5 generalizes each transaction t in D according to the generalization rules *GenRules*. For each generalized transaction t, line 6 adds all i-subsets of t to a new count-tree and increases the support of each i-subset. Line 7 identifies all i-subsets with a support below k and finds a set of generalization rules to eliminate all such i-subsets. This step runs *Direct Anonymization* (*DA*) on the count-tree, another heuristic algorithm proposed in [220] that operates directly on i-itemsets violating the anonymity requirement. After the mth iteration, all i-

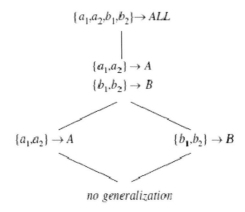

FIGURE 13.6: Possible generalizations and cut hierarchy

subsets of items with support below k are removed, $i \leq m$. The final *GenRules* is the set of generalization rules that will transform D into k^m-anonymity.

The benefit of this algorithm is that it exploits the generalizations performed in iteration i, to reduce the search space in iteration $i+1$. This is because earlier generalizations reduce the size of the taxonomy, pruning detailed items, for later iterations. As the algorithm progresses to larger values of i, the effect of pruned detailed items increases because (i) more generalization rules are expected to be in *GenRules* and (ii) the total number of i-itemsets increases exponentially with i. Terrovitis et al. [220] also present *Optimal Anonymization (OA)* that explores in a bottom-up fashion all possible cuts and picks the best one. Although optimal, OA cannot be applied for realistic databases because it has very high computational cost due to the exhaustive search nature.

13.4.3 Discussion

The k^m-anonymity approach only handles record linkage attacks, not attribute linkage attacks. For record linkage attacks, the privacy notion is the same as the notion of coherence when all items are public items, as shown in Proposition 13.1. Both models consider a bounded adversary having background knowledge limited by the maximum number of items. The main difference lies at the anonymization operator. The coherence approach uses total item suppression, whereas the k^m-anonymization approach uses global item generalization. Another difference is that the coherence approach also handles attribute linkage attacks, but the k^m-anonymity approach does not.

Item suppression and item generalization each have its own strengths and weaknesses. Item suppression is effective in dealing with "outliers" that cause violation of the privacy requirement, but may have a large information loss if the data is sparse. In contrast, global generalization is vulnerable to "outlier"

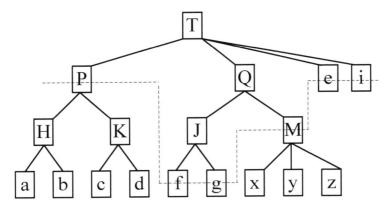

FIGURE 13.7: Outliers e and i cause generalization to top item T

items because the generalization of such items causes the generalization of other items. We show this point in Figure 13.7. The dashed curve represents a cut through the taxonomy, which corresponds to a solution by the generalization approach. Suppose that the items e and i are contained in less than k transactions, the global generalization will cause all items to be generalized to the top level, even though the other items do not cause violation. In contrast, suppressing the items e and i is all we need, which incurs less information loss. In general, global generalization incurs high information loss for a "shallow" and "wide" taxonomy because each generalization step tends to generalize many items. Moreover, the generalization approach is applicable only when an item taxonomy is available.

Fewer items will be generalized if local generalization is used instead of global generalization because local generalization does not have to generalize all occurrences of an item and all sibling items. However, like total item suppression, global generalization preserves the truthfulness of analysis results, i.e., the results derived from the generalized data also hold on the original data. Partial generalization does not have this property, as discussed in Chapter 13.2.5. For example, suppose that five transactions bought both "cream" and "chicken," which causes violation of 6^2-anonymity. Suppose that global generalization removes this violation by generalizing "cream" (and all siblings) to "dairy product." Suppose now that ten transactions contain both "dairy product" and "chicken," so the violation is eliminated. The analysis on the generalized data remains truthful of the original data. For example, the count 10 of the itemest { "dairy product," "chicken" } indicates that ten transactions contain some items from the category "dairy product" and the item "chicken," which is true of the original data.

13.5   Transactional k-Anonymity

A key assumption made in (h, k, p)-coherence and k^m-anonymity is the maximum number of items that an adversary can acquire as background knowledge, which is p for (h, k, p)-coherence and m for k^m-anonymity. There are scenarios where it may not be possible to determine this bound in advance. If all background knowledge is limited to the presence of items, this case may be addressed by setting p or m to the maximum transaction length in the database since any subset of items that is more than this length does not match any transaction. However, if background knowledge may be on the absence of items, the adversary may exclude transactions using this knowledge and focus on fewer than k transactions. For example, an adversary may know that Alice has purchased "milk," "beer," and "diapers," but has not purchased "snow tires." Suppose that three transactions contain "milk," "beer," and "diapers," but only two of them contain "snow tires." Then the adversary could exclude the two transactions containing "snow tires" and link the remaining transaction to Alice. In this example, k^m privacy with $k = 2$ and $m = 4$ is violated, even m is the maximum transaction length.

13.5.1 k-Anonymity for Set Valued Data

One way to address these scenarios is to make each transaction *indistinguishable* from $k - 1$ other transactions. The following transactional k-anonymity, proposed in [112], is an adoption of the k-anonymity originally proposed for relational data to set-valued data.

DEFINITION 13.4 Transactional k-anonymity   A transaction database D is *k-anonymous* if every transaction in D occurs at least k times. A transaction database D_0 with some instances of items generalized from D using a taxonomy is a *k-anonymization* of D if D_0 is k-anonymous. ∎

Intuitively, a transaction database is k-anonymous if each transaction is identical to at least $k - 1$ others in the database. This partitions transactions into equivalence classes, where all transactions in the same equivalence class are exactly identical. This model is different from the (h, k, p)-coherence and k^m-anonymity models, which states that, for any set of up to m (or p) items (that occur in some transaction), there are at least k transactions that contain these items, but these transactions are not required to be identical to each other. Also, the k-anonymity model does not have the parameter m because it requires all transactions in the same equivalence class to be identical.

It follows that every database D that satisfies k-anonymity also satisfies k^m-anonymity for all m. Indeed, if any n-itemset, where $n \leq m$, is contained

Table 13.5: Original database

Owner	TID	Items Purchased
Alice	T_1	$\{a_1, b_1\}$
Bob	T_2	$\{a_2, b_1, b_2\}$
Chris	T_3	$\{a_1, a_2, b_2\}$
Dan	T_4	$\{a_1, a_2, b_1, b_2\}$

Table 13.6: Generalized 2-anonymous database

Owner	TID	Items Purchased
Alice	T_1	$\{A, B\}$
Bob	T_2	$\{A, B\}$
Chris	T_3	$\{a_1, a_2, B\}$
Dan	T_4	$\{a_1, a_2, B\}$

in some transaction $t \in D$, the k-anonymity of D implies that there are at least $k-1$ other transactions identical to t, thus, this n-itemset has a support of at least k. So D is k^m-anonymous. The next example from [112] shows that there exists a database D such that for any m, D satisfies k^m-anonymity but not k-anonymity.

Example 13.5

The original database D in Table 13.5 is not 2-anonymous, but satisfies 2^2-anonymity. Assuming that the taxonomy in Figure 13.4 is used, Table 13.6 gives a possible 2-anonymization. To further illustrate that there exists a database that satisfies k^m-anonymity for any m but not k-anonymity, we add an additional transaction T_5 in Table 13.5 which is identical to T_4. This new database is 2^m-anonymous for any m given the existence of T_4 and T_5, but not 2-anonymous due to T_1, T_2, and T_3. □

He and Naughton [112] present a generalization approach to transform D into k-anonymization, assuming that a taxonomy of items is available. If several items are generalized to the same item, only one occurrence of the generalized item will be kept in the generalized transaction. Thus the information loss now comes from two types: a detailed child item is replaced with a general parent item, and duplicate general items are eliminated. To see the second type, in the above example, from the generalized transaction, we know that the transaction originally contains some items from the A category, but we will not know the number of such items in the original transaction. As a result, count queries pertaining to the number of items in an original transaction, such as the average number of items per transaction, will not be supported by this type of generalization. This second type of information loss was not measured by a usual information loss metric for relational data where no attribute value will be eliminated by generalization.

Algorithm 13.5.12 Top-Down, Local Partitioning Algorithm

Anonymize(partition)

1: **if** no further drill down possible for *partition* **then**
2:      return and put *partition* in global list of returned partitions;
3: **else**
4:      *expandNode* ← *pickNode(partition)*;
5: **end if**
6: **for all** transaction *t* in *partition* **do**
7:      distribute *t* to a proper *subpartition* induced by *expandNode*;
8: **end for**
9: merge small *subpartitions*;
10: **for all** *subpartition* **do**
11:     *Anonymize(subpartition)*;
12: **end for**

13.5.2   Top-Down Partitioning Anonymization

A greedy top-down partitioning algorithm, presented in [112], is described in Algorithm 13.5.12. This algorithm is essentially Mondrian [149] but extended to transaction data. It starts with the single partition containing all transactions with all items generalized to the topmost item ALL. Since duplicate items are removed, each transaction at this level contains the single item ALL. Then it recursively splits a partition by specializing a node in the taxonomy for all the transactions in the partition. For each partition, there is a choice of which node to specialize. This choice is determined by the *pick_node* subroutine. Then all the transactions in the partition with the same specialized item are distributed to the same subpartition. At the end of data distribution phase, (small) subpartitions with fewer than k transactions are merged into a special leftover subpartition, and if necessary, some large transactions with over k transactions will be re-distributed to the leftover partition to make sure that the leftover partition has at least k transactions. The partitioning stops when violation of k-anonymity occurs. Since the specialization is determined independently for each partition, the recoding for generalization is local.

13.5.3   Discussion

Like the k^m-anonymity approach, the k-anonymity approach deals with only record linkage attacks. He and Naughton [112] show that k-anonymization has a small information loss. This is because local generalization is employed where the partitioning decision is made independently for each partition without forcing it in other partitions. This flexibility, however, creates the anonymized data that does not have the value exclusiveness property discussed in Chapter 13.1.4. For example, it is possible to have two partitions such that one has the item "North America" and the other has the item "Canada." The first partition is obtained by expanding a node other than "North America" and the second partition is produced by expanding the node for "North America." With the data containing both "North America" and "Canada" (in different partitions), it is not possible to count the number of transactions containing "Canada" because "North America" covers "Canada." On the other hand, the k^m-anonymity approach and coherence approach preserve value exclusiveness, due to global recoding and total item suppression. In summary, which anonymization scheme retains more data utility depends on the actual use of the data and the data mining algorithms available.

13.6 Anonymizing Query Logs

As discussed in Chapter 13.1, query log anonymization is an important problem and several recent works from the web community have studied this problem. In many cases, these studies identify the attacks arising from publishing query logs and motivate the need for a solution. There is a lack of a formal problem statement and privacy guarantee. One solution to this problem is to model a query log as a transaction database where each query is a transaction and each query term is an item. Since each query is usually very short, it makes sense to merge all queries by the same user into one transaction. Now, each transaction corresponds to a user, instead of a query, and such transactions can be used to analyze user's behaviors. Then we can anonymize query logs by applying the methods discussed previously. Below we discuss several works on query log anonymization from the web community.

13.6.1 Token-Based Hashing

[146] is one of the first few works considering attacks on query logs. It studied a natural anonymization technique called *token based hashing* and shows that serious privacy leaks are possible in this technique. First, a query log is anonymized by tokenizing each query term and securely hashing each token to an identifier. It assumes that an unanonymized "reference" query log has been released previously and is available to the adversary. The adversary first employs the reference query log to extract statistical properties of query terms in the log-file. The adversary then processes the anonymized log to invert the hash function based on co-occurrences of tokens within queries. Their study shows that serious leaks are possible in token-based hashing even when the order of the underlying tokens is hidden. For example, suppose that the term "Tom" has a frequency of 23% in the unanonymized reference log. The adversary may find a small number of hashes in the anonymized log with a frequency similar to 23%. If "Tom" also occurs in the anonymized log, the

adversary can infer that one of these hashes corresponds to "Tom," therefore, inverting the hashing with a high probability. A more powerful attack can make use of combinations of several terms. Their study focuses the accuracy of such attacks. No prevention solution is proposed.

13.6.2   Secret Sharing

The standard logging system for enforcing k-anonymity requires buffering all queries until there are k users for the same query, and anonymizes them in less than real time. This means that the logs are being held as unencrypted data for some period which may be undesirable for certain scenarios. To solve this probelm, a *secret sharing* scheme is proposed in [4]. The main idea is to split a query into k random shares and publish a new share for each distinct user issuing the same query. Once all k shares for the same query are presented in the published log, which happens when at least k distinct users have issued the query, the query can be decoded by summing up all its k shares. This technique ensures k-anonymity.

More specifically, a secret S corresponding to a query is split into k random shares using some predefined function. Each share is useless on its own, and all the k shares are required to decode the secret. The scheme works essentially by generating k -1 random numbers $S_1, \ldots, S_{k-1}$ in the range of 0 and $m-1$. A final secret, S_k, is generated as:

$$S_k = S - \sum_{i=1}^{k-1} S_i \mod m. \tag{13.4}$$

A query must appear k times (for k unique users) before S can be decoded using

$$S = \sum_{i=1}^{k} S_i \mod m. \tag{13.5}$$

For each query q_i, we need to keep track of the share S_{ji} for the user j issuing the query. To achieve this, k hash buckets are created and the user ID is mapped to one of these buckets (e.g., UserID mod k). The bucket indicates which secret share is to be used for the present user u_j, and the query q_i is replaced with the appropriate share S_{ji} and a query ID. Thus the string for any given query, q_i, by user u_j, is replaced with S_{ji}, the secret for user j for query i:

$$\langle u_j, q_i \rangle = \langle u_j, H(q_i), S_{ji} \rangle.$$

Here $H(q_i)$ is the hash that identifies a query. If all the shares of a particular query are present in the log, they can be combined to form the exact query. More precisely, to decode the query q_i, we compute $\sum S_{ji}$ over the entries $\langle u_j, H(q_i), S_{ji} \rangle$. At least k entries for the same $H(q_i)$ but different u_j must be present. To avoid the need to remember all the previously generated shares S_{ji} for a query q_i and user u_i, it is possible to seed the random number generator deterministically for q_i and user u_i. A disadvantage of this scheme is that it is possible that initially more than k unique users might be required to make the query before it can be decoded. This is due to the fact that more than one unique user might get hashed into the same bucket. One solution is to keep a distinct hash bucket for each of the *first k users* of each query. Once we have seen k users issuing the same query, the query will be decoded, therefore, there is no need to retrieve the share for additional users of the same query.

An alternative scheme suggested in the same paper is the Threshold Scheme in which the secret is split up into n pieces where any k of those pieces can be combined to decode this secret. By choosing a sufficiently large n, the probability of getting any k distinct secrets can be ensured to be very high, thus, reducing the probability of the above disadvantages.

13.6.3 Split Personality

This technique, also proposed by Adar [4], splits the logs of each user on the basis of "interests" so that the users become dissimilar to themselves, thus reducing the possibility of reconstructing a full user trace (i.e., search history of a user) and finding subsets of the data that can be used to identify the user. Using a similarity measure, a number of profiles are built for each of the users. Each user profile is then given a different user ID, so that two profiles cannot be linked to the same individual. As an example, if a particular user is interested in Tennis and Music, then two different profiles would be created for him, one containing the queries concerning Tennis, and the other containing queries related to Music. This reduces the probability of finding the complete search history of an individual by an adversary, thus increasing the privacy. The privacy gain by making it difficult for an adversary to relate multiple profiles to the same person is exactly a utility loss because it limits us to one specific facet of an individual. If a researcher is interested in correlating different facets, they will not be able to use a data set encoded in this way.

13.6.4 Other Related Works

Finally, Jones et al. [129] use classifiers to map a sequence of queries into demographic information and shows that candidate users can be identified using query logs. Korolova [142] proposes the concept of minimizing the increase in privacy risk as the result of using search engines. They propose to add random noise and suppress sensitive information. Instead of privacy for the users, Poblete et al. [188] deal with the privacy for the web sites, which are being clicked using search engines, and whose URLs are mentioned in the query logs. Xiong and Agichtein [253] put forward the need of query log publishing and the challenges that need to be faced.

Table 13.7:   Summary of approaches

	coherence [255, 256]	band matrix [101]	k^m-anonymity [220]	k-anonymity [112]
Record linkage	Yes	No	Yes	Yes
Attribute linkage	Yes	Yes	No	No
Adversary type	bounded	unbounded	bounded	unbounded
Truthfulness	Yes	No	Yes	No
Inferences	Yes	No	N/A	N/A
Itemset utility	Yes	Yes	No	No
Value exclusiveness	Yes	Yes	Yes	No

13.7   Summary

We summarize the transaction anonymization works in Table 13.7. We characterize them according to several properties discussed in Chapter 13.1.4: type of attacks (record linkage or attribute linkage attacks), type of adversary (bounded or unbounded background knowledge), truthfulness with respect to the original data, whether permitting inferences on sensitive items, whether modeling itemset based utility, whether guaranteeing value exclusiveness. A detailed discussion of these properties can be found at the Discussion section for each of these approaches. Among the approaches in Table 13.7, the coherence approach is the only approach that can be used to prevent record linkage attacks as well as attribute linkage attacks, and is the only approach that permits inferences on sensitive items. The coherence approach and k^m-anonymity approach guarantees truthful analysis with respect to the original data.

On information loss, the item suppression of the coherence approach could better deals with "outliers," but may suffer a large information loss if the data is too sparse. The item generalization of the k^m-anonymization approach and the transactional k-anonymity approach could work better if the data is sparse and the taxonomy is "slim" and "tall," but have a large information loss if the taxonomy is "short" and "wide." The local generalization of transactional k-anonymity approach has a smaller information loss than global generalization, however, the anonymized data does not have the value exclusiveness, a property assumed by most existing data mining algorithms. This means that either existing algorithms must be modified or new algorithms must be designed to analyze such data.

The works on query log anonymization somewhat focus on features specific to query logs, such as query history, temporal information like query time, terms of certain types such as those on demographic information, "vanity" queries [4], privacy of URL mentioned in queries, and reducing privacy risk through search engines. Unlike the works on transaction anonymization, there is a lack of a formal notion of privacy and problem formulation in this body of works. The difficulty comes from factors such as the lack of a generally agreeable taxonomy, the extreme sparseness of the data, and the lack of practical utility notions. So far, the research from the two different communities have taken different approaches, although the problems considered share much similarity in structure. It would be interesting to see how these fields could benefit by taking an integral approach.

Chapter 14

Anonymizing Trajectory Data

14.1 Introduction

Location-aware devices are used extensively in many network systems, such as mass transportation, car navigation, and healthcare management. The collected spatio-temporal data capture the detailed movement information of the tagged objects, offering tremendous opportunities for mining useful knowledge. Yet, publishing the *raw* data for data mining would reveal specific sensitive information of the tagged objects or individuals. In this chapter, we study the privacy threats in trajectory data publishing and show that traditional anonymization methods are not applicable for trajectory data due to its challenging properties: high-dimensional, sparse, and sequential. In this chapter, we study several trajectory data anonymization methods to address the anonymization problem for trajectory data.

14.1.1 Motivations

In recent years, there has been an explosive growth of location-aware devices such as RFID tags, GPS-based devices, cell phones, and PDAs. The use of these devices facilitates new and exciting location-based applications that consequently generate a huge collection of trajectory data. Recent research reveals that these trajectory data can be used for various data analysis purposes to improve current systems, such as city traffic control, mobility management, urban planning, and location-based service advertisements. Clearly, publication of these trajectory data threatens individuals' privacy since these raw trajectory data provide location information that identifies individuals and, potentially, their sensitive information. Below, we present some real-life applications of publishing trajectory data.

- **Transit company:** Transit companies have started to use smart cards for passengers, such as the Oyster Travel card in London. The company says they do not associate journey data with named passengers, although they do provide such data to government agencies on request [222].

- **Hospital:** Some hospitals have adopted Radio Frequency IDentification (RFID) sensory system to track the positions of patients, doctors, and medical equipment inside the hospital with the goals of minimizing life-threatening medical errors and improving the management of patients and resources [240]. Analyzing trajectory data, however, is a non-trivial task. Hospitals often do not have the expertise to perform the analysis themselves but outsource this process and, therefore, require granting a third party access to the patient-specific location and health data.

- **LBS provider:** Many companies provide location-based services (LBS) for mobile devices. With the help of triangulation and GPS devices, the location information of users can be precisely determined. Various data mining tasks can be performed on these trajectory data for different applications, such as traffic analysis and location-based advertisements. However, these trajectory data contain people's visited locations and thus reveal identifiable sensitive information such as social customs, religious preferences, and sexual preferences.

In this chapter, we study privacy threats in the data publishing phase and define a practical privacy model to accommodate the special challenges of anonymizing trajectory data. We illustrate an anonymization algorithm in [91, 170] to transform the underlying raw data into a version that is immunized against privacy attacks but still useful for effective data mining tasks. Data "publishing" includes sharing the data with specific recipients and releasing the data for public download; the recipient could potentially be an adversary who attempts to associate sensitive information in the published data with a target victim.

14.1.2 Attack Models on Trajectory Data

We use an example to illustrate the privacy threats and challenges of publishing trajectory data.

Example 14.1

A hospital wants to release the patient-specific trajectory and health data (Table 14.1) to a data miner for research purposes. Each record contains a *path* and some patient-specific information, where the *path* is a sequence of *pairs* $(loc_i t_i)$ indicating the patient's visited location loc_i at time t_i. For example, $ID\#2$ has a path $\langle f6 \rightarrow c7 \rightarrow e8 \rangle$, meaning that the patient has visited locations f, c, and e at time 6, 7, and 8, respectively. Without loss of generality, we assume that each record contains only one sensitive attribute, namely, diagnosis, in this example. We address two types of privacy threats:

- *Record linkage*: If a path in the table is so specific that not many patients match it, releasing the trajectory data may lead to linking the victim's record and, therefore, her diagnosed disease. Suppose the adversary knows that the data record of a target victim, Alice, is in Table 14.1, and Alice has visited $b2$ and $d3$. Alice's record, together with

Table 14.1: Raw trajectory and health data

ID	Path	Diagnosis	...
1	$\langle b2 \rightarrow d3 \rightarrow c4 \rightarrow f6 \rightarrow c7 \rangle$	AIDS	...
2	$\langle f6 \rightarrow c7 \rightarrow e8 \rangle$	Flu	...
3	$\langle d3 \rightarrow c4 \rightarrow f6 \rightarrow e8 \rangle$	Fever	...
4	$\langle b2 \rightarrow c5 \rightarrow c7 \rightarrow e8 \rangle$	Flu	...
5	$\langle d3 \rightarrow c7 \rightarrow e8 \rangle$	Fever	...
6	$\langle c5 \rightarrow f6 \rightarrow e8 \rangle$	Diabetes	...
7	$\langle b2 \rightarrow f6 \rightarrow c7 \rightarrow e8 \rangle$	Diabetes	...
8	$\langle b2 \rightarrow c5 \rightarrow f6 \rightarrow c7 \rangle$	AIDS	...

Table 14.2: Traditional 2-anonymous data

EPC	Path	Disease	...
1	$\langle f6 \rightarrow c7 \rangle$	AIDS	...
2	$\langle f6 \rightarrow c7 \rightarrow e8 \rangle$	Flu	...
3	$\langle f6 \rightarrow e8 \rangle$	Fever	...
4	$\langle c7 \rightarrow e8 \rangle$	Flu	...
5	$\langle c7 \rightarrow e8 \rangle$	Fever	...
6	$\langle f6 \rightarrow e8 \rangle$	Diabetes	...
7	$\langle f6 \rightarrow c7 \rightarrow e8 \rangle$	Diabetes	...
8	$\langle f6 \rightarrow c7 \rangle$	AIDS	...

her sensitive value (AIDS in this case), can be uniquely identified because $ID\#1$ is the *only* record that contains $b2$ and $d3$. Besides, the adversary can also determine the other visited locations of Alice, such as $c4$, $f6$, and $c7$.

- *Attribute linkage*: If a sensitive value occurs frequently together with some sequence of pairs, then the sensitive information can be inferred from such sequence even though the exact record of the victim cannot be identified. Suppose the adversary knows that Bob has visited $b2$ and $f6$. Since two out of the three records ($ID\#1,7,8$) containing $b2$ and $f6$ have sensitive value AIDS, the adversary can infer that Bob has AIDS with $2/3 = 67\%$ confidence.

□

Many privacy models, such as k-anonymity [201, 217] and its extensions [162, 247, 250], have been proposed to thwart privacy threats caused by record and attribute linkages in the context of relational databases. These models are based on the notion of *quasi-identifier* (*QID*), which is a set of attributes that may be used for linkages. The basic idea is to disorient potential linkages by generalizing the records into equivalent groups that share values on QID. These privacy models are effective for anonymizing relational data, but they are not applicable to trajectory data due to two special challenges.

Table 14.3: Anonymous data with
$L = 2$, $K = 2$, $C = 50\%$

ID	Path	Diagnosis	...
1	$\langle d3 \rightarrow f6 \rightarrow c7 \rangle$	AIDS	...
2	$\langle f6 \rightarrow c7 \rightarrow e8 \rangle$	Flu	...
3	$\langle d3 \rightarrow f6 \rightarrow e8 \rangle$	Fever	...
4	$\langle c5 \rightarrow c7 \rightarrow e8 \rangle$	Flu	...
5	$\langle d3 \rightarrow c7 \rightarrow e8 \rangle$	Fever	...
6	$\langle c5 \rightarrow f6 \rightarrow e8 \rangle$	Diabetes	...
7	$\langle f6 \rightarrow c7 \rightarrow e8 \rangle$	Diabetes	...
8	$\langle c5 \rightarrow f6 \rightarrow c7 \rangle$	AIDS	...

1. **High dimensionality:** Consider a hospital with 200 rooms functioning 24 hours a day. There are $200 \times 24 = 4800$ possible combinations (dimensions) of locations and timestamps. Each dimension could be a potential QID attribute used for record and attribute linkages. Traditional k-anonymity would require every path to be shared by at least k records. Due to *the curse of high dimensionality* [6], most of the data have to be suppressed in order to achieve k-anonymity. For example, to achieve 2-anonymity on the path data in Table 14.1, all instances of $\{b2, d3, c4, c5\}$ have to be suppressed as shown in Table 14.2 even though k is small.

2. **Data sparseness:** Consider the patients in a hospital or the passengers in a public transit system. They usually visit only a few locations compared to all available locations, so each trajectory path is relatively short. Anonymizing these short, little-overlapping paths in a high-dimensional space poses a significant challenge for traditional anonymization techniques because it is difficult to identify and group the paths together. Enforcing traditional k-anonymity on high-dimensional and sparse data would render the data useless.

14.2 *LKC*-Privacy

Traditional k-anonymity and its extended privacy models assume that an adversary could potentially use any or even all of the QID attributes as background knowledge to perform record or attribute linkages. However, in real-life privacy attacks, it is very difficult for an adversary to acquire *all* the visited locations and timestamps of a victim because it requires non-trivial effort to gather each piece of background knowledge from so many possible locations at different times. Thus, it is reasonable to assume that the adversary's background knowledge is bounded by at most L pairs of $(loc_i t_i)$ that the victim has visited.

Based on this assumption, we can employ the LKC-*privacy* model studied in Chapter 6 for anonymizing high-dimensional and sparse spatio-temporal data. The general intuition is to ensure that every sequence q with maximum length L of any path in a data table T is shared by at least K records in T, and the confidence of inferring any sensitive value in S from q is not greater than C, where L and K are positive integer thresholds, C is a positive real number threshold, and S is a set of sensitive values specified by the data holder. LKC-privacy bounds the probability of a successful record linkage to be $\leq 1/K$ and the probability of a successful attribute linkage to be $\leq C$. Table 14.3 shows an example of an anonymous table that satisfies $(2, 2, 50\%)$-privacy by suppressing $b2$ and $c4$ from Table 14.1. Every possible sequence q with maximum length 2 in Table 14.3 is shared by at least 2 records and the confidence of inferring the sensitive value AIDS from q is not greater than 50%.

While protecting privacy is a critical element in data publishing, it is equally important to preserve the utility of the published data because this is the primary reason for publication. In this chapter, we aim at preserving the *maximal frequent sequences* (*MFS*) because MFS often serves as the information basis for different primitive data mining tasks on sequential data. MFS is useful for trajectory pattern mining [102], workflow mining [105] and it also captures the major paths of moving objects in the trajectory data [30].

In Chapter 14.2.1, we explain the special challenges of anonymizing high-dimensional, sparse, and sequential trajectory data. In Chapter 14.2.2, we present an efficient anonymization algorithm to achieve LKC-privacy on trajectory data while preserving maximal frequent sequences in the anonymous trajectory data.

14.2.1 Trajectory Anonymity for Maximal Frequent Sequences

We first describe the trajectory database and then formally define the privacy and utility requirements.

14.2.1.1 Trajectory Data

A trajectory data table T is a collection of records in the form

$$\langle (loc_1 t_1) \rightarrow \ldots \rightarrow (loc_n t_n) \rangle : s_1, \ldots, s_p : d_1, \ldots, d_m,$$

where $\langle (loc_1 t_1) \rightarrow \ldots \rightarrow (loc_n t_n) \rangle$ is the path, $s_i \in S_i$ are the sensitive values, and $d_i \in D_i$ are the quasi-identifying (QID) values of an object. A *pair* $(loc_i t_i)$ represents the visited location loc_i of an object at time t_i. An object may revisit the same location at different times. At any time, an object can appear at only one location, so $\langle a1 \rightarrow b1 \rangle$ is not a valid sequence and timestamps in a path increase monotonically.

The sensitive and QID values are the object-specific data in the form of relational data. Record and attribute linkages via the QID attributes can be avoided by applying existing anonymization methods for relational data [96, 148, 151, 162, 237]. In this chapter, we focus on eliminating record and attribute linkages via trajectory data as illustrated in Example 14.1.

14.2.1.2   Privacy Model

Suppose a data holder wants to publish the trajectory data table T (e.g., Table 14.1) to recipients for data mining. Explicit identifiers, e.g., name, and SSN, are removed. (Note, we keep the ID in our examples for discussion purpose only.)

We assume that the adversary knows at most L pairs of location and time-stamp that V has previously visited. We use q to denote such an a priori known sequence of pairs, where $|q| \leq L$. $T(q)$ denotes a group of records that contains q. A record in T *contains* q if q is a subsequence of the path in the record. For example in Table 14.1, $ID\#1, 2, 7, 8$ contains $q = \langle f6 \rightarrow c7 \rangle$, written as $T(q) = \{ID\#1, 2, 7, 8\}$. Based on background knowledge q, the adversary could launch record and attribute linkage attacks. To thwart the record and attribute linkages, we require that every sequence with a maximum length L in the trajectory data table has to be shared by at least a certain number of records, and the ratio of sensitive value(s) in every group cannot be too high. The presented privacy model, *LKC-privacy* [91, 170], reflects this intuition.

DEFINITION 14.1 *LKC-privacy*   Let L be the maximum length of the background knowledge. Let S be a set of sensitive values. A trajectory data table T satisfies *LKC-privacy* if and only if for any sequence q with $|q| \leq L$,

1. $|T(q)| \geq K$, where $K > 0$ is an integer anonymity threshold, and

2. $P(s|q) \leq C$ for any $s \in S$, where $0 < C \leq 1$ is a real number confidence threshold. ∎

LKC-privacy has several nice properties that make it suitable for anonymizing high-dimensional sparse trajectory data. First, it only requires subsequences of a path to be shared by at least K records. This is a major relaxation from traditional k-anonymity based on a very reasonable assumption that the adversary has limited power. Second, *LKC*-privacy generalizes several traditional privacy models, such as k-anonymity (Chapter 2.1.1), confidence bounding (Chapter 2.2.2), (α, k)-anonymity (Chapter 2.2.5), and ℓ-diversity (Chapter 2.2.1). Refer to Chapter 6.2 for a discussion on the generalization of these privacy models. Third, it is flexible to adjust the trade-off between data privacy and data utility, and between an adversary's power and data utility.

Increasing L and K, or decreasing C, would improve the privacy at the expense of data utility. Finally, LKC-privacy is a general privacy model that thwarts both identity linkage and attribute linkage, i.e., the privacy model is applicable to anonymize trajectory data with or without sensitive attributes.

In the attack models studied in this chapter, we assume that the adversary can acquire both the time and locations of a target victim as background knowledge. In a real-life attack, it is possible that the adversary's background knowledge q' contains only the location loc_i or only the timestamp t_i. This type of attack is obviously weaker than the attack based on background knowledge q containing $(loc_i t_i)$ because the identified group $|T(q')| \geq |T(q)|$. Thus, an LKC-privacy preserved table that can thwart linkages on q can also thwart linkages on q'.

14.2.1.3 Utility Measure

The measure of data utility varies depending on the data mining task to be performed on the published data. In this chapter, we aim at preserving the maximal frequent sequences. A sequence $q = \langle (loc_1 t_1) \rightarrow \ldots \rightarrow (loc_n t_n) \rangle$ is an ordered set of locations. A sequence q is *frequent* in a trajectory data table T if $|T(q)| \geq K'$, where $T(q)$ is the set of records containing q and K' is a minimum support threshold. Frequent sequences (FS) capture the major paths of the moving objects [30], and often form the information basis for different primitive data mining tasks on sequential data, e.g., association rules mining. In the context of trajectories, association rules can be used to determine the subsequent locations of the moving object given the previously visited locations. This knowledge is important for traffic analysis.

There is no doubt that FS are useful. Yet, mining all FS is a computationally expensive operation. When the data volume is large and FS are long, it is infeasible to identify all FS because all subsequences of an FS are also frequent. Since trajectory data is high-dimensional and in large volume, a more feasible solution is to preserve only the *maximal frequent sequences (MFS)*.

DEFINITION 14.2 Maximal frequent sequence For a given minimum support threshold $K' > 0$, a sequence x is *maximal frequent* in a trajectory data table T if x is frequent and no super sequence of x is frequent in T. ∎

The set of MFS in T, denoted by $U(T)$, is much smaller than the set of FS in T given the same K'. MFS still contains the essential information for different kinds of data analysis [155]. For example, MFS captures the longest frequently visited paths. Any subsequence of an MFS is also a FS. Once all the MFS have been determined, the support counts of any particular FS can be computed by scanning the data table once. The data utility goal is to preserve as many MFS as possible, i.e., maximize $|U(T)|$, in the anonymous trajectory data table.

One frequently raised question is: why do we want to publish sensitive attributes at all when the goal is to preserve maximal frequent sequences? It is because some applications may require publishing the sensitive attributes for data mining purpose, such as to find association rules between frequent sequences and sensitive attributes. However, if there is no such data mining purpose, the sensitive attributes should be removed. LKC-privacy, together with the anonymization algorithm presented in Chapter 14.2.2, is flexible enough to handle trajectory data with or without sensitive attributes.

14.2.1.4   Problem Statement

LKC-privacy can be achieved by performing a sequence of suppressions on selected pairs from T. In this chapter, we employ *global suppression*, meaning that if a pair p is chosen to be suppressed, *all* instances of p in T are suppressed. For example, Table 14.3 is the result of suppressing $b2$ and $c4$ from Table 14.1. Global suppression offers several advantages over generalization and local suppression. First, suppression does not require a predefined taxonomy tree for generalization, which often is unavailable in real-life databases. Second, trajectory data could be extremely sparse. Enforcing global generalization on trajectory data will result in generalizing many sibling location or time values even if there is only a small number of outlier pairs, such as $c4$ in Table 14.1. Suppression offers the flexibility of removing those outliers without affecting the rest of the data. Note, we do not intend to claim that global suppression is always better than other schemes. For example, LeFevre et al. [148] present some local generalization schemes that may result in less data loss depending on the utility measure. Third, global suppression retains exactly the same support counts of the preserved MFS in the anonymous trajectory data as there were in the raw data. In contrast, a local suppression scheme may delete *some* instances of the chosen pair and, therefore, change the support counts of the preserved MFS. The property of data truthfulness is vital in some data analysis, such as traffic analysis.

DEFINITION 14.3 Trajectory anonymity for MFS   Given a trajectory data table T, a LKC-privacy requirement, a minimum support threshold K', a set of sensitive values S, the problem of *trajectory anonymity for maximal frequent sequences (MFS)* is to identify a transformed version of T that satisfies the LKC-privacy requirement while preserving the maximum number of MFS with respect to K'. ∎

Theorem 14.2, given in Chapter 14.2.2.3, proves that finding an optimum solution for LKC-privacy is NP-hard. Thus, we propose a greedy algorithm to efficiently identify a reasonably "good" sub-optimal solution.

14.2.2 Anonymization Algorithm for LKC-Privacy

Given a trajectory data table T, the first step is to identify all sequences that violate the given LKC-privacy requirement. Chapter 14.2.2.1 describes a method to identify violating sequences efficiently. Chapter 14.2.2.2 presents a greedy algorithm to eliminate the violating sequences with the goal of preserving as many maximal frequent sequences as possible.

14.2.2.1 Identifying Violating Sequences

An adversary may use any sequence with length not greater than L as background knowledge to launch a linkage attack. Thus, any non-empty sequence q with $|q| \leq L$ in T is a *violating sequence* if its group $T(q)$ does not satisfy condition 1, condition 2, or both in LKC-privacy in Definition 14.1.

DEFINITION 14.4 Violating sequence   Let q be a sequence of a path in T with $|q| \leq L$. q is a *violating sequence* with respect to a LKC-privacy requirement if (1) q is non-empty, and (2) $|T(q)| < K$ or $P(s|q) > C$ for any sensitive value $s \in S$. ∎

Example 14.2
Let $L = 2$, $K = 2$, $C = 50\%$, and $S = \{AIDS\}$. In Table 14.1, a sequence $q_1 = \langle b2 \rightarrow c4 \rangle$ is a violating sequence because $|T(q_1)| = 1 < K$. A sequence $q_2 = \langle b2 \rightarrow f6 \rangle$ is a violating sequence because $P(AIDS|q_2) = 67\% > C$. However, a sequence $q_3 = \langle b2 \rightarrow c5 \rightarrow f6 \rightarrow c7 \rangle$ is not a violating sequence even if $|T(q_3)| = 1 < K$ and $P(AIDS|q_3) = 100\% > C$ because $|q_3| > L$. ☐

A trajectory data table satisfies a given LKC-privacy requirement, if all violating sequences with respect to the privacy requirement are removed, because all possible channels for record and attribute linkages are eliminated. A naive approach is to first enumerate all possible violating sequences and then remove them. This approach is infeasible because of the huge number of violating sequences. Consider a violating sequence q with $|T(q)| < K$. Any super sequence of q, denoted by q'', in the data table T is also a violating sequence because $|T(q'')| \leq |T(q)| < K$.

Another *inefficient* and *incorrect* approach to achieve LKC-privacy is to ignore the sequences with size less than L and assume that if a table T satisfies LKC-privacy, then T satisfies $L'KC$-privacy where $L' < L$. Unfortunately, this monotonic property with respect to L does not hold in LCK-privacy.

THEOREM 14.1
LKC-privacy is not monotonic with respect to adversary's knowledge L.

PROOF   To prove that LKC-privacy is not monotonic with respect to L, it is sufficient to prove that one of the conditions of LKC-privacy in Definition 14.1 is not monotonic.

Condition 1: Anonymity threshold K is monotonic with respect to L. If $L' \leq L$ and $C = 100\%$, a data table T satisfying LKC-privacy must satisfy $L'KC$-privacy because $|T(q')| \geq |T(q)| \geq K$, where q' is subsequence of q.

Condition 2: Confidence threshold C is not monotonic with respect to L. If q is a non-violating sequence with $P(s|q) \leq C$ and $|T(q)| \geq K$, its subsequence q' may or may not be a non-violating sequence. We use a counter example to show that $P(s|q') \leq P(s|q) \leq C$ does not always hold. In Table 14.4, the sequence $q = \langle a1 \rightarrow b2 \rightarrow c3 \rangle$ satisfies $P(AIDS|q) = 50\% \leq C$. However, its subsequence $q' = \langle a1 \rightarrow b2 \rangle$ does not satisfy $P(AIDS|q') = 100\% > C$. $\square$

To satisfy condition 2 in Definition 14.1, it is insufficient to ensure that every sequence q with only length L in T satisfies $P(s|q) \leq C$. Instead, we need to ensure that every sequence q with length not greater than L in T satisfies $P(s|q) \leq C$. To overcome this bottleneck of violating sequence enumeration, the insight is that there exists some "minimal" violating sequences among the violating sequences, and it is sufficient to achieve LKC-privacy by removing only the minimal violating sequences.

DEFINITION 14.5 Minimal violating sequence   A violating sequence q is a *minimal violating sequence* (*MVS*) if every proper subsequence of q is not a violating sequence.   ∎

Example 14.3
In Table 14.1, given $L = 3$, $K = 2$, $C = 50\%$, $S = \{AIDS\}$, the sequence $q = \langle b2 \rightarrow d3 \rangle$ is a MVS because $\langle b2 \rangle$ and $\langle d3 \rangle$ are not violating sequences. The sequence $q = \langle b2 \rightarrow d3 \rightarrow c4 \rangle$ is a violating sequence but not a MVS because its subsequence $\langle b2 \rightarrow d3 \rangle$ is a violating sequence. $\square$

Every violating sequence is either a MVS or it contains a MVS. Thus, if T contains no MVS, then T contains no violating sequences.

Observation 14.2.1 A trajectory data table T satisfies LKC-privacy if and only if T contains no MVS.   ∎

Table 14.4:   Counter example for monotonic property

ID	Path	Diagnosis	...
1	$\langle a1 \rightarrow b2 \rangle$	AIDS	...
2	$\langle a1 \rightarrow b2 \rightarrow c3 \rangle$	AIDS	...
3	$\langle a1 \rightarrow b2 \rightarrow c3 \rangle$	Fever	...

Algorithm 14.2.13 MVS Generator

Input: Raw trajectory data table T
Input: Thresholds L, K, and C
Input: Sensitive values S
Output: Minimal violating sequence $V(T)$

 1: $X_1 \leftarrow$ set of all distinct pairs in T;
 2: $i = 1$;
 3: **while** $i \leq L$ or $X_i \neq \emptyset$ **do**
 4:     Scan T to compute $|T(q)|$ and $P(s|q)$, for $\forall q \in X_i$, $\forall s \in S$;
 5:     **for** $\forall q \in X_i$ where $|T(q)| > 0$ **do**
 6:         **if** $|T(q)| < K$ or $P(s|q) > C$ **then**
 7:             Add q to V_i;
 8:         **else**
 9:             Add q to W_i;
10:         **end if**
11:     **end for**
12:     $X_{i+1} \leftarrow W_i \bowtie W_i$;
13:     **for** $\forall q \in X_{i+1}$ **do**
14:         **if** q is a super sequence of any $v \in V_i$ **then**
15:             Remove q from X_{i+1};
16:         **end if**
17:     **end for**
18:     $i{+}{+}$;
19: **end while**
20: **return** $V(T) = V_1 \cup \cdots \cup V_{i-1}$;

Next, we present an algorithm to efficiently identify all MVS in T with respect to a LKC-privacy requirement. Based on Definition 14.5, we generate all MVS of size $i + 1$, denoted by V_{i+1}, by incrementally extending a non-violating sequence of size i, denoted by W_i, with an additional pair.

Algorithm 14.2.13 presents a method to efficiently generate all MVS. Line 1 puts all the size-1 sequences, i.e., all distinct pairs, as candidates X_1 of MVS. Line 4 scans T once to compute $|T(q)|$ and $P(s|q)$ for each sequence $q \in X_i$ and for each sensitive value $s \in S$. If the sequence q violates the LKC-privacy requirement in Line 6, then we add q to the MVS set V_i (Line 7); otherwise, add q to the non-violating sequence set W_i (Line 9) for generating the next candidate set X_{i+1}, which is a self-join of W_i (Line 12). Two sequences $q_x = \langle (loc_1^x t_1^x) \rightarrow \ldots \rightarrow (loc_i^x t_i^x) \rangle$ and $q_y = \langle (loc_1^y t_1^y) \rightarrow \ldots \rightarrow (loc_i^y t_i^y) \rangle$ in W_i can be joined only if the first $i-1$ pairs of q_x and q_y are identical and $t_i^x < t_i^y$. The joined sequence is $\langle (loc_1^x t_1^x) \rightarrow \ldots \rightarrow (loc_i^x t_i^x) \rightarrow (loc_i^y t_i^y) \rangle$. Lines 13-17 remove a candidate q from X_{i+1} if q is a super sequence of any sequence in V_i because any proper subsequence of a MVS cannot be a violating sequence. The set of MVS, denoted by $V(T)$, is the union of all V_i.

Example 14.4

Consider Table 14.1 with $L = 2$, $K = 2$, $C = 50\%$, and $S = \{AIDS\}$.

$$X_1 = \{b2, d3, c4, c5, f6, c7, e8\}.$$

After scanning T, we divide X_1 into $V_1 = \emptyset$ and

$$W_1 = \{b2, d3, c4, c5, f6, c7, e8\}.$$

Next, from W_1 we generate the candidate set

$$X_2 = \{b2d3, b2c4, b2c5, b2f6, b2c7, b2e8, d3c4, d3c5, d3f6, d3c7, d3e8, c4c5,$$
$$c4f6, c4c7, c4e8, c5f6, c5c7, c5e8, f6c7, f6e8, c7e8\}.$$

We scan T again to determine

$$V_2 = \{b2d3, b2c4, b2f6, c4c7, c4e8\}.$$

We do not further generate X_3 because $L = 2$.   □

14.2.2.2   Eliminating Violating Sequences

We present a greedy algorithm to transform the raw trajectory data table T to an anonymous table T' with respect to a given LKC-privacy requirement by a sequence of suppressions. In each iteration, the algorithm selects a pair p for suppression based on a greedy selection function. In general, a suppression on a pair p in T increases privacy because it removes minimal violating sequences (MVS), and decreases data utility because it eliminates maximal frequent sequences (MFS) in T. Therefore, we define the greedy function, $Score(p)$, to select a suppression on a pair p that maximizes the number of MVS removed but minimizes the number of MFS removed in T. $Score(p)$ is defined as follows:

$$Score(p) = \frac{PrivGain(p)}{UtilityLoss(p) + 1} \tag{14.1}$$

where $PrivGain(p)$ and $UtilityLoss(p)$ are the number of minimal violating sequences (MVS) and the number of maximal frequent sequences (MFS) containing the pair p, respectively. A pair p may not belong to any MFS, resulting in $|UtilityLoss(p)| = 0$. To avoid dividing by zero, we add 1 to the denominator. The pair p with the highest $Score(p)$ is called the *winner* pair, denoted by w.

Algorithm 14.2.14 summarizes the anonymization algorithm that removes all MVS. Line 1 calls Algorithm 14.2.13 to identify all MVS, denoted by $V(T)$, and then builds a MVS-tree with a PG table that keeps track of the $PrivGain$ of all candidate pairs for suppressions. Line 2 calls a maximal frequent sequence mining algorithm (see Chapter 14.2.2.3) to identify all MFS, denoted by $U(T)$, and then builds a MFS-tree with a UL table that keeps track of the $UtilityLoss$ of all candidate pairs. At each iteration in Lines 3-9, the algorithm selects the winner pair w that has the highest $Score(w)$ from

---

Algorithm 14.2.14 Trajectory Data Anonymizer

Input: Raw trajectory data table T
Input: Thresholds L, K, C, and K'
Input: Sensitive values S
Output: Anonymous T' that satisfies LKC-privacy

1: generate $V(T)$ by Algorithm 14.2.13 and build MVS-tree;
2: generate $U(T)$ by MFS algorithm and build MFS-tree;
3: **while** PG table is not empty **do**
4:   select a pair w that has the highest *Score* to suppress;
5:   delete all MVS and MFS containing w from MVS-tree and MFS-tree;
6:   update the $Score(p)$ if both w and p are contained in the same MVS or MFS;
7:   remove w from PG Table;
8:   add w to Sup;
9: **end while**
10: **for** $\forall w \in Sup$, suppress all instances of w from T;
11: **return** the suppressed T as T';

Table 14.5: Initial *Score*

	b2	d3	c4	f6	c7	e8
PrivGain	3	1	3	1	1	1
UtilityLoss (+1)	4	4	2	5	6	5
Score	0.75	0.25	1.5	0.2	0.16	0.2

the PG table, removes all the MVS and MFS that contain w, incrementally updates the *Score* of the affected candidates, and adds w to the set of suppressed values, denoted by Sup. Values in Sup are collectively suppressed in Line 10 in one scan of T. Finally, Algorithm 14.2.14 returns the anonymized T as T'. The most expensive operations are identifying the MVS and MFS containing w and updating the *Score* of the affected candidates. Below, we propose two tree structures to efficiently perform these operations.

DEFINITION 14.6 MVS-tree   MVS-tree is a tree structure that represents each MVS as a tree path from root-to-leaf. Each node keeps track of a count of MVS sharing the same prefix. The count at the root is the total number of MVS. MVS-tree has a PG table that maintains every candidate pair p for suppression, together with its $PrivGain(p)$. Each candidate pair p in the PG table has a link, denoted by $Link_p$, that links up all the nodes in an MVS-tree containing p. $PrivGain(p)$ is the sum of the counts of MVS on $Link_p$. ∎

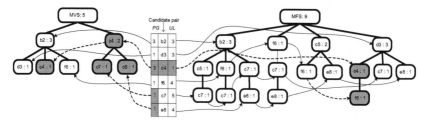

FIGURE 14.1: MVS-tree and MFS-tree for efficient *Score* updates

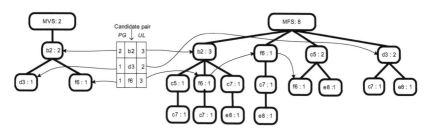

FIGURE 14.2: MVS-tree and MFS-tree after suppressing $c4$

DEFINITION 14.7 MFS-tree   MFS-tree is a tree structure that represents each MFS as a tree path from root-to-leaf. Each node keeps track of a count of MFS sharing the same prefix. The count at the root is the total number of MFS. MFS-tree has a UL table that keeps the $UtilityLoss(p)$ for every candidate pair p. Each candidate pair p in the UL table has a link, denoted by $Link_p$, that links up all the nodes in MFS-tree containing p. $UtilityLoss(p)$ is the sum of the counts of MFS on $Link_p$. ∎

Example 14.5
Figure 14.1 depicts both an MVS-tree and an MFS-tree generated from Table 14.1, where

$V(T) = \{b2d3,\ b2c4,\ b2f6,\ c4c7,\ c4e8\}$ and
$U(T) = \{b2c5c7,\ b2f6c7,\ b2c7e8,\ d3c4f6,\ f6c7e8,\ c5f6,\ c5e8,\ d3c7,\ d3e8\}$

with $L = 2$, $K = 2$, $C = 50\%$, and $K' = 2$. Each root-to-leaf path represents one sequence of MVS or MFS. To find all the MVS (or MFS) containing $c4$, follow $Link_{c4}$ starting from the PG (or UL) table. For illustration purposes, we show PG and UL as a single table. □

Table 14.5 shows the initial $Score(p)$ of every candidate in the PG table in the MVS-tree. Identify the winner pair $c4$ from the PG table. Then traverse $Link_{c4}$ to identify all MVS and MFS containing $c4$ and delete them from the MVS-tree and MFS-tree accordingly. These links are the key to efficient *Score* updates and suppressions. When a winner pair w is suppressed

Table 14.6:   *Score* after suppressing *c4*

	b2	d3	f6
PrivGain	2	1	1
UtilityLoss (+1)	4	3	4
Score	0.5	0.33	0.25

from the trees, the entire branch of *w* is trimmed. The trees provide an efficient structure for updating the counts of MVS and MFS. For example, when *c4* is suppressed, all its descendants are removed as well. The counts of *c4*'s ancestor nodes are decremented by the counts of the deleted *c4* node. If a candidate pair *p* and the winner pair *w* are contained in some common MVS or MFS, then $UtilityLoss(p)$, $PrivGain(p)$, and $Score(p)$ have to be updated by adding up the counts on $Link_p$. A pair *p* is removed from the *PG* table if $PrivGain(p) = 0$. The shaded blocks in Figure 14.1 represent the nodes to be deleted after suppressing *c4*. The resulting MVS-tree and MFS-tree are shown in Figure 14.2. Table 14.6 shows the updated *Score* of the remaining candidate pairs. In the next iteration, *b2* is suppressed and thus all the remaining MVS are removed. Table 14.3 shows the resulting anonymized table T' for $(2, 2, 50\%)$-privacy.

14.2.2.3   Analysis

THEOREM 14.2
Given a trajectory data table T and a LKC-privacy requirement, it is NP-hard to find the optimum anonymous solution.

PROOF   The problem of finding the optimum anonymous solution can be converted into the *vertex cover problem*. The vertex cover problem is a well-known problem in which, given an undirected graph $G = (V, E)$, it is NP-hard to find the smallest set of vertices S such that each edge has at least one endpoint in S. To reduce the problem into the vertex cover problem, we consider the set of candidate pairs as the set of vertices V. The set of MVS, denoted by $V(T)$, is analogous to the set of edges E. Hence, the optimum vertex cover, S, means finding the smallest set of candidate pairs that must be suppressed to obtain the optimum anonymous data set T'. Given that it is NP-hard to determine the smallest set of vertices S, it is also NP-hard to find the optimum set of candidate pairs for suppression.   □

The presented trajectory anonymization method has two steps. In the first step, we determine the set of MVS and the set of MFS. In the second step, we build the MVS-tree and MFS-tree, and suppress the winner pairs iteratively according to their *Score*. We modified *MAFIA* [39], which is originally designed for mining maximal frequent itemsets, to mine MFS. Any alternative MFS algorithm can be used as a plug-in to the presented anonymization method. The most expensive operation of the method is scanning the raw trajectory data table T once to compute $|T(q)|$ and $P(s|q)$ for all sequence q in the candidate set X_i. This operation takes place during MVS generation. The cost of this operation is approximated as $Cost = \sum_{i=1}^{L} m_i i$, where $m_i = |X_i|$. Note that the searching cost depends on the value of L and size of the candidate set. When $i = 1$, the candidate set X_i is the set of all distinct pairs in T. Hence, the upper limit of $m_i = |d|$, where $|d|$ is the number of dimensions. It is unlikely to have any single pair violating the LKC-privacy; therefore, $m_2 = |d|(|d| - 1)/2$. In practice, most of the candidate sets are of size-2; therefore, the lower bound of the $Cost \leq m_1 + 2m_2 = |d|^2$. Finally, including the dependence on the data size, the time complexity of the presented anonymization algorithm is $O(|d|^2 n)$.

In the second step, we insert the MVS and MFS into the respective trees and delete them iteratively afterward. This operation is proportional to the number of MVS and thus in the order of $O(|V(T)|)$. Due to MVS-tree and MFS-tree data structures, the anonymization method can efficiently calculate and update the the the score of the candidate pairs.

14.2.3   Discussion

14.2.3.1   Applying LKC-Privacy on RFID Data

Radio Frequency IDentification (RFID) is a technology of automatic object identification. Figure 14.3 illustrates a typical RFID information system, which consists of a large number of tags and readers and an infrastructure for handling a high volume of RFID data. A tag is a small device that can be attached to a person or a manufactured object for the purpose of unique identification. A reader is an electronic device that communicates with the RFID tag. A reader broadcasts a radio signal to the tag, which then transmits its information back to the reader [204]. Streams of RFID data records, in the format of $\langle EPC, loc, t \rangle$, are then stored in an RFID database, where EPC (Electronic Product Code) is a unique identifier of the tagged person or object, loc is the location of the reader, and t is the time of detection. The path of an object, like the path defined in Chapter 14.2.1, is a sequence of pairs that can be obtained by first grouping the RFID records by EPC and then sorting the records in each group by timestamps. A data recipient (or a data analysis module) could obtain the information on either specific tagged objects or general workflow patterns [105] by submitting data requests to the query engine. The query engine then responds to the requests by joining the RFID data with some object-specific data.

Retailers and manufacturers have created compelling business cases for deploying RFID in their supply chains, from reducing out-of-stocks at Wal-Mart to up-selling consumers in Prada. Yet, the uniquely identifiable objects pose a privacy threat to individuals, such as tracing a person's movements, and pro-

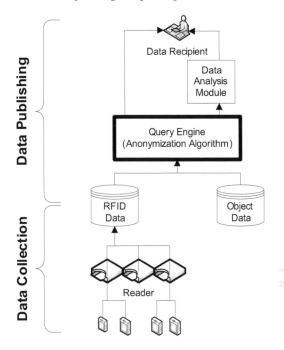

FIGURE 14.3: Data flow in RFID system

filing individuals becomes possible. Most previous work on privacy-preserving RFID technology [204] focus on the threats caused by the physical RFID tags. Techniques like EPC re-encryption and killing tags [130] have been proposed to address the privacy issues in the *data collection* phase, but these techniques cannot address the privacy threats in the *data publishing* phase, when a large volume of RFID data is released to a third party.

Fung et al. [91] present the first work to study the privacy threats in the data publishing phase and define a practical privacy model to accommodate the special challenges of RFID data. Their privacy model, LKC-privacy which is also studied in this chapter, ensures that every RFID moving paths with length not greater than L is shared by least $K-1$ other moving paths, and the confidence of inferring any pre-specified sensitive values is not greater than C. Fung et al. [91] propose an anonymization algorithm for the query engine (see Figure 14.3) to transform the underlying raw object-specific RFID data into a version that is immunized against privacy attacks. The general assumption is that the recipient could be an adversary, who attempts to associate some target victim(s) to his/her sensitive information from the published data. The general idea is very similar to the privacy model and anonymization method studied in this chapter.

14.2.3.2   Comparing with Anonymizing Transaction Data

Chapter 13 discusses some works on anonymizing high-dimensional transaction data [101, 220, 255, 256]. Ghinita et al. [101] divide the transaction data into public and private items. Then the public items are grouped together based on similarity. Each group is then associated with a set of private items such that probabilistically there are no linkages between the public and private items. The idea is similar to the privacy model of *Anatomy* [249] in Chapter 3.2, which disorients the linkages between QID and sensitive attributes by putting them into two tables.

The methods presented in [220, 255, 256] model the adversary's power by a maximum number of known items as background knowledge. This assumption is similar to LKC-privacy studied above, but with two major differences. First, a transaction is a *set* of items, but a moving object's path is a *sequence* of visited location-time pairs. Sequential data drastically increases the computational complexity for counting the support counts as compared transaction data because $\langle a \rightarrow b \rangle$ is different from $\langle b \rightarrow a \rangle$. Hence, their proposed models are not applicable to spatio-temporal data studied in this chapter. Second, the privacy and utility measures are different. Terrovitis et al.'s privacy model [220] is based on only k-anonymity and does not consider attribute linkages. Xu et al. [255, 256] measure their data utility in terms of preserved item instances and frequent itemsets, respectively. In contrast, the method studied in Chapter 14.2 aims at preserving frequent sequences.

14.3 (k, δ)-Anonymity

Many mobile devices, such as GPS navigation device on cell phones, have very limited energy. To reduce energy consumption, some methods [124] have been developed to predict the location of a mobile device at a given time. A mobile device has to report its new location only if its actual location differs more than an uncertainty threshold δ from the predicted location [1]. Abul et al. [1] propose a new privacy model called (k, δ)-*anonymity* that exploits the inherent uncertainty of moving objects' locations. The trajectory can be considered as polylines in a cylindrical volume with some uncertainty; therefore, the anonymity is achieved if k different trajectories co-exist within the radius δ of any trajectory, as depicted in Figure 14.4. δ could be the result of inaccuracy in a positioning device.

14.3.1   Trajectory Anonymity for Minimal Distortion

Enforcing (k, δ)-anonymity on a data set of paths D requires every path in D to be (k, δ)-anonymous; otherwise, we need to transform D into another

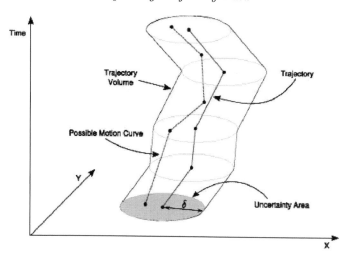

FIGURE 14.4: Time and spatial trajectory volume ([1] ©2008 IEEE)

version D' that satisfies the given (k, δ)-anonymity requirement. Let τ be trajectory. Let $(x, y, t) \in \tau$ be the (x, y) position of τ at time t. The problem of (k, δ)-anonymity is formally defined as follows.

DEFINITION 14.8 Co-localization   Two trajectories τ_1 and τ_2 defined in time interval $[t_1, t_n]$ *co-localize*, written as $Coloc_{[t_1,t_n]}^{\delta}(\tau_1, \tau_2)$, with respect to a uncertainty threshold δ if and only if for each point (x_1, y_1, t) in τ_1 and (x_2, y_2, t) in τ_2 with $t \in [t_1, t_n]$, it holds that $Dist((x_1, y_1), (x_2, y_2)) \leq \delta$ [1]. ∎

$Dist$ can be any function that measures the distance between two points. For example, Euclidean distance:

$$Dist((x_1, y_1), (x_2, y_2)) = \sqrt{(x_1 - x_2)^2 + (y_1 - y_2)^2} \qquad (14.2)$$

Intuitively, a trajectory is anonymous if it shares a similar path with other trajectories.

DEFINITION 14.9 Anonymity group of trajectories   Given an uncertainty threshold δ and an anonymity threshold k, a group G of trajectories is (k, δ)-anonymous if and only if $|G| \geq k$, $\forall \tau_i, \tau_j \in G$, and $Coloc_{[t_1,t_n]}^{\delta}(\tau_i, \tau_j)$ [1]. ∎

The trajectory anonymity problem is to transform a data set such that every group of trajectories is (k, δ)-anonymous with minimal distortion.

DEFINITION 14.10 Trajectory anonymity for minimal distortion
Given a data set of trajectory paths D, an uncertainty threshold δ, and an
anonymity threshold k, the problem of *trajectory anonymity for minimal distortion* is to transform D into a (k, δ)-anonymous data set D', such that for
trajectory $\tau \in D'$, there exists a (k, δ)-anonymous group $G \subseteq D'$, $\tau \in G$, and
the distortion between D and D' is minimized [1]. ∎

14.3.2   The Never Walk Alone Anonymization Algorithm

The *Never Walk Alone* (*NWA*) anonymization algorithm in [1] can be summarized in three phases. The first phase, *preprocessing*, is to trim the starting
and ending portions of the trajectories to ensure that they share the same time
span. The second phase, *clustering*, is to group nearby trajectories together
into clusters. The third phase, *space translation*, is to "push" some locations
of a trajectory that fall outside cylindrical volume into the cluster. Each phase
is described in details below.

14.3.2.1   Preprocessing

In real-world moving object databases, trajectories are very unlikely to have
the same starting and ending points. Consider a city transport system. Many
passengers travel from their home in uptown area to their workplaces in downtown area in the morning and go back home in the evening. Though they share
a similar path and direction during the same period of time, their homes and
workplaces are different. Enforcing (k, δ)-anonymity on these scattered trajectories will result in poor data quality. Thus, the first step of NWA is to
partition the input trajectories into groups of trajectories that have the same
starting time and the same ending time.

The preprocessing is controlled by an integer parameter π: only one timestamp every π can be the starting or ending point of a trajectory [1]. For
example, if the original data was sampled at a frequency of one minute, and
$\pi = 60$, all trajectories are preprocessed in such a way that their starting and
ending timestamps are mapped to full hours. We can first determine the starting timestamp t_s and the ending timestamp t_e of each trajectory, and then all
the points of trajectory that do not fall between t_s and t_e are discarded. After
this preprocessing step, trajectories are partitioned into equivalence classes
with respect to their new starting and ending timestamps.

14.3.2.2   Clustering

Next, NWA clusters the trajectories into groups. First, NWA selects a sequence of *pivot* trajectories as cluster centers. The first pivot trajectory chosen
is the farthest one from the center of the entire data set D. Then, the next
pivot trajectory chosen is the farthest trajectory from the previous pivot. After
a pivot trajectory is determined, a cluster is formed by taking the $(k - 1)$-
nearest neighbor trajectories as its elements. Then, assign remaining trajec-

tories to the closest pivot. Yet, NWA enforces an additional constraint: the radius of every cluster must not be larger than a threshold *max_radius*. In case a cluster cannot be formed on the pivot due to lack of nearby trajectories, it will not be used as pivot but it can be used in the subsequent iterations as member of some other cluster. The remaining trajectories that cannot be added to any cluster without violating the *max_radius* constraint, such outlier trajectories are discarded. If there are too many outlier trajectories, NWA restarts the clustering procedure by increasing *max_radius* until not too many trajectories are discarded.

14.3.2.3 Space Translation

Space translation is the last phase to achieve (k, δ)-anonymity. This operation involves moving some trajectory points from the original location to another location. The objective is to achieve (k, δ)-anonymity while minimizing the distortion on the original routes. For each cluster formed in the the clustering phase, compute the cluster center, form a cylindrical volume based on the cluster center, and move points lying outside of the cylindrical volume onto the perimeter of the cylindrical volume, from the original location towards the cluster center with minimal distortion. A natural choice of minimal distortion on trajectories is the sum of point-wise distances between the original and translated trajectories. The problem of space translation is to achieve a given (k, δ)-anonymity with the goal minimizing the total translation distortion cost defined below.

DEFINITION 14.11 Space translation distortion   Let $\tau' \in D'_T$ be the translated version of raw trajectory $\tau \in D_T$. The *translation distortion cost* of τ' with respect to τ is:

$$DistortCost(\tau, \tau') = \sum_{t \in T} Dist(\tau[t], \tau'[t]) \qquad (14.3)$$

where $\tau[t]$ is the location of τ in the form of (x, y) at time t. The *total translation distortion cost* of the translated data set D'_T with respect to the raw data set D_T is:

$$TotalDistortCost(D_T, D'_T) = \sum_{\tau \in D_T} DistortCost(\tau, \tau'). \quad \blacksquare \qquad (14.4)$$

14.3.3   Discussion

Abul et al. [1] present an interesting trajectory anonymization algorithm, Never Walk Alone (NWA), by exploiting the inherent uncertainty of mobile devices. Some new RFID devices, however, are highly accurate with error less than a couple of centimeters. In that, the inherent uncertainty may not be present. Also, NWA relies on the basic assumption that every trajectory is continuous. Though this assumption is valid for GPS-iike devices where the object can be traced all the time, it does not hold for RFID-based moving objects. For example, when a passenger uses his smart card in a subway station, the smart card or RFID tag is detected once at the entrance. The system may not know the next location of the passenger until hours later, so the time on a RFID path may not be continuous.

The clustering approach employed in NWA has to restart again everytime when too many trajectories are discarded as outliers. As a result, it is very difficult to predict when the algorithm will terminate. Furthermore, the anonymity is achieved by space translation, which changes the actual location of an object, resulting in the publication of untruthful data.

14.4   MOB k-Anonymity

In contrast to (k, δ)-anonymity, which bypasses the fundamental concept of QID and relies on the concept of co-localization to achieve k-anonymity, Yarovoy et al. [263] present a novel notion of k-anonymity in the context of *moving object databases* (MOD) based on the assumption that different moving objects may have different QIDs.

14.4.1   Trajectory Anonymity for Minimal Information Loss

Unlike in relational data, where all tuples share the same set of quasi-identifier (QIDs), Yarovoy et al. argue that in MOD there does not exist a fixed set of QID attributes for all the MOBs. Hence it is of importance to model the concept of quasi-identifier on an individual basis. Specifically, Yarovoy et al. [263] consider timestamps as the QIDs with MOBs' positions forming their values. A group of moving objects with the same QID values is called an *anonymization group*. In a MOD, the anonymization groups associated with different moving objects may not be disjoint.

Example 14.6
Consider a raw moving object database (Table 14.7) with 4 moving objects, in which the explicit identifiers (e.g. I_1, I_2, I_3, I_4) have been suppressed. Each row represents the trajectory of a moving object. Suppose $k = 2$ and $QID(O_1) = QID(O_4) = \{t_1\}$, $QID(O_2) = QID(O_3) = \{t_2\}$. Clearly the best anonymization group for O_1 with respect to its $QID\{t_1\}$ is $AS(O_1) = \{O_1, O_3\}$ as O_3 is closest to O_1 at time t_1. Similarly, the best anonymization group for O_2 and O_3 with respect to their $QID\{t_2\}$ is $\{O_2, O_3\}$, and for O_4 with respect to its $QID\{t_1\}$ is $\{O_2, O_4\}$. The anonymization groups are illustrated in Figure 14.5 by dark rectangles. Obviously, the anonymization groups of O_1 and O_3 as well as O_2 and O_4 overlap. □

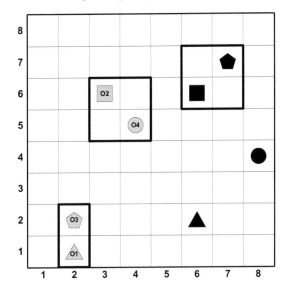

FIGURE 14.5: Graphical representation of MOD D

Due to this fact, the most obvious but *incorrect* way of defining k-anonymity is that an anonymous version D^* of a MOD D satisfies k-anonymity provided that $\forall O \in D$ and $\forall t \in QID(O)$, there are at least $k-1$ other distinct MOBs in D^* indistinguishable from O at time t. Under such definition, an adversary is able to conduct a privacy attack based on an *attack graph* formalized below.

DEFINITION 14.12 Attack graph   *[263]* An attack graph associated with a MOD D and its anonymous version D^* is a bipartite graph that consists of nodes for every individual I in D, called *I-nodes*, and nodes for every MOB id O in D^*, called *O-nodes*. If and only if $\forall t \in QID(I)[D(O,t) \sqsubseteq D^*(O,t)]$, there is an edge (I, O) in G, where $\sqsubseteq$ denotes spatial containment. ∎

Example 14.7
Table 14.8 provides an *incorrect* 2-anonymity release of the MOD D (Table 14.7) based on space generalization. For example, all objects in $AS(O_1) = \{O_1, O_3\}$ are generalized to the smallest common region $[(2, 1), (2, 2)]$ at time t_1. Figure 14.6 presents the corresponding attack graph. An adversary can re-identify both I_1 and I_4 because there exist perfect matchings in the attack graph, that is, there are some O-nodes with degree 1. As a result, the adversary knows that O_1 must map to I_1 and O_4 must map to I_4.   □

In some subtler cases, the adversary can iteratively identify and prune edges that can not be part of any perfect matching to discover perfect matchings,

Table 14.7: Raw moving
object database D

MOB	t_1	t_2
O_1	$(2,1)$	$(6,2)$
O_2	$(3,6)$	$(6,6)$
O_3	$(2,2)$	$(7,7)$
O_4	$(4,5)$	$(8,4)$

Table 14.8: A 2-anonymity scheme of D
that is not safe

MOB	t_1	t_2
O_1	$[(2,1),(2,2)]$	$(6,2)$
O_2	$[(3,5),(4,6)]$	$[(6,6),(7,7)]$
O_3	$[(2,1),(2,2)]$	$[(6,6),(7,7)]$
O_4	$[(3,5),(4,6)]$	$(8,4)$

and finally intrude a record owner's privacy. To avoid privacy attacks based on the notion of attack graph, *MOB k-anonymity* is formally defined as follows.

DEFINITION 14.13 MOB k-anonymity   *[263]* Let D be a MOD and D^* its anonymized version. Given a set of $QIDs$ for the MOBs in D, let G be the attack graph with respect to D and D^*. D^* satisfies the MOB k-anonymity provided that: (i) every I-node in G has at least degree k; and (ii) G is *symmetric*, i.e. whenever G contains an edge (I_i, O_j), it also contains the edge (I_j, O_i). ∎

For MOB k-anonymity, the *information loss* is measured as the reduction in the probability of accurately determining the position of an object over all timestamps between the raw MOD D and its anonymous version D^*. It is formally defined as follows:

$$IL(D, D^*) = \sum_{i=1}^{n} \sum_{j=i}^{m} (1 - 1/area(D^*(O_i, t_j))),$$

where $area(D^*(O_i, t_j))$ denotes the area of the region $D^*(O_i, t_j)$. For example, in Table 14.8, $area(D^*(O_1, t_1))$ is 2 while $area(D^*(O_2, t_2))$ is 4.

14.4.2   Anonymization Algorithm for MOB k-Anonymity

The MOB anonymization algorithm in [263] is composed of two steps: identifying anonymization groups and generalizing the groups to common regions according to the QIDs while achieving minimal information loss.

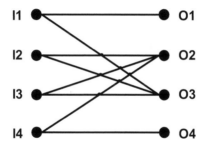

FIGURE 14.6: Attack graph of the unsafe 2-anonymity scheme of D in Table 14.8

14.4.2.1 Identifying anonymization groups

The first step of identifying anonymization groups is for each MOB O in a given MOD D to find the top-K MOBs whose aggregate distance (e.g., sum of distance, average distance) from O over all $QID(O)$ timestamps is minimun. The distance between two MOBs is measured by *Hilbert index*, which makes sure that points close in the multi-dimensional space remain close in the linear Hilbert ordering. Given a MOB O, its Hilbert index at time t is denoted as $H_t(O)$. The list of MOBs and their Hilbert index at time t is referred as the *Hilbert list of MOBs* at time t, denoted by L_t. The distance between two MOBs, O and O', can therefore be approximated as $|H_t(O) - H_t(O')|$. Thus, the problem of finding the top-K MOBs with closest distance from O is to find the top-K MOBs with the lowest overall *score*, $\sum_{t \in QID(O)} |H_t(O) - H_t(O')|$. Yarovoy et al. [263] adapt the *Threshold Algorithm* (TA) [85] by keeping the list L_t in ascending order of the Hilbert index. For every MOB O, we consider the top-K MOBs as its anonymization group $AG(O)$.

However, simply generalizing a moving object O with the MOBs in $AG(O)$ with respect to $QID(O)$ may not ensure k-anonymity. Two algorithms, *extreme union* and *symmetric anonymization*, are consequently proposed to expand the anonymization groups in order to ensure k-anonymity. In extreme union, for every moving object O in D, we take the union of the QIDs of all MOBs in $AG(O)$ and then generalize all of them with respect to every time point in this union in the later stage (Chapter 14.4.2.2). For example, in the running example, $AG(O_1)$ with respect to $QID(O_1) = \{t_1\}$ is $\{O_1, O_3\}$. It is insufficient to guarantee k-anonymity by generalizing only on t_1. In contrast, the extreme union will generalize O_1 and O_2 together with respect to the union of their QIDs, $\{t_1, t_2\}$. Since the distance between a moving object O and another object $O' \in AG(O)$ for the timestamps outside $QID(O)$ but in the timestamp union (e.g. O_1 and O_3 at time t_2) could be arbitrarily far, the generalizations over such timestamps could incur significant information loss. Table 14.9 shows the timestamp unions of the MOBs in Table 14.7.

An alternative approach, symmetric anonymization, keeps the timestamps

Table 14.9:   Extreme union over Table 14.7

MOB	QID	AG(O)	Timestamp Union
O_1	t_1	O_1, O_3	t_1, t_2
O_2	t_2	O_2, O_3	t_2
O_3	t_2	O_2, O_3	t_2
O_4	t_1	O_2, O_4	t_1, t_2

Table 14.10:   Symmetric
anonymization over Table 14.7

MOB	QID	HS(O)
O_1	t_1	O_1, O_3
O_2	t_2	O_2, O_3, O_4
O_3	t_2	O_1, O_2, O_3
O_4	t_1	O_2, O_4

of an object O w.r.t. which all objects in $AG(O)$ are generalized together fixed to $QID(O)$ only, instead of the union of the QIDs of all objects in $AG(O)$. To enforce symmetry, it controls the composition of the anonymization groups. Thus, the anonymization groups generated by symmetric anonymization may not be the same as the ones produced by top-K MOBs, and will be referred as *hiding sets* (HS) for clarity. To compute the HS of a moving object O_i, first, we add O_i itself to $HS(O_i)$; second, if the number of distinct objects in $HS(O_i)$ is less than k, we add the top-$(k - |HS(O_i)|)$ MOBs to $HS(O_i)$; third, to enforce the symmetry for each object O_j in $HS(O_i)$, where $i \neq j$, we further add O_i to $HS(O_j)$. For example, assume we consider 2-anonymity in the MOD given in Table 14.7. $HS(O_1)$ is initialized to $\{O_1\}$, then $\{O_3\}$ as the top-1 MOBs with respect to O_1 at time t_1 is added to $HS(O_1)$. To enforce symmetry, O_1 is added to $HS(O_3)$. Now both O_1 and O_3 have 2 objects in their hiding sets, so we can move to O_2 and set $HS(O_2) = \{O_2, O_3\}$. Due to the symmetry requirement, we need to add O_2 to $HS(O_3)$ in spite of the fact that there are already 2 objects in $HS(O_3)$. Finally, we compute $HS(O_4) = \{O_2, O_4\}$, which requires to add O_4 to $HS(O_2)$ due to the symmetry. Table 14.10 shows the hiding sets of the MOBs in Table 14.7.

14.4.2.2   Generalizing anonymization groups

The last step of the anonymization algorithm is to perform the *space generalization* over either all objects in $AG(O)$ together with respect to every timestamp in its timestamp union for every object O in the MOD D (for extreme union) or all objects in $HS(O)$ together with respect to $QID(O)$ for every object O in D (for symmetric anonymization). The main challenge is that *overlapping anonymization groups can force us to revisit earlier generalizations* [263]. The concept of *equivalence class* is consequently proposed.

Table 14.11: Equivalence classes produced by extreme union and symmetric union over Table 14.7

t	EC_t by Extreme Union	EC_t by Symmetric Anonymization
t_1	$\{O_1, O_3\}, \{O_2, O_4\}$	$\{O_1, O_3\}, \{O_2, O_4\}$
t_2	$\{O_2, O_3\}$	$\{O_1, O_2, O_3, O_4\}$

DEFINITION 14.14 *Equivalence class* Two MOBs O_i and O_j are equivalent at time t, denoted by $O_i \equiv_t O_j$, if and only if:

1. $t \in QID(O_j)$ and $O_i \in S(O_j)$, or

2. $t \in QID(O_i)$ and $O_j \in S(O_i)$, or

3. there exists a MOB $O_k \neq O_i, O_j$ such that $O_i \equiv_t O_k$ and $O_k \equiv_t O_j$, where $S(O)$ is either $AG(O)$ or $HS(O)$ [263]. ∎

For all $O_i \in D$, let $S(O_i)$ be the anonymization group or the hiding set of O_i, let $T(O_i)$ be the set of timestamps associated with $S(O_i)$, and let QIT be the union of all timestamps in D. The equivalence classes with respect to time t, denoted by EC_t, can be computed by going through every MOB O_i with $t \in QID(O_i)$ and then adding $S(O_i)$ to the collection EC_t. When a new $S(O_i)$ is added to EC_t, if it has overlaps with an existing set in EC_t, we merge it with the existing set, otherwise, we make a new set. Table 14.11 presents the equivalence classes produced by both extreme union and symmetric anonymization on Table 14.7. Achieving a k-anonymous D^* of D is, therefore, for each time $t \in QIT$, for each equivalence class set $C \in EC_t$ to generalize the position of every MOB $O \in C$ to the smallest common region in order to minimize the information loss.

Though symmetric anonymization overcomes the aforementioned disadvantage of extreme union, from Table 14.7 we can observe that its resulting equivalence classes could be larger than those produced by extreme union, depending on the relative positions of the moving objects. Typically, the smaller the classes, the less general the regions. Thus, theoretically extreme union and symmetric anonymization are incomparable in terms of the information loss they result in [263]. However, the experimental results in [263] indicate that symmetric anonymization outperforms extreme union in terms of both efficiency and efficacy.

14.4.2.3 Discussion

An underlying assumption of the MOB k-anonymity is that the data publisher must be aware of the $QIDs$ of all moving objects in the MOD to publish, that is, all adversaries' possible background knowledge. However, the paper left the acquisition of QIDs for a data publisher unsolved. An attacker may obtain a moving object's $QIDs$ from various sources beyond the data publisher's perception. Recall that usually data publishers are not experts, so the fact may hinder the application of the MOB k-anonymity.

The approach proposed in [263] is limited to protection from only identity linkage attacks (k-anonymity). However, in the context of MODs, there are also requirements of protecting attribute linkage attacks (see Chapter 14.1.2), thus the approach is not applicable to such scenarios. In addition, space generalization based on coordinates sometimes may impose additional efforts on the data publisher. For example, a transit company needs preprocessing to get all station's coordinates.

14.5   Other Spatio-Temporal Anonymization Methods

Different solutions have been proposed to protect the privacy of location-based service (LBS) users. The anonymity of a user in LBS is achieved by mixing the user's identity and request with other users. Example of such techniques are Mix Zones [31], cloaking [106], and location-based k-anonymity [98]. The objective of these techniques is very different from the problem studied in this chapter. First, their goal is to anonymize an individual user's identity resulting from a set of LBS requests, but the problem studied in this chapter is to anonymize a high-dimensional trajectory data. Second, they deal with small dynamic groups of users at a time, but we anonymize a large static data set. Hence, their problem is very different from spatio-temporal data publishing studied in this chapter.

The privacy model proposed by Terrovitis and Mamoulis [219] assumes that different adversaries have different background knowledge about the trajectories, and thus their objective is to prevent adversaries from gaining any further information from the published data. They consider the locations in a trajectory as sensitive information and assume that the data holder has the background knowledge of all the adversaries. In reality, such information is difficult to obtain.

Papadimitriou et al. [185] study the privacy issue on publishing time series data and examined the trade-offs between time series compressibility and partial information hiding and their fundamental implications on how one should introduce uncertainty about individual values by perturbing them. The study found that by making the perturbation "similar" to the original data, we can both preserve the structure of the data better, while simultaneously making breaches harder. However, as data become more compressible, a fraction of the uncertainty can be removed if true values are leaked, revealing how they were perturbed. Malin and Airoldi [163] study the privacy threats in location-based data in the environment of hospitals.

14.6   Summary

We have studied the problem of anonymizing high-dimensional trajectory data and shown that traditional QID-based anonymization methods, such as k-anonymity and its variants, are not suitable for anonymizing trajectories, due to the curse of high dimensionality. Applying k-anonymity on high-dimensional data would result in a high utility loss. To overcome the problem, we discuss the LKC-privacy model [91, 170], where privacy is ensured by assuming that an adversary has limited background knowledge about the victim. We have also presented an efficient algorithm for achieving LKC-privacy with the goal of preserving maximal frequent sequences, which serves as the basis of many data mining tasks on sequential data.

The Never Walk Alone (NWA) [1] algorithm studied in Chapter 14.3 employs clustering and space translation to achieve the anonymity. The drawback of the clustering phase in NWA is that it may have to restart a number of times in order to find a suitable solution. Another drawback is that the space translation produces untruthful data. In contrast, the LKC-privacy approach presented in Chapter 14.2 does not require continuous data and employs suppression for anonymity. Thus, the LKC-privacy approach preserves the data truthfulness and maximal frequent sequences with true support counts. Preserving data truthfulness is important if the data will be examined by human users for the purposes of auditing and data interpretation. Moreover, NWA does not address the privacy threats caused by attribute linkages. Yarovoy et al. [263] consider time as a QID attribute. However, there is no fixed set of time for all moving objects, or rather each trajectory has its own set of times as its QID. It is unclear how the data holder can determine the QID attributes for each trajectory.

Chapter 15

Anonymizing Social Networks

15.1 Introduction

In 2001, Enron Corporation filed for bankruptcy. With the related legal investigation in the accounting fraud and corruption, the Federal Energy Regulatory Commission has made public a large set of email messages concerning the corporation. This data set is known as the *Enron corpus*, and contains over 600,000 messages that belong to 158 users, mostly senior management of Enron. After removing duplicates, there are about 200,000 messages. This data set is valuable for researchers interested in how emails are used in an organization and better understanding of organization structure. If we represent each user as a node, and create an edge between two nodes when there exists sufficient email correspondence between the two corresponding individuals, then we arrive at a data graph, or a social network.

It is natural that when such data are made public, the involved individuals will be concerned about the disclosure of their personal information, which should be kept private. This data set is quoted in [111] as a motivating example for the study of privacy in social networks. Such a set of data can be visualized as a graph as shown in Figure 15.1.

It is observed that social networks are abundant on the Internet, corporate correspondences, networks of collaborating authors, etc. Social networking websites such as Friendster, MySpace, Facebook, Cyworld, and others have become very popular in recent years. The information in social networks becomes an important data source, and sometimes it is necessary or beneficial to release such data to the public. Other than the above utilities of the Enron email data set, there can be other kinds of utility for social network data. Kumar et al. [147] study the structure and evolution of the network. Getor and Diehl [100] prepare a survey on link mining for data sets that resemble social networks. McCallum et al. [167] consider topic and role discovery in social networks.

To this date, not many data sets have been made public because of the associated privacy issues. It is obvious that no employee of Enron would like his/her identity in the data set to be disclosed since it means that their messages to others, which were written only for the recipient(s), would be disclosed. Anonymous web browsing is an example where people want to conceal any behavior that is deemed unethical or disapproved by society. It becomes important to ensure that any published data about the social networks would not violate individual privacy. In this chapter we examine the related issues and explore some of the existing mechanisms.

15.1.1   Data Models

Different models have been proposed with respect to social network data that are published or made available to the public. The following are some of such models

- *A simple model*: The data set is given by a graph $G = (V, E)$, where V is a set of nodes, and E is a set of edges. Each node is an entity of interest. In social networks, each node typically corresponds to an individual or a group of individuals. An edge represents a relationship between two individuals.

- *Labeled nodes*: In [271], the graph $G = (V, E)$ is enriched with labels, let L be a set of labels, there is a mapping function $\mathcal{L} : V \rightarrow L$ which assigns to each node in V a label from L. For example, the occupation of an individual can be used as a label. Figure 15.2 shows a social network with labeled nodes, where A, B, C are the labels.

- *Nodes with attached attributes or data*: Each node typically is an individual, so each node is associated with some personal information. In the Enron data set, the emails sent or received by an individual can be seen as attached data to the corresponding node.

- *Sensitive edges*: The data set is a multi-graph $G = (V, E_1, E_2, \ldots, E_s)$, where V is a set of nodes, and E_i are sets of edges. E_s correspond to the sensitive relationships. There can be different sets of edges where each set belongs to a particular class. Edges can also be labeled with more information about the relationships.

15.1.2   Attack Models

The anonymization problem of social networks depends on the background knowledge of the adversary and the model of privacy attack, which can be the identification of individuals in the network or the relationship among individuals.

Li et al. [153] suggest that there are two types of privacy attacks on social networks:

- *identity disclosure*: With a social network, this is to link the nodes in the anonymized network to real world individuals or entities. Conceptually, the system may choose a value of k, and make sure that in the released

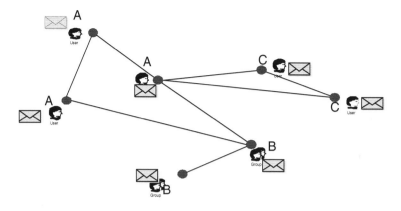

FIGURE 15.1: A social network

social network G', which can be different from the original data G, no node v in G' can be re-identified with a probability of greater than $1/k$, based on the assumption of the adversary's background knowledge. Most existing mechanisms would try to ensure that at least k different nodes are similar in terms of the adversary's knowledge about the target of attack, so that each of the k nodes has the same chance of being the culprit.

- *attribute disclosure*: With a social network, each node represents an individual or a group of individuals. There can be attributes attached to each node, such as personal or group information. Sometimes, such information can be considered sensitive or private to some individuals.

With graph data, another type of attack is identified:

- *link re-identification*: Links or edges in a social network can represent sensitive relationships. In cases where the identity of nodes are released to some user groups, some individuals may not want their relationship to some other individuals to be discovered.

15.1.2.1 Passive Attacks

The terms passive versus active attacks are used to differentiate between cases where the adversary only observes the data and does not tamper with the data versus the cases where the adversary may change the data for attack purposes.

Basis of Attacks: Background Knowledge of Adversary

In a social network, an individual may be identified based on the attribute values and also the relationships with other individuals [235]. Before we introduce the kinds of adversary's knowledge, we need some definitions.

DEFINITION 15.1 Induced subgraph   Given a graph $G = (V, E)$, with node set V and edge set E, let S be a set of nodes in V, the *induced subgraph* of G on S is $G(S) = (S, E')$, where $E' = \{(u, v) | (u, v) \in E, u \in V, v \in V\}$. ∎

DEFINITION 15.2 1-neighborhood   Given a graph, $G = (V, E)$, if $(u, v) \in E$, then v and v are neighbors to each other. Suppose $u \in V$, let W be the set of neighbors of u. The *1-neighborhood* of $u \in V$ is the induced subgraph of G on $\{u\} \cup W$. ∎

$\mathcal{H}_i$: Neighborhood Knowledge

Hay et al. [111, 110] consider a class of queries, of increasing power, which report on the local structure of the graph a target node. For example, Hay et al. [111, 110] define that

- $\mathcal{H}_0(x)$ returns the label of a node x (in case of unlabeled social network, the nodes are not labeled, $\mathcal{H}_0(x) = \epsilon$),

- $\mathcal{H}_1(x)$ returns the degree of node x, and

- $\mathcal{H}_2(x)$ returns the multiset of the degrees of each neighbor of x.

For example, consider the node $x1$ in Figure 15.2.

$\mathcal{H}_0(x1) = A$
$\mathcal{H}_1(x1) = 2$
$\mathcal{H}_2(x1) = \{2, 4\}$

The queries can be defined iteratively, where $\mathcal{H}_i(x)$ could return the multiset of values which are the result of evaluating $\mathcal{H}_{i-1}(x)$ on the set of nodes adjacent to x. For example,

- $\mathcal{H}_i(x) = \{\mathcal{H}_{i-1}(z_1), \mathcal{H}_{i-1}(z_2), \ldots, \mathcal{H}_{i-1}(z_m)\}$,

where $z_1, \ldots, z_m$ are the neighbors of x.

Subgraph Knowledge

Hay et al. [110] suggest that other than $\mathcal{H}_i$, a stronger and more realistic class of query is *subgraph query*, which asserts the existence of a subgraph

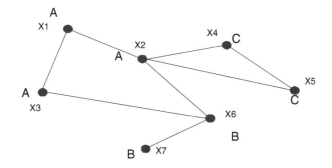

FIGURE 15.2: A social network

around the target node. The descriptive power of the query is counted by the number of edges in the subgraph. Note that this class of adversary's knowledge covers also the 1-neighborhood since the 1-neighborhood is one possible subgraph around the target node.

In Figure 15.2, if the adversary knows that the target individual is at the center of a star with 4 neighbors, then the adversary can pinpoint the node $x2$ in the network as the target, since $x2$ is the only node with 4 neighbors. However, if the adversary knows only that the target is labeled A and has a neighbor with label A, then nodes $x1$, $x2$, and $x3$ all qualify as the possible node for the target, and the adversary cannot succeed in a sure attack.

Zhou and Lei [271] consider an adversary's background knowledge of the 1-neighborhood of the target node. Backstrom et al. [25] describe a type of passive attack, in which a small group of colluding social network users discover their nodes in the anonymized network by utilizing the knowledge of the network structure around them. This attack is feasible, but only works on a small scale because the colluding users can only compromise the privacy of some of the users who are already their friends.

For link re-identification, Korolova et al. [143] assume that each user can have the knowledge of the neighborhood within a distance ℓ, and with this knowledge, an adversary can try to bribe other nodes in the network to gain information about a significant portion of the links in the network.

Recently, Zou et al. [272] propose a *k-automorphism model* that can prevent any types of structural attacks. The intuition of the method is described as follows: Assume that there are $k - 1$ automorphic functions F_a for $1 \leq a \leq k - 1$ in the published network, and for each vertex v, $F_{a_x}(v) \neq F_{a_y}(v)$ $(a_x \neq a_y)$. Thus, for each vertex v in published network, there are always $k - 1$ other symmetric vertices. This means that there are no structural differences between v and each of its $k - 1$ symmetric vertices. Thus, the adversary cannot distinguish v from the other $k - 1$ symmetric vertices using any structural information. Therefore, the target victim cannot be identified with a probability higher than $1/k$.

15.1.2.2　Active Attacks

Backstrom et al. [25] study the problem of active attacks aiming for identity disclosure and node re-identification with an assumption that the adversary has the ability to modify the network prior to it release. The general idea is first choose an arbitrary set of target victim users from the social network, create a small number of new "sybil" social network user accounts and link these new accounts with target victims, and create a pattern of links among the new accounts such that they can be uniquely identified in the anonymized social network structure. The attack involves creating $O(logN)$ number of sybil accounts, where N is the total number of users in the social network.

Alternatively, an adversary would find or create k nodes in the network namely $\{x_1, \ldots, x_k\}$, and next create the edge (x_i, x_j) independently with probability $1/2$. This produces a random graph H. The graph will be included into the given social network forming a graph G. The first requirement of H is such that there is no other subgraph S in G that is isomorphic to H (meaning that H can result from S by relabeling the nodes). In this way H can be uniquely identified in G. The second requirement of H is that there is no automorphism, which is an isomorphism from H to itself. With H, the adversary can link a target node w to a subset of nodes N in H so that once H is located, w is also located. From results in random graph theory [34], the chance of achieving the two requirements above is very high by using the random graph generation method.

Fortunately, active attacks are not practical for large scale privacy attacks due to three limitations suggested by Narayanan and Shmatikov [175].

1. *Online social networks only*: Active attacks are restricted to online social networks only because the adversary has to create a large number fake user accounts in the social network *before* its release. Many social network providers, such as Facebook, ensure that each social network account associates with at least one e-mail account, making creation of a large number of fake social network user accounts difficult.

2. *Sybil accounts have low in-degree*: The adversary may be able to plant the fake user accounts and link the fake accounts to the target victims. Yet, the adversary has little control to increase the in-degree of the fake user accounts. As a result, sybil accounts may be identified with low in-degree. Yu et al. [266] develop some techniques to identify sybil attacks from social networks.

3. *Mutual links*: Many online social network providers consider two users are linked only if *both* users mutually agree to be "friends." For example, in Facebook, user A initiates a friendship with user B. The friendship is established only if B confirms the relationship. Due to the restriction of mutual links, the target victims will not agree to link back to the fake accounts, so the links are not established, thereby do not appear in the released network.

Note that since the attack is based on a subgraph in the network, it can be defended in the same manner as for passive attack based on subgraph knowledge.

15.1.3 Utility of the Published Data

For privacy-preserving data publishing, the other side of the coin is the utility of the published data. Most of the utility measures for social networks are related to graph properties. The following are some examples.

- **Properties of interest in network data**: Hay et al. [110] use the following properties for the utility measure.

  - Degree: distribution of degrees of all nodes in the graph
  - Path length: distribution of the lengths of the shortest paths between 500 randomly sampled pairs of nodes in the network
  - Transitivity: distributions of the size of the connected component that a node belongs to.
  - Network resilience: number of nodes in the largest connected component of the graph as nodes are removed.
  - Infectiousness: proportion of nodes infected by a hypothetical disease, first randomly pick a node for the first infection, and then spread the disease with a specific rate.

- **Aggregate query answering**: Korolova et al. [143] consider queries of the following form: for two labels l_1, l_2, what is the average distance from a node with label l_1 to its nearest node with label l_2.

15.2 General Privacy-Preserving Strategies

In order to avoid privacy breach, there can be different strategies. The first method, the most widely adopted approach is to publish an anonymized network. In other cases, such as Facebook, the data holder may choose to allow only subgraphs to be known to individual users. For example, the system may let each user see one level of the neighbors of the node of the user. Another approach is not to release the network, but to return an approximate answer to any query that is issued about the network.

To preserve privacy, we can release a data set that deviates from the original data set, but which still contains useful information for different usages of the data. In this Chapter 15.2, we introduce two different approaches: graph modification and equivalence class of nodes.

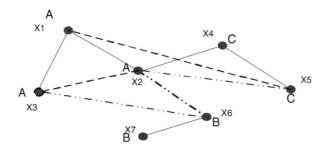

FIGURE 15.3: Anonymization by addition and deletion of edges

15.2.1   Graph Modification

One way to anonymize a social network is to modify the network by adding or deleting nodes, adding or deleting edges, and changing (generalize) the labels of nodes. The network is release only after sufficient changes have been made to satisfy certain privacy criteria.

In Figure 15.3, we show an anonymization of Figure 15.1 by adding and deleting edges only. The aim is to resist attacks from adversaries with knowledge of the 1-neighborhood of some target node. We would like the resulting graph to be 2-anonymous with respect to this neighborhood knowledge, meaning that for any 1-neighborhood N, there are at least 2 nodes with a 1-neighborhood of N. In the anonymization, one edge $(x2, x3)$ is added, while 4 edges are deleted, namely, $(x2, x4), (x2, x5), (x2, x6), (x3, x6)$. If the target victim node is $x1$, which is labeled A and is connected to 2 neighbors also labeled A, we find that in the resulting graph in Figure 15.3, there are 3 nodes, namely $x1$, $x2$, and $x3$ that have the same 1-neighborhood. If the target node is $x7$, with label B, we find that both $x7$ and $x6$ have the same 1-neighborhood. The graph is 2-anonymous with respect to attacks by 1-neighborhood.

15.2.2   Equivalence Classes of Nodes

With this method, clusters of nodes are formed and selected linkages can be hidden, or the linkages among nodes for two different clusters can be "generalized" to links among the clusters instead. The clusters form equivalence classes of nodes, so that within any cluster or equivalence class, the nodes are indistinguishable from each other. For example, Figure 15.4 shows three clusters formed from Figure 15.2. An earlier work that proposes such a method is [270], the aim of this work is to protect the re-identification of the links. Some links are classified as sensitive and they need to be protected.

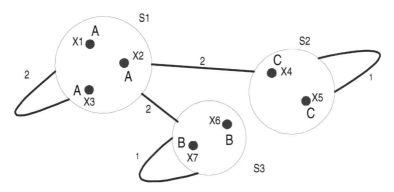

FIGURE 15.4: Anonymization by clustering nodes

15.3 Anonymization Methods for Social Networks

In the rest of the chapter, we will describe in more details some of the existing anonymization methods.

15.3.1 Edge Insertion and Label Generalization

Zhou and Pei [271] consider the 1-neighborhood of a node as a possible adversary's background knowledge. The aim of protection is node re-identification. Here graph changes by edge addition and change of labels are allowed in the algorithm.

There are two main steps in the anonymization:

1. Find the 1-neighborhood of each node in the network.

2. Group the nodes by similarity and modify the neighborhoods of the nodes with the goal of having at least k nodes with the same 1-neighborhood in the anonymized graph.

The second step in the above faces the difficult problem of graph isomorphism, which is one of a very small number of known problems in NP with uncertainty in NP-completeness, that is, there is no known polynomial algorithm and also no known proof of NP-completeness. Hence only exponential time algorithms are available. To solve this problem, Zhou and Pei [271] use a minimum depth-first-search coding for each node, which is adopted from [257].

15.3.2   Clustering Nodes for k-Anonymity

Hay et al. [110] propose to form clusters or equivalent classes of nodes. Clusters of nodes of size at least k are formed. The aim is to make the nodes inside each cluster indistinguishable, so that node re-identification is not possible. This method can resist attacks based on different kinds of adversary's knowledge, including $\mathcal{H}_i$, neighboring subgraph, and 1-neighborhood.

In the terminology of [110], each cluster of nodes is called a *supernode*, and an edge between two supernodes is called a *superedge*. The superedges include self-loops and are labeled with a non-negative weight, which indicates the density of edges within and across supernodes.

In the graph $G = (V, E)$ in Figure 15.4, there are 3 supernodes, $S1$, $S2$, $S3$. That is, $V = \{S1, S2, S3\}$. The superedge between $S1$ and $S2$ has a weight of 2, since there are 2 edges in the original graph of Figure 15.1 linking nodes in $S1$ to nodes in $S2$. We say that $d(S1, S2) = 2$. Similarly the weight of the superedge between $S1$ and $S3$, given by $d(S1, S3)$, is 2. Each node can have a self-loop also. The self-loop of $S1$ has a weight of 2 since within $S1$, there are two edges in the original graph among the nodes in $S1$. In a similar manner, the self-loops for $S2$ and $S3$ are given weights of $d(S2, S3) = 1$.

Since each supernode in Figure 15.4 has at least 2 nodes in the original graph, and the nodes inside each supernode are indistinguishable from each other, this graph is 2-anonymous.

In order to preserve the utility, we examine the likelihood of recovering the original graph given the anonymized graph. If the graph $G = (V, E)$ in Figure 15.4 is published instead of that in Figure 15.1, there will be multiple possibilities of the original graphs, each being a possible world. Let $W(G)$ be the set of all possible worlds. If we assume equal probability for all possible worlds, then the probability of the original graph, which is one of the possible worlds, is given by $1/|W(G)|$. This probability should be high in order to achieve high utility of the published data.

We can formulate $|W(G)|$ by

$$|W(G)| = \prod_{X \in V} \binom{\frac{1}{2}|X|(|X|-1)}{d(X, X)} \prod_{X, Y \in V} \binom{|X||Y|}{d(X, Y)} \qquad (15.1)$$

For example, in Figure 15.4,

$$|W(G)| = \binom{\frac{1}{2}3 \cdot 2}{2} \binom{\frac{1}{2}2 \cdot 1}{1} \binom{\frac{1}{2}2 \cdot 1}{1} \binom{3 \cdot 2}{2} \binom{3 \cdot 2}{2} = 675$$

The algorithm in [110] follows a simulated annealing method to search for a good solution. Starting with a graph with a single supernode which contains all the original nodes, the algorithm repeatedly tries to find alternatives by splitting a supernode, merging two supernodes, or moving an original node from one supernode to another. If the above probability of $1/|W(G)|$ increases with the newly form alternative, the alternative is accepted to be explored.

The termination criterion is that fewer than 10% of the current alternatives are accepted.

15.3.3 Supergraph Generation

In the model proposed by Liu and Terzi [159], the adversary attack is based on the degree of the target node, that is the knowledge of the adversary is given by $\mathcal{H}_1$. Both edge insertion and deletion are allowed to modify the given graph to form an anonymized graph. Given a graph $G = (V, E)$, if we sort the degrees of each node, then the sorted list is a degree sequence for G. Anonymization is based on the construction of a graph that follows a given degree sequence.

DEFINITION 15.3 k-anonymous graph   The degree sequence d of a graph G is k-*anonymous* if and only if each degree value in d appears at least k times in d. ■

For example $d = \{5, 5, 3, 3, 2, 2, 2\}$ is 2-anonymous, but not 3-anonymous. The degree sequence of Figure 15.1 is given by $\{4, 3, 2, 2, 2, 1\}$, which is not k-anonymous for any k greater than 1.

In Figure 15.1, if we delete edge $(x2, x6)$ and add edge $(x3, x7)$, then the degree sequence of the modified graph becomes $\{3, 3, 2, 2, 2, 2, 2\}$ and it is 2-anonymous. Obviously, if an adversary only knows the degree of a target node, then there are always at least 2 nodes that have the same degree and they are not distinguishable.

To preserve the utility of the published data, we measure the distance of a degree sequence $\hat{d}$ from the original sequence d by the following:

$$L_1(\hat{d} - d) = \sum_i |\hat{d}(i) - d(i)| \qquad (15.2)$$

where $d(i)$ refers to the i-th value in the list d.

There are two main steps in the anonymization:

1. Given a degree sequence d, construct a new degree sequence $\hat{d}$ that is k-anonymous and such that the degree-anonymization cost

$$D_A(\hat{d}, d) = L_1(\hat{d} - d) \qquad (15.3)$$

   is minimized.

2. With $\hat{d}$, try to construct a graph $\hat{G}(V, \hat{E})$ such that $d_{\hat{G}} = \hat{d}$ and $\hat{E} \cap E = E$.

A dynamic programming algorithm is proposed for Step 1, which solves the problem in polynomial time. For the second step an algorithm Construct-Graph is taken from [80] as the backbone, this algorithm constructs a graph given a degree sequence. After Step 1, we obtain a k-anonymous degree sequence $\hat{d}$. This is input to the algorithm ConstructGraph. If the resulting graph $G1$ is a supergraph of G, then we can return $G1$. However, Step 2 may fail so that some edges in G are not in $G1$. The degree sequence can be relaxed to increase the values of some degrees while maintaining the k-anonymity. ConstructGraph is run again on the new sequence. If it is still not successful, we consider deletion of edges that violate the supergraph condition.

15.3.4   Randomized Social Networks

In the report [111], an anonymization technique based on random *edge deletions and insertions* is proposed, which can resist $\mathcal{H}_1$ attacks. However, the utility degradation from this anonymization is steep.

Ying and Wu [264] quantify the relationship between the amount of randomization and the protection against link re-identification. A randomization strategy is proposed that preserves the spectral properties of the graph. With this method, the utility of the published graph is enhanced.

15.3.5   Releasing Subgraphs to Users: Link Recovery

Korolova et al. [143] consider link privacy: the goal of an adversary is to find a fraction of the links in the network. The links represent the relationship among users and it is deemed sensitive. Here the graph is not released, and the owner of the network would like to hide the links. Each user can see its neighborhood in the network. An adversary can bribe a number of users to gain information about other linkages.

For example on Facebook, each user can determine if they allow their friends to see his/her friend list, and also maybe allow the friends of friends to see it.

15.3.6   Not Releasing the Network

Rastogi et al. [192] propose a different scenario that does not publish the social network. Instead, from the system point of view, the input is the network I, and a query q on I, the output is an approximation $A(I, q)$ of the query answer $q(I)$. I is considered a relation database containing tuples. The adversary can revise the estimate of any tuple in I given the values of $A(I, q)$. The aim is to resist the attack where the estimate becomes close to the actual values.

15.4   Data Sets

In almost all existing works, the proposed ideas or methods have been tested on some data sets. It is important to show that the methods work on some real data. Here we list some of the data sets that have been used.

In [111], three sets of real data are tested:

1. *Hep-Th*: data from the arXiv archive and the Stanford Linear Accelerator Center SPRIES-HEP database. It describes papers and authors in theoretical high-energy physics.

2. *Enron*: we have introduced this data set in the beginning of the chapter.

3. *Net-trace*: this data set is derived from an IP-level network trace collected at a major university, with 201 internal address from a single campus and over 400 external addresses. Another set Net-common is derived from Net-trace with only the internal nodes.

Zhou and Pei [271] adopt a data set from the KDD cup 2003 on co-authorship for a set of papers in high-energy physics. In the co-authorship graphs, each node is an author and an edge between two authors represents a co-authorship for one or more papers. There are over 57,000 nodes and 120,000 edges in the graph, with an average degree of about 4. There is in fact no privacy issue with the above data set but it is a real social network data set.

In addition to real data sets, synthetic data from R-MAT graph model has been used which follows the power law [86] on node degree distribution and the small-world characteristics [224].

15.5   Summary

We have seen a number of techniques for privacy-preserving publishing of social networks in this chapter. The research is still at an early stage and there are different issues to be investigated in the future; we list some such directions in the following.

- Enhancing the utility of the published social networks

  With known methods, privacy is achieved with trade off of the utility of the published data. Since the problems are typically very hard and an optimal solution is not possible, there is the possibility to find better solutions that involve less information loss.

- Multiple releases for updated social networks

  Social networks typically evolve continuously and quickly, so that they keep changing each day, with new nodes added, new edges added, or old edges deleted. It would be interesting to consider how privacy may be breached and how it can be protected when we release the social networks more than once.

- Privacy preservation on attributes of individuals

  So far most of the existing works assume a simple network model, where there are no attributes attached to a node. It is interesting to consider the case where additional attributes are attached and when such attributes can be sensitive.

- k-anonymity is not sufficient to protect privacy in some cases. Suppose a published network is k-anonymous so that there are k nodes that can be the target node. However, if all of these k nodes have the same sensitive property, then the adversary is still successful in breaching the privacy.

In conclusion, privacy-preserving publishing of social networks remains a challenging problem, since graph problems are typically difficult and there can be many different ways of adversary attacks. It is an important problem and it will be interesting to look for new solutions to the open issues.

Chapter 16

Sanitizing Textual Data

16.1 Introduction

All works studied in previous chapters focused on anonymizing the structural relational and transaction data. What about the sensitive, person-specific information in unstructural text documents?

Sanitization of text documents involves removing sensitive information and potential linking information that can associate an individual person to the sensitive information. Documents have to be sanitized for a variety of reasons. For example, government agencies have to remove the sensitive information and/or person-specific identifiable information from some classified documents before making them available to the public so that the secrecy and privacy are protected. Hospitals may need to sanitize some sensitive information in patients' medical reports before sharing them with other healthcare agencies, such as government health department, drugs companies, and research institutes.

To guarantee that the privacy and secrecy requirements are met, the process of document sanitization is still performed manually in most of the government agencies and healthcare institutes. Automatic sanitization is still a research area in its infancy stage. An earlier work called *Scrub* [214] finds and replaces identifying information of individuals, identifying information such as name, location, and medical terms with other terms of similar type, such as fake names and locations. In this chapter, we focus on some recently developed text sanitization techniques in privacy protection. We can broadly categorize the literature in text sanitization into two categories:

1. *Association with structural or semi-structural data.* Textual data itself is unstructural, but some of its information could be associated with some structural or semi-structural data, such as, a relational database. The database could keep track of a set of individuals or entities. The general idea of document sanitization in this scenario is to remove some terms in documents so that the adversary cannot link a document to an entity in the structural data. This problem is studied in Chapter 16.2.

2. *No association with structural or semi-structural data.* This family of sanitization methods rely on information extraction tool to identify en-

tities, such as names, phone number, and diseases, etc., from the textual documents. Then, suppress or generalize of the terms if they contain identifiable or sensitive information. The reliability of the sanitization and quality of the resulting documents pretty much depend on the quality of the information extraction modules. This problem is studied in Chapter 16.3.

16.2   ERASE

Chakaravarthy et al. [44] introduce the *ERASE* system to sanitize documents with the goal of minimal distortion. External knowledge is required to associate a database of entities with their context. *ERASE* prevents disclosure of protected entities by removing certain terms of their context so that no protected entity can be inferred from remaining document text. *K-safety*, in the same spirit of k-anonymity, is thereafter defined. A set of terms is *K-safe* if its intersection with every protected entity contains at least K entities. Then the proposed problem is to find the maximum cardinality subset of a document satisfying K-safety. Chakaravarthy et al. [44] propose and evaluate both a global optimal algorithm and an efficient greedy algorithm to achieve K-safety.

16.2.1   Sanitization Problem for Documents

Chakaravarthy et al. [44] model public knowledge as a database of *entities*, denoted by E, such as persons, products, and diseases, etc. Each entity $e \in E$ is associated with a set of *terms*, which forms the *context* of e, denoted by $C(e)$. For instance, the context of a person entity could include his/her name, age, city of birth, and job. The database can be in the form of structured relational data or unstructured textual data, for example, an employee list in a company or Wikipedia [44]. The database can be composed manually or extracted automatically using an information extraction method [15].

16.2.2   Privacy Model: K-Safety

The data holder specifies some entities $P \subseteq E$ to be *protected*. These are the entities that need to be protected against *identity linkage*. For instance, in a database of diseases, certain diseases, e.g., AIDS, can be marked as protected. Let D be the input document to be sanitized. A document contains a set of terms. We assume that D contains only the terms that are in the context of some protected entity, i.e., $D \subseteq \cup_{e \in P} C(e)$. Any other terms in D but not in $\cup_{e \in P} C(e)$ has no effect on privacy, therefore, need not be removed.

Suppose a document D contains a set of terms S that appears in the context of some protected entity e. $S \subseteq D$ and $S \subseteq C(e)$ for some $e \in P$. The adversary may use S to link the protected entity e with the document D. The likelihood of a successful identity linkage depends on how many entities $E - e$ contain S in their context as well. Chakaravarthy et al.'s privacy model [44] assumes that the adversary has no other external knowledge on the target victim, therefore, the adversary cannot confirm whether or not the linkage is correct as long as the number of entities in $E - e$ containing S in their context is large. The intuition of K-safety is to ensure that there are at least K entities in E, other than e, that can link to D, where $K > 0$ is an anonymity threshold specified by the data holder.

DEFINITION 16.1 K-safety Let E be a set of entities. Let $T \subseteq D$ be a set of terms. Let $P \subseteq E$ be a set of protected entities. For a protected entity $\bar{e} \in P$, let $A_T(\bar{e})$ be the number of entities other than $\bar{e}$ that contain $C(\bar{e}) \cap T$ in their context. The set of terms T is K-*safe* with respect to a protected entity $\bar{e}$ if $A_T(\bar{e}) \geq K$. This set T is said to be K-safe if T is K-safe with respect to every protected entity [44]. ∎

16.2.3 Problem Statement

The sanitization problem for K-safety can be defined as follows.

DEFINITION 16.2 Sanitization problem for K-safety Given a set of entities E, where each entity $e \in E$ is associated with a set of terms $C(e)$, a set of protected entities $P \in E$, a document D, and an anonymity threshold K, the *sanitization problem for K-safety* is to find the maximum cardinality subset of D that is K-safe. ∎

The following example, borrowed from [44], illustrates this problem.

Example 16.1
Consider a set of entities $E = \{\bar{e}_1, \bar{e}_2, \bar{e}_3, e_4, e_5, e_6, e_7\}$, where $P = \{\bar{e}_1, \bar{e}_2, \bar{e}_3\}$ is a set of protected entities. Suppose their contexts contain the following terms:

$C(\bar{e}_1) = \{t_a, t_b, t_c\}$
$C(\bar{e}_2) = \{t_b, t_d, t_e, t_f\}$
$C(\bar{e}_3) = \{t_a, t_d, t_g\}$
$C(e_4) = \{t_a, t_b, t_d, t_g\}$
$C(e_5) = \{t_c, t_e, t_f\}$
$C(e_6) = \{t_b, t_g\}$
$C(e_7) = \{t_a, t_b, t_c, t_e, t_f, t_g\}$

Suppose the data holder wants to achieve 2-safety on a document $D = \{t_a, t_b, t_d, t_e, t_f, t_g\}$. The subset $T_1 = \{t_b, t_d, t_g\}$ is not 2-safe because $C(\bar{e}_2) \cap T_1 = t_b, t_d$ is contained in the context of only one other entity $\bar{e}_1$, and therefore, $A_{T_1}(\bar{e}_2) = 1$.

The subset $T_2 = \{t_a, t_e, t_f, t_g\}$ is 2-safe because:

$\bar{e}_1 : C(\bar{e}_1) \cap T_2 = t_a$ contained in $\bar{e}_3$, e_4, e_7
$\bar{e}_2 : C(\bar{e}_2) \cap T_2 = t_e, t_f$ contained in e_5, e_7
$\bar{e}_3 : C(\bar{e}_3) \cap T_2 = t_a, t_g$ contained in e_4, e_7

Since $A_{T_2}(\bar{e}_i) \geq 2$ for every $\bar{e}_i \in P$, T_2 is 2-safe with respect to P. It can be verified that for any $T_x \supset T_2$ is not 2-safe, so T_2 is an optimal solution. $\qquad \square$

16.2.4 Sanitization Algorithms for K-Safety

Chakaravarthy et al. [44] present several sanitization algorithms to achieve K-safety on a given document D.

16.2.4.1 Levelwise Algorithm

A set of terms T_i is K-safe only if all its subsets are K-safe. The *Levelwise* algorithm [44] exploits this Apriori-like property to enumerate the maximal K-safe subsets of the given document, and find the maximum cardinality K-safe subset. The algorithm proceeds in a level-wise manner starting with safe subsets of cardinality $r = 1$. In each iteration, the algorithm generates the candidate subsets of cardinality $r + 1$ based on the K-safe subsets of cardinality r generated by the previous iteration. A subset of cardinality $r+1$ is a candidate only if all it subsets of cardinality r are K-safe. The algorithm terminates when none of the subsets considered are K-safe, or after $r = |D|$. The idea of the algorithm is very similar to the Apriori algorithm for mining frequent itemsets [18].

This Apriori-like approach computes *all* the maximal K-safe subsets, which is in fact unnecessary. For document sanitization, it is sufficient to find one of the maximal safe subsets. Thus, Chapter 16.2.4.2 presents a more efficient branch and bound strategy, called *Best-First* [44], that systematically prunes many unnecessary choices and converges on an optimal solution quickly.

16.2.4.2 Best-First Algorithm

Consider a document D with n terms $\{t_1, \ldots, t_n\}$. We can build a binary tree of depth n such that each level represents a term and each root-to-leaf represents a subset of D. The Best-First algorithm [44] performs a pruned-search over this binary tree by expanding the most promising branch in each iteration.

For $i \leq j$, we use $D_{[i,j]}$ to denote the substring $t_i t_{i+1} \ldots t_j$. The Best-First algorithm maintains a collection $\mathcal{C}$ of K-safe subsets of the prefixes of D, where each element in $\mathcal{C}$ is a pair $\langle s, r \rangle$ such that $s \subseteq D_{[1,r]}$ and $r \leq n$. A K-safe set $T \subseteq D$ *extends* (s, r) if $T \cap D_{[1,r]} = s$. For each pair $\langle s, r \rangle$, the algorithm keeps track of the upperbound value $UB(\langle s, r \rangle)$ on the largest K-safe subset extending $\langle s, r \rangle$. The Best-First iteratively extend the maximum cardinality $\mathcal{C}$ by choosing terms with the maximum $UB(\langle s, r \rangle)$.

16.2.4.3 Greedy Algorithm

Chakaravarthy et al. [44] also suggest a greedy algorithm, called *Fast-BTop*, to accommodate the requirement of sanitizing a large document. The heuristic aims to ensure that only a minimum number of terms are removed from the document, but may occasionally remove a larger number of terms. The general idea is to iteratively delete terms from the document until it is K-safe. In each iteration, the algorithm selects a term for deletion by estimating the amount of progress made with respect to the K-safety goal. Refer to [44] for different heuristic functions.

16.3   Health Information DE-identification (HIDE)

Gardner and Xiong [97] introduce a prototype system, called *Health Information DE-identification (HIDE)*, for removing the personal identifying information from healthcare-related text documents. We first discuss their employed privacy models, followed by the framework of HIDE.

16.3.1   De-Identification Models

According to the Health Insurance Portability and Accountability Act (HIPAA) in the United States, identifiable information refers to data explicitly linked to a particular individual and the data that enables individual identification. These notions correspond to the notion of explicit identifiers, such as names and SSN, and the notion of quasi-identifiers, such as age, gender, and postal code. The framework of HIDE [97] considers three types of de-identification models:

- *Full de-identification.* According to HIPAA, information is considered *fully de-identified* if all the explicit (direct) identifiers and quasi-(indirect-) identifiers have been removed. Enforcing full de-identification often renders the data useless for most data mining tasks.

- *Partial de-identification.* According to HIPAA, information is considered partially de-identified if all the explicit (direct) identifiers have been removed. This model yields better data utility in the resulting anonymized data.

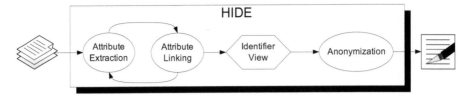

FIGURE 16.1: Health Information DE-identification (HIDE)

- *Statistical de-identification.* This type of de-identification model guarantees the probability of identifying an individual from the released information to be under certain probability while also aiming at preserving as much information as possible for some data mining tasks.

16.3.2 The HIDE Framework

Figure 16.1 shows an overview of the HIDE framework in three phases: attribute extraction, attribute linking, and anonymization.

Phase 1: Attribute extraction. Use a statistical learning approach for extracting and sensitive information from the text documents. To facilitate the overall attribute extraction process, HIDE uses an iterative process for classifying and retagging which allows the construction of a large training data set. Specifically, this attribute extraction process consists of four steps:

- User tags the identifying information and sensitive attributes for building the training data set.
- Extract features from text documents for the classifier.
- Classify terms extracted from the text documents into multiple classes. Different types of identifiers and sensitive attributes could be classified into different classes.
- Feed the classified data back to the tagging step for retagging and corrections.

Phase 2: Attribute linking. Link the extracted identifying and sensitive information to an individual. This step is challenging for text documents because, in most cases, there does not exist a unique identifier that can link all the relevant information to an individual. To improve the accuracy of linking relevant information to an individual, HIDE employs an iterative two-step solution involving attribute linking and attribute extraction. The extraction component (Phase 1) extracts relevant attributes from the text and links or adds them to the existing or new entities in the database. The linking component (Phase 2) links and merges the records based on the extracted attributes using existing record linkage techniques [107].

Phase 3 Anonymization. After the first two phases, HIDE has transformed the unstructured textual data into a structured *identifier view*, which facilitates the application of privacy models for relational data, such as k-anonymity [201, 217] and ℓ-diversity, in this final phase. Refer to Chapter 2 for details of different privacy models. Finally, the information in text documents is sanitized according to the anonymized identifier view.

16.4   Summary

Text sanitization is a challenging problem due to its unstructural nature. In this chapter, we have studied two major categories of text sanitization methods.

The first model assumes that the information in text documents is associated with some entities in a structural or semi-structural database. The goal is to sanitize some terms in the documents so that the adversary can no longer accurately associate the documents to any entities in the associated database.

The second model does not associate with a database, and depends on some information extraction methods to retrieve entities from the text documents, and sanitize them accordingly. The second category has a more general application because it does not assume the presence of an associated database, but the sanitization reliability relies on the quality of the information extraction tools. In contrast, the sanitization reliability is more reliable in the first model because the privacy guarantee can be measured based on number of associated entities in a well-structured database.

There are several other sanitization methods illustrated on real-life medical text documents. Kokkinakis and Thurin [141] implement a system for automatically anonymizing hospital discharge letters by identifying and deliberately removing all phrases from clinical text that satisfy some pre-defined types of sensitive entities. The identification phase is achieved by collaborating with an underlying generic Named Entity Recognition (NER) system. Saygin et al. [205] describe implicit and explicit privacy threats in text document repositories.

Chapter 17

Other Privacy-Preserving Techniques and Future Trends

17.1 Interactive Query Model

Closely related, but orthogonal to PPDP, is the extensive literature on inference control in multilevel secure databases [87, 125]. Attribute linkages are identified and eliminated either at the database design phase [104, 115, 116], by modifying the schemes and meta-data, or during the interactive query time [59, 223], by restricting and modifying queries. These techniques, which focus on query database answering, are not readily applicable to PPDP, where the data holder may not have sophisticated database management knowledge, or does not want to provide an interface for database query. A data holder, such as a hospital, has no intention to be a database server. Answering database queries is not part of its normal business. Therefore, query answering is quite different from the PPDP scenarios studied in this book. Here, we briefly discuss the interactive query model.

In the interactive query model, the user can submit a sequence of queries based on previously received query results. Although this query model could improve the satisfaction of the data recipients' information needs [77], the dynamic nature of queries makes the returned results even more vulnerable to attacks, as illustrated in the following example. Refer to [32, 33, 76, 62] for more privacy-preserving techniques on the interactive query model.

Example 17.1

Suppose that an examination center allows a data miner to access its database, Table 17.1, for research purposes. The attribute *Score* is sensitive. An adversary wants to identify the *Score* of a target victim, Bob, who is a student from the computer science department at Illinois. The adversary can first submit the query

$Q1$: COUNT ($University = Illinois$) AND ($Department = CS$)

Since the count is 1, the adversary can determine Bob's *Score* = 96 by the following query

$Q2$: AVERAGE *Score* WHERE ($University = Illinois$) AND ($Department = CS$).

Table 17.1:   Interactive query model: original examination data

ID	University	Department	Score
1	Concordia	CS	92
2	Simon Fraser	EE	91
3	Concordia	CS	97
4	Illinois	CS	96

Table 17.2:   Interactive query model: after adding one new record

ID	University	Department	Score
1	Concordia	CS	92
2	Simon Fraser	EE	91
3	Concordia	CS	97
4	Illinois	CS	96
5	Illinois	CS	99

Suppose that the data holder has inserted a new record as shown in Table 17.2. Now, the adversary tries to identify another victim by re-submitting query $Q1$. Since the answer is 2, the adversary knows another student from the computer science department of Illinois took this exam and can then submit query

$Q3$: SUM *Score* WHERE (*University* = *Illinois*) AND (*Department* = *CS*)

Benefiting from this update, the adversary can learn the *Score* of the new record by calculating $Q3 - Q2 = 99$. □

Query auditing has a long history in statistical disclosure control. It can be broadly divided into two categories: *online auditing* and *offline auditing*.

Online Auditing: The objective of online query auditing is to detect and deny queries that violate privacy requirements. Miklau and Suciu [169] measure information disclosure of a view set V, with respect to a secret view S. S is secure if publishing V does not alter the probability of inferring the answer to S. Deutsch and Papakonstantinou [60] study whether a new view disclosed more information than the existing views with respect to a secret view. To put the data publishing scenario considered in this book into their terms, superficially the anonymous release can be considered as the "view" and the underlying data can be considered as the "secret query." However, the two problems have two major differences: First, the anonymous release is obtained by anonymization operations, not by conjunctive queries as in [60, 169]. Second, the publishing scenarios employ anonymity as the privacy measure, whereas [169] and [60] adopt the *perfect secrecy* for the security measure. The released data satisfies perfect secrecy if the probability that the adversary finds the original data after observing the anonymous data is the same as the probability or difficulty of getting the original data before observing the anonymous data.

Kenthapadi et al. [137] propose another privacy model called *stimulatable auditing* for an interactive query model. If the adversary has access to all previous query results, the method denies the new query if it leaks any information beyond what the adversary has already known. Although this "detect and deny" approach is practical, Kenthapadi et al. [137] point out that the denials themselves may implicitly disclose sensitive information, making the privacy protection problem even more complicated. This motivates the offline query auditing.

Offline Auditing: In offline query auditing [82], the data recipients submit their queries and receive their results. The auditor checks if a privacy requirement has been violated *after* the queries have been executed. The data recipients have no access to the audit results and, therefore, the audit results do not trigger extra privacy threats as in the online mode. The objective of offline query audition is to check for compliance of privacy requirement, not to prevent the adversaries from accessing the sensitive information.

17.2 Privacy Threats Caused by Data Mining Results

The release of data mining results or patterns could pose privacy threats. There are two broad research directions in this family.

The first direction is to anonymize the data so that sensitive data mining patterns cannot be generated. Aggarwal et al. [7] point out that simply suppressing the sensitive values chosen by individual record owners is insufficient because an adversary can use association rules learnt from the data to estimate the suppressed values. They proposed a heuristic algorithm to suppress a minimal set of values to combat such attacks. Vassilios et al. [233] propose algorithms for hiding sensitive association rules in a transaction database. The general idea is to hide one rule at a time by either decreasing its support or its confidence, achieved by removing items from transactions. Rules satisfying a specified minimum support and minimum confidence are removed. However, in the notion of anonymity, a rule applying to a small group of individuals (i.e., low support) presents a more serious threat because record owners from a small group are more identifiable.

The second direction is to directly anonymize the data mining patterns. Atzori et al. [22] propose the insightful suggestion that if the goal is to release data mining results, such as frequent patterns, then it is sufficient to anonymize the patterns rather than the data. Their study suggested that anonymizing the patterns yields much better information utility than performing data mining on anonymous data. This opens up a new research direction for privacy-preserving patterns publishing. Kantarcioglu et al. [135]

Table 17.3:   3-anonymous patient data

Job	Sex	Age	Disease
Professional	Male	[35-40)	Hepatitis
Professional	Male	[35-40)	Hepatitis
Professional	Male	[35-40)	HIV
Artist	Female	[30-35)	Flu
Artist	Female	[30-35)	HIV
Artist	Female	[30-35)	HIV
Artist	Female	[30-35)	HIV

define an evaluation method to measure the loss of privacy due to releasing data mining results.

The *classifier attack* is a variant type of attribute linkage attack. Suppose a data miner has released a classifier, not the data, that models a sensitive attribute. An adversary can make use of the classifier to infer sensitive values of individuals. This scenario presents a dilemma between privacy protection and data mining because the target attribute to be modeled is also the sensitive attribute to be protected. A naive solution is to suppress sensitive classification rules, but it may defeat the data mining goal. Another possible solution is to build a classifier from the anonymous data that has bounded confidence or breach probability on some selected sensitive values. Alternatively, record owners may specify some guarding nodes on their own records, as discussed in Chapter 2.2.

Example 17.2
A data recipient has built a classifier on the target attribute *Disease* from Table 17.3, and then released two classification rules:

$$\langle Professional, Male, [35\text{-}40) \rangle \rightarrow Hepatitis$$
$$\langle Artist, Female, [30\text{-}35) \rangle \rightarrow HIV$$

The adversary can use these rules to infer that *Emily*, who is a female artist at age 30, has *HIV*. Even though the data recipient has not released any data, the adversary can confidently make such inference if the adversary knows the *qid* of *Emily* who comes from the same population where the classifier was built from. Even though the inference may not be correct, the adversary can make decision based on such inference.   □

17.3   Privacy-Preserving Distributed Data Mining

Privacy-preserving distributed data mining (PPDDM) is a cousin research topic of privacy-preserving data publishing (PPDP). PPDDM assumes a scenario that multiple data holders want to collaboratively perform data mining on the union of their data without revealing their sensitive information. PPDDM usually employs cryptographic solutions. Although the ultimate goal of both PPDDM and PPDP is to perform data mining, they have very different assumptions on data ownerships, attack models, privacy models, and solutions, so PPDDM is out of the scope of this book. We refer readers interested in PPDDM to these works [50, 132, 187, 227, 248].

17.4   Future Directions

Information sharing has become part of the routine activities of many individuals, companies, organizations, and government agencies. Privacy-preserving data publishing is a promising approach to information sharing, while preserving individual privacy and protecting sensitive information. In this book, we reviewed the recent developments in the field. The general objective is to transform the original data into some anonymous form to prevent inferring its record owners' sensitive information. We presented our views on the difference between privacy-preserving data publishing and privacy-preserving data mining, and a list of desirable properties of a privacy-preserving data publishing method. We reviewed and compared existing methods in terms of privacy models, anonymization operations, information metrics, and anonymization algorithms. Most of these approaches assumed a single release from a single publisher, and thus only protected the data up to the first release or the first recipient. We also reviewed several works on more challenging publishing scenarios, including multiple release publishing, sequential release publishing, continuous data publishing, and collaborative data publishing.

Privacy protection is a complex social issue, which involves policy making, technology, psychology, and politics. Privacy protection research in computer science can provide only technical solutions to the problem. Successful application of privacy-preserving technology will rely on the cooperation of policy makers in governments and decision makers in companies and organizations. Unfortunately, while the deployment of privacy-threatening technology, such as RFID and social networks, grows quickly, the implementation of privacy-preserving technology in real-life applications is *very limited*. As the gap becomes larger, we foresee that the number of incidents and the scope of privacy breach will increase in the near future. Below, we identify a few potential research directions in privacy preservation, together with some desirable properties that could facilitate the general public, decision makers, and systems engineers to adopt privacy-preserving technology.

- *Privacy-preserving tools for individuals.* Most previous privacy-preserving techniques were proposed for data holders, but individual record owners should also have the rights and responsibilities to protect their own private information. There is an urgent need for personalized privacy-preserving tools, such as privacy-preserving web browser and minimal information disclosure protocol for e-commerce activities. It is important that the privacy-preserving notions and tools developed are intuitive for novice users. Xiao and Tao's work [250] on "Personalized Privacy Preservation" provides a good start, but little work has been conducted on this direction.

- *Privacy protection in emerging technologies.* Emerging technologies, like location-based services [23, 114, 265], RFID [240], bioinformatics, and mashup web applications, enhance our quality of life. These new technologies allow corporations and individuals to have access to previously unavailable information and knowledge; however, they also bring up many new privacy issues. Nowadays, once a new technology has been adopted by a small community, it can become very popular in a short period of time. A typical example is the social network application Facebook. Since its deployment in 2004, it has acquired 70 million active users. Due to the massive number of users, the harm could be extensive if the new technology is misused. One research direction is to customize existing privacy-preserving models for emerging technologies.

- *Incorporating privacy protection in engineering process.* The issue of privacy protection is often considered after the deployment of a new technology. Typical examples are the deployments of mobile devices with location-based services [1, 23, 114, 265], sensor networks, and social networks. Preferably, the privacy issue should be considered as a primary requirement in the engineering process of developing new technology. This involves formal specification of privacy requirements and formal verification tools to prove the correctness of a privacy-preserving system.

Finally, we emphasize that privacy-preserving technology solves only one side of the problem. It is equally important to identify and overcome the non-technical difficulties faced by decision makers when they deploy a privacy-preserving technology. Their typical concerns include the degradation of data/service quality, loss of valuable information, increased costs, and increased complexity. We believe that cross-disciplinary research is the key to remove these obstacles, and urge computer scientists in the privacy protection field to conduct cross-disciplinary research with social scientists in sociology, psychology, and public policy studies. Having a better understanding of the privacy problem from different perspectives can help realize successful applications of privacy-preserving technology.

References

[1] O. Abul, F. Bonchi, and M. Nanni. Never walk alone: Uncertainty for anonymity in moving objects databases. In *Proc. of the 24th IEEE International Conference on Data Engineering (ICDE)*, pages 376–385, April 2008.

[2] D. Achlioptas. Database-friendly random projections. In *Proc. of the 20th ACM Symposium on Principles of Database Systems (PODS)*, pages 274–281, May 2001.

[3] N. R. Adam and J. C. Wortman. Security control methods for statistical databases. *ACM Computer Surveys*, 21(4):515–556, December 1989.

[4] E. Adar. User 4xxxxx9: Anonymizing query logs. In *Proc. of the 16th International Conference on World Wide Web (WWW)*, 2007.

[5] E. Adar, D. S. Weld, B. N. Bershad, and S. D. Gribble. Why we search: Visualizing and predicting user behavior. In *Proc. of the 16th International Conference on World Wide Web (WWW)*, pages 161–170, 2007.

[6] C. C. Aggarwal. On *k*-anonymity and the curse of dimensionality. In *Proc. of the 31st Very Large Data Bases (VLDB)*, pages 901–909, Trondheim, Norway, 2005.

[7] C. C. Aggarwal, J. Pei, and B. Zhang. On privacy preservation against adversarial data mining. In *Proc. of the 12th ACM International Conference on Knowledge Discovery and Data Mining (SIGKDD)*, Philadelphia, PA, August 2006.

[8] C. C. Aggarwal and P. S. Yu. A condensation approach to privacy preserving data mining. In *Proc. of the International Conference on Extending Database Technology (EDBT)*, pages 183–199, 2004.

[9] C. C. Aggarwal and P. S. Yu. A framework for condensation-based anonymization of string data. *Data Mining and Knowledge Discovery (DMKD)*, 13(3):251–275, February 2008.

[10] C. C. Aggarwal and P. S. Yu. On static and dynamic methods for condensation-based privacy-preserving data mining. *ACM Transactions on Database Systems (TODS)*, 33(1), March 2008.

[11] C. C. Aggarwal and P. S. Yu. *Privacy-Preserving Data Mining: Models and Algorithms*. Springer, March 2008.

[12] G. Aggarwal, T. Feder, K. Kenthapadi, R. Motwani, R. Panigrahy, D. Thomas, and A. Zhu. Anonymizing tables. In *Proc. of the 10th International Conference on Database Theory (ICDT)*, pages 246–258, Edinburgh, UK, January 2005.

[13] G. Aggarwal, T. Feder, K. Kenthapadi, R. Motwani, R. Panigrahy, D. Thomas, and A. Zhu. Achieving anonymity via clustering. In *Proc. of the 25th ACM SIGMOD-SIGACT-SIGART Symposium on Principles of Database Systems (PODS)*, Chicago, IL, June 2006.

[14] G. Aggarwal, N. Mishra, and B. Pinkas. Secure computation of the kth-ranked element. In *Proc. of the Eurocyrpt*, 2004.

[15] E. Agichtein, L. Gravano, J. Pavel, V. Sokolova, and A. Voskoboynik. Snowball: A prototype system for extracting relations from large text collections. *ACM SIGMOD Record*, 30(2):612, 2001.

[16] D. Agrawal and C. C. Aggarwal. On the design and quantification of privacy preserving data mining algorithms. In *Proc. of the 20th ACM Symposium on Principles of Satabase Systems (PODS)*, pages 247–255, Santa Barbara, CA, May 2001.

[17] R. Agrawal, A. Evfimievski, and R. Srikant. Information sharing across private databases. In *Proc. of ACM International Conference on Management of Data (SIGMOD)*, San Diego, CA, 2003.

[18] R. Agrawal, T. Imielinski, and A. N. Swami. Mining association rules between sets of items in large databases. In *Proc. of ACM International Conference on Management of Data (SIGMOD)*, 1993.

[19] R. Agrawal and R. Srikant. Privacy preserving data mining. In *Proc. of ACM International Conference on Management of Data (SIGMOD)*, pages 439–450, Dallas, Texas, May 2000.

[20] R. Agrawal, R. Srikant, and D. Thomas. Privacy preserving olap. In *Proc. of ACM International Conference on Management of Data (SIGMOD)*, pages 251–262, 2005.

[21] S. Agrawal and J. R. Haritsa. A framework for high-accuracy privacy-preserving mining. In *Proc. of the 21st IEEE International Conference on Data Engineering (ICDE)*, pages 193–204, Tokyo, Japan, April 2005.

[22] M. Atzori, F. Bonchi, F. Giannotti, and D. Pedreschi. Anonymity preserving pattern discovery. *International Journal on Very Large Data Bases (VLDBJ)*, 17(4):703–727, July 2008.

[23] M. Atzori, F. Bonchi, F. Giannotti, D. Pedreschi, and O. Abul. Privacy-aware knowledge discovery from location data. In *Proc. of the International Workshop on Privacy-Aware Location-based Mobile Services (PALMS)*, pages 283–287, May 2007.

[24] R. Axelrod. *The Evolution of Cooperation*. Basic Books, New York, 1984.

[25] L. Backstrom, C. Dwork, and J. Kleinberg. Wherefore art thou r3579x? Anonymized social networks, hidden patterns and structural steganography. In *Proc. of the International World Wide Web Conference (WWW)*, Banff, Alberta, May 2007.

[26] B. Barak, K. Chaudhuri, C. Dwork, S. Kale, F. McSherry, and K. Talwar. Privacy, accuracy, and consistency too: A holistic solution to contingency table release. In *Proc. of the 26th ACM Symposium on Principles of Database Systems (PODS)*, pages 273–282, Beijing, China, June 2007.

[27] M. Barbaro and T. Zeller. A face is exposed for aol searcher no. 4417749. *New York Times*, August 9, 2006.

[28] M. Barbaro, T. Zeller, and S. Hansell. A face is exposed for aol searcher no. 4417749. *New York Times*, August 2006.

[29] R. J. Bayardo and R. Agrawal. Data privacy through optimal k-anonymization. In *Proc. of the 21st IEEE International Conference on Data Engineering (ICDE)*, pages 217–228, Tokyo, Japan, 2005.

[30] Z. Berenyi and H. Charaf. Retrieving frequent walks from tracking data in RFID-equipped warehouses. In *Proc. of Conference on Human System Interactions*, pages 663–667, May 2008.

[31] A. R. Beresford and F. Stajano. Location privacy in pervasive computing. *IEEE Pervasive Computing*, 1:46–55, 2003.

[32] A. Blum, C. Dwork, F. McSherry, and K. Nissim. Practical privacy: The sulq framework. In *Proc. of the 24th ACM Symposium on Principles of Database Systems (PODS)*, pages 128–138, Baltimore, MD, June 2005.

[33] A. Blum, K. Ligett, and A. Roth. A learning theory approach to non-interactive database privacy. In *Proc. of the 40th annual ACM Symposium on Theory of Computing (STOC)*, pages 609–618, Victoria, Canada, 2008.

[34] B. Bollobas. *Random Graphs*. Cambridge, 2001.

[35] F. Bonchi, F. Giannotti, and D. Pedreschi. Blocking anonymity threats raised by frequent itemset mining. In *Proc. of the 5th IEEE International Conference on Data Mining (ICDM)*, 2005.

[36] R. Brand. Microdata protection through noise addition. In *Inference Control in Statistical Databases, From Theory to Practice*, pages 97–116, London, UK, 2002.

[37] S. Brin, R. Motwani, and C. Silverstein. Beyond market basket: Generalizing association rules to correlations. In *Proc. of ACM International Conference on Management of Data (SIGMOD)*, 1997.

[38] Y. Bu, A. W. C. Fu, R. C. W. Wong, L. Chen, and J. Li. Privacy preserving serial data publishing by role composition. *Proc. of the VLDB Endowment*, 1(1):845–856, August 2008.

[39] D. Burdick, M. Calimlim, J. Flannick, J. Gehrke, and T. Yiu. MAFIA: A maximal frequent itemset algorithm. *IEEE Transactions on Knowledge and Data Engineering (TKDE)*, 17(11):1490–1504, 2005.

[40] L. Burnett, K. Barlow-Stewart, A. Pros, and H. Aizenberg. The gene trustee: A universal identification system that ensures privacy and confidentiality for human genetic databases. *Journal of Law and Medicine*, 10:506–513, 2003.

[41] Business for Social Responsibility. BSR Report on Privacy, 1999. http://www.bsr.org/.

[42] J.-W. Byun, Y. Sohn, E. Bertino, and N. Li. Secure anonymization for incremental datasets. In *Proc. of the VLDB Workshop on Secure Data Management (SDM)*, 2006.

[43] D. M. Carlisle, M. L. Rodrian, and C. L. Diamond. California inpatient data reporting manual, medical information reporting for california, 5th edition. Technical report, Office of Statewide Health Planning and Development, July 2007.

[44] V. T. Chakaravarthy, H. Gupta, P. Roy, and M. Mohania. Efficient techniques for documents sanitization. In *Proc. of the ACM 17th Conference on Information and Knowledge Management (CIKM)*, 2008.

[45] D. Chaum. Untraceable electronic mail, return addresses, and digital pseudonyms. *Communications of the ACM*, 24(2):84–88, 1981.

[46] S. Chawla, C. Dwork, F. McSherry, A. Smith, and H. Wee. Toward privacy in public databases. In *Proc. of Theory of Cryptography Conference (TCC)*, pages 363–385, Cambridge, MA, February 2005.

[47] S. Chawla, C. Dwork, F. McSherry, and K. Talwar. On privacy-preserving histograms. In *Proc. of Uncertainty in Artificial Intelligence (UAI)*, Edinburgh, Scotland, July 2005.

[48] B.-C. Chen, R. Ramakrishnan, and K. LeFevre. Privacy skyline: Privacy with multidimensional adversarial knowledge. In *Proc. of the 33rd International Conference on Very Large Databases (VLDB)*, 2007.

[49] C. Clifton. Using sample size to limit exposure to data mining. *Journal of Computer Security*, 8(4):281–307, 2000.

[50] C. Clifton, M. Kantarcioglu, J. Vaidya, X. Lin, and M. Y. Zhu. Tools for privacy preserving distributed data mining. *ACM SIGKDD Explorations Newsletter*, 4(2):28–34, December 2002.

[51] Confidentiality and Data Access Committee. Report on statistical disclosure limitation methodology. Technical Report 22, Office of Management and Budget, December 2005.

[52] L. H. Cox. Suppression methodology and statistical disclosure control. *Journal of the American Statistical Association*, 75(370):377–385, June 1980.

[53] H. Cui, J. Wen, J. Nie, and W. Ma. Probabilistic query expansion using query logs. In *Proc. of the 11th International Conference on World Wide Web (WWW)*, 2002.

[54] E. Cuthill and J. McKee. Reducing the bandwidth of sparse symmetric matrices. In *4th National ACM Conference*, 1969.

[55] T. Dalenius. Towards a methodology for statistical disclosure control. *Statistik Tidskrift*, 15:429–444, 1977.

[56] T. Dalenius. Finding a needle in a haystack - or identifying anonymous census record. *Journal of Official Statistics*, 2(3):329–336, 1986.

[57] R. N. Dave and R. Krishnapuram. Robust clustering methods: A unified view. *IEEE Transactions on Fuzzy Systems*, 5(2):270–293, May 1997.

[58] U. Dayal and H. Y. Hwang. View definition and generalization for database integration in a multidatabase system. *IEEE Transactions on Software Engineering (TSE)*, 10(6):628–645, 1984.

[59] D. E. Denning. Commutative filters for reducing inference threats in multilevel database systems. In *Proc. of the IEEE Symposium on Security and Privacy (S&P)*, Oakland, CA, April 1985.

[60] A. Deutsch and Y. Papakonstantinou. Privacy in database publishing. In *Proc. of the 10th International Conference on Database Theory (ICDT)*, pages 230–245, Edinburgh, UK, January 2005.

[61] C. Diaz, S. Seys, J. Claessens, and B. Preneel. Towards measuring anonymity. In *Proc. of the 2nd Internationl Workshop on Privacy Enchancing Technologies (PET)*, pages 54–68, San Francisco, CA, April 2002.

[62] I. Dinur and K. Nissim. Revealing information while preserving privacy. In *Proc. of the 22nd ACM Symposium on Principles of Database Systems (PODS)*, pages 202–210, San Diego, June 2003.

[63] J. Domingo-Ferrer. *Confidentiality, Disclosure and Data Access: Theory and Practical Applications for Statistical Agencies*, chapter Disclosure

Control Methods and Information Loss for Microdata, pages 91–110. 2001.

[64] J. Domingo-Ferrer. *Privacy-Preserving Data Mining: Models and Algorithms*, chapter A Survey of Inference Control Methods for Privacy-Preserving Data Mining, pages 53–80. Springer, 2008.

[65] J. Domingo-Ferrer and V. Torra. *Theory and Practical Applications for Statistical Agencies*, chapter A Quantitative Comparison of Disclosure Control Methods for Microdata, Confidentiality, Disclosure and Data Access, pages 113–134. North-Holland, Amsterdam, 2002.

[66] J. Domingo-Ferrer and V. Torra. A critique of k-anonymity and some of its enhancements. In *Proc. of the 3rd International Conference on Availability, Reliability and Security (ARES)*, pages 990–993, 2008.

[67] G Dong and J. Li. Efficient mining of emerging patterns: discovering trends and differences. In *Proc. of 5th ACM International Conference on Knowledge Discovery and Data Mining (SIGKDD)*, 1999.

[68] Z. Dou, R. Song, and J. Wen A large-scale evaluation and analysis of personalized search strategies. In *Proc. of the 16th International Conference on World Wide Web (WWW)*, 2007.

[69] W. Du, Y. S. Han, and S. Chen. Privacy-preserving multivariate statistical analysis: Linear regression and classification. In *Proc. of the SIAM International Conference on Data Mining (SDM)*, Florida, 2004.

[70] W. Du, Z. Teng, and Z. Zhu. Privacy-MaxEnt: Integrating background knowledge in privacy quantification. In *Proc. of the 34th ACM International Conference on Management of Data (SIGMOD)*, 2008.

[71] W. Du and Z. Zhan. Building decision tree classifier on private data. In *Workshop on Privacy, Security, and Data Mining at the 2002 IEEE International Conference on Data Mining*, Maebashi City, Japan, December 2002.

[72] W. Du and Z. Zhan. Using randomized response techniques for privacy preserving data mining. In *Proc. of the 9the ACM International Conference on Knowledge Discovery and Data Mining (SIGKDD)*, pages 505–510, 2003.

[73] G. Duncan and S. Fienberg. Obtaining information while preserving privacy: A Markov perturbation method for tabular data. In *Statistical Data Protection*, pages 351–362, 1998.

[74] C. Dwork. Differential privacy. In *Proc. of the 33rd International Colloquium on Automata, Languages and Programming (ICALP)*, pages 1–12, Venice, Italy, July 2006.

[75] C. Dwork. Ask a better question, get a better answer: A new approach to private data analysis. In *Proc. of the Interntaional Conference on Database Theory (ICDT)*, pages 18–27, Barcelona, Spain, January 2007.

[76] C. Dwork. Differential privacy: A survey of results. In *Proc. of the 5th International Conference on Theory and Applications of Models of Computation (TAMC)*, pages 1–19, Xian, China, April 2008.

[77] C. Dwork, F. McSherry, K. Nissim, and A. Smith. Calibrating noise to sensitivity in private data analysis. In *Proc. of the 3rd Theory of Cryptography Conference (TCC)*, pages 265–284, New York, March 2006.

[78] C. Dwork and K. Nissim. Privacy-preserving data mining on vertically partitioned databases. In *Proceedings of the 24th International Cryptology Conference (CRYPTO)*, pages 528–544, Santa Barbara, August 2004.

[79] K. E. Emam. Data anonymization practices in clinical research: A descriptive study. Technical report, Access to Information and Privacy Division of Health Canada, May 2006.

[80] P. Erdos and T. Gallai. Graphs with prescribed degrees of vertices. *Mat. Lapok*, 1960.

[81] A. Evfimievski. Randomization in privacy-preserving data mining. *ACM SIGKDD Explorations Newsletter*, 4(2):43–48, December 2002.

[82] A. Evfimievski, R. Fagin, and D. P. Woodruff. Epistemic privacy. In *Proc. of the 27th ACM Symposium on Principles of Database Systems (PODS)*, pages 171–180, Vancouver, Canada, 2008.

[83] A. Evfimievski, J. Gehrke, and R. Srikant. Limiting privacy breaches in privacy preserving data mining. In *Proc. of the 22nd ACM SIGMOD-SIGACT-SIGART Symposium on Principles of Database Systems (PODS)*, pages 211–222, 2002.

[84] A. Evfimievski, R. Srikant, R. Agrawal, and J. Gehrke. Privacy preserving mining of association rules. In *Proc. of 8th ACM International Conference on Knowledge Discovery and Data Mining (SIGKDD)*, pages 217–228, Edmonton, AB, Canada, July 2002.

[85] R. Fagin, Amnon Lotem, and Moni Naor. Optimal aggregation algorithms for middleware. In *Proc. of the 20th ACM Symposium on Principles of Database Systems (PODS)*, pages 102–113, Santa Barbara, CA, 2001.

[86] M. Faloutsos, P. Faloutsos, and C. Faloutsos. On power-law relationships of the internet topology. In *Proc. of the Conference on Applications, Technologies, Architectures, and Protocols for Computer Communication (SIGCOMM)*, pages 251–262, 1999.

[87] C. Farkas and S. Jajodia. The inference problem: A survey. *ACM SIGKDD Explorations Newsletter*, 4(2):6–11, 2003.

[88] T. Fawcett and F. Provost. Activity monitoring: Noticing interesting changes in behavior. In *Proc. of the 5th ACM International Conference on Knowledge Discovery and Data Mining (SIGKDD)*, pages 53–62, San Diego, CA, 1999.

[89] A. W. C. Fu, R. C. W. Wong, and K. Wang. Privacy-preserving frequent pattern mining across private databases. In *Proc. of the 5th IEEE International Conference on Data Mining (ICDM)*, pages 613–616, Houston, TX, November 2005.

[90] W. A. Fuller. Masking procedures for microdata disclosure limitation. *Official Statistics*, 9(2):383–406, 1993.

[91] B. C. M. Fung, M. Cao, B. C. Desai, and H. Xu. Privacy protection for RFID data. In *Proc. of the 24th ACM SIGAPP Symposium on Applied Computing (SAC)*, pages 1528–1535, Honolulu, HI, March 2009.

[92] B. C. M. Fung, K. Wang, R. Chen, and P. S. Yu. Privacy-preserving data publishing: A survey on recent developments. *ACM Computing Surveys*, 42(4), December 2010.

[93] B. C. M. Fung, K. Wang, A. W. C. Fu, and J. Pei. Anonymity for continuous data publishing. In *Proc. of the 11th International Conference on Extending Database Technology (EDBT)*, pages 264–275, Nantes, France, March 2008.

[94] B. C. M. Fung, K. Wang, L. Wang, and P. C. K. Hung. Privacy-preserving data publishing for cluster analysis. *Data & Knowledge Engineering (DKE)*, 68(6):552–575, June 2009.

[95] B. C. M. Fung, K. Wang, and P. S. Yu. Top-down specialization for information and privacy preservation. In *Proc. of the 21st IEEE International Conference on Data Engineering (ICDE)*, pages 205–216, Tokyo, Japan, April 2005.

[96] B. C. M. Fung, Ke Wang, and P. S. Yu. Anonymizing classification data for privacy preservation. *IEEE Transactions on Knowledge and Data Engineering (TKDE)*, 19(5):711–725, May 2007.

[97] J. Gardner and L. Xiong. An integrated framework for de-identifying heterogeneous data. *Data and Knowledge Engineering (DKE)*, 68(12):1441–1451, December 2009.

[98] B. Gedik and L. Liu. Protecting location privacy with personalized k-anonymity: Architecture and algorithms. *IEEE Transactions on Mobile Computing (TMC)*, 7(1):1–18, January 2008.

[99] J. Gehrke. Models and methods for privacy-preserving data publishing and analysis. In *Tutorial at the 12th ACM International Conference on Knowledge Discovery and Data Mining (SIGKDD)*, Philadelphia, PA, August 2006.

[100] L. Getor and C. P. Diehl. Link mining: A survey. *ACM SIGKDD Explorations Newsletter*, 7(2):3–12, 2005.

[101] G. Ghinita, Y. Tao, and P. Kalnis. On the anonymization of sparse high-dimensional data. In *Proc. of the 24th IEEE International Conference on Data Engineering (ICDE)*, pages 715–724, April 2008.

[102] F. Giannotti, M. Nanni, D. Pedreschi, and F. Pinelli. Trajectory pattern mining. In *Proc. of the 13th ACM International Conference on Knowledge Discovery and Data Mining (SIGKDD)*, 2007.

[103] N. Gibbs, W. Poole, and P. Stockmeyer. An algorithm for reducing the bandwidth and profile of a sparse matrix. *SIAM Journal on Numerical Analysis (SINUM)*, 13:236–250, 1976.

[104] J. Goguen and J. Meseguer. Unwinding and inference control. In *Proc. of the IEEE Symposium on Security and Privacy (S&P)*, Oakland, CA, 1984.

[105] H. Gonzalez, J. Han, and X. Li. Mining compressed commodity workflows from massive RFID data sets. In *Proc. of the 16th ACM Conference on Information and Knowledge Management (CIKM)*, 2006.

[106] M. Gruteser and D. Grunwald. Anonymous usage of location-based services through spatial and temporal cloaking. In *Proc. of the 1st International Conference on Mobile Systems, Applications, and Services (MobiSys)*, 2003.

[107] L. Gu, R. Baxter, D. Vickers, and C. Rainsford. Record linkage: Current practice and future directions. Technical report, CSIRO Mathematical and Information Sciences, 2003.

[108] K. Hafner. Researchers yearn to use aol logs, but they hesitate. *New York Times*, 2006.

[109] Jiawei Han and Micheline Kamber. *Data Mining: Concepts and Techniques*. Morgan Kaufmann, 2 edition, November 2005.

[110] M. Hay, G. Miklau, D. Jensen, D. Towsley, and P. Weis. Resisting structural re-identification in anonymized social networks. In *Proc. of the Very Large Data Bases (VLDB)*, Auckland, New Zealand.

[111] M. Hay, G. Miklau, D. Jensen, P. Weis, and S. Srivastava. Anonymizing social networks. Technical report, University of Massachusetts Amherst, 2007.

[112] Y. He and J. Naughton. Anonymization of set valued data via top down, local generalization. In *Proc. of the Very Large Databases (VLDB)*, 2009.

[113] M. Hegland, I. Mcintosh, and B. A. Turlach. A parallel solver for generalized additive models. *Computational Statistics & Data Analysis*, 31(4):377–396, 1999.

[114] U. Hengartner. Hiding location information from location-based services. In *Proc. of the International Workshop on Privacy-Aware Location-based Mobile Services (PALMS)*, pages 268–272, Mannheim, Germany, May 2007.

[115] T. Hinke. Inference aggregation detection in database management systems. In *Proc. of the IEEE Symposium on Security and Privacy (S&P)*, pages 96–107, Oakland, CA, April 1988.

[116] T. Hinke, H. Degulach, and A. Chandrasekhar. A fast algorithm for detecting second paths in database inference analysis. *Journal of Computer Security*, 1995.

[117] R. D. Hof. Mix, match, and mutate. *Business Week*, July 2005.

[118] Z. Huang, W. Du, and B. Chen. Deriving private information from randomized data. In *Proc. of ACM International Conference on Management of Data (SIGMOD)*, pages 37–48, Baltimore, ML, 2005.

[119] Z. Huang and W. Du. OptRR: Optimizing randomized response schemes for privacy-preserving data mining. In *Proc. of the 24th IEEE International Conference on Data Engineering (ICDE)*, pages 705–714, 2008.

[120] A. Hundepool and L. Willenborg. μ- and τ-argus: Software for statistical disclosure control. In *Proc. of the 3rd International Seminar on Statistical Confidentiality*, Bled, 1996.

[121] Ali Inan, Selim V. Kaya, Yucel Saygin, Erkay Savas, Ayca A. Hintoglu, and Albert Levi. Privacy preserving clustering on horizontally partitioned data. *Data & Knowledge Engineering (DKE)*, 63(3):646–666, 2007.

[122] T. Iwuchukwu and J. F. Naughton. K-anonymization as spatial indexing: Toward scalable and incremental anonymization. In *Proc. of the 33rd International Conference on Very Large Data Bases (VLDB)*, 2007.

[123] V. S. Iyengar. Transforming data to satisfy privacy constraints. In *Proc. of the 8th ACM International Conference on Knowledge Discovery and Data Mining (SIGKDD)*, pages 279–288, Edmonton, AB, Canada, July 2002.

[124] A. Jain, E. Y. Chang, and Y.-F. Wang. Adaptive stream resource management using Kalman filters. In *Proc. of 2004 ACM International Conference on Management of Data (SIGMOD)*, pages 11–22, 2004.

[125] S. Jajodia and C. Meadows. Inference problems in multilevel database management systems. *IEEE Information Security: An Integrated Collection of Essays*, pages 570–584, 1995.

[126] M. Jakobsson, A. Juels, and R. L. Rivest. Making mix nets robust for electronic voting by randomized partial checking. In *Proc. of the 11th USENIX Security Symposium*, pages 339–353, 2002.

[127] W. Jiang and C. Clifton. Privacy-preserving distributed k-anonymity. In *Proc. of the 19th Annual IFIP WG 11.3 Working Conference on Data and Applications Security*, pages 166–177, Storrs, CT, August 2005.

[128] W. Jiang and C. Clifton. A secure distributed framework for achieving k-anonymity. *Very Large Data Bases Journal (VLDBJ)*, 15(4):316–333, November 2006.

[129] R. Jones, R. Kumar, B. Pang, and A. Tomkins. I know what you did last summer. In *Proc. of the 16th ACM Conference on Information and Knowledge Management (CIKM)*, 2007.

[130] A. Juels. RFID security and privacy: A research survey. 2006.

[131] P. Jurczyk and L. Xiong. Distributed anonymization: Achieving privacy for both data subjects and data providers. In *Proc. of the 23rd Annual IFIP WG 11.3 Working Conference on Data and Applications Security (DBSec)*, 2009.

[132] M. Kantarcioglu. *Privacy-Preserving Data Mining: Models and Algorithms*, chapter A Survey of Privacy-Preserving Methods Across Horizontally Partitioned Data, pages 313–335. Springer, 2008.

[133] M. Kantarcioglu and C. Clifton. Privacy preserving data mining of association rules on horizontally partitioned data. *IEEE Transactions on Knowledge and Data Engineering (TKDE)*, 16(9):1026–1037, 2004.

[134] M. Kantarcioglu and C. Clifton. Privately computing a distributed k-nn classifier. In *Proc. of the 8th European Conference on Principles and Practice of Knowledge Discovery in Databases (PKDD)*, volume LNCS 3202, pages 279–290, Pisa, Italy, September 2004.

[135] M. Kantarcioglu, J. Jin, and C. Clifton. When do data mining results violate privacy? In *Proc. of the 2004 ACM International Conference on Knowledge Discovery and Data Mining (SIGKDD)*, pages 599–604, Seattle, WA, 2004.

[136] H. Kargupta, S. Datta, Q. Wang, and K. Sivakumar. On the privacy preserving properties of random data perturbation techniques. In *Proc.*

of the 3rd IEEE International Conference on Data Mining (ICDM), pages 99–106, Melbourne, FL, 2003.

[137] K. Kenthapadi, Nina Mishra, and Kobbi Nissim. Simulatable auditing. In *Proc. of the 24th ACM Symposium on Principles of Database Systems (PODS)*, pages 118–127, Baltimore, MD, June 2005.

[138] D. Kifer. Attacks on privacy and deFinetti's theorem. In *Proc. of the 35th ACM International Conference on Management of Data (SIGMOD)*, pages 127–138, Providence, RI, 2009.

[139] D. Kifer and J. Gehrke. Injecting utility into anonymized datasets. In *Proc. of ACM International Conference on Management of Data (SIGMOD)*, Chicago, IL, June 2006.

[140] J. Kim and W. Winkler. Masking microdata files. In *Proc. of the ASA Section on Survey Research Methods*, pages 114–119, 1995.

[141] D. Kokkinakis and A. Thurin. Anonymisation of Swedish clinical data. In *Proc. of the 11th Conference on Artificial Intelligence in Medicine (AIME)*, pages 237–241, 2007.

[142] A. Korolova. Releasing search queries and clicks privately. In *Proc. of the 18th International Conference on World Wide Web (WWW)*, 2009.

[143] A. Korolova, R. Motwani, U.N. Shubha, and Y. Xu. Link privacy in social networks. In *Proc. of IEEE 24th International Conference on Data Engineering (ICDE)*, April 2008.

[144] B. Krishnamurthy. Privacy vs. security in the aftermath of the September 11 terrorist attacks, November 2001. http://www.scu.edu/ethics/publications/briefings/privacy.html.

[145] J. B. Kruskal and M. Wish. *Multidimensional Scaling.* Sage Publications, Beverly Hills, CA, USA, 1978.

[146] R. Kumar, J. Novak, B. Pang, and A. Tomkins. On anonymizing query logs via token-based hashing. In *Proc. of the 16th International Conference on World Wide Web (WWW)*, pages 628–638, May 2007.

[147] R. Kumar, K. Punera, and A. Tomkins. Hierarchical topic segmentation of websites. In *Proc. of the 12th ACM International Conference on Knowledge Discovery and Data Mining (SIGKDD)*, pages 257–266, 2006.

[148] K. LeFevre, D. J. DeWitt, and R. Ramakrishnan. Incognito: Efficient full-domain k-anonymity. In *Proc. of ACM International Conference on Management of Data (SIGMOD)*, pages 49–60, Baltimore, ML, 2005.

[149] K. LeFevre, D. J. DeWitt, and R. Ramakrishnan. Mondrian multidimensional k-anonymity. In *Proc. of the 22nd IEEE International Conference on Data Engineering (ICDE)*, Atlanta, GA, 2006.

[150] K. LeFevre, D. J. DeWitt, and R. Ramakrishnan. Workload-aware anonymization. In *Proc. of the 12th ACM International Conference on Knowledge Discovery and Data Mining (SIGKDD)*, Philadelphia, PA, August 2006.

[151] K. LeFevre, D. J. DeWitt, and R. Ramakrishnan. Workload-aware anonymization techniques for large-scale data sets. *ACM Transactions on Database Systems (TODS)*, 33(3), 2008.

[152] J. Li, Y. Tao, and X. Xiao. Preservation of proximity privacy in publishing numerical sensitive data. In *Proc. of the ACM International Conference on Management of Data (SIGMOD)*, pages 437–486, Vancouver, Canada, June 2008.

[153] N. Li, T. Li, and S. Venkatasubramanian. t-closeness: Privacy beyond k-anonymity and ℓ-diversity. In *Proc. of the 21st IEEE International Conference on Data Engineering (ICDE)*, Istanbul, Turkey, April 2007.

[154] T. Li and N. Li. Modeling and integrating background knowledge. In *Proc. of the 23rd IEEE International Conference on Data Engineering (ICDE)*, 2009.

[155] G. Liang and S. S. Chawathe. Privacy-preserving inter-database operations. In *Proc. of the 2nd Symposium on Intelligence and Security Informatics (ISI)*, Tucson, AZ, June 2004.

[156] B. Liu, W. Hsu, and Y. Ma. Integrating classification and association rule mining. In *Proc. of 4th ACM International Conference on Knowledge Discovery and Data Mining (SIGKDD)*, 1998.

[157] J. Liu and K. Wang. On optimal anonymization for ℓ^{+}-diversity. In *Proc. of the 26th IEEE International Conference on Data Engineering (ICDE)*, 2010.

[158] K. Liu, H. Kargupta, and J. Ryan. Random projection-based multiplicative perturbation for privacy preserving distributed data mining. *IEEE Transactions on Knowledge and Data Engineering (TKDE)*, 18(1):92–106, January 2006.

[159] K. Liu and E. Terzi. Towards identity anonymization on graphs. In *Proc. of ACM International Conference on Management of Data (SIGMOD)*, Vancouver, Canada, 2008.

[160] A. Machanavajjhala, J. Gehrke, D. Kifer, and M. Venkitasubramaniam. ℓ-diversity: Privacy beyond k-anonymity. In *Proc. of the 22nd IEEE International Conference on Data Engineering (ICDE)*, Atlanta, GA, 2006.

[161] A. Machanavajjhala, D. Kifer, J. M. Abowd, J. Gehrke, and L. Vilhuber. Privacy: Theory meets practice on the map. In *Proc. of the 24th IEEE*

International Conference on Data Engineering (ICDE), pages 277–286, 2008.

[162] A. Machanavajjhala, D. Kifer, J. Gehrke, and M. Venkitasubramaniam. ℓ-diversity: Privacy beyond k-anonymity. *ACM Transactions on Knowledge Discovery from Data (TKDD)*, 1(1), March 2007.

[163] B. Malin and E. Airoldi. The effects of location access behavior on re-identification risk in a distributed environment. In *Proc. of 6th Workshop on Privacy Enhancing Technologies (PET)*, pages 413–429, 2006.

[164] B. Malin and L. Sweeney. How to protect genomic data privacy in a distributed network. In *Journal of Biomed Info, 37(3): 179-192*, 2004.

[165] D. Martin, D. Kifer, A. Machanavajjhala, J. Gehrke, and J. Halpern. Worst-case background knowledge in privacy-preserving data publishing. In *Proc. of the 23rd IEEE International Conference on Data Engineering (ICDE)*, April 2007.

[166] N. S. Matloff. Inference control via query restriction vs. data modification: A perspective. In *Database Security: Status and Prospects*, pages 159–166, Annapolis, ML, 1988.

[167] A. McCallum, A. Corrada-Emmanuel, and X. Wang. Topic and role discovery in social networks. In *Proc. of International Joint Conference on Artificial Intelligence (IJCAI)*, 2005.

[168] A. Meyerson and R. Williams. On the complexity of optimal k-anonymity. In *Proc. of the 23rd ACM SIGMOD-SIGACT-SIGART PODS*, pages 223–228, Paris, France, 2004.

[169] G. Miklau and D. Suciu. A formal analysis of information disclosure in data exchange. In *Proc. of ACM International Conference on Management of Data (SIGMOD)*, pages 575–586, Paris, France, 2004.

[170] N. Mohammed, B. C. M. Fung, and M. Debbabi. Walking in the crowd: Anonymizing trajectory data for pattern analysis. In *Proc. of the 18th ACM Conference on Information and Knowledge Management (CIKM)*, pages 1441–1444, Hong Kong, November 2009.

[171] N. Mohammed, B. C. M. Fung, P. C. K. Hung, and C. K. Lee. Anonymizing healthcare data: A case study on the blood transfusion service. In *Proc. of the 15th ACM SIGKDD International Conference on Knowledge Discovery and Data Mining (SIGKDD)*, pages 1285–1294, Paris, France, June 2009.

[172] N. Mohammed, B. C. M. Fung, K. Wang, and P. C. K. Hung. Privacy-preserving data mashup. In *Proc. of the 12th International Conference on Extending Database Technology (EDBT)*, pages 228–239, Saint-Petersburg, Russia, March 2009.

[173] R. A. Moore, Jr. Controlled data-swapping techniques for masking public use microdata sets. Statistical Research Division Report Series RR 96-04, U.S. Bureau of the Census, Washington, DC., 1996.

[174] R. Motwani and Y. Xu. Efficient algorithms for masking and finding quasi-identifiers. In *Proc. of SIAM International Workshop on Practical Privacy-Preserving Data Mining (P3DM)*, Atlanta, GA, April 2008.

[175] A. Narayanan and V. Shmatikov. De-anonymizing social networks. In *Proc. of the IEEE Symposium on Security and Privacy (S&P)*, 2009.

[176] M. Ercan Nergiz, M. Atzori, and C. W. Clifton. Hiding the presence of individuals from shared databases. In *Proc. of ACM International Conference on Management of Data (SIGMOD)*, pages 665–676, Vancouver, Canada, 2007.

[177] M. Ercan Nergiz and C. Clifton. Thoughts on k-anonymization. *Data & Knowledge Engineering*, 63(3):622–645, Decemeber 2007.

[178] M. Ercan Nergiz, C. Clifton, and A. Erhan Nergiz. Multirelational k-anonymity. In *Proc. of the 23rd International Conference on Data Engineering (ICDE)*, pages 1417–1421, Istanbul, Turkey, 2007.

[179] D. J. Newman, S. Hettich, C. L. Blake, and C. J. Merz. UCI repository of machine learning databases, 1998.

[180] N. Nisan. Algorithms for selfish agents. In *Proc. of the 16th Symposium on Theoretical Aspects of Computer Science*, Trier, Germany, March 1999.

[181] A. Ohrn and L. Ohno-Machado. Using Boolean reasoning to anonymize databases. *Artificial Intelligence in Medicine*, 15:235–254, 1999.

[182] S. R. Oliveira and O. R. Zaiane. A privacy-preserving clustering approach toward secure and effective data analysis for business collaboration. *Journal on Computers and Security*, 26(1):81–93, 2007.

[183] M. J. Osborne and A. Rubinstein. *A Course in Game Theory*. Cambridge, MA: The MIT Press, 1994.

[184] G. Ozsoyoglu and T. Su. On inference control in semantic data models for statistical databases. *Journal of Computer and System Sciences*, 40(3):405–443, 1990.

[185] S. Papadimitriou, F. Li, G. Kollios, and P. S. Yu. Time series compressibility and privacy. In *Proc. of the 33rd International Conference on Very Large Data Bases (VLDB)*, pages 459–470, Vienna, Austria, September 2007.

[186] J. Pei, J. Xu, Z. Wang, W. Wang, and K. Wang. Maintaining k-anonymity against incremental updates. In *Proc. of the 19th Inter-*

national Conference on Scientific and Statistical Database Management (SSDBM), Banff, Canada, 2007.

[187] B. Pinkas. Cryptographic techniques for privacy-preserving data mining. *ACM SIGKDD Explorations Newsletter*, 4(2):12–19, January 2002.

[188] B. Poblete, M. Spiliopoulou, and R. Baeza-Yates. *Website privacy preservation for query log publishing*. Privacy, Security, and Trust in KDD. Springer Berlin / Heidelberg, 2007.

[189] S. C. Pohlig and M. E. Hellman. An improved algorithm for computing logarithms over gf(p) and its cryptographic significance. *IEEE Transactions on Information Theory (TIT)*, IT-24:106–110, 1978.

[190] President Information Technology Advisory Committee. Revolutionizing health care through information technology. Technical report, Executive Office of the President of the United States, June 2004.

[191] J. R. Quinlan. *C4.5: Programs for Machine Learning*. Morgan Kaufmann, 1993.

[192] V. Rastogi, M. Hay, G. Miklau, and D. Suciu. Relationship privacy: Output perturbation for queries with joins. In *Proc. of the 28th ACM SIGMOD-SIGACT-SIGART Symposium on Principles of Database Systems (PODS)*, Providence, Rhode Island, USA, July 2009.

[193] V. Rastogi, D. Suciu, and S. Hong. The boundary between privacy and utility in data publishing. In *Proc. of the 33rd International Conference on Very Large Data Bases (VLDB)*, pages 531–542, Vienna, Austria, September 2007.

[194] K. Reid and J. A. Scott. Reducing the total bandwidth of a sparse unsymmetric matrix. In *SIAM Journal on Matrix Analysis and Applications*, volume 28, pages 805–821, 2006.

[195] S. P. Reiss. Practical data-swapping: The first steps. *ACM Transactions on Database Systems (TODS)*, 9(1):20–37, 1984.

[196] Steven P. Reiss, Mark J. Post, and Tore Dalenius. Non-reversible privacy transformations. In *Proc. of the 1st ACM Symposium on Principles of Database Systems (PODS)*, pages 139–146, 1982.

[197] M. K. Reiter and A. D. Rubin. Crowds: Anonymity for web transactions. *ACM Transactions on Information and System Security (TISSEC)*, 1(1):66–92, November 1998.

[198] S. Rizvi and J. R. Harista. Maintaining data privacy in association rule mining. In *Proc. of the 28th International Conference on Very Large Data Bases (VLDB)*, pages 682–693, 2002.

[199] B. E. Rosen, J. M. Goodwin, and J. J. Vidal. Process control with adaptive range coding. *Biological Cybernetics*, 67:419–428, 1992.

[200] D. B. Rubin. Discussion statistical disclosure limitation. *Journal of Official Statistics*, 9(2).

[201] P. Samarati. Protecting respondents' identities in microdata release. *IEEE Transactions on Knowledge and Data Engineering (TKDE)*, 13(6):1010–1027, 2001.

[202] P. Samarati and L. Sweeney. Generalizing data to provide anonymity when disclosing information. In *Proc. of the 17th ACM SIGACT-SIGMOD-SIGART Symposium on Principles of Database Systems (PODS)*, page 188, Seattle, WA, June 1998.

[203] P. Samarati and L. Sweeney. Protecting privacy when disclosing information: k-anonymity and its enforcement through generalization and suppression. Technical report, SRI International, March 1998.

[204] S. E. Sarma, S. A. Weis, and D. W. Engels. RFID systems and security and privacy implications. In *Proc. of the 4th International Workshop on Cryptographic Hardware and Embedded Systems (CHES)*, pages 454–469, 2003.

[205] Y. Saygin, D. Hakkani-Tur, and G. Tur. *Web and Information Security*, chapter Sanitization and Anonymization of Document Repositories, pages 133–148. IRM Press, 2006.

[206] Y. Saygin, V. S. Verykios, and C. Clifton. Using unknowns to prevent discovery of association rules. In *Conference on Research Issues in Data Engineering*, 2002.

[207] B. Schneier. *Applied Cryptography*. John Wiley & Sons, 2 edition, 1996.

[208] J. W. Seifert. Data mining and homeland security: An overview. *CRS Report for Congress*, (RL31798), January 2006. http://www.fas.org/sgp/crs/intel/RL31798.pdf.

[209] A. Serjantov and G. Danezis. Towards an information theoretic metric for anonymity. In *Proc. of the 2nd Internationl Workshop on Privacy Enchancing Technologies (PET)*, pages 41–53, San Francisco, CA, April 2002.

[210] C. E. Shannon. A mathematical theory of communication. *The Bell System Technical Journal*, 27:379 and 623, 1948.

[211] W. Shen, X. Li, and A. Doan. Constraint-based entity matching. In *Proc. of the 20th National Conference on Artificial Intelligence (AAAI)*, 2005.

[212] A. Shoshani. Statistical databases: Characteristics, problems and some solutions. In *Proc. of the 8th Very Large Data Bases (VLDB)*, pages 208–213, September 1982.

[213] A. Skowron and C. Rauszer. *Intelligent Decision Support: Handbook of Applications and Advances of the Rough Set Theory*, chapter The Discernibility Matrices and Functions in Information Systems. 1992.

[214] L. Sweeney. Replacing personally-identifying information in medical records, the scrub system. In *Proc. of the AMIA Annual Fall Symposium*, pages 333–337, 1996.

[215] L. Sweeney. Datafly: A system for providing anonymity in medical data. In *Proc. of the IFIP TC11 WG11.3 11th International Conference on Database Securty XI: Status and Prospects*, pages 356–381, August 1998.

[216] L. Sweeney. Achieving k-anonymity privacy protection using generalization and suppression. *International Journal of Uncertainty, Fuzziness, and Knowledge-based Systems*, 10(5):571–588, 2002.

[217] L. Sweeney. k-Anonymity: A model for protecting privacy. *International Journal of Uncertainty, Fuzziness and Knowledge-based Systems*, 10(5):557–570, 2002.

[218] Y. Tao, X. Xiao, J. Li, and D. Zhang. On anti-corruption privacy preserving publication. In *Proc. of the 24th IEEE International Conference on Data Engineering (ICDE)*, pages 725–734, April 2008.

[219] M. Terrovitis and N. Mamoulis. Privacy preservation in the publication of trajectories. In *Proc. of the 9th International Conference on Mobile Data Management (MDM)*, pages 65–72, April 2008.

[220] M. Terrovitis, N. Mamoulis, and P. Kalnis. Privacy-preserving anonymization of set-valued data. *Proc. of the VLDB Endowment*, 1(1):115–125, August 2008.

[221] The House of Commons in Canada. The personal information protection and electronic documents act, April 2000. http://www.privcom.gc.ca/.

[222] The RFID Knowledgebase. Oyster transport for London TfL card UK, January 2007. http://www.idtechex.com/knowledgebase/en/ casestudy.asp?casestudyid=227.

[223] B. M. Thuraisingham. Security checking in relational database management systems augmented with inference engines. *Computers and Security*, 6:479–492, 1987.

[224] J. Travers and S. Milgram. An experimental study of the small world problem. *Sociometry*, 32(4):425–443, 1969.

[225] T. Trojer, B. C. M. Fung, and P. C. K. Hung. Service-oriented architecture for privacy-preserving data mashup. In *Proc. of the 7th IEEE International Conference on Web Services (ICWS)*, pages 767–774, Los Angeles, CA, July 2009.

[226] T. M. Truta and V. Bindu. Privacy protection: p-sensitive k-anonymity property. In *Proc. of the Workshop on Privacy Data Management (PDM)*, page 94, April 2006.

[227] J. Vaidya. *Privacy-Preserving Data Mining: Models and Algorithms*, chapter A Survey of Privacy-Preserving Methods Across Vertically Partitioned Data, pages 337–358. Springer, 2008.

[228] J. Vaidya and C. Clifton. Privacy preserving association rule mining in vertically partitioned data. In *Proc. of the 8th ACM International Conference on Knowledge Discovery and Data Mining (SIGKDD)*, pages 639–644, Edmonton, AB, Canada, 2002.

[229] J. Vaidya and C. Clifton. Privacy-preserving k-means clustering over vertically partitioned data. In *Proc. of the 9th ACM International Conference on Knowledge Discovery and Data Mining (SIGKDD)*, pages 206–215, Washington, DC, 2003.

[230] J. Vaidya, C. W. Clifton, and M. Zhu. *Privacy Preserving Data Mining*. Springer, 2006.

[231] C. J. van Rijsbergen. *Information Retrieval, 2nd edition*. London, Butterworths, 1979.

[232] V. S. Verykios, E. Bertino, I. N. Fovino, L. P. Provenza, Y. Saygin, and Y. Theodoridis. State-of-the-art in privacy preserving data mining. *ACM SIGMOD Record*, 3(1):50–57, March 2004.

[233] V. S. Verykios, A. K. Elmagarmid, A. Bertino, Y. Saygin, and E. Dasseni. Association rule hiding. *IEEE Transactions on Knowledge and Data Engineering (TKDE)*, 16(4):434–447, 2004.

[234] S. A. Vinterbo. Privacy: A machine learning view. *IEEE Transactions on Knowledge and Data Engineering (TKDE)*, 16(8):939–948, August 2004.

[235] D.-W. Wang, C.-J. Liau, and T.-S. Hsu. Privacy protection in social network data disclosure based on granular computing. In *Proc. of IEEE International Conference on Fuzzy Systems*, Vancouver, BC, July 2006.

[236] K. Wang and B. C. M. Fung. Anonymizing sequential releases. In *Proc. of the 12th ACM SIGKDD International Conference on Knowledge Discovery and Data Mining (SIGKDD)*, pages 414–423, Philadelphia, PA, August 2006.

[237] K. Wang, B. C. M. Fung, and P. S. Yu. Handicapping attacker's confidence: An alternative to k-anonymization. *Knowledge and Information Systems (KAIS)*, 11(3):345–368, April 2007.

[238] K. Wang, Y. Xu, A. W. C. Fu, and R. C. W. Wong. ff-anonymity: When quasi-identifiers are missing. In *Proc. of the 25th IEEE International Conference on Data Engineering (ICDE)*, March 2009.

[239] K. Wang, P. S. Yu, and S. Chakraborty. Bottom-up generalization: A data mining solution to privacy protection. In *Proc. of the 4th IEEE International Conference on Data Mining (ICDM)*, pages 249–256, November 2004.

[240] S.-W. Wang, W.-H. Chen, C.-S. Ong, L. Liu, and Y. W. Chuang. RFID applications in hospitals: a case study on a demonstration RFID project in a taiwan hospital. In *Proc. of the 39th Hawaii International Conference on System Sciences*, 2006.

[241] T. Wang and X. Wu. Approximate inverse frequent itemset mining: Privacy, complexity, and approximation. In *Proc. of the 5th IEEE International Conference on Data Mining (ICDM)*, 2005.

[242] S. L. Warner. Randomized response: A survey technique for eliminating evasive answer bias. *Journal of the American Statistical Association*, 60(309):63–69, 1965.

[243] D. Whitley. The genitor algorithm and selective pressure: Why rank-based allocation of reproductive trials is best. In *Proc. of the 3rd International Conference on Genetic Algorithms*, pages 116–121, 1989.

[244] G. Wiederhold. Intelligent integration of information. In *Proc. of ACM International Conference on Management of Data (SIGMOD)*, pages 434–437, 1993.

[245] R. C. W. Wong, A. W. C. Fu, K. Wang, and J. Pei. Minimality attack in privacy preserving data publishing. In *Proc. of the 33rd International Conference on Very Large Data Bases (VLDB)*, pages 543–554, Vienna, Austria, 2007.

[246] R. C. W. Wong, J. Li., A. W. C. Fu, and K. Wang. (α,k)-anonymity: An enhanced k-anonymity model for privacy preserving data publishing. In *Proc. of the 12th ACM International Conference on Knowledge Discovery and Data Mining (SIGKDD)*, pages 754–759, Philadelphia, PA, 2006.

[247] R. C. W. Wong, J. Li., A. W. C. Fu, and K. Wang. (α,k)-anonymous data publishing. *Journal of Intelligent Information Systems*, in press.

[248] R. N. Wright, Z. Yang, and S. Zhong. Distributed data mining protocols for privacy: A review of some recent results. In *Proc. of the Secure Mobile Ad-hoc Networks and Sensors Workshop (MADNES)*, 2005.

[249] X. Xiao and Y. Tao. Anatomy: Simple and effective privacy preservation. In *Proc. of the 32nd Very Large Data Bases (VLDB)*, Seoul, Korea, September 2006.

[250] X. Xiao and Y. Tao. Personalized privacy preservation. In *Proc. of ACM International Conference on Management of Data (SIGMOD)*, Chicago, IL, 2006.

[251] X. Xiao and Y. Tao. m-invariance: Towards privacy preserving republication of dynamic datasets. In *Proc. of ACM International Conference on Management of Data (SIGMOD)*, Beijing, China, June 2007.

[252] X. Xiao, Y. Tao, and M. Chen. Optimal random perturbation at multiple privacy levels. In *Proc. of the 35th Very Large Data Bases (VLDB)*, pages 814–825, 2009.

[253] L. Xiong and E. Agichtein. Towards privacy-preserving query log publishing. In *Query Logs Workshop at the 16th International Conference on World Wide Web*, 2007.

[254] J. Xu, W. Wang, J. Pei, X. Wang, B. Shi, and A. W. C. Fu. Utility-based anonymization using local recoding. In *Proc. of the 12th ACM International Conference on Knowledge Discovery and Data Mining (SIGKDD)*, Philadelphia, PA, August 2006.

[255] Y. Xu, B. C. M. Fung, K. Wang, A. W. C. Fu, and J. Pei. Publishing sensitive transactions for itemset utility. In *Proc. of the 8th IEEE International Conference on Data Mining (ICDM)*, Pisa, Italy, December 2008.

[256] Y. Xu, K. Wang, A. W. C. Fu, and P. S. Yu. Anonymizing transaction databases for publication. In *Proc. of the 14th ACM International Conference on Knowledge Discovery and Data Mining (SIGKDD)*, August 2008.

[257] X. Yan and J. Han. gSpan: Graph-based substructure pattern mining. In *Proc. of the 2nd IEEE International Conference on Data Mining (ICDM)*, 2002.

[258] Z. Yang, S. Zhong, and R. N. Wright. Anonymity-preserving data collection. In *Proc. of the 11th ACM International Conference on Knowledge Discovery and Data Mining (SIGKDD)*, pages 334–343, 2005.

[259] Z. Yang, S. Zhong, and R. N. Wright. Privacy-preserving classification of customer data without loss of accuracy. In *Proc. of the 5th SIAM International Conference on Data Mining (SDM)*, pages 92–102, Newport Beach, CA, 2005.

[260] A. C. Yao. Protocols for secure computations. In *Proc. of the 23rd IEEE Symposium on Foundations of Computer Science*, pages 160–164, 1982.

[261] A. C. Yao. How to generate and exchange secrets. In *Proc. of the 27th Annual IEEE Symposium on Foundations of Computer Science*, pages 162–167, 1986.

[262] C. Yao, X. S. Wang, and S. Jajodia. Checking for k-anonymity violation by views. In *Proc. of the 31st Very Large Data Bases (VLDB)*, pages 910–921, Trondheim, Norway, 2005.

[263] R. Yarovoy, F. Bonchi, L. V. S. Lakshmanan, and W. H. Wang. Anonymizing moving objects: How to hide a MOB in a crowd? In *Proc. of the 12th International Conference on Extending Database Technology (EDBT)*, pages 72–83, 2009.

[264] X. Ying and X. Wu. Randomizing social networks: a spectrum preserving approach. In *Proc. of SIAM International Conference on Data Mining (SDM)*, Atlanta, GA, April 2008.

[265] T.-H. You, W.-C. Peng, and W.-C. Lee. Protect moving trajectories with dummies. In *Proc. of the International Workshop on Privacy-Aware Location-based Mobile Services (PALMS)*, pages 278–282, May 2007.

[266] H. Yu, P. Gibbons, M. Kaminsky, and F. Xiao. Sybil-limit: A near-optimal social network defense against sybil attacks. In *Proc. of the IEEE Symposium on Security and Privacy*, 2008.

[267] L. Zayatz. Disclosure avoidance practices and research at the U.S. census bureau: An update. *Journal of Official Statistics*, 23(2):253–265, 2007.

[268] P. Zhang, Y. Tong, S. Tang, and D. Yang. Privacy-preserving naive bayes classifier. *Lecture Notes in Computer Science*, 3584, 2005.

[269] Q. Zhang, N. Koudas, D. Srivastava, and T. Yu. Aggregate query answering on anonymized tables. In *Proc. of the 23rd IEEE International Conference on Data Engineering (ICDE)*, April 2007.

[270] E. Zheleva and L. Getoor. Preserving the privacy of sensitive relationships in graph data. In *Proc. of the 1st ACM SIGKDD International Workshop on Privacy, Security and Trust in KDD*, San Jose, USA, Aug 2007.

[271] B. Zhou and J. Pei. Preserving privacy in social networks against neighborhood attacks. In *Proc. of IEEE 24th International Conference on Data Engineering (ICDE)*, April 2008.

[272] L. Zou, L. Chen, and M. T. Özsu. K-automorphism: A general framework for privacy preserving network publication. *Proc. of the VLDB Endowment*, 2(1):946–957, 2009.

Index

Printed and bound by CPI Group (UK) Ltd, Croydon, CR0 4YY

23/10/2024

01777670-0016